Sex, Sexuality, and the Constitution

Sex, Sexuality, and the Constitution

Enshrining the Right to Sexual Autonomy in Japan

SHIGENORI MATSUI

UBCPress · Vancouver · Toronto

© UBC Press 2023

All rights reserved. No part of this publication may be reproduced, stored in a retrieval system, or transmitted, in any form or by any means, without prior written permission of the publisher, or, in Canada, in the case of photocopying or other reprographic copying, a licence from Access Copyright, www.accesscopyright.ca.

32 31 30 29 28 27 26 25 24 23   5 4 3 2 1

Printed in Canada on FSC-certified ancient-forest-free paper (100% post-consumer recycled) that is processed chlorine- and acid-free.

Library and Archives Canada Cataloguing in Publication

Title: Sex, sexuality, and the constitution : enshrining the right to sexual autonomy in Japan / Shigenori Matsui.
Names: Matsui, Shigenori, author.
Identifiers: Canadiana (print) 20220497133 | Canadiana (ebook) 20220497192 |
  ISBN 9780774868150 (hardcover) | ISBN 9780774868181 (EPUB) |
  ISBN 9780774868174 (PDF)
Subjects: LCSH: Sexual rights – Japan. | LCSH: Sex and law – Japan.
Classification: LCC HQ65.5.J37 M38 2023 | DDC 305.30952 – dc23

UBC Press gratefully acknowledges the financial support for our publishing program of the Government of Canada and the British Columbia Arts Council.

This book has been published with the help of the University of British Columbia through the K.D. Srivastava Fund.

The publication of this book was also made possible by the grant from the UBC Scholarly Publishing Fund.

Printed and bound in Canada by Friesens
Set in Sabon Next LT Pro and Myriad Pro by Apex CoVantage, LLC
Copy editor: Deborah Kerr
Proofreader: Sophie Pouyanne

UBC Press
The University of British Columbia
2029 West Mall
Vancouver, BC V6T 1Z2
www.ubcpress.ca

*To everyone who is suffering an infringement
on sexual autonomy*

Contents

Acknowledgments / ix

Introduction / 3

1 Sexual Autonomy: Sex, Childbirth, and the Constitution / 16

2 Sexual Freedom: The Right to Decide One's Sexual Identity and the Right to Have Sex / 35

3 Rape: The Right Not to Be Forced to Have Sex / 84

4 Childbirth: The Right to Have a Child / 117

5 Abortion: The Right Not to Be Forced to Have a Child / 154

6 Sex, Childbirth, and the Government: Sexual Freedom, Freedom of Choice, and Population Policy / 192

Conclusion / 221

List of Caselaw, Legislation, and Treaties / 225

Notes / 235

Index / 323

Acknowledgments

As with all my previous work, I could not have finished this book without the support of my family: Chika, Ayana, and Haruto. I would also like to thank my students Alexander Bres, Taylor Stone, Gabrielle Barron-Styan, Jaime Prins, and Kirsty Hogg for their editorial assistance and useful comments on each chapter. In addition, I would like to thank professor Mai Sugaya of Takushoku University for reading all of the chapters and for providing a very insightful feminist critique. Finally, I am especially grateful to Joy Lin Salzberg and her family. Her husband, Professor Stephan M. Salzberg, was a predecessor of mine as director of the Japanese legal studies program at the Peter A. Allard School of Law at the University of British Columbia and a very good friend too, who unfortunately passed away suddenly in 2004. We shared an academic interest in law and medicine, which is one of the reasons I began the research for this book. Moreover, Joy Salzberg gifted the Peter A. Allard School of Law with the Stephan M. Salzberg Endowment Fund to allow us to get access to a database for Japanese court judgments, which was essential for my research. I am deeply thankful for their contribution.

Sex, Sexuality, and the Constitution

Introduction

This book examines the legal status of sexual autonomy in Japan. More specifically, it discusses sexual freedom – the right to decide one's own sexual or gender identity and whether to have sex or not to have sex. Everyone should possess these rights. The legal status of choice in connection with childbirth – the right to have a child or not to have one – will also be explored. The right to give birth should be untrammelled, as should the right to refuse to give birth to a child.

In what follows, I suggest that these issues must be examined in light of the Constitution of Japan and should not be regarded solely as matters of legislative policy. Moreover, I advance "sexual autonomy" as a foundational right or coordinating principle to contextualize them. Every aspect of sex and childbirth is only part of the foundational right of sexual autonomy. My aim is to draw the right to this autonomy from the Constitution and to critically examine all the issues outlined above as interrelated aspects of it.

Although this book discusses issues in Europe and North America, it focuses largely on Japan and will, therefore, trace its history of government regulation of sex and childbirth. It critically examines the current legal status of sexual freedom and the right of choice on childbirth, based on the constitutional protection of sexual autonomy. This discussion is particularly relevant in Japan, since sex and childbirth have traditionally been seen as community matters and were not left to personal choice. There is definitely a need to revisit these issues as individual rights and also as parts of the principle of sexual autonomy. Such an examination is vital for the final topic of this book: whether and how much government population policies can limit sexual autonomy. In Japan, the population is aging, the birthrate shrinking, and population numbers are declining overall. As a result, the government has generated various policies to encourage marriage and childbirth. The investigation of the right to sexual autonomy is vital in determining their legitimacy and limits.

Aims of the Book
This book has two primary aims. One is to provide a detailed analysis of Japan's current predicament as regards sex and childbirth, a situation that is perhaps more fraught than in any other country. Very little research has dealt with this topic, which means that *Sex, Sexuality, and the Constitution* will break new ground.

The other primary aim is to draw important lessons from the Japanese predicament. Since many developed countries are now struggling with the same kinds of serious social issues, Japan's experience will prove educational for them. Perhaps the most important lesson here is the need to place sexual autonomy as *the* foundational constitutional mandate and to re-examine all restrictions on sex and childbirth before determining how to cope with the diminishing birthrate and shrinking population. The population policy of the government needs to be squarely examined in light of the constitutional command of sexual autonomy (a constitutional obligation in the form of a mandate, beyond a simple endorsement or request for respect, which obliges the government not to unreasonably restrict it).

Sexual Freedom
In most countries, including Japan, the government has traditionally assumed that sex is predetermined biologically at the time of birth and that all individuals are either male or female. As a result, there was no serious argument that an individual has a right to decide or change sexual or gender identity. In many countries, sex is seen as a freedom that people can enjoy. After all, it is a natural part of love, and it is essential to the

survival of the human species. However, no country leaves it completely unregulated. Aside from the criminalization of sexual assault, various laws proscribe certain behaviours, including seemingly consensual acts, such as sex with a child, incest, adultery, and sodomy, or other atypical or so-called deviant sex, necrophilia, and bestiality. Most of these bans are rooted in the assumption that people will naturally choose heterosexual sex and that "normal" relations between husband and wife in the bedroom are the only legitimate and proper version. In other words, sexual orientation and sexual preferences have not been much respected, and sex is seen as a social matter to be controlled. In some countries, prostitution is also criminalized. In the past, this ban was rarely subject to constitutional scrutiny, probably because there was no consensus on whether sex should be constitutionally protected or because no one doubted the government's power to regulate it. Public discussions of sex were largely taboo, with the result that many people were hesitant to debate openly on whether such prohibitions could be justified.

On the other hand, the freedom not to be forced to have sex has generally been respected. As a result, forcible sex without consent is banned as rape or sexual assault in most countries, but the relevant legislation varies considerably from one country to the next. Some countries impose extraordinary and almost insurmountable hurdles for the criminal punishment of sex offenders, thus preventing their conviction. In other countries, even though punishment is possible, many barriers impede conviction, and it is not easy for victims to obtain justice. In those countries, it could be argued that the freedom from sexual coercion is not sufficiently protected, raising the question of whether the laws need revision. However, almost all discussions of rape or sexual assault have been framed as matters of criminal policy, not as constitutional issues.

Freedom of Choice on Childbirth
In most parts of the world, giving birth is among the freedoms that individuals can enjoy, and few attempt to limit it through bans or restrictions. In some instances, however, the government has implemented mandatory castration for violent sex offenders or sterilization for persons with mental disabilities; in others, it has limited the number of offspring a couple can legally have. Nevertheless, there has been little discussion

on whether such measures or regulations can be justified. Moreover, with the significant increase in infertility, growing numbers of people have turned to assisted reproductive technology (ART) or medically assisted reproduction (MAR) to have children. Sexual intercourse is no longer the only means of producing a child. It is therefore important to allow access to ART/MAR to achieve the freedom to procreate. In most countries, however, discussions of ART/MAR have tended to focus on its regulation to ensure that it is both safe and ethical. Little attention has been paid to whether the denial of access to ART/MAR could be constitutionally justified. Moreover, the law of parentage, the law to decide who should be regarded as parent of a child, might present a challenge for a couple who want to become parents. However, there has been no examination of the law of parentage from the constitutional perspective of the right to have a child.

Furthermore, freedom of choice on childbirth also needs to include the right not to be forced to have a child. This includes the right to use contraceptives to prevent or delay pregnancy, as well as the right to abortion. However, some countries limit the use of contraceptives and many ban or restrict abortion. The appropriateness of such measures has been highly controversial in many countries. However, contraception and abortion have been debated as matters of constitutional law in only a few, such as the United States, Canada, and Germany. Elsewhere, they have been debated only as criminal policy issues for the legislature.

The Need for Constitutional Discussion
Of course, most of these topics, such as prostitution, rape, ART/MAR, or abortion, have been thoroughly discussed in the past. On the whole, however, such discussions are deeply inadequate, a fact that prompted me to write this book.

First, almost all these subjects have typically been approached as matters of legislative policy. It is obviously simply wrong to view them solely as freedoms that can be regulated and restricted by legislation. Indeed, sex and childbirth have become increasingly personal and deeply felt individual choices that people can and should make for themselves. Moreover, they are an important aspect of family and are foundational to society, necessary in sustaining a democratic country. Given this, it is imperative that questions regarding sex and childbirth be examined as constitutional matters, not just as legislative or government policy issues.

When these freedoms are accepted as constitutional rights, then, any law that unreasonably bans or restricts them needs to be abolished or revised in the name of the Constitution. In other words, enshrining these freedoms in the Constitution limits legislatures as to what kind of policies they can implement and how they can be implemented.

In addition, whereas courts have the power to review the constitutionality of legislation, judges can review any statute that prohibits or limits these freedoms. Since in most countries, policies on sex and childbirth are debated in the legislative process, constitutionalization would allow for the judicialization of these issues and would therefore create another arena for debate. Moreover, it would structure these debates in terms of the justification as a matter of the Constitution, not only as a matter of policy, completely changing the framework and structure of discussion.

Integrating Issues under Sexual Autonomy
Second, discussions of sex and childbirth have tended to focus on each individual topic separately, without attempting to connect them or to integrate them into a coherent framework. It is a tragic failure to lose sight of the very strong ties among these issues: all are closely linked to the sexuality of individuals. Instead of concentrating narrowly on discrete topics, such as prostitution, rape, ART/MAR, or abortion, we need to draw a coherent foundational framework of principles to connect them.

Therefore, this book will consider them in light of the constitutional command of "sexual autonomy." Instead of addressing each one as a separate and distinct subject, the book aims to apply the common framework and subject them to uniform analysis because all are interrelated and connected. This is the most important aspect of my research.

The focus on sexual autonomy will reveal that earlier discussions of the individual topics are deeply inadequate since they fail to see the close connections among them and the necessary implications to each other. All these issues on sex and childbirth are parts of the foundational principle of sexual autonomy, which lies at the heart of this book and will be elaborated in the following chapters. Briefly, it refers to the right of individuals to determine their sexuality and make sexual decisions as they choose. It includes sexual freedom – the right to decide one's sexual identity and the freedom of sex (including the right to have sex and the right not to be forced to have sex). It also includes the right of choice on childbirth (including the right to have a child and the right not to be forced to have a child). This foundational right should inform all discussions of sex and childbirth under the Constitution. Although few countries have adopted it, accepting and confirming it as a guiding right or guiding principle is now imperative.

Vital Reconsiderations
This examination is vital in facing the most daunting question this book will address: the legitimacy and limits of government population policies. Since both birthrates and population numbers are declining in many countries, governments must now grapple with the challenge of maintaining economic growth and sustaining the tax revenues that fund pensions, health care, and senior care. Many will be forced to adopt some kind of measures to cope.

As will be closely examined in this book, the most likely of these are attempting to increase childbirth and taking in more immigrants. The latter, however, involves various challenges, and thus governments might be tempted to concentrate on the former. This would raise the complicated issues of sex and childbirth. If deciding whether to engage in sex and have a child is truly an individual freedom, how would it be possible for a government to promote childbirth? Are there any limits on what it can do?

Why Japan?
This book focuses on Japan. One reason for this is because Japan has traditionally lacked a strong commitment to individual freedom when it comes to sexuality. The government has never officially accepted sexual freedom and freedom of choice as individual rights. It sees sexual identity as determined at birth, with no room for change. Although it has made some rare exceptions for certain transgender persons, the exceptions were very narrow. However, this fact prompted no serious discussion. Government restrictions on the freedom to have sex have generally remained unopposed, and virtually no constitutional arguments have

been raised against any criminalization of that freedom. There has been no discussion as to whether the rape and sexual assault laws sufficiently protect against coercion to have sex or of whether the current ban can be justified as appropriate. Furthermore, with respect to freedom of choice in childbirth, virtually no arguments have been based on the right to bear a child or to be a parent. The same is true in connection with the right not to be forced to have a child (the right to abortion). In the past, Japanese society almost universally accepted that the government should have the power to regulate sex and childbirth from the standpoint of morality and population policy. Sex and childbirth have always been seen as social matters, not as matters of individual rights.

Indeed, for many centuries in Japan's long history, they were not viewed as personal. During the third or fourth centuries BCE, people began to live and work together in farming communities.[1] The primary focus of their labour was the production of rice, a key food staple. Since growing this crop necessitates a group effort in planting, weeding, and harvesting, communities were naturally closely bound by family and work. For many centuries, Japanese society was largely agrarian, focused on rice production. During the Tokugawa period, or so-called Edo Period, from 1600 to 1867, Japan was ruled by a military elite of samurai warriors.[2] Rice remained the main food, and indeed taxes to the government were paid in the form of rice. Therefore, most farmers maintained the traditional group orientation, and people had no strong perception of individualism. Local communities, families, and society played a more important role for them. There was no notion of individual freedoms or rights until the government launched a sweeping modernization program. Indeed, during the Edo Period, the family had been jointly liable for criminal wrongdoing by a relative: an entire family would be punished if one member committed a crime.[3] All family members were legally obliged to report any offence by a relative, and failure to do so could make them liable too. Everyone was expected to keep an eye on the behaviour of everyone else.[4] Moreover, the family and the village were jointly responsible for collecting and submitting taxes. If an individual or a village failed to submit the allocated amount of rice, family members or the village itself were required to make up the shortfall.[5] In such a society, there was no room to create and foster individualistic freedom or liability.[6]

The Meiji Restoration of 1868 ended the Tokugawa shogunate and restored power to the emperor.[7] Created under his authority, the Meiji government wished to fend off Western colonization, feeling the need to modernize and to build an economically robust country with a strong military. It also replaced the traditional legal system with elements imported from the various Western examples. The modernization campaign extended to architecture, fashion, culture, and lifestyle, as people were urged to follow Western precedents.[8] The Meiji Constitution of 1889, the first in Japan, was, however, strongly conservative, granting sovereign authority to the emperor and vesting all government power in him.[9] It did declare that the people possessed certain constitutional rights. However, even after modernization, the government placed society, the interests of the community, and public commitment to the emperor above any individual. Indeed, the people were regarded as "subjects" of the Emperor, and they were granted these rights based only on the benevolent grace of their master, the Emperor.[10] Furthermore, the constitutional protection of their rights and freedoms existed only "within the limits of law."[11] Therefore, if the Imperial Diet, the newly created legislative body, together with the Emperor passed a statute restricting such rights and freedoms, there was no room to claim infringement. Individuals had never had any personal freedom regarding sex or childbirth. The government promoted the birth of healthy boys to sustain the military.

Family relationships were decidedly hierarchical, structured around the *ie* (the house), which was headed by a housemaster.[12] They were also highly patriarchal since the housemaster was typically a father and husband. Under the Meiji family law system, members of an extended family belonged to a house, whose housemaster exercised strong authority over them. He could admit new members, decide where they would live, and grant his permission for younger members to marry. The estate also belonged to the house and was supposed to be inherited by the firstborn son of the housemaster. In this system, women could not manage property, choose a husband, or make their own decisions on virtually any important matter, such as whether to pursue an education or to work. Many married the man whom the housemaster or their parents had selected, entered his house, took its name, and were expected to bear sons. As we will see more fully, they were prohibited from having extramarital sex, though this ban did not apply to married men wanting to have sex with unmarried women. A wife could not refuse her husband exercising his conjugal rights, and if she failed to bear a son, she could be evicted from the house. Women did not have the right to abort a child.

After the Second World War, Japan was placed under Allied occupation, and the new Constitution of Japan was enacted in 1946.[13] It was totally new, profoundly different from the Meiji Constitution.[14] Built on the principle of popular sovereignty, it declared that the people were sovereign.[15] Now merely a symbol of the state and the people, the Emperor had no political power.[16] The Constitution established a liberal democracy, enshrining many rights for citizens. It declared that the people "shall not be prevented from enjoying any of the fundamental human rights. These fundamental human rights guaranteed to the people by this Constitution shall be conferred upon the people of this and future generations as eternal and inviolate rights."[17] Moreover, it baldly proclaimed that "all of the people shall be respected as individuals."[18] It also stated that "all of the people are equal under the law and there shall be no discrimination in political, economic or social relations because of race, creed, sex, social status or family origin."[19] In a radical denial of the family law system that existed under the Meiji Constitution, it specifically provided that "marriage shall be based only on the mutual consent of both sexes and it shall be maintained through mutual cooperation with the equal rights of husband and wife as a basis" and that "with regard to choice of spouse, property rights, inheritance, choice of domicile, divorce and other matters pertaining to marriage and the family, laws shall be enacted from the standpoint of individual dignity and the essential equality of the sexes."[20] Finally, it asserted that "the fundamental human rights by this Constitution guaranteed to the people of Japan are fruits of the age-old struggle of man to be free; they have survived the many exacting tests for durability and are conferred upon this and future generations in trust, to be held for all time inviolate."[21]

As a result of this development, the entire legal system of Japan was overhauled. The family law and inheritance law sections of the Civil Code were rewritten, and the Criminal Code was revised in several important ways. Especially, there was no longer a house headed by a housemaster. As we will see in the following chapters, individuals could now choose a marriage partner, and husband and wife were granted equal rights, even with respect to matters on family. Under its new Constitution, Japan placed a stronger emphasis on the individual than on society. Indeed, individualism lay at the core of the document.

However, these fundamental human rights are protected only so long as they do not interfere with public welfare. This is made clear in article 12 of the Constitution: "The freedoms and rights guaranteed to the people by this Constitution shall be maintained by the constant endeavor of the people, who shall refrain from any abuse of these freedoms and rights and shall always be responsible for utilizing them for the public welfare." Article 13 also states that the "right to life, liberty, and the pursuit of happiness shall, to the extent that it does not interfere with the public welfare, be the supreme consideration in legislation and in other governmental affairs."

Moreover, even though society and the Constitution were greatly changed after the Second World War, a strong group orientation still persists in Japan, which has not embraced the highly individualistic ideal of the Constitution.[22] Although sex and childbirth have been significantly liberalized, they are not viewed as purely personal matters. As a result, their regulation has been discussed without constitutional scrutiny. Although this might also be the case in other countries, a critical examination of these issues in the context of Japan is especially useful due to its strong society and group orientation.

The focus on Japan is also particularly relevant because the country has the highest old-age dependency ratio in the world, as well as one of the lowest total fertility rates. Indeed, its population is rapidly aging. As of October 1, 2020, the population of Japan was 125,710,000, and the number of adults sixty-five years of age or older was 36,190,000, representing 28.8 percent of the population.[23] The number of seniors is projected to increase, expected to reach 33.3 percent of the population in 2036, meaning that one in three residents of Japan will be sixty-five or older.[24] With its significant population decline, Japan has the highest dependency ratio of seniors (aged sixty-five and older) to working-aged individuals (aged twenty to sixty-four).[25]

At the same time, its birthrate is rapidly declining. In 2006, 1,093,000 children were born in Japan, a number that decreased to only 902,000 in 2020.[26] It is estimated that the birthrate will drop to 782,000 in 2035 and to 557,000 in 2065.[27] In terms of total fertility, Japan ranks among the lowest countries.[28] There is no doubt that its population is shrinking. It is estimated to reach less than 120,000,000 in 2029, close to 99,240,000 in 2053, and approximately 88,080,000 in 2065.[29]

These numbers are especially concerning for Japan because, if left unaddressed, they will have serious social and economic impacts. As increasing numbers of seniors retire and fewer babies are born, the proportion of the working-age population is shrinking. In 1950, there were 12.1 working people for every senior, but this ratio significantly decreased to 2.3 to 1 in 2015. It is estimated that in 2065, it will be 1.3 to 1.[30] This number is entirely unsustainable. Therefore, the Japanese government is now faced with one of the most daunting tasks: increasing the rate of childbirth.

As we will see in the following chapters, the government has implemented a number of measures to encourage marriage and childbirth, all of which will have a significant impact on sexual autonomy. Specifically, they will inevitably place a great deal of pressure on women. It is important that, in light of the right to sexual autonomy, these measures do not place undue burdens on women. Women should still have the option to remain childless. However, for those who wish to have children, we must determine whether the government initiatives actually do facilitate childbirth. It is essential to discuss the measures that are available to the government and what limitations the Constitution places on it.

Roadmap of the Book

Chapter 1 of this book starts with the examination of sexual autonomy, elucidating the relevant issues and trying to extrapolate the fundamental principles to be applied. It initially looks at various American Supreme Court cases to determine whether this privacy jurisprudence can supply comprehensive and coherent fundamental principles. It closes by switching the focus to the Constitution of Japan, attempting to discover whether it protects the right to sexual autonomy.

Chapter 2 explores sexual freedom, showing both how it was treated in the past and the need to protect it under the Constitution of Japan.

The chapter concentrates on the right to decide one's sexual or gender identity and to have sex, inquiring whether current and possible restrictions on these rights can be justified. It picks up sex with children and prostitution as the most controversial issues to be discussed in terms of sexual freedom.

In Chapter 3, we will turn to the right not to be forced to have sex, which is a corollary to the right to have sex. Indeed, in most countries, including Japan, rape is a criminal offence. This chapter focuses on how the crime of rape is punished in Japan and on some of the impediments to that punishment, revealing that the rape law has many serious defects.

Chapter 4 discusses the right to have children. Japan has no legal restrictions on the right to reproduce, though it did sterilize the mentally ill in the past, and some countries still do. Moreover, some countries castrate sex offenders, and some limit the number of children a couple can have. We will see whether such measures can be justified. The chapter also examines ART/MAR. Although Japan places very few legal restrictions on its use, obtaining it can be very difficult. We will consider whether this can be constitutionally justified.

In Chapter 5, we will examine the right not to be forced to have a child, which encompasses the right to use contraceptives and to access abortion. Although these topics are highly controversial all over the world, the situation is complicated and nuanced in Japan. There is no legal ban on the use of contraceptives, but acquiring them is not always easy, thus resulting in unwanted pregnancies. The Criminal Code flatly bans abortion, but a different statute, which refers to it as "artificial termination of pregnancy (ATP)," permits it under certain circumstances. However, regardless of what the statutes may say, abortion in the early stage of pregnancy is freely available in practice. As a result, it is not a particularly controversial topic in Japan. However, it does not mean that there is no abortion issue in Japan.

Finally, Chapter 6 considers the most daunting challenge for the government: how to increase the birthrate. In an attempt to reach this goal, it has instigated many measures, none of which have proven especially effective. Raising the numbers of immigrants could potentially solve the problem, but this is unlikely to be popular in Japan, so finding successful ways of amplifying the birthrate appears to be the only viable approach at the moment. Whatever population policies the government may generate, the right to sexual autonomy must always be a starting point, and the government should not have a free hand in its efforts to promote childbirth.

Lessons for the Future
Examining the predicament and challenges of Japan can provide some very important lessons. The most vital of these is that viewing sex and childbirth solely as legislative policy choices is inappropriate. Legislatures should not be allowed to decide on these issues merely on policy grounds. They need to be viewed as constitutional rights, and any government attempt to restrict them must be constitutionally justified. This would prompt a radical reconsideration of various government limitations on sexual autonomy. The second-most important lesson is that the issues of sex and childbirth need to be seen only as parts of the most foundational constitutional right of "sexual autonomy." In other words, the right to sexual autonomy needs to be accepted as the grounding principle to guide our analysis. It is imperative for the government to realize that this right must be respected whenever it attempts to influence, let alone regulate, sex and childbirth in the service of a population policy. These are the major arguments of this book.

Japan is not alone in experiencing a declining fertility rate coupled with an aging population. Some countries are doing better at coping with the problem, but others are doing much worse. Some have attempted to bump up their population figures by accepting huge numbers of immigrants, and though this alternative may solve the immediate crisis, it also creates many new issues. Moreover, as in Japan, it may not be universally popular in every country, which means that working to increase the birthrate will be the only available course. For such countries, the lessons provided in this book will be especially relevant. The necessity of using the constitutional mandate of sexual autonomy as a baseline and then examining possible countermeasures to the declining birthrate is most vividly shown in Japan, but it needs to be accepted in other countries as well.

Sexual Autonomy: Sex, Childbirth, and the Constitution

1

Although no clause in the Constitution of Japan protects sexual freedom, Japanese society perceives it as one of the numerous freedoms an individual can enjoy. However, it has also been subject to many limitations in both the past and the present. Historically, Japan has assumed that sex and gender are established at birth.[1] Every person will be born either male or female, the sex or gender of newborns were to be registered, and no individual could subsequently change that identification. Throughout the years, Japanese law imposed several bans on sexual freedoms, and though some were later removed, others remain in place today, including sex with children, rape and sexual assault, and prostitution. Many countries prohibit other kinds of sexual activities. Across Europe and North America, the Christian belief that sex is a sin was the foundation for various legal bans, including on sodomy and homosexuality.[2] Japan's two leading religions, Shintoism and Buddhism, do not condemn sex in the same way. Therefore, the religious censure of certain sexual activities is not as strong in Japan as in Christian countries. Nevertheless, moral condemnation and social prejudice could work to curb some sexual behaviour and could fuel statutory restrictions. Moreover, the family system – especially the marriage system – limits sexual freedom on a practical level. For example, bigamy is illegal in Japan. Even if a marriage has totally broken down, the spouses cannot remarry without first obtaining a divorce. The marriage system also accepts heterosexual relationships only and does not allow same-sex marriage. Furthermore, husband and wife are mandated to carry the same surname. These regimes necessarily exclude certain people from legal marriage. Without its blessing, an individual's sexual freedom could be hugely curtailed. We therefore need to examine whether these bans and restrictions can be justified.

A corollary of the right to sexual freedom is the right not to be coerced to have sex. In Japan, this right is protected by the rape and sexual assault provisions in the Criminal Code, which impose punishment for forcible sexual intercourse or obscene (indecent) sexual conduct with assault or intimidation. These provisions are, however, quite controversial. Many argue that they are too restrictive and that they fail to protect victims. It is imperative to determine whether the laws are adequate.

The right to have sex also encompasses the right to have a child. At the time of writing, Japan had practically no restrictions on the right to procreate, though it once imposed the mandatory sterilization of patients with mental disabilities. Other countries have castrated sex offenders or limited the number of children a family can have. We need to ask whether such measures could ever be justified in Japan. Moreover, the use of assisted reproductive technology (ART) and medically assisted reproduction (MAR) is not illegal, but access is seriously limited. Furthermore, the law of parentage, which developed long before the rise of ART/MAR, is out of touch with modern conceptions of family. We need to explore these practical barriers to exercising the right to have children.

Finally, the right to have a child gives rise to the right not to be forced to have one. Contraception and abortion should be accepted as means to prevent pregnancy and childbirth. Contraceptives are not banned in Japan, but the lack of access creates a huge practical barrier. Although abortion per se is illegal, it is widely practised. This ease of access despite the legal ban is troublesome. We need to inquire whether this position can be justified.

The right to have sex or to refuse sex and the right to have children or not to have them are important social issues in many countries. Japan needs to squarely face these hard issues too. They tend to be addressed as legislative or policy issues in many countries, but they need to be treated as constitutional issues instead. The Constitution is the foundational law of the country. It sets out the basic rules for government. We need to consider sex and childbirth as constitutional issues because they are fundamental to the most intimate part of life and play a vital role in human and social survival. Moreover, it is imperative to see them as interrelated. They are not stand-alone issues that can be assessed independently of each other. This book, therefore, sets out to examine them as interconnected constitutional issues to be approached as a matter of sexual autonomy.

The Reason for Focusing on Sexual Autonomy

The Need for an Integrated Framework

One may ask why the issues of sex and childbirth would be best analyzed as a matter of sexual autonomy. The term "sexual autonomy" is used to signify both sexual freedom and freedom of choice in childbirth. Sexual freedom includes the right to decide or change one's sex or gender, the right to have sex, and the right not to be forced to have sex. It represents the idea that sex should be consensual and that all consensual sex should be respected. Freedom of choice in childbirth includes the right to have a child (or to become a parent), as well as the right not to have one, via the use of contraceptives and access to abortion. In the United States, some of these issues have been discussed as privacy rights, furnishing important lessons for everyone.

A Lesson from the United States

The Supreme Court of the United States (SCOTUS) has interpreted the right to privacy under the Constitution as including various freedoms of the individual under the due process clause of the Fourteenth Amendment, which stipulates that "no State shall deprive any person of life, liberty, or property, without due process of law."[3] The SCOTUS thus accepts procreation as a fundamental right that is protected under the Constitution.[4] It also recognizes the right to use contraceptives as a constitutionally protected privacy right in *Griswold v Connecticut*.[5] It also used to recognize the right to an abortion as a constitutionally protected privacy right as well, in *Roe v Wade*.[6] The exact scope of the right to privacy is still unclear. It probably would have included the right to make deeply personal sexual and reproductive decisions, such as whether to have a child or an abortion.

In the past, however, there were doubts over whether the right to privacy could also include the right to sexual activity itself, especially non-reproductive sex. In *Bowers v Hardwick*, for example, the SCOTUS declined to recognize a right to homosexual sex under the Constitution, opting to uphold a Georgia statute that criminalized sodomy.[7] In *Lawrence v Texas*, however, the SCOTUS struck down a statute that criminalized homosexual sodomy and clarified that the right to privacy included the right to engage in private, consensual sexual activities.[8]

Moreover, in *Obergefell v Hodges*, the SCOTUS invoked the Constitution in striking down the exclusion of same-sex marriage.[9] The SCOTUS held that "under the Due Process Clause of the Fourteenth Amendment, no State shall 'deprive any person of life, liberty, or property, without due process of law.'" The fundamental liberties protected by this clause "extend to certain personal choices central to individual dignity and autonomy, including intimate choices that define personal identity and beliefs."[10] In holding that the right to marry is indeed protected by the Constitution, and that it should also be extended to same-sex couples, the SCOTUS stated that "like choices concerning contraception, family relationships, procreation, and childrearing, all of which are protected by the Constitution, decisions concerning marriage are among the most intimate that an individual can make."[11]

It therefore appeared that the SCOTUS was ready to define the right to privacy as including autonomous decisions on personal matters such as family relationships, reproduction, and childbearing. Nevertheless, these judgments are filled with ambiguity, and their reach remains unclear. For instance, the SCOTUS in *Lawrence* criticized *Bowers* by quoting the key part of its opinion:

> "The issue presented is whether the Federal Constitution confers a fundamental right upon homosexuals to engage in sodomy and hence invalidates the laws of the many States that still make such conduct illegal and have done so for a very long time." Id., at 190. That statement, we now conclude, discloses the Court's own failure

> to appreciate the extent of the liberty at stake. To say that the issue in Bowers was simply the right to engage in certain sexual conduct demeans the claim the individual put forward, just as it would demean a married couple were it to be said marriage is simply about the right to have sexual intercourse. The laws involved in Bowers and here are, to be sure, statutes that purport to do no more than prohibit a particular sexual act. Their penalties and purposes, though, have more far-reaching consequences, touching on the most private human conduct, sexual behaviour, and in the most private of places, the home. The statutes do seek to control a personal relationship that, whether or not entitled to formal recognition in the law, is within the liberty of persons to choose without being punished as criminals.
>
> This, as a general rule, should counsel against attempts by the State, or a court, to define the meaning of the relationship or to set its boundaries absent injury to a person or abuse of an institution the law protects. It suffices for us to acknowledge that adults may choose to enter upon this relationship in the confines of their homes and their own private lives and still retain their dignity as free persons. When sexuality finds overt expression in intimate conduct with another person, the conduct can be but one element in a personal bond that is more enduring. The liberty protected by the Constitution allows homosexual persons the right to make this choice.[12]

According to this, the liberty at stake encompasses more than simply having sex with a partner of the same gender. Instead, it extends to a much more fundamental freedom: the right to define a personal relationship and to set its boundaries.

Again, in summarizing recent SCOTUS decisions on the right to privacy, it confirmed in *Obergefell* that the rulings had protected

> personal decisions relating to marriage, procreation, contraception, family relationships, child rearing, and education. In explaining the respect the Constitution demands for the autonomy of the person in making these choices, we stated as follows: These matters, involving the most intimate and personal choices a person may make in a lifetime, choices central to personal dignity and autonomy, are central to

the liberty protected by the Fourteenth Amendment. At the heart of liberty is the right to define one's own concept of existence, of meaning, of the universe, and of the mystery of human life.[13]

Sexual Autonomy: The Better Alternative

Therefore, the SCOTUS has already developed the right to privacy doctrine to analyze these matters. It might be argued that other countries, including Japan, could use this approach. However, the SCOTUS understanding of the underlying right to privacy is too broad and could potentially include all personal rights that an individual can enjoy under the Constitution. The boundaries of this right are too vague.

It is important to point out that the SCOTUS in *Lawrence* believed that homosexual sodomy was sexual conduct, though it was not traditional sexual intercourse. The SCOTUS stated that its other recent judgments "show an emerging awareness that liberty gives substantial protection to adult persons in deciding how to conduct their private lives in matters pertaining to *sex*."[14] Apparently, the SCOTUS has now accepted that homosexual acts between two male adults do constitute "sex." It reiterated that *Lawrence*

> does involve two adults who, with full and mutual consent from each other, engaged in *sexual practices* common to a homosexual lifestyle. The petitioners are entitled to respect for their private lives. The State cannot demean their existence or control their destiny by making their private *sexual conduct* a crime. Their right to liberty under the Due Process Clause gives them the full right to engage in their conduct without intervention of the government. It is a promise of the Constitution that there is a realm of personal liberty which the government may not enter.[15]

This statement is another indication that the SCOTUS has expanded the traditional understanding of sex to include much broader sex-related activities, including between a gay couple. However, the SCOTUS has not provided a definition of sex.

Moreover, in distinguishing consensual homosexual activities from other sexual activities that have been subject to statutory bans, the

SCOTUS explicitly made the following reservation: *Lawrence* "does not involve minors. It does not involve persons who might be injured or coerced or who are situated in relationships where consent might not easily be refused. It does not involve public conduct or prostitution."[16] This suggests that sex involving minors, coercion, or a person who is in an unequal relationship, or that takes place in public or with a prostitute may not be constitutionally protected. However, the SCOTUS has not indicated how to distinguish which sexual activities fall outside the protection of the Constitution.

Moreover, in totally reversing this trend of expanding the right to privacy and, in overturning *Roe*, which started this revolutionary change, and *Planned Parenthood v Casey*,[17] which confirmed *Roe* on *stare decisis* grounds, the SCOTUS in *Dobbs v Jackson Women's Health Organization*,[18] cast a serious doubt on the validity of these precedents. The SCOTUS declares that

> Even though the Constitution makes no mention of abortion, the Court held that it confers a broad right to obtain one. It did not claim that American law or the common law had ever recognized such a right, and its survey of history ranged from the constitutionally irrelevant ... to the plainly incorrect ... After cataloging a wealth of other information having no bearing on the meaning of the Constitution, the opinion concluded with a numbered set of rules much like those that might be found in a statute enacted by a legislature.[19]

It thus concluded that "[w]e hold that *Roe* and *Casey* must be overruled. The Constitution makes no reference to abortion, and no such right is implicitly protected by any constitutional provision, including the one on which the defenders of *Roe* and *Casey* now chiefly rely – the Due Process Clause of the Fourteenth Amendment. That provision has been held to guarantee some rights that are not mentioned in the Constitution, but any such right must be "deeply rooted in this Nation's history and tradition" and "implicit in the concept of ordered liberty." The right to abortion does not fall within this category.[20] In the end, it was held, that

Roe was egregiously wrong from the start. Its reasoning was exceptionally weak, and the decision has had damaging consequences. And far from bringing about a national settlement of the abortion issue, *Roe* and *Casey* have enflamed debate and deepened division. It is time to heed the Constitution and return the issue of abortion to the people's elected representatives. "The permissibility of abortion, and the limitations, upon it, are to be resolved like most important questions in our democracy: by citizens trying to persuade one another and then voting" ... That is what the Constitution and the rule of law demand.[21]

The SCOTUS now made clear that "[c]onstitutional analysis must begin with 'the language of the instrument,' which offers a 'fixed standard' for ascertaining what our founding document means ... The Constitution makes no express reference to a right to obtain an abortion, and therefore those who claim that it protects such a right must show that the right is somehow implicit in the constitutional text."[22] It concedes that the Due Process Clause of the Fourteenth Amendment protects two categories of rights. The first one consists of rights guaranteed by the first eight Amendments. The second category comprises a "select list of fundamental rights that are not mentioned anywhere in the Constitution." "In deciding whether a right falls into either of these categories," the SCOTUS declares, "the Court has long asked whether the right is 'deeply rooted in [our] history and tradition' and whether it is essential to our Nation's 'scheme of ordered liberty.' ... And in conducting this inquiry, we have engaged in a careful analysis of the history of the right at issue."[23] "Historical inquiries of this nature are essential," the SCOTUS continues, "whenever we are asked to recognize a new component of the 'liberty' protected by the Due Process Clause because the term 'liberty' alone provides little guidance. 'Liberty' is a capacious term."[24] In interpreting what is meant by the Fourteenth Amendment's reference to liberty, it admonishes,

> we must guard against the natural human tendency to confuse what that Amendment protects with our own ardent views about the liberty that Americans should enjoy. That is why the Court has long been

"reluctant" to recognize rights that are not mentioned in the Constitution ... Substantive due process has at times been a treacherous field for this Court ... and it has sometimes led the Court to usurp authority that the Constitution entrusts to the people's elected representatives ... As the Court cautioned ... "[w]e must ... exercise the utmost care whenever we are asked to break new ground in this field, lest the liberty protected by the Due Process Clause be subtly transformed into the policy preferences of the Members of this Court." The Court must not fall prey to such an unprincipled approach. Instead, guided by the history and tradition that map the essential components of our Nation's concept of ordered liberty, we must ask what the Fourteenth Amendment means by the term "liberty." When we engage in that inquiry in the present case, the clear answer is that the Fourteenth Amendment does not protect the right to an abortion.[25]

Shrugging off the argument based on *stare decisis* to keep the *Roe* holding,[26] the SCOTUS explicitly overruled it.

The *Dobbs* holding triggered the suspicion that the SCOTUS might totally rewrite the whole privacy jurisprudence.[27] The Justice Alito's majority opinion carefully emphasized the uniqueness of abortion[28] and explicitly reject any such suspicion.[29] Thus, although the right to an abortion was now rejected by the SCOTUS, the rest of the cases still remains valid law.

The *Dobbs* holding is in one sense inevitable. The right to privacy, which the SCOTUS has relied on in these cases, is so amorphous and so undefined. It does not have any clear definition and any boundaries.[30] The right to create and maintain an intimate personal relationship adopted by the *Lawrence* and *Obergefell* is apparently too unprincipled.

In light of these ambiguities and the difficulty in generating a precise definition of the right to privacy, as well as the fact that the SCOTUS has now concluded that the right to an abortion was not included in the definition of the right to privacy, analyzing issues of sex and childbirth in terms of sexual autonomy, rather than privacy, would be the best course. All these issues are part of a single right to sexual autonomy, which deserves to be constitutionally protected. Whereas the SCOTUS focuses on the broader right to define a personal relationship and to set its boundaries, it is better to focus specifically on sexual autonomy – that is, sexual freedom and the freedom of choice regarding childbirth.[31]

Moreover, it is best to accept that sexual autonomy encompasses all kinds of decisions on sex and childbirth. We can then examine whether bans and restrictions can be justified on the assumption that all these decisions, at least at face value, fall within the definition of sexual autonomy.

Sexual Autonomy and the Constitution

Constitutional Protection

The starting point of my analysis is whether sexual autonomy should be constitutionally protected. Sexual autonomy is deeply personal. It is an essential part of love, integral to individual development, and vital for the reproduction of children. Securing it is also vital for people as both individuals and citizens. In a liberal democratic country, sex, childbirth, and raising children are essential in furthering that system into the future. Obviously, therefore, sexual autonomy needs to be constitutionally protected.

Sexual Autonomy and the Constitution of Japan

The Constitution of Japan has no provisions that explicitly protect sexual autonomy.[32] Although many Japanese people see sex and childbirth as individual freedoms, there is no clear consensus regarding whether they are constitutionally protected.

If sexual autonomy were a protected right under the Constitution, the government could not unreasonably interfere with it. Japan's national legislature, the Diet, wields legislative power.[33] It enacted the Criminal Code, the Civil Code, and other statutes. Both of these codes have a significant impact on the sexual autonomy of individuals. The judiciary exercises judicial power.[34] Furthermore, the Constitution stipulates that the Supreme Court of Japan (SCOJ) has ultimate authority over all constitutional questions.[35] All courts can review the constitutionality of legislative decisions, but the SCOJ, as the highest court, has the final say.

Thus, if sexual autonomy were constitutionally protected, the judiciary would need to determine whether any legislative restrictions on sexual autonomy could be justified. To examine various issues related to the right to sexual autonomy, we must define precisely what is meant by "sex" and must determine what should be included in the definition of sexual autonomy. Furthermore, it is important to consider how the right to sexual autonomy should be safeguarded by the judiciary, what kinds of interests the government can invoke in regulating it, and to what extent such government interference can be justified. These examinations will lead to important constraints on the government.[36]

How should we infer the right to sexual autonomy from the Constitution? The most natural approach is to follow the lead of the SCOTUS and accept sexual autonomy as a "privacy right" that is protected under the due process clause.[37] In Japan, however, article 13 of the Constitution declares that "all of the people shall be respected as individuals." In this, it mandates the adoption of individualism and prioritizes individuals ahead of the state or society, stipulating also that their "right to life, liberty, and the pursuit of happiness" shall be the "supreme consideration in legislation and in other governmental affairs."[38] Most academics agree that article 13 should include unenumerated fundamental human rights, one of which should be some kind of right to autonomy.[39] This should encompass family affairs, including the right to marry, divorce, have children, and cohabitate.[40] This constitutes an acceptance of the right to privacy, as developed by the SCOTUS in the United States. Therefore, it is a natural step to enshrine the right to sexual autonomy in article 13, rather than relying on the due process clause.

On the other hand, article 24 of the Constitution makes a special provision on family matters and family law:

> Marriage shall be based only on the mutual consent of both sexes and it shall be maintained through mutual cooperation with the equal rights of husband and wife as a basis. With regard to choice of spouse, property rights, inheritance, choice of domicile, divorce and other matters pertaining to marriage and the family, laws shall be enacted from the standpoint of individual dignity and the essential equality of the sexes.[41]

Article 14 already provides that "all of the people are equal under the law and there shall be no discrimination in political, economic or social relations because of race, creed, sex, social status or family origin." Article 24 has thus been viewed as a special equality provision on family matters and family law.

Although article 24 has not been interpreted as a substantive right provision, it explicitly mandates the government to enact family laws based on "individual dignity and the essential equality of the sexes." Thus, it could and should be construed in a way that grants individuals the right to autonomy in family affairs as a substantive right.[42] Since article 24 is a specific provision on family matters and family law, it could be seen as superior to article 13 in protecting sexual autonomy as a substantive right.

Either way, there is ample textual support for granting constitutional protection to the right to autonomy in family affairs. But given that the original intent of article 24 was to reject the family law system of the Meiji government, it is apparent that it is better designed than article 13 to secure individual dignity and the essential equality of sexes in all aspects of law relevant to family affairs.

The SCOTUS, in rejecting the right to an abortion and casting doubt on why it should be constitutionally protected, now focuses on the text and history. If we exclusively focus on the history, the right to sexual autonomy would likely not be justified. Unlike the right to privacy, which the SCOTUS had relied on to justify these decisions, however, the right to sexual autonomy is much defined and principled. It can be considered an integral part of individuals' lives, and it constitutes the very essence of one's personhood. Moreover, if liberal democratic society is to survive, the right to sexual autonomy is indispensable. Without sexual autonomy, no one can create a family and participate in democratic process. Thus, although history may not be on the side of sexual autonomy, there are ample reasons to grant constitutional protection to such a right. Moreover, unlike in the US, there is an ample textual support for sexual autonomy in Japan.

Article 24 does not define "marriage and the family." Apparently, however, it guarantees the autonomy right with respect to all aspects of family, including whether to have an intimate relationship with someone, whether and where to cohabit, whether a couple attempt to have a child, whether they welcome it, and what kind of relationship they want to have with it. It should also entail an individual's decision on what kind of relationship to have with parents, siblings, and other relatives. In this sense, the guaranteed right to autonomy in family affairs should be broad enough to include sexual autonomy, which should be a primary part of autonomy on family affairs. It must also be noted that the right to have sex should be protected regardless of whether sex occurs within a legal marriage. Sex can be part of marriage, but it is not necessarily exclusive to marriage. Rather, it is an essential aspect of life, often a manifestation of love, and integral in creating human life. Therefore, the right to have sex should be seen as an aspect of sexual autonomy and should be protected under article 24, but this protection should extend to sexual freedom in general without regard to marriage and family.

The right to sexual autonomy should thus be broad enough to encompass all personal decisions on sexual matters. It should include the right to decide or change one's sexual or gender identity and the right to decide whether to have sex, with whom, when, where, and how.[43] Additionally, sexual autonomy should mean that anyone can refuse sex, giving rise to a right not to be forced to have it.[44] Sex must be voluntary and consensual. Any forced sex without consent is a violation of this right.

Sexual autonomy should also include the right to have a child or to become a parent. Of course, as sex was once the only means of reproduction, this right was a natural corollary to the right to have sex. But as we will see later, women can now become pregnant using technological assistance, and therefore the right to become a parent should be independent of the right to have sex. Additionally, it should include the right to access ART/MAR. It should also include the right to be treated as parents under the law.

Also, the right to become a parent includes the right not to do so. This means that an individual should have the right to use contraceptives and to terminate a pregnancy. As discussed later on, the right to abortion should therefore be recognized as a part of sexual autonomy protected under the Constitution.

The Standard of Review

In countries where courts are empowered to review the constitutionality of legislation or other government actions, citizens can use them to challenge government restrictions of sexual autonomy. However, the way in which courts review and scrutinize such bans or restrictions differs from country to country.

In the United States, the SCOTUS initially closely scrutinized any restriction on the right to abortion. This principle originated in *Roe*, a landmark 1973 case in which the SCOTUS held that the right to abortion was included in the privacy rights under the due process clause of the Fourteenth Amendment and that it was a "fundamental" right.[45] Although it is not an absolute right, as was claimed, any restriction was subject to strict scrutiny: only a compelling and specific government interest can justify a restriction. Any overbroad or underinclusive restrictions would be deemed impermissible. Therefore, the SCOTUS struck down a Texas statute that prohibited abortion except to save the life of the mother, finding it overbroad.

This adoption of strict scrutiny has significant implications for other right-to-privacy cases. If it is applied in other cases, there is very little room for government restriction. In cases involving economic liberty, the SCOTUS usually applies a rationality review: it will uphold economic regulation so long as it serves a legitimate rational goal, and its means have a rational connection to that goal. If legislative judgments on the necessity of regulation and on the choice of means are susceptible to objection, courts generally defer to the judgments of the legislature. Under this very lenient standard of review, almost any restriction can be justified. It is therefore unsurprising that the SCOTUS, which had used strict scrutiny on restrictions on liberty of contract in the early twentieth century, came to apply this lenient standard and upheld all economic regulations dating from 1938 following the fierce criticism against its judicial activism.

As a result, when a restriction on sex or childbirth is challenged in the United States, the argument is usually framed as an infringement of the right to privacy, as this calls for the court to apply strict scrutiny and increases the likelihood that it will strike down the restriction. Although the SCOTUS later applied a somewhat more lenient standard of scrutiny in abortion cases,[46] many lawyers still expect courts to apply strict scrutiny in cases involving the right to privacy. Although the *Dobbs* judgment used such a lenient standard of review to examine the rationality of an abortion ban, since the SCOTUS found no ground to protect the right to an abortion,[47] all other cases still remain valid, which applies heightened scrutiny to the infringement of other privacy rights.

In Canada and many European countries, the courts are not mandated to apply such strict scrutiny. Instead, they usually apply a single standard in all cases: the proportionality review.[48] According to the Supreme Court of Canada (SCOC), if a restriction on individual rights is to be justifiable, it must serve a "pressing and substantial" government interest, and its means must be proportionate: a rational connection must exist between the means and the aim, impairment must be minimal, and the overall balance must be preserved.[49] The review standard does not differ depending on the right involved. However, the SCOC emphasizes that courts need to consider contextual factors in applying it. This means that it is sometimes easy to satisfy but sometimes difficult.[50] It has much in common with the proportionality review adopted by the Federal Constitutional Court of Germany (FCCG). It is highly ad hoc and extremely unpredictable.

Japan has not accepted either the dichotomy adopted by the SCOTUS or the proportionality review of the SCOC.[51] As a result, the SCOJ framework of analysis is unclear and unpredictable. Moreover, the SCOJ has never squarely faced the constitutional questions raised in this book.

Although scholars who study constitutional matters agree that the right to sexual autonomy should be constitutionally protected, there is little discussion over what kind of judicial standard should be applied in reviewing the constitutionality of restrictions on sexual autonomy. If we follow the lead of the SCOTUS and take the strict scrutiny approach, the government will probably have difficulty in justifying limitations. On the other hand, if we adopt the more lenient review, as applied by the SCOTUS to economic liberties, courts will probably uphold all sorts of restrictions. If we follow the proportionality review of the SCOC or the FCCG, the results will be highly unpredictable.

Of course, the adoption of a review standard may not be as critical as is often assumed. For instance, in the United States, the SCOTUS has struck down legislation even under the lenient rationality standard. Specifically, when a case involves discrimination against homosexuals, it has indicated that homophobia can never be acceptable, and the SCOTUS uses the baseline rationality review to determine if this restriction can be justified for reasons other than mere prejudice.[52] Therefore, even under the lenient rationality standard, some kinds of restrictions could be struck down as unreasonable.

Nevertheless, the choice of review standard is still important as it affects judicial scrutiny and the way in which courts reach their decisions. From this perspective, strict scrutiny is very demanding and could have a huge impact on sexual autonomy cases. Since sexual autonomy is so essential in a liberal democracy, adoption of strict scrutiny in cases involving it would be justified. Moreover, many sexual autonomy cases involve sexual minorities whose values and views on sexual relationships may not to be shared by the mainstream. Therefore, these cases appear to involve "isolated and insular" minorities,[53] leading to an expectation that the political process is not available for redress. The judiciary, politically independent, is their only avenue to seek redress. Therefore, the strict scrutiny approach is best for sexual autonomy cases.

Government Restrictions on Sexual Autonomy

Even if the right to sexual autonomy is constitutionally protected, this does not mean that the government cannot regulate or limit it. Certain constraints can be justified, and sexual autonomy has been subjected to all kinds of limits in the past. By reviewing them, we can identify government interests that could be invoked to justify such restrictions. We can clearly see the legitimacy and limits of government justification in cases involving sexual freedom.

First, in aid of facilitating its various programs, the government might have a legitimate interest in collecting information on the sex or gender of individuals. This might restrict an individual's right to identify his or her sex or gender, at least until that person might choose to change it, but it should be allowed for the accomplishment of compelling interests.

Second, the government has a legitimate interest in protecting the freedom of everyone not to be coerced into sex. The punishment for rape and sexual assault can thus be justified as a means to protect the sexual autonomy of others. Banning sex with someone who is incapable of giving consent is also justifiable. For instance, a person who is unconscious or semi-conscious, or who is extremely intoxicated, is not capable of understanding the situation and agreeing to sex. Therefore, sex with that person is defined as forced.

The corollary to this principle is the necessity to protect those who have a diminished capacity to consent. Some examples here include children, persons with mental disabilities, and those who are at a disadvantage in a relationship where power is unbalanced. These individuals are vulnerable to exploitation, and many consider them to be in need of protection. As a result, a ban or other kind of restriction could sometimes be called for to shield them from unwanted sex.

Though intended to be beneficial, such measures are paternalistic, in that they remove the freedom to give consent. Generally, they cannot be applied to adults who are not categorized as vulnerable. Most adults are assumed to have the capacity to understand and to give or refuse consent, and they therefore do not need such protection. Thus, any paternalistic restrictions need to be carefully justified, based on the degree of vulnerability, the extent of the protection, and whether the need for it outweighs the freedom that such individuals should have.

Sexual freedom could be restricted for other compelling reasons. Everyone has a right to engage in sex, but everyone should also have a right not be disturbed by sex in public places. No one should be forced to watch someone having sex in public. The government would have a legitimate interest in protecting the rights and interests of others in this regard.

Furthermore, it has a legitimate and compelling interest in securing public safety and public health. Bans or restrictions on private activities, including sex, should be allowed if they are necessary to secure safety or health.

On the other hand, governments have regulated sex for moral reasons, which still sometimes occurs. For instance, the prohibition on having sex in public was at least partially justified in the name of defending morality. Group sex might be forbidden for the same reason. The ban on sex with an unmarried person was justified on the assumption that sex was reserved solely for married couples. The ban on adultery was intended to protect family order and monogamous sexual relationships – being unfaithful to a partner was seen as immoral. In Europe and North America, prohibitions on various kinds of "deviant" and "atypical" sex,[54] such as sodomy, were grounded in Christian beliefs. However, this resort to morality was eventually viewed as indefensible. In *Lawrence*, the SCOTUS made clear that restrictions on sexual activities cannot be justified simply because mainstream society does not perceive them as moral or even because it condemns them as immoral. Sexual autonomy, if it means anything, must mean that people can make their own decisions about their sexuality so long as this does not restrict the rights and interests of others. Various sexual activities should not be banned simply because they are deemed immoral or because they disturb the moral sense of a community.

In *R. v Labaye*, a case involving a brothel in which indecent acts were committed, the SCOC stated that

> historically, the legal concepts of indecency ... as applied to conduct ... have been *inspired and informed by the moral views of the community. But over time, courts increasingly came to recognize that morals and taste were subjective, arbitrary and unworkable in the criminal context, and that a diverse society could function only with a generous measure of tolerance for minority mores and practices.* This led to a legal norm of objectively ascertainable harm instead of subjective disapproval.[55]

The SCOC held that only "conduct which society formally recognizes as incompatible with its proper functioning" could be subject to criminal punishment.[56] It elaborated:

> Two general requirements emerge from this description of the harm required for criminal indecency. First, the words "formally recognize" suggest that the harm must be grounded in norms which our society has recognized in its Constitution or similar fundamental laws. This means that the inquiry is not based on individual notions of harm, nor on the teachings of a particular ideology, but on what society, through its laws and institutions, has recognized as essential to its proper functioning. Second, the harm must be to a serious degree. It must not only detract from proper societal functioning but must be *incompatible* with it.[57]

The SCOC explained different types of the relevant harms:

> Three types of harm have thus far emerged from the jurisprudence as being capable of supporting a finding of indecency: (1) harm to those whose autonomy and liberty may be restricted by being confronted with inappropriate conduct; (2) harm to society by predisposing others to anti-social conduct; and (3) harm to individuals participating in the conduct. Each of these types of harm is grounded in values recognized by our Constitution and similar fundamental laws. The list is not closed; other types of harm may be shown in the future to meet the standards of criminality ... But thus far, these are the types of harm recognized by the cases.[58]

The SCOC went on to declare that

> reference to the fundamental values of our Constitution and similar fundamental laws also eliminates types of conduct that do not constitute harm in the required sense. Bad taste does not suffice ... *Moral views, even if strongly held, do not suffice. Similarly, the fact that most members of the community might disapprove of the conduct does not suffice* ... In each case, more is required to establish the necessary harm for criminal indecency.[59]

This holding is remarkable because it explicitly rules out the possibility of invoking morality as a justification for regulating sex. Any such infringement on sexual activity needs to be justified by specific harms that the government has a legitimate interest to prohibit.[60]

This reasoning should be applicable to all sexual autonomy cases. We should follow the SCOTUS and the SCOC and deny morality as a justification for regulating sexual autonomy. All individuals have different opinions and attitudes toward sexual autonomy, which cannot be restricted merely because mainstream society sees certain conduct as immoral, indecent, or unethical. To determine whether a restriction is acceptable, we need to assess the objective harms to people or to a community. When we examine each instance in which sexual autonomy is regulated, we need to carefully sort out what interests the government can invoke to justify the ban or restriction, and whether they are legitimate and sufficient.

Sexual Freedom: The Right to Decide One's Sexual Identity and the Right to Have Sex   2

Sexual freedom means that people are at liberty to decide their own sexual or gender identity and to have sex without criminal punishment, civil liability, or government regulation of any kind. Although sex is regarded as a freedom, all governments, including that of Japan, start from the premise that sexual or gender identity is predetermined by biological characteristics at birth. There is no freedom to change it. Moreover, every country restricts or regulates sex in some way. Rape is universally prohibited, and some forms of consensual sexual behaviour have been limited.

Sexual Freedom

History of Sexual Freedom in Japan
Before the Meiji Restoration of 1868, the beginning of the modern era in Japan, the country had no integrated legal system. Japan's two major religions, Shintoism and Buddhism, have no meaningful implications regarding sex, so there were no religious motivations to restrict it. This is a stark contrast to Western countries, where Christianity deems sex to be sinful and promotes its regulation for religious reasons.[1]

The military government of the Edo Period, which spanned three centuries, established a family system for samurai warriors that was based on Confucian traditions. It regulated the behaviour of local lords, local leaders of these samurai warriors, and their families.[2] The most important role of the lord was to maintain the military house and to pass it on to a male successor. Thus, it was imperative for a lord to produce a son who could inherit the house, which included a huge number of retainers. As a result, lords were allowed to have secondary wives (*sokushitsu*), and sometimes their illegitimate children could inherit the military house. Lower-ranking samurai were required to live humbly and to follow the Confucian code of ethics. Their sexual activities were similarly strictly regulated.[3]

The people who were not samurai were treated somewhat differently from the samurai warriors. The Kujikata osadamegaki was compiled in 1742 to allow judges to adjudicate criminal liability of the public,[4] but it was meant to be confidential and has never been officially published. However, there were several crimes related to sex, such as sex outside of marriage, rape, and adultery by a married woman for which she could be executed together with her lover. But these bans were rarely enforced, and the sexual behaviour of the public was not strictly regulated.[5]

After the Meiji Restoration, the government embarked on a program of modernization. It introduced a legal system similar to that of France and enacted the first Criminal Code in 1880.[6] Then it shifted its focus from France to Germany and enacted the Civil Code in 1896,[7] followed by its second Criminal Code in 1907.[8] Japanese law is predominantly a civil system, regulated by various codes.[9] Since the Western legal tradition was heavily influenced by Christianity, some of the laws imported into Japan showed evidence of this. But there was no strong incentive to fully incorporate and implement Christian beliefs into the Japanese system.

In 1871, the Meiji government passed the original Family Registration Act to establish a national family registry for all Japanese citizens.[10] It collected information from housemasters on their household, making a distinction between men and women. This was Japan's first nation-wide family registry. Since only male citizens possessed the right to vote,[11] and under the Civil Code men and women were treated differently in various other situations,[12] distinguishing between the sexes was important for the government.

The 1880 Criminal Code included several bans on sexual freedom, prohibiting forcible indecent conduct (obscene conduct) against anyone under the age of twelve, as well as forcible indecent conduct against anyone twelve years of age or older, with assault or intimidation.[13] Forcible indecent conduct with assault and intimidation against anyone under the age of twelve was separately banned.[14] In addition, the rape of women twelve years of age or older,[15] sexual intercourse as well as rape of girls under age twelve,[16] rape resulting in death or injury,[17] and adultery were also separately forbidden.[18]

When the Meiji government passed the first Criminal Code in 1880, the Constitution did not yet exist. However, when the public demanded that a representative body be established, it was forced to create the Meiji Constitution in 1889 and to establish the Imperial Diet.[19] The Constitution was premised on the sovereignty of the Emperor, who possessed all government power.[20] It was highly patriarchal since only a man could become an Emperor,[21] who was regarded as the father of all Japanese subjects.[22] The Constitution protected various rights, but because the people were regarded as subjects of the Emperor, these rights were granted only as the rights of subjects.[23] Moreover, they were granted by the gracious gift of the sovereign Emperor to his subjects, and they were protected only "within the law."[24] Therefore, when the Imperial Diet together with the Emperor passed legislation that restricted these rights, there was no recourse. Nor was there any provision for judicial review, which would have empowered the courts to determine the constitutionality of legislation. Moreover, the rights to equality, to have sex, or to sexual autonomy were not protected. Instead, it was believed that sex and family relationships needed to be regulated to promote state power. As the government was committed to building a "wealthy and strong state,"[25] one that could compete with European nations, it naturally came to restrict sex and sexual autonomy for the good of the country.[26]

The most conspicuous restriction of sex and sexual freedom was incorporated into the family law sections of the Civil Code.[27] Intending to follow precedents set during the Edo Period, the government based the family system on the house system, as mandated for the samurai and local lords. As a result, family law prioritized the house – a family consisting of several generations that was headed by a housemaster.[28] He was granted sweeping power, including the right to accept a new member,[29] to decide where members would live,[30] and to approve the marriage of girls.[31] However, in return he was obliged to support everyone.[32]

Under Meiji law, wives and girls occupied a subsidiary position.[33] Women did not possess the right to vote.[34] They had no right to manage the house property.[35] Moreover, as stated above, girls needed to obtain approval from the housemaster to get married. They were not provided with higher education, due to the belief that they should learn domestic skills rather than studying at school. They were strongly encouraged to marry at a young age, bear children, and devote their lives to homemaking and child rearing. They rarely held white-collar jobs, and those who did filled secretarial positions and were pressured to resign once they married.

There was no sexual autonomy for women. They were expected to be chaste until marriage, and a wife could not refuse sex with her husband. There was no concept of domestic rape. A man expected to have sex with his wife regardless of her wishes. In practice, many girls were forced to marry the man chosen by their housemaster or father and did not have the freedom to say no. Marriage was a union between two houses, not simply between two individuals, and thus it was very important to the house and housemaster. The preferences of the women rarely mattered to the housemaster. Wives were prohibited from having extra-marital sex. If a house were extremely poor and could not afford to sustain all its members, many girls were sold to brothels by the housemaster, and many others ended up working in factories, with advance payment to the housemaster. Working conditions were often poor in the factories, and many women died of illnesses contracted on the job.

The estate of the house was inherited by the first-born son of the housemaster.[36] As a result, giving birth to a boy was considered the primary role of a wife. If she failed in this respect, she could be divorced or kicked out of the house. At the time, women were largely seen as a means of producing an heir.

In contrast, though sex was subject to all kinds of social restraints, men were granted far more freedom than women. They could have sexual relationships with single women (only adultery with married women was prohibited). They could have sex with prostitutes and could have mistresses.

Therefore, under the family law system of the Meiji government, women had no sexual autonomy. However, even the sexual freedoms that men enjoyed had no constitutional protection but were merely created and granted by law. Essentially, men and women were supposed to devote their lives to the welfare of the Emperor and the state. There were no inherent individual freedoms. During times of war, everyone was expected to give his or her life in service of the Emperor and the state. Men were conscripted and sent overseas as soldiers. All other persons, properties, and natural resources were mobilized for the war effort, and there was no room to refrain from actively supporting it. Anyone who failed to do so or who cast doubt on the wisdom of the Emperor or the government, even the slightest hint of skepticism, was condemned as anti-Japanese and subjected to violent questioning and torture by the secret police. There was simply no individual freedom left.

Sex under the Current Constitution
Under the Constitution of Japan, promulgated in 1946, the people were granted a full list of rights and liberties that were deemed "fundamental human rights."[37] These were "guaranteed to the people by [the] Constitution [and were] conferred upon the people of this and future generations as eternal and inviolate rights."[38] Moreover, these fundamental human rights are "conferred upon this and future generations in trust, to be held for all time inviolate."[39] They were no longer a gracious gift from the Emperor, and the Constitution declared that the people now held sovereign power.[40] The Constitution became the supreme law of the land, and every government institution (including the Diet) was bound by it.[41] Furthermore, it explicitly granted the power of judicial review to the judiciary, making the Supreme Court of Japan (SCOJ) the final determinant of the constitutionality of legislation and other government measures.[42]

Although the Supreme Court of the United States (SCOTUS) is somewhat ambivalent on whether the right to have sex is constitutionally protected, it did imply that such was the case when it struck down a ban on homosexual sodomy in *Lawrence v Texas*.[43] However, as the previous chapter revealed, the right to have sex or to exercise sexual freedom should be granted constitutional protection as a part of sexual autonomy. Indeed, as mentioned, articles 13[44] and 24[45] of the Constitution of Japan should be construed as providing protection for sexual freedom.

In particular, it must be emphasized that article 24 was inserted into the Constitution primarily to reject the family law system of the Meiji government.[46] The Constitution was based on a draft prepared by the occupation forces. In the Occupation Headquarters under General Douglas MacArthur, a team was appointed to prepare a preliminary draft that the Japanese government would use to craft the Constitution.[47] Beate Sirota Gordon, a female American citizen who had grown up in Japan, was a team member. As the only one who had first-hand experience of sexual discrimination in Japan, she was a strong advocate for sexual equality.[48] She tried to insert various equality provisions into the draft that would be handed over to the government. Ultimately, only article 24 was included, but it was pivotal in that it mandated the government to assure individual dignity and equality of the sexes in matters of family law.

As a result, the Constitution completely revamped family law. The Civil Code of 1896 was reworked to state that its own provisions must be interpreted in accordance with individual dignity and the essential equality of both sexes.[49] Its family law and inheritance law sections were totally rewritten. The prominence of the house and the overwhelming power of the housemaster were removed, and a new era of family law began. Family law was now based on the new Family Registration Act of 1947, which defined a family as consisting of a married couple and their unmarried children.[50] There was no longer a housemaster. The Civil Code also introduced various new measures to secure sexual equality and individual dignity. Men could marry at age eighteen and women at sixteen.[51] Although parental approval was necessary for the marriage of minors, only one parent needed to approve.[52] If the engaged couple had reached the age of majority, no approval was required. The newlyweds could take the surname of either the husband or the wife.[53] Both were granted equal status, and both were mandated to cooperate on family affairs.[54] There was no house estate and all property belonged to individuals. The law governing inheritance was now totally egalitarian: the surviving spouse and the children inherited the estate, and all legitimate children had the equal share in it.[55]

Moreover, sex was substantially liberalized. The Criminal Code prohibited rape and sexual assault but did not include any ban on sex between consenting adults.[56] Sex with girls under age thirteen was regarded as statutory rape and was illegal regardless of their consent.[57] The Prostitution Prevention Act was created in 1956 to prohibit prostitution and sex with prostitutes.[58] But there was no criminal punishment for either the woman or her customers. The adultery ban was removed from the Criminal Code,[59] and adultery was no longer criminalized. In 1999, the Child Prostitution Prohibition Act was passed to prohibit sex with minors, with payment or the promise of payment.[60] Also, "indecent sexual conduct" (*inkō*), including sex, with minors was forbidden under local youth protection ordinances.[61] The Child Welfare Act bans making children engage in "indecent sexual conduct."[62] The Child Abuse Prevention Act also prohibits child abuse,[63] including sexual abuse.[64] These are the only legal prohibitions on sex in Japan.

The Critical Failure to Examine Sexual Autonomy

Amid all these reforms, there was no serious discussion of whether the right to decide one's own sex or gender should be protected. As mentioned, the sex of newborns is to be reported and recorded in the family registry.[65] This identification is generally made by the doctor or midwife who attended the birth.[66] It is mostly based on physical characteristics: whether the baby has a penis or a vagina. Once the sex is registered, changing it was not possible. In response to criticism from the transgender community, the government allowed a few transgender individuals to change their recorded sex or gender under very tight conditions.[67] However, aside from these few exceptions, the listing cannot be revised. Although many transgender people are precluded from changing it, neither the registration system itself nor the difficulty of changing sex or gender on the registry have been seriously questioned.

Moreover, there has been no serious discussion on whether or not sexual freedom itself is constitutionally protected. The various restrictions on sexual freedom have rarely been questioned or challenged before the courts. In 1953, for example, the rape provision of the

Criminal Code was challenged before the Supreme Court of Japan (SCOJ), but only on the grounds that it punished rape of "a female person," thus applying solely to protect women.[68] The SCOJ rejected the challenge, holding that special protection for women was justified, but it did not consider whether forcible sexual intercourse with assault or intimidation should be banned in the first place, although from the decision, this appeared to be taken for granted.[69] A 1985 Supreme Court case challenged the constitutionality of the youth protection ordinance that prohibited indecent sexual conduct with youth. The SCOJ read down the ban and rejected the challenge. It simply excluded non-exploitative romantic relationships with minors from punishment.[70] It did not confront the question of whether the right to have sex is constitutionally protected or whether the ban on exploitative sex with minors could be justified.

Even if sex is constitutionally protected, there has been no serious discussion of what should actually be counted as "sex." As a result, there is no consensus on the meaning of "sex" in the Constitution. We will see that the rape provision of the Criminal Code once banned only sexual intercourse in the traditional sense: penile penetration of a vagina.[71] It was revised in 2017 to prohibit "sexual intercourse, anal intercourse or oral intercourse," which it lumped under the heading of "sexual intercourse et al."[72] The Prostitution Prevention Act defines "prostitution" as encompassing only "sexual intercourse" in the traditional sense.[73] The Child Prostitution Prohibition Act protects children from "sexual intercourse et al.," meaning "sexual intercourse, sexual intercourse analogous conducts, and sexual touching of sexual organ et al. of the child (sexual organ, anus or nipple) for the purpose of satisfying one's own sexual desire."[74] It does not explain what is meant by conduct that is analogous to sexual intercourse. The Child Welfare Act forbids "indecent sexual conduct" with a child, though it does not specify what such conduct might be.[75] The Child Abuse Prevention Act forbids indecent sexual conduct with a child or making a child perform "indecent sexual conduct."[76] The local youth protection ordinance also prohibits "indecent sexual conduct" with youth, again without clarifying.[77] This vagueness demonstrates the difficulty of the legislature in determining exactly what conduct needs to be targeted. Moreover, advocates have suggested that the rape provision in the Criminal Code and the definition of "prostitution" in the Prostitution Prevention Act should be revised to include broader sexual conduct.[78] Obviously, there is little consensus on what kind of conduct should be regarded as sex.[79]

However, people do have sexual freedom, which is one aspect of sexual autonomy that is protected by the Constitution. We need to start our examination from that premise.

Sexual or Gender Identity

Sexual or Gender Identity and the Law

In most countries, the distinction between a man and a woman has traditionally been taken as a given. Indeed, many countries record "male" or "female" on their official documents, such as birth certificates, drivers' licences, and passports, without giving the matter a second thought. But in most countries, there is no legal ban on changing one's sexual or gender identity markers on official documents.

In this regard, the Japanese family registry system and the inability to change its listings are unusual and highly restrictive. As noted above, the government has allowed a few transgender people to change their listing, with the permission of the family court. To qualify for this, a person must satisfy the following criteria:

(a) be over the age of eighteen
(b) be unmarried
(c) have no minor children
(d) have no genital gland or be permanently lacking function of a genital gland, and
(e) have the body structure with the appearance resembling the sexual organs of the other sex.[80]

As a result, unless a transgender person is diagnosed by a physician as having a sexual identity disorder, has undergone sex reconstruction surgery, and is single with no minor children, he or she cannot change the family registry listing. Aside from these exceptions, there is no way to change sexual or gender identity in the registry.

In the past, certain differential treatments depended on sex or gender. For example, rape was defined solely as forcible sexual intercourse with a "female person,"[81] and Japanese citizenship was granted only to children of a Japanese father, not to those of a Japanese mother.[82] All these differential treatments have been removed, and maintaining the distinction between male and female no longer seems necessary for the purpose of law, except for precluding same-sex marriage. Since it is highly questionable whether the exclusion of same-sex marriage can be justified, as discussed below, there is practically no need to maintain the distinction of sex or gender for legal purposes. Nevertheless, many public application forms and documents identify individuals by noting whether they are male or female.[83] Transgender people who have not satisfied the stringent requirements and legally changed their sex experience discrimination, embarrassment, and humiliation in daily life.

The Right to Decide One's Sexual or Gender Identity
The right to determine one's own sexual or gender identity should entail deciding whether one is a man or a woman but should also encompass not being forced to choose. Instead, individuals may opt for "undecided," "non-binary," or "neither a man nor a woman." They should also be at liberty to decide their sexual or gender identity if they wish. Given that many people now see sexual or gender identity as a matter of individual decision, it is questionable whether parents can be forced to choose only whether their baby is a boy or girl. It is even more questionable whether the government can justifiably preclude legal sexual or gender identity change. Japan's current narrow exception for some transgender people is obviously too restrictive.[84] The distinction between male and female does not have to be based on physical characteristics at the time of birth, and there is no compelling interest to preclude the change of sex or gender on the family registry.[85]

The Right to Have Sex

Defining "Sex"
Sexual freedom includes the right to have sex, but what is "sex"? Is there a difference between sex, sexual activity, and sexual conduct? If sexual

activity or sexual conduct are not synonymous with sex, how are they different? What criteria should be employed in deciding whether a particular conduct is a sexual freedom that warrants constitutional protection?

When the SCOTUS in *Lawrence* struck down the ban on homosexual sodomy,[86] it granted constitutional protection to that conduct. As the couple was gay, penile penetration of a vagina was obviously not involved. However, the SCOTUS understood that their sexual conduct would meet the definition of sex under the Constitution. The SCOTUS has been quite ambivalent about sex for a long time. For example, in 1965 *Griswold v Connecticut* challenged a state law that prohibited the use of any contraceptive drug or device, as well as counselling or aiding and abetting the use of contraceptives.[87] The SCOTUS struck down the law as an infringement of the right to privacy. It emphasized sex within marriage and the need to protect the privacy of the marital bedroom, but it did not specifically declare that sex itself was to be protected.[88] In *Lawrence*, however, as mentioned above, the SCOTUS condemned *Bowers v Hardwick* for its focus on whether the Constitution conferred "a fundamental right upon homosexuals to engage in sodomy." It commented that perceiving the issue solely as "the right to engage in certain *sexual conduct*" demeaned the claim put forward by the individual. It proclaimed that the statute at issue purported to do "no more than prohibit a particular *sexual act*" and that it had more far-reaching consequences, touching on the "most private human conduct, *sexual behaviour*."[89] The SCOTUS also added that "individual decisions by married persons, concerning the intimacies of their physical relationship, even when not intended to produce offspring, are a form of 'liberty' protected by the Due Process Clause of the Fourteenth Amendment. Moreover, this protection extends to intimate choices by unmarried as well as married persons."[90]

Therefore, although the SCOTUS accepted that gay couples did engage in "sex" or "sexual conduct," it failed to provide a precise definition of what that might actually be. While excluding various other cases in reaching its judgment, the SCOTUS stressed that *Lawrence* did not involve minors, anyone who might be injured or coerced, or who could not easily refuse consent. Nor did it involve public behaviour or prostitution. Instead, it involved "two adults who, with full and mutual consent from each other, engaged in *sexual practices* common to a homosexual lifestyle. The petitioners are entitled to respect for their private lives. The State cannot demean their existence or control their destiny by making their private *sexual conduct* a crime."[91]

However, the SCOTUS gave no reason as to why these instances differed from the situation at hand or why they lay beyond the reach of *Lawrence*. As a result, it is totally unclear what kind of private intimate conduct between individuals should be protected as "sex" or "sexual conduct" and which should not.

Understandings of Sex and Sexual Activity

Obviously, there is no consensus on what should be regarded as "sex" and "sexual conduct" or "sexual activity" for the purposes of legislation in the United States. Most American rape laws define rape as sexual intercourse.[92] Other sexual conduct is also regulated, but it is treated somewhat differently from rape.[93] However, there is no nation-wide uniform definition of rape. The definition of prostitution, on the other hand, could be very broad, including all kinds of sexual behaviour.[94] But again, there is no uniform definition of prostitution.

Moreover, state criminal codes, penal codes, and revenge porn legislation show major discrepancies in the understanding of what should be counted as sexual organs and sexual activities. For instance, the California Penal Code forbids the distribution of images of "a person depicted engaging in an act of sexual intercourse, sodomy, oral copulation, sexual penetration, or an image of masturbation by the person depicted or in which the person depicted participates."[95] The Arizona revenge porn legislation bans the distribution of images of "specific sexual activities," which it defines as either "(a) human genitals in a state of sexual stimulation or arousal, or (b) sex acts, normal or perverted, actual or simulated, including acts of human masturbation, sexual intercourse, oral copulation or sodomy."[96] Delaware's revenge porn legislation bars the distribution of images of "sexual conduct," meaning

a   sexual contact;
b   sexual intercourse;
c   sexual penetration;
d   masturbation;

e   bestiality;
f   sadism;
g   masochism; or
h   explicit representations of the defecation or urination functions.[97]

Here, "sexual contact" means "any touching by 1 person of uncovered anus, breast, buttocks, or genitalia of another person or any touching of a person with the uncovered anus, breasts, buttocks or genitalia of another person." And "sexual intercourse" refers to "any act of physical union of the genitalia or anus of a person with the mouth, anus, or genitalia of another person."[98] Apparently, the Delaware legislature believed that all these activities should be protected as "sexual activities" against unwanted disclosure.

These discrepancies indicate that "sex" and "sexual conduct" or "sexual activity" could be defined significantly differently and that there is no universal definition.

A Better Definition
Therefore, to sufficiently protect "sex" under the Constitution, we need to move beyond the traditional concentration on sexual intercourse (penile penetration of the vagina) to include various sex-related behaviours. However, it is extremely difficult to precisely define sex, sexual conduct, or sexual activity for the purpose of constitutional protection.

For now, it is agreed that traditional sexual intercourse is sex (sex in the narrow sense) and that the right to engage in it or to refuse it should be constitutionally protected. In addition, most people would probably agree that oral and anal sex, whether heterosexual or homosexual, is sex as well. Most would also consider lesbian sex (the union of female genitalia with other female genitalia or mouths, with or without using sexual devices) as sex. These forms of conduct could be termed as sex in the broader sense.

A third category, sex in the broadest sense, would incorporate all other sexual activities. These would cover a great deal of territory and would include, but not be limited to, inserting fingers, a fist, or other objects into the vagina; licking a penis or vagina; nude contact between penis and vulva via nude body washing; kissing; groping and touching the breasts, buttocks, or other parts of the body; and masturbation or helping masturbation (hand jobs). All three categories should be protected by the Constitution as encompassed within the definition of "sex" in the constitutional sense. But when a legislature enacts a Criminal Code, it might be allowed to distinguish the first two categories from the third to prohibit these activities when they occur without consent or with the use of force. In that respect, the necessary degree of protection might differ for each category.

Other activities that might potentially end in sex, such as cuddling together in bed, enjoying a meal or a conversation, going for a walk or shopping, are not necessarily sex-bound and should be treated separately. Watching women who are naked, undressing, or masturbating, or watching people having sex would also be included in this category, as would watching a stripper dance. Certain forms of conduct can be sexual, private, and personal, but they do not necessarily lead to sex. Thus, they could be described as activities that might stimulate sexual desire.

It is tempting to view these as "sex," as protected under the Constitution, but broadening the definition to encompass all of them may prove difficult to protect. People can be sexually aroused by so many different things, such as various parts of the body and diverse forms of conduct. It is hard to view any kind of conduct as "sexual" simply because someone sees it as such. Accepting this approach would make the constitutional definition totally unstable. Thus, it would be better to limit the constitutional meaning of "sex" to sex in the narrow, broader, and broadest senses.

Restrictions on the Right to Have Sex

All around the world, countries place various limits on the right to have sex.[99] We need to examine whether they can be justified. This chapter discusses some typical restrictions, including on sex in public, involving violence, in a group, among unmarried persons (fornication), adultery, incest, atypical or "deviant" sex (including sodomy, oral sex, or anal sex), necrophilia, and sex with animals (bestiality). The ban on sex with children raises somewhat different issues from sex with adult. In most countries, such limitations listed above have not been thought to raise constitutional questions, as there is no agreement that sexual autonomy is constitutionally protected. However, if it is seen as such, the issue of whether such limitations can be justified must be addressed.

Sex in Public

In most jurisdictions, having sex in a public place is a crime. For example, article 174 of Japan's Criminal Code prohibits obscene acts in public and imposes up to six months of imprisonment with labour or a fine.[100] Having sex in public is largely perceived as obscene. In the United States, some jurisdictions explicitly ban sex in public places or even in private places where it may reasonably be expected to be viewed by members of the public as indecency.[101] Most jurisdictions simply ban indecency, lewdness, or exposure without specifically referring to sex or sexual intercourse,[102] but having sex in public is probably defined as lewdness or exposure.

In the past, sex in public was banned on moral grounds, but as discussed earlier, this is no longer acceptable. However, individuals who engage in it are essentially forcing people to witness it, and though everyone should have sexual freedom, anyone who has no wish to become an onlooker deserves to be protected. As a result, a ban on sex in public places could be justified. The possibility that children might be among the viewers is an all the more convincing reason to justify such a prohibition for their protection.

Violent and Dehumanizing or Degrading Sex

Some sexual activities can involve violence, such as torture or erotic asphyxiation, usually featuring some type of physical harm. In *Lawrence*, the court explicitly limited its holding to sex *without* harm, thus excluding constitutional protection for violent sex. That form of sex can result in being charged with rape, battery or aggravated battery, sexual assault, or aggravated sexual assault, even when both parties give full consent.[103]

However, in *R. v J.A.*,[104] the SCOC held that an "individual must be conscious throughout the sexual activity in order to provide the requisite consent. Parliament requires ongoing, conscious consent to ensure that women and men are not the victims of sexual exploitation, and to ensure that individuals engaging in sexual activity are capable of asking their partners to stop at any point."[105] At issue was sexual conduct during erotic asphyxiation. With her consent, a husband choked his wife until she passed out. On regaining consciousness, she discovered that he was inserting a dildo into her anus. She later claimed that she had not consented to this, and he was charged with sexual assault. The SCOC rejected his argument that she had given advance consent to sexual acts that might occur while she was unconscious. The SCOC held that "these provisions indicate that Parliament viewed consent as requiring a 'capable' or operating mind, able to evaluate each and every sexual act committed ... I cannot accept the respondent's contention that an individual may consent in advance to sexual activity taking place while she is unconscious."[106] The SCOC left open the issue of whether individuals could consent to bodily harm during sexual activity (at least, it did not consider erotic asphyxiation to be unlawful). However, it may signal that a person can consent to some form of violence or use of force so long as he or she is conscious throughout and is actively providing ongoing consent.

Usually, battery or injury is not a crime if it occurs in a consensual context. For example, engaging in the potentially injurious sports of boxing or wrestling is lawful if the participants consent. If violent sex with full and active consent is regarded as illegal, we need to explain why such a ban should apply to sex and not to other violent consensual activities. It may be normal to expect that sex will not involve violence, but when it does and when the partners give their active and full consent, there may be little excuse to condemn it. Indeed, it should be viewed as permissible.

Some sado-masochistic sex may involve dehumanization and degradation rather than corporeal harm. Treating one's partner as a slave and tying or cuffing the hands, for example, deprives freedom of movement but may not cause physical damage. It remains an open question as to whether consent to such activities should be accepted as consent, thus nullifying any subsequent charges of sexual assault or rape. If dehumanizing or degrading treatment during sex is illegal, we need to ask why. We may not approve of it, but if both parties consent to it, why would we care? The individuals should be at liberty to decide on their own sex lives, and we should not deny constitutional protection simply because we find certain practices objectionable, as long as there is ongoing and full consent.

Some commentators assert that because women are usually weaker than their male partners and may thus potentially be forced to acquiesce at any time, they cannot give truly voluntary consent, a reality that would also apply to sex. However, this argument constitutes a total denial of the sexual autonomy of women. It is true that some women are vulnerable and may be forced to consent. The government should be allowed to protect them. But this does not justify the conclusion that no woman can ever give true and voluntary consent to sex.

Group Sex
Some people choose to partake in group sex, as, for example, at "sex parties," where individuals or couples gather and freely have sex with any willing partner. Some people see group sex as particularly immoral. However, as long as there is consent, it is doubtful that the government could prohibit it. In *R. v Labaye*,[107] for instance, the SCOC dealt with the issue of whether the defendant could be convicted under section 210(1) of the Criminal Code for keeping a "common bawdy-house" for the "practice of acts of indecency" and whether the acts committed in his establishment were indecent, as defined by the code.[108] The defendant operated a club in which couples and single people met for group sex. Applying the objective harm test, the SCOC eventually concluded that there would be no justifiable harms in the case and thus set aside the defendant's conviction.

Indeed, there is no constitutional justification for banning group sex as indecent conduct so long as all the parties know the nature of the activity, give full and active consent, and no one is harmed. The SCOC did not address the constitutionality of such a prohibition. Yet, since there is no justification for it, it should be struck down as invalid.

Sex Involving Unmarried Persons: Fornication
Some countries and jurisdictions ban sexual intercourse involving an unmarried person.[109] Japan is an exception, although having sex before marriage was once seen as immoral. Unless one of the partners is a child, there is now no legal barrier to non-marital sex. Indeed, many people engage in casual sex or begin a sexual relationship before marriage. As long as both parties are fully consenting adults, why should

such behaviour be banned? Moral objections should not be accepted as a legitimate reason to proscribe sexual conduct.

An increasing number of American states have recently repealed their fornication laws. In light of *Lawrence*, it is natural to question their constitutionality. There is no justification for such a ban, which is utterly unconstitutional.

Adultery

Although rarely enforced, the Criminal Codes of some countries and jurisdictions criminalize adultery.[110] Before the end of the Second World War, it was a crime in Japan as well.[111] Under the Criminal Code of the Meiji era, adultery with married women was illegal. This was found to be discriminatory because it allowed married men to have sex with single women. A wife was required to remain faithful to her husband. When the Japanese government formulated the new Constitution, which prohibited sexual discrimination, it was faced with a choice: either abolish the ban on adultery or revise it to be sexually neutral. In the end, the government decided to remove the ban, which is why adultery is no longer criminalized in Japan.[112]

Nonetheless, adultery can still result in civil liability. It is a statutory reason for seeking a divorce,[113] and if it leads to the breakdown of the marriage, the unfaithful partner may be liable in tort law. His or her lover can also be liable for damages. Moreover, the moral condemnation of adultery remains strong in Japan. Some adulterous celebrities have been removed from television programs and left without jobs, though people have increasingly come to accept adultery as a part of life. However, moral expectations for celebrities and public figures apparently remain high.

Anyone who discovers the unfaithfulness of a spouse will commonly be deeply upset and hurt, but this does not justify criminal punishment. Defining the marital relationship is up to the couple, and it can be irrevocably damaged if a spouse cheats. Using criminal law in an attempt to force couples to stay together and to force public respect for marriage is not legitimate. It is no wonder that an increasing number of jurisdictions are heading toward abolishing criminal bans on adultery.[114]

Incest

Some countries and jurisdictions criminalize incest – sexual intercourse with a close relative.[115] Although Japan has no such prohibition, its Criminal Code now has a special ban on sexual intercourse between legal guardians and minor children.[116] As a result, this behaviour could be unlawful even if assault or intimidation are not involved. In other words, it is subject to criminal punishment. Other than this, there is no criminal ban on sexual intercourse between family members.[117]

Incest may be considered morally wrong, but so long as both parties are adults, there should be no objection to it. However, one could argue that even if the parties are adults, a power imbalance may exist between them, as for an older brother and a younger sister or father and daughter. One may be tempted to justify forbidding incest to protect such vulnerable individuals. But if both parties are adults, capable of understanding their situation and giving consent, objecting to their relationship might be difficult. In situations where neither person is aware of their blood tie, it is even more difficult to prove that a power imbalance exists.

It is true that incest can increase the risk of producing a baby with a disability, a fact that one could ostensibly invoke in arguing that it be banned. But, if the couple are diligent in the use of contraceptives or are incapable of giving birth, justifying such a prohibition becomes difficult. Moreover, people with inheritable genetic disorders or who carry a disease that can be transmitted to an unborn baby are not barred from having sex. In other words, the possibility of producing a baby with a disability cannot be a legitimate reason for prohibiting sex. It is hard to justify a total ban on incest simply because a disabled baby might possibly result from it.

Incest also disturbs family relationships. The need to prevent this could be cited as a reason for banning it, but this logic is unlikely to prove sufficient. The public might have an interest in maintaining good family relationships, but it is questionable whether criminal law is the proper vehicle to achieve this, given that it is generally a means to protect the rights and interests of individuals and society. The government should not be allowed to invoke criminal law due to moral concerns. As a result, it is doubtful that punishing all incestuous relationships would be reasonable, which means that the criminalization of incest needs to be questioned.

Atypical Sex

Some countries and jurisdictions ban atypical or so-called deviant sex, sodomy, oral sex or anal sex. This attitude is a reflection of the denial of sexual orientation as a personal choice. As we saw in *Bowers v Hardwick*, the SCOTUS upheld a Georgia statute that banned "sexual acts involving sex organs of one person and the mouth or anus of another person." This ban applied to everyone, including heterosexual couples.[118] The SCOTUS reasoned that such acts were not rooted in the fundamental traditions of the United States.

However, the SCOTUS in *Lawrence* struck down a ban on sodomy between a homosexual couple in Texas as unconstitutional.[119] In light of the *Lawrence* holding, it is likely that all prohibitions of sodomy between homosexual couples would be invalidated.[120] Although the SCOTUS declared that the state had no legitimate interest to interfere with the sexual relationship of two consenting adults, whether it is ready to wipe out the ban on atypical heterosexual sex is unknown. It is likely, however, that there would be no legitimate interest to bar it even among heterosexuals since the only possible legitimate interest would involve morality, and moral objections are not sufficient to forbid sexual conduct. Therefore, criminal bans on atypical sex would probably be struck down.

In Japan, there is no ban on this form of sexual behaviour, as long as it is consensual.[121] As a result, the issue has never come up for discussion. But following the lead of the SCOTUS, any potential ban on it should be struck down as a violation of sexual autonomy. Sexual orientation is included in sexual autonomy to be protected by the Constitution, and there is no legitimate reason to preclude certain sexual orientations from protection. The Constitution encompasses more than heterosexual relationships and typical sexual intercourse. It is up to the parties involved to decide what kind of sex they want to have.

This issue has huge implications for members of the 2SLGBTQ+ community. For 2SLGBTQ+ couples, it is vital that their sexual activities are viewed as sex and are protected by the Constitution. In Japan, homosexuality per se is not a criminal offence, but the law does discriminate against homosexual people. A gay couple cannot legally marry and cannot receive social security benefits, unlike heterosexual common law spouses, who are eligible. Further, 2SLGBTQ+ couples have difficulty in asking for technological assistance to have children. They are also subject to serious prejudice. It is vital to accept that they are just people who have their own sexual orientation or sexual identity and that there is no justification to treat them differently.

Necrophilia and Bestiality

Necrophilia is illegal in some countries and jurisdictions. In New York, for instance, it is termed sexual misconduct.[122] Similarly, the Washington state penal code criminalizes the sexual violation of human remains.[123] Some jurisdictions ban necrophilia as an abuse of a dead body.[124]

Why necrophilia needs to be forbidden is ambiguous. The person is already dead, and thus sex with the corpse does not infringe on any of his or her rights or interests, unless the dead still possess rights and legal interests. The issue of consent is also irrelevant, as the dead can neither provide consent nor refuse it. As a result, necrophiliacs might be able to claim that it was not needed and that no one was harmed. It is unclear whether the corpse is part of the estate to be inherited by the heirs. The only government interest to ban necrophilia is to protect the sexual decency or dignity of the deceased. But again, unless one holds that the dead person maintains a legal interest in decency or dignity, the government interest could be seen as based on moral grounds (unless the surviving family could invoke that right to decency or dignity on the side of the dead). Moreover, it is questionable whether the government can justify such a ban solely on necrophilia, since the decency or integrity of the corpse can be violated in many other ways.

If the government were to widen its protection to encompass all kinds of abuses involving a cadaver, such as theft, mutilation, destruction, or consumption, it may be able to include a ban on necrophilia among them. In that case, the prohibition would be directed, not at sex with the corpse, but at protecting its decency and integrity in general. Then, the government might be able to justify the ban on destruction or infringement of the corpse by invoking the general interest in preserving the decency or dignity of the corpse, since its interest is not directed at sex.

Some countries and jurisdictions also ban bestiality: sex with an animal. For instance, the New York Penal Law forbids it as sexual misconduct.[125] The Virginia Criminal Code also bans bestiality as a crime against nature.[126] An increasing number of states have recently decided to disallow it.[127]

This prohibition may be justified on public health grounds; various zoonotic diseases can be transmitted during sex with an animal.[128] Yet, it is questionable whether a total ban can be justified on these grounds, especially if a person uses adequate protection. The prohibition may be justified also on moral grounds, as the practice is commonly seen as immoral and disgusting. But recently, it has been justified as a protection of animal welfare. In *Warren v Commonwealth*, the Virginia Court of Appeal sustained the constitutionality of its ban on bestiality even after the *Lawrence* holding.[129] In *Warren*, the defendant argued that in light of *Lawrence*, the state should not be allowed to ban bestiality, because it was nothing more than private sexual conduct between consenting adults. The court rejected equating sex between consenting adults to sex with an animal and held that there was no established fundamental right to engage in it. Moreover, it easily concluded that the ban was reasonable, since the government had a legitimate interest in protecting animals from cruelty and in protecting public health.

The government may have a legitimate interest in protecting both animal welfare and public health, but if a general ban on animal cruelty is already in place, one that specifically targets bestiality needs to be justified. It may be questioned whether there is a separate and independent government interest in protecting the sexual integrity of an animal.

Practical Difficulties Caused by the Family System

Even in circumstances where there is no legal ban, the family system can sometimes limit sexual freedom. As mentioned above,[130] in Japan, all citizens must be registered as either male or female, and virtually no change is permitted. As a result of this, many transgender people are unable to marry the partner of their choice. Moreover, bigamy is illegal in Japan.[131] As long as both husband and wife agree, a divorce is relatively easy to obtain: they simply file the relevant application.[132] However, in the absence of agreement, the spouse who wishes to be divorced must acquire permission from the court, citing one of the listed legitimate reasons to do so.[133] Adultery is included in this list, but a cheating spouse cannot cite it as a reason to ask for a divorce.[134] Thus, many people remain trapped in failed marriages, even when the relationship has totally broken down, and cannot remarry. Furthermore, same-sex marriage is not legal in Japan.[135] As a result, same-sex partners are precluded from marriage. Finally, the Civil Code mandates that husband and wife must carry the same surname.[136] Although they can choose which name they prefer, women are virtually always forced to give up their maiden name. Because of the serious inconvenience and reluctance to abandon their maiden names, some choose not to legally marry and opt for a de facto marriage. Of course, none of this prevents anyone from having sex, but the absence of the blessing of marriage surely leads to the practical restriction on sexual freedom because of social prejudice.

Since sexual autonomy should include the right to decide one's sexual or gender identity, it is highly questionable whether the family registration system can be sustained. Transgender people should be free to decide and change their sex or gender. Moreover, there is no legitimate reason to preclude same-sex marriage. The marriage system provides government recognition of and protection for the strong mutual commitment between two partners. There is simply no reason why this cannot extend to same-sex couples. Some commentators point to the specific wording of the Constitution in voicing their opposition to same-sex marriage. Article 24 states that marriage shall be based on the consent of "both sexes" and that it is to be maintained through mutual cooperation with the equal rights of "husband and wife as a basis." With regard to choice of spouse, property rights, inheritance, choice of domicile, divorce, and other matters pertaining to marriage and the family, laws shall be enacted from the standpoint of individual dignity and the essential equality of the "sexes." The people who drafted article 24 were motivated by a desire to eradicate the sexual discrimination existed under the Meiji Constitution.[137] Given the norms of the 1940s, when the new Constitution was written, it was natural for them to see marriage in terms of heterosexuality. Yet, there was no argument to exclude same-sex couples from constitutional protection, and nor does the language demonstrate such an intent. Given that the purpose of the Constitution was to protect equality and individual dignity for both spouses, accepting same-sex marriage is far more consistent with this underlying objective.

It is understandable that the courts would wish to protect a wronged spouse from a cheating partner: they are reluctant to lend their aid to dirty hands. But withholding divorce even when a marriage has broken down also stops the discontented partner from remarrying, which is an unacceptable sacrifice. The protection of the wronged spouse should be provided by means other than denying a divorce application. As for the requirement that husband and wife must share the same surname, the SCOJ sustained it as constitutional for preserving the family bond and avoiding confusion over the children's surname.[138] Whether it is necessary to mandate husband and wife to bear the same name is highly doubtful. The marital bond can be achieved by other means, and the assumption that all family members must carry the same surname is simply unsustainable.

Removing all these barriers to legal marriage and providing the blessing of marriage to all those who are precluded will surely work to advance sexual freedom.[139]

Sex with Children

The Ban on Sex with Children
Sexual autonomy is premised on the assumption that sex is consensual. If there is no consent, it could be deemed rape or sexual assault. The issue of sex with children is thus a complicated one. It is generally believed that children are not mature enough to fully understand the meaning and implications of sex; therefore, almost all countries place some limitations on sex with them. Specific restrictions vary. In some countries, sex with children is defined as statutory rape even when the child gives consent.[140] In other countries, it is a separate crime or a violation of child welfare laws.[141] Many nations also ban prostitution involving children.[142]

In Japan, sexual intercourse, anal intercourse, or oral intercourse (sexual intercourse et al.) with any person that involves assault or intimidation is subject to criminal punishment. But sexual intercourse et al. with a child under the age of thirteen is illegal, regardless of whether assault or intimidation is used.[143] As a result, it would constitute forcible sexual intercourse et al. and could lead to criminal punishment. In this sense, this part of the forcible sexual intercourse et al. provision is statutory rape.

Moreover, sexual intercourse, conduct analogous to it, or the sexual touching of a child for payment or with the promise of payment is child prostitution. Anyone who engages in this behaviour is subject to criminal punishment.[144]

Furthermore, youth protection ordinances in most prefectures ban indecent sexual conduct with anyone under the age of eighteen.[145] Although the ordinances do not define indecent sexual conduct, it is generally agreed that sexual intercourse, conduct analogous to it, and sexual touching all come under this heading. However, most ordinances exempt the young people themselves from criminal punishment. Thus, when sexual intercourse occurs between two young people under age eighteen, the ordinance is violated, but no punishment will be imposed. Although there is no other exemption to this ban, the SCOJ created a judicial exemption for sexual intercourse with someone under age eighteen when the partners are involved in a genuine romantic relationship.[146] Given that the Civil Code allowed sixteen-year-old women to marry, this exemption was logical.[147] If this exemption did not exist, a husband married to a sixteen-year old wife would be breaking the law every time he had sex with her. The construction adopted by the SCOJ thus made sense, although the ordinances did not include any explicit exemptions.

As a result of these limitations, no one is allowed to have sex with anyone under age thirteen, and no indecent sexual conduct with anyone under age eighteen is allowed unless the partners are involved in a genuine romantic relationship. On the other hand, children under thirteen are prevented from having sex, and youth under eighteen are also prevented from having sex even when they believe they are capable of giving consent. This limitation is designed to protect them from exploitation. As a result, sex will be prohibited even when youth are capable of giving consent.

The Permissibility of the Ban
Bans on sex with children are widely seen as justified because children have not developed an understanding of sex and therefore are not fully capable of consenting to it. Even if they do consent, their agreement should not be regarded as voluntary and informed, as they don't have the capacity to understand sex. Moreover, since they lack this understanding,

they can be taken advantage of or exploited by adults. To guard against such situations, it is necessary to ban sex with children. The protection of children is certainly a legitimate and compelling government interest. Therefore, even if we accept that the right to have sex is constitutionally protected, prohibiting adults from having sex with children is amply justified.

If sex with children is forbidden, this would apply not only to adults, but to the children themselves. For them, the ban is a paternalistic restriction on their constitutional rights and freedoms, whose purpose is to protect them. In general, such restrictions are impermissible, but it is widely believed that they can be justified when children are involved.

Nevertheless, a child might ostensibly be capable of understanding sex and giving consent, especially a sixteen- or seventeen-year-old, who can probably argue convincingly on this point. As girls were allowed to marry at sixteen, such an argument could be more persuasive for them. Nevertheless, neither the Criminal Code nor local youth protection ordinances anticipate an individual inquiry regarding the maturity and capability of a child. Nor do they permit a defendant to plead that a child is mature and therefore capable of understanding sex and giving consent. Is this justifiable? Or should the government be obliged to provide for individual inquiry and leave room for this defence?

If the answer to the second question is yes, an offender might take advantage of the vulnerability of a child or erroneously believe that the child had sufficient capability and gave consent. In light of the grave consequences of sex, there is a significant risk. In some situations, individual exemptions are made for a mature child, whereas in others, they are not. For example, in all democratic countries the franchise is granted solely to adult citizens, and no exceptions are made for any minor. Therefore, an absolute ban on sex with children under a certain age could probably be justified as well.

Whether the government should allow minors to have sex with other minors is a very important distinction. Japan does not make it. Any sexual intercourse, anal intercourse, or oral intercourse with a person who is twelve or younger is punishable under the Criminal Code, and any indecent sexual conduct with a person under age eighteen, unless a genuine romantic relationship exists, can violate local youth protection ordinances (despite the fact that most ordinances exempt punishment for youth). In Canada, however, children who are between the ages of twelve and fifteen can legally have sex with anyone who is less than two years younger or five years older than they and who is not in a position of trust or authority.[148] Sex that does not fall within these limits is regarded as sexual assault, even if the child consents.[149] The age exception is generally called the Romeo-Juliet exception or the Romeo and Juliet law. It is based on the assumption that children of approximately the same age will have reached a roughly equivalent level of maturity and that the older partner is unlikely to exploit the vulnerability of the younger one.

But if sex with children is banned on the assumption that they lack the necessary understanding and therefore cannot give consent, allowing a twelve-year-old to engage in sex at all might be somewhat questionable. Moreover, even if the partners are similar in age, the older partner could potentially exploit the vulnerability of the younger one. Therefore, introducing the Romeo and Juliet law into Japan may not be a good idea. It is hard to criticize the Japanese ban on sex with children because of the absence of such an exception.

Prostitution

A History of Prostitution and Its Regulation
Prostitution, the world's oldest profession, has a long history in Japan.[150] During the Heian period, prostitutes were often called *asobime* or *yūjo*, which means "women providing enjoyment for men."[151] In 1617, the Tokugawa shogunate issued an order restricting prostitution to certain areas on the outskirts of cities, known as *yūkaku* (pleasure quarter). Prostitutes were licensed as yūjo, and they were ranked according to an elaborate hierarchy, with *tayū* and later *oiran* at the top. Many lower-ranked prostitutes sat behind a lattice-screened window and solicited men who happened to be passing by.[152] The yūkaku districts were walled and guarded for taxation and control of access.[153] Many women were sold by their poor families to a yūkaku, where they were forced to serve as prostitutes.[154] Their only means of escape was to find a rich patron who could obtain their release by paying a substantial sum to the yūkaku manager (*miuke*). Although it was illegal to run a brothel

in other areas, the government gradually came to tolerate them. Called *okabasho*, they became very popular because of the popularization of prostitution.[155]

After the Meiji modernization, the government had to face criticism from foreign countries regarding human trafficking in prostitution.[156] In 1872, it enacted new legislation, emancipating prostitutes from bondage labour: the Emancipation Order for Playing Girls.[157] In 1900, it promulgated the Regulation to Control Playing Girls to regulate the labour conditions of prostitution.[158] In 1908, it penalized unregulated prostitution.[159] Nevertheless, prostitution simply continued.[160] Many girls and women were practically sold to brothels by their father or housemaster. In legal terms, this involved a fixed-term service contract with an advance payment of money. The women had no freedom to refuse or to escape. During the Second World War, the government collected many Japanese and other Asian women to send overseas, now known as "comfort women," which allowed them to service soldiers in mainland China and other Asian countries.[161]

Immediately after the end of the Second World War, Japan was placed under occupation. In preparation for this, the government formed the Recreation and Amusement Association (RAA) to organize brothels that would cater to the occupying forces that would soon arrive. On August 19, 1945, the government ordered local government offices to establish a prostitution service for Allied soldiers, hoping that they would confine their attentions to prostitutes and leave other women alone, thus preserving the "purity" of the Japanese race.[162]

The Supreme Commander of the Allied Powers, who directed the occupation, abolished this licensed prostitution system (as well as the RAA) in 1946, which led to the repeal of the Regulation to Control Playing Girls. Certain districts were created in which licensed nightlife establishments, known as *pan-pan*, were allowed to offer sexual services under the guise of being ordinary clubs or cafes. Local police determined their location by drawing red lines on a map, thus producing what was called a "red-line" district (*akasen*). In other areas, so-called blue-line establishments offered sexual services under the guise of being restaurants, bars, or other less strictly regulated venues than ones in the red-line districts. In 1947, the government imposed a punishment on persons who forced or enticed women to act as prostitutes,[163] but prostitution itself remained legal.

On May 24, 1956, the Diet passed the Prostitution Prevention Act, which came into force in April 1958.[164] Banning sexual intercourse in exchange for actual or promised compensation as "prostitution," it prohibited both prostitution and being a customer of prostitution.[165] This eliminated the distinction between red-line and blue-line facilities and forced any establishment that wished to remain in the sex industry to operate as an "entertainment business," where it could legally offer sexual services that did not extend to sexual intercourse.[166]

The Current Legal Status of Prostitution

The purpose of the Prostitution Prevention Act of 1956 is to "prevent prostitution, by imposing criminal punishment on activities that facilitate prostitution and by adopting rehabilitation measures for women who will plausibly engage in prostitution in light of their behaviours or environments, since prostitution infringes the dignity of humans, violates sexual morality and disturbs the good morality of society."[167] According to the act, "prostitution" consists of "offering sexual intercourse with unspecified persons while receiving compensation or with the promise of compensation."[168] It declares that "no person may either perform prostitution or become its customer,"[169] but it does not mention how those who violate this clause are to be punished.[170] In other words, providing prostitution and patronizing a prostitute are both illegal, but neither offence will be punished. Instead, the following conduct is prohibited with criminal punishment: soliciting for the purposes of prostitution;[171] procuring a person for prostitution;[172] deceiving, harassing, or coercing using the family relationship to influence a person into prostitution;[173] receiving or demanding a part or total compensation from prostitution after procuring or forcing it;[174] inducing a person to be a prostitute by paying an "advance";[175] concluding a contract for making a person a prostitute;[176] furnishing a place for prostitution;[177] engaging in the business of making a person a prostitute;[178] and providing the funds, place, or facility for a prostitution business.[179]

A woman over the age of twenty who violates the solicitation ban can be sent to a rehabilitation centre.[180] Moreover, the local authority is mandated to establish women's counselling centres to offer protection and rehabilitation services for "women and girls in need of protection,"[181] those who are defined as in danger of engaging in prostitution. Local authorities are also authorized to build women's shelters to accept and protect such women.[182]

Sexual services other than sexual intercourse are regulated by the Entertainment Business Regulation Act of 1948.[183] It lists five business categories that can offer sexual services: for example, cabarets, restaurants, cafes, and other facilities that entertain or provide food for the treatment of guests are classed as category 1; cafes, bars, or other facilities with dim lighting under 10 lux specified by the National Public Safety Commission are in category 2; and cafes, bars, or other facilities that serve food in individual rooms under five square metres that are shielded from the rest are in category 3.[184] In this context, "treatment" means entertaining guests by creating an enjoyable atmosphere.[185]

The act also created the category of the "sexual services special business." This includes the "sexual service special business with a store"; "sexual service special business without a store"; "sexual service video streaming special business"; "telephone dating service with a store"; and "telephone dating service without a store."[186] The first of these, a business with a store, can provide individual rooms for sexual touching or facilities in which customers watch others undress. The category also encompasses strip clubs; adult stores that sell or lease pictures, videos, and other goods solely to entice sexual curiosity; and other businesses that provide similar sexual services.[187]

Businesses without a store also provide the sexual touching of customers.[188] The telecommunication streaming of images of sexual conduct involving undressed persons is a "sexual service streaming special business."[189] Enabling customers to enjoy a telephone conversation is a "telephone dating service," which can function either with or without a store.[190]

Under the act, anyone who wishes to open such an entertainment business must obtain a licence from the local public safety commission, according to each local store depending on the type of business to be offered.[191] The act tightly regulates these businesses, stipulating the layout of the store, its hours, necessary light level, acceptable noise or vibration, and advertising. It also mandates that a sign indicating "no minors under the age of eighteen" is posted at the front door.[192] It prohibits pimping, harassing or blocking passersby to solicit them, allowing persons under age eighteen to "treat" guests, or allowing a guest under age eighteen to enter the premises.[193]

Curiously, however, a person who plans to operate a "sexual service special business with a store" is required to register with the local public safety commission and does not need to acquire a licence.[194] This is odd because of the ease with which such venues could violate the Prostitution Prevention Act. It is believed that the legislature intentionally opted for registration rather than licensing because issuing a licence could be interpreted as condoning these services. This indicates that the legislature knows that these businesses are providing illegal prostitution and has simply decided to ignore it.

The Prostitution Prevention Act and the Entertainment Business Regulation Act employ differing terms for sexual services.[195] The Prostitution Prevention Acts prohibits sexual intercourse, and any other sexual services can be offered under the Entertainment Business. "Soaplands" are very popular; they are bathhouses in which female staff soap up the bodies of their customers and assist them in masturbating. Each staff member leases her own bathroom, which she manages herself. She is not supposed to provide sexual intercourse for payment, but if she agrees to it, that is her choice and the owner or manager of the facility can pretend ignorance. Other businesses, such as fashion health shops and pink salons, are officially massage or esthetic treatment parlours, but female staff might offer sexual services there as well, including sexual intercourse.

Escort services (operate via what is known as a delivery health service). Allows a customer to call the service, which dispatches someone to his or her house or hotel room. Technically, women who work for escort services are not supposed to offer sex,[196] but if they do, the operators can again claim ignorance. Various Internet dating sites are also available, ostensibly to enable single people to meet for a date,[197] but in reality, they offer various sexual services, including sex. Store managers are not supposed to know if the girls who date customers agree to have sex.

Some young girls, mostly high school students, participate in a service called *enjokōsai*, or "compensated dating." To avoid entanglements with the law, operators present it solely as a date, perhaps for supper or conversation, and the girl is paid for her participation. Sometimes, however, the date ends with sexual intercourse.[198] Online or smartphone booking is generally used, and operators typically don't have an office or storefront.

There are all kinds of other sexual services. Peeping rooms enable paying customers to peep into a secluded room, typically to watch girls undress and masturbate. A paying customer can also sleep with a young girl, without engaging in sexual contact. Retail outlets sell the used underwear of young girls. In various night clubs, cabarets, or bars, a man can have a drink and enjoy a conversation with a female hostess. Dressed in revealing clothes, she often sits close to him, and although many of these venues prohibit him from touching her, casual contact is usually tolerated. Customers can spend large sums of money and are sometimes assigned to a particular hostess to entice and attract them. They may shower her with expensive gifts, usually with the expectation of sex in return. In dancing clubs, men can dance with girls and can sing along with them in karaoke stores. None of these venues offer sexual services, but all include an erotic element.

At host clubs, handsome male hosts "treat" guests, most of whom are female, over drinks. Sometimes, they provide sexual services to their customers. Gay people can meet over drinks at a gay club, and transgender female dancers dance for guests at "new-half pubs." None of these establishments offer sexual services to clients, but they provide an opportunity to hook up with staff or other customers, prompting sexual intercourse. In short, sex is significantly commercialized in Japan, and there are many places where some form of erotic encounter can be purchased in the name of entertainment rather than prostitution.

Serious concerns have been raised about the increasing participation of young girls,[199] especially high school students, who want quick money.[200] In fact, their involvement is so notorious that what are known as *joshi kosei* (JK) businesses, in which they provide various types of sexual services to adult men, take their name from the Japanese word for high school girl. If a JK business charges a customer for sexual intercourse with a girl, it could be liable under the Prostitution Prevention

Act, and if she is younger than eighteen, it could violate the indecent sexual conduct prohibition of the local youth protection ordinance. But as long as no one files a complaint, the police cannot arrest either girls or customers (the Japanese police do not engage in sting operations). There is a tendency to justify such behaviour on the grounds that teenage girls should be permitted to make their own decisions.[201]

International Comparison

Countries throughout the world have adopted quite different approaches to prostitution.[202] In some instances, they impose criminal punishment on both prostitutes and their clients in an attempt to eradicate it. Most American states, for example, ban both performing the act and purchasing it, enforcing their prohibition through criminal punishment. The New York Penal Law thus provides that "a person is guilty of prostitution when such person engages or agrees or offers to engage in sexual conduct with another person in return for a fee." Anyone who pays a prostitute to engage in "sexual conduct" is also guilty of violating this law.[203]

The New York Penal Law's definition of banned "sexual conduct" for the purpose of prostitution is very broad. It means "sexual intercourse, oral sexual conduct, anal sexual conduct, aggravated sexual contact, or sexual contact."[204] "Sexual intercourse" has "its ordinary meaning and occurs upon any penetration, however slight"; "oral sexual conduct" involves "contact between the mouth and the penis, the mouth and the anus, or the mouth and the vulva or vagina"; and "anal sexual conduct" is "contact between the penis and anus." Further, "sexual contact" refers to "any touching of the sexual or other intimate parts of a person for the purpose of gratifying the sexual desire of either party. It includes touching by both participants, whether directly or through clothing, as well as emission of ejaculate by the actor upon any part of the victim, clothed or unclothed." Finally, "aggravated sexual contact" means "inserting, other than for a valid medical purpose, a foreign object in the vagina, urethra, penis, rectum or anus of a child, thereby causing physical injury to such child." However, the definition of prohibited sexual activities differs significantly from state to state.[205]

Alternatively, some countries and jurisdictions have legalized prostitution and attempt to regulate it as they would any other business.

In the Netherlands,[206] Germany,[207] and New Zealand,[208] for example, prostitutes are viewed as "sex workers" who are entitled to protection under the labour laws and are eligible for social security benefits. These countries often subject brothels and sex workers to health and sanitary checks, but there are no criminal punishments for engaging in the sex work or paying for their services.

Finally, some parts of the world see prostitution as sexual exploitation of women and attempt to eradicate it by punishing the customers alone. Sweden, Norway, Iceland, and Finland all take this approach, which is often called the Nordic model. According to the Swedish Criminal Code, "A person who ... obtains casual sexual relations in return for a payment, is guilty of purchase of sexual services and is sentenced to a fine or imprisonment for at most one year. The provision in the first paragraph also applies if the payment was promised or made by another person."[209]

The code also bans procuring prostitutes.[210] But there is no ban or criminal punishment on the prostitutes themselves.

Constitutionality Challenged: Canada
The constitutionality of prostitution bans has rarely been challenged in court. In Canada, however, *Bedford* challenged prostitution-related offences before the SCOC.[211] Prostitution per se has never been illegal in Canada, but several prostitution-related conducts have been criminalized. These include running a brothel, living on the avails of prostitution, and public solicitation.[212] In *Bedford*, sex workers argued that these prohibitions exposed them to significant danger and increased the chances that they could be killed by a customer. They felt unable to ask for help from police due to fear that their identities might be revealed and that police could harass them. They also felt that the police would not take their complaints seriously and that laying a complaint ultimately achieved nothing.

The SCOC agreed. It held that the bans infringed the constitutional right to security of the person, as protected under section 7 of the Canadian Charter of Rights and Freedoms.[213] The SCOC stated that the bans "do not merely impose conditions on how prostitutes operate. They go a critical step further, by imposing dangerous conditions on prostitution;

they prevent people engaged in a risky – but legal – activity from taking steps to protect themselves from the risks."[214] It added

> that laws run afoul of our basic values when the means by which the state seeks to attain its objective is fundamentally flawed, in the sense of being arbitrary, overbroad, or having effects that are grossly disproportionate to the legislative goal. To deprive citizens of life, liberty, or security of the person by laws that violate these norms is not in accordance with the principles of fundamental justice.[215]

The SCOC supported the lower court's finding on the evidence that working in a bawdy house would improve the safety of prostitutes by providing the "benefits of proximity to others, familiarity with surroundings, security staff, closed-circuit television and other such monitoring that a permanent indoor location can facilitate." Noting that "complaints about nuisance arising from indoor prostitution establishments are rare," it concluded that the harmful impact of the provision was grossly disproportionate to its purpose. Thus, a ban on a brothel could not be justified.[216] Moreover, it held that the prohibition on "living on the avails" of prostitution was overbroad because it captured a number of non-exploitative relationships that were not connected to the law's purpose.[217] It also found that although the solicitation ban was intended, "not to eliminate street prostitution for its own sake, but to take prostitution 'off the streets and out of public view' in order to prevent the nuisances that street prostitution can cause,"[218] it was grossly disproportionate to its objective because its ability to screen clients was an "essential tool" in avoiding violent or drunken customers and the total ban simply precludes it.[219] In the end, the SCOC concluded that these infringements were not justified under section 1 of the Charter,[220] declaring them unconstitutional but suspending the declaration of invalidity for one year, thus giving Parliament time to revise them.

Sex workers called for the total legalization of prostitution. In response, Parliament removed the prohibition on brothels and on living on the avails of prostitution, but it opted to follow the Nordic model and introduced a criminal ban on purchasing sex services. It thus created a new section of the Criminal Code on the commodification of sexual activity:

Obtaining sexual services for consideration
s. 286.1 (1) Everyone who, in any place, obtains for consideration, or communicates with anyone for the purpose of obtaining for consideration, the sexual services of a person is guilty of

(a)   an indictable offence and liable to imprisonment for a term of not more than five years ...
(b)   an offence punishable on summary conviction and liable to a fine of not more than $5,000 or to imprisonment for a term of not more than two years less a day, or to both ...

Obtaining sexual services for consideration from person under 18 years
(2) Everyone who, in any place, obtains for consideration, or communicates with anyone for the purpose of obtaining for consideration, the sexual services of a person under the age of 18 years is guilty of an indictable offence and liable to imprisonment for a term of not more than 10 years and to a minimum punishment of imprisonment for a term of

(a)   six months for a first offence; and
(b)   one year for each subsequent offence.[221]

It also banned receiving "a financial or other material benefit, knowing that it is obtained by or derived directly or indirectly from the commission of an offence under subsection 286.1(1)," with certain exceptions including the prostitutes themselves.[222] Further, it prohibited both procuring and advertisement,[223] with the exception of the prostitutes themselves.[224] Finally, it revised the communication ban as follows:

Stopping or impeding traffic
s. 213 (1) Everyone is guilty of an offence punishable on summary conviction who, in a public place or in any place open to public view, for the purpose of offering, providing or obtaining sexual services for consideration,

(a) stops or attempts to stop any motor vehicle; or
(b) impedes the free flow of pedestrian or vehicular traffic or ingress to or egress from premises adjacent to that place.

Communicating to provide sexual services for consideration
(1.1) Everyone is guilty of an offence punishable on summary conviction who communicates with any person – for the purpose of offering or providing sexual services for consideration – in a public place, or in any place open to public view, that is or is next to a school ground, playground or daycare center.

Definition of public place
(2) In this section, public place includes any place to which the public have access as of right or by invitation, express or implied, and any motor vehicle located in a public place or in any place open to public view.[225]

As a result, sex workers would not face criminal punishment for engaging in prostitution, though it was now illegal.[226] However, the Canadian approach differed slightly from the Nordic model, as sex workers can be criminally charged if they advertise their services in "a public place, or in any place open to public view, that is or is next to a school ground, playground or daycare center." "Sexual services" were not defined in the Criminal Code but could be very broad, since they meant any "service that is sexual in nature and whose purpose is to sexually gratify the person who receives it," including "sexual intercourse; masturbation; oral sex; lap-dancing, which involves sitting in a person's lap and simulating sexual intercourse; and sadomasochistic activities, provided that the acts can be considered to be sexually stimulating or gratifying."[227]

Constitutionality Challenged: The United States
Before the advent of *Lawrence* in 2003, American courts were reluctant to accept constitutional challenges based on the due process clause.[228]

Following the *Lawrence* decision, the constitutionality of the prostitution ban was again challenged. However, courts were not receptive to striking down anti-prostitution laws.

In California, for instance, the Erotic Service Provider Legal, Education and Research Project (ESP) challenged the constitutionality of the prostitution prohibition, but the United States Court of Appeal for the 9th Circuit rejected the challenge.[229] The court noted that ESP's primary argument was that in *Lawrence,* the Supreme Court ruled that laws forbidding homosexual sodomy were unconstitutional and that a state should therefore not be permitted to criminalize prostitution involving adults. In support of its argument, ESP made two related contentions: 1) *Lawrence* guarantees consenting adults a fundamental liberty interest to engage in private sexual activity; and 2) the State cannot wholly outlaw a commercial exchange related to the exercise of such a liberty interest. However, the court held that

> *Lawrence* has not previously been interpreted as creating a liberty interest that invalidates laws criminalizing prostitution. As we have observed before, "the bounds of *Lawrence*'s holding are unclear." The nature of the right *Lawrence* protects – be it a right to private sexual activity among consenting adults, or the right to achieve "a personal bond that is more enduring," by the use of private sexual conduct – is never stated explicitly and has not been elaborated upon by the Supreme Court since. But whatever the nature of the right protected in *Lawrence;* one thing *Lawrence* does make explicit is that the *Lawrence* case "does not involve prostitution."
>
> We have considered whether a fundamental due process right to engage in prostitution exists. In *IDK, Inc. v Clark C'nty.,* 836 F.2d 1185, 1193 (9th Cir. 1988), the court upheld a regulation which infringed on the right of escorts and clients to associate with one another, and determined that the relationship between a prostitute and a client is not protected by the due process clause of the Fourteenth Amendment.
>
> ESP argues that *Lawrence* overruled *IDK* by establishing a fundamental right among consenting adults to engage in sexual activity

in private. But, as already noted, *Lawrence* explicitly stated that it did not "involve prostitution." Absent clearer language from the Court regarding the nature of the right *Lawrence* actually does protect, we cannot rule that *IDK*, binding Ninth Circuit precedent, is no longer good law.

Due to *IDK*, we conclude that laws invalidating prostitution may be justified on a rational basis review, rather than the more searching review called for when a right protected by *Lawrence* is infringed.[230]

The court thus applied a lenient deferential rationality review to judge the constitutionality of the prostitution ban and found that the law served a legitimate purpose, as the state supplied specific and legitimate reasons for criminalizing prostitution in California. These purposes were found to include discouraging human trafficking, violence against women, and illegal drug use, and to prevent the spread of contagious and infectious diseases. The court concluded that California provided adequate arguments to establish that section 647(b) of its Penal Code promoted these purposes. Therefore, it sustained the constitutionality of the prostitution ban.[231]

Such a stance is quite understandable, as *Lawrence* explicitly left prostitution out of reach of its decision. However, the court never explained why it had done so, and one could argue that so long as sexual intercourse occurs between two consenting adults, the state has no legitimate reason to forbid it.[232]

Divided Opinions
Throughout the world, there is wide disagreement on whether prostitution should be illegal.[233] In the United States and Canada, few academics and experts support a total ban that would punish both sex workers and customers. The US Department of State vindicates its stance by stating that prostitution is inherently harmful and that it provides a "façade behind which traffickers for sexual exploitation operate."[234] Therefore, those who hold conservative views often support a total ban on prostitution, as well as criminal punishment. On the other hand, sex workers and allies often strongly advocate for its legalization or, at a

minimum, its decriminalization. In the middle camp, many feminists support decriminalization, thus leaving prostitutes unpunished, while retaining criminal punishment for customers. They thus argue against total legalization.[235]

People who support legalization generally point to various negative consequences to the prostitutes or sex workers. For instance, Human Rights Watch observed in 2019 that criminalizing adult, voluntary, and consensual sex – including the commercial exchange of sexual services – was incompatible with the human right to personal autonomy and privacy. It exposes sex workers to abuse and exploitation by law enforcement officials, such as police officers. It also heightens their vulnerability to violence, including rape, assault, and murder, by attackers who see them as easy targets because they are stigmatized and unlikely to receive help from the police. This undermines their ability to seek justice for crimes against them and has a negative effect on their right to health.[236] Moreover, they might not be able to rent an apartment or may be evicted from their current one, and they may not be able to send their children to school without them being harassed. Only by total legalization or decriminalization could prostitution be regarded as a lawful occupation, which would make all sex workers eligible for labour law protections and social security benefits. Further, if legalization were to occur, governments could potentially regulate prostitution as a legitimate business.[237]

In contrast, those who oppose legalization question whether it would greatly increase the safety of sex workers. It might increase competition, pressuring them to partake in unsafe or uncommon forms of sex, and may not improve safety for those who work in brothels.[238] Legalization might also simply make it more difficult for the police to discover abuse. The opponents of legalization point out that an overwhelming number of sex workers are forced into the industry by poverty, sexual and racial discrimination, sexual abuse during childhood,[239] or human and sex trafficking. To stop the trafficking, they argue, prostitution must be eliminated. Legalization, from their viewpoint, would necessarily increase it.[240]

Moreover, some claim that prostitution is inherently exploitative and discriminatory.[241] It is well known that the overwhelming majority of sex workers are women. Therefore, prostitution allows men to sexually exploit them and forces them to act as an object of sex. Thus, some argue that it enables men to treat all women as objects, leading to further sexual violence and discrimination in society. Those who take this view insist that banning prostitution is essential to stopping sexual discrimination. They also often claim that prostitution is a violation of human dignity and should not be legalized.[242] Sex should not be commodified or traded on the market.

However, supporters of legalization counteract these objections. First, studies have shown that when prostitution is criminalized and when police enforce this ban, the level of violence from clients and other parties increases, and prostitutes are at greater risk of being forced to accept condomless sex.[243] Given the results of these studies, it is logical to assume that legalization would facilitate safer working conditions for sex workers.

Second, with respect to trafficking, though the government has a legitimate interest in combatting it, there may be no need to prohibit prostitution altogether. Instead, the government can simply enforce a ban on trafficking. It is true that such a measure may be ineffective and may not save everyone who is trafficked. But, to justify a blanket ban on prostitution, it is necessary to argue that, to eradicate trafficking, the deprivation of the rights of the women who are not forced to serve as prostitutes or who are not the victims of human or sex trafficking can be justified for the sake of other vulnerable women. Women who are not victims might question why their freedom of choice needs to be curtailed for the sake of women who could be victims.

Third, it is true that prostitution can be viewed as sexually discriminatory, and it is understandable that it could facilitate sexual discrimination. On the basis of this, one might ostensibly argue that it needs to be disallowed if sexual discrimination is to be eliminated. However, sex workers are not necessarily engaging in sexual discrimination. Paying for sex might be viewed as discriminatory since prostitutes are overwhelmingly women and their customers are overwhelmingly men. But it is not clear why this imbalance automatically renders such service discriminatory. Moreover, a total ban on prostitution is highly unlikely to eradicate sexual discrimination. Further, it can be argued that criminalizing prostitution makes sex workers easier targets of discrimination. The ban could even work to justify this discrimination to prevent possible discrimination against other women: prostitutes would be sacrificed for the sake of other women.

Fourth, it may be worth asking why the commodification of sex is seen as such an egregious violation of human dignity.[244] Many people assert that prostitution violates human dignity but rarely go on to explain why. Some claim that economically speaking, there is little difference between sex work and being a housewife, as wives run the family home and raise the children in exchange for financial support from the husband, a kind of compensation for sex.[245] This logic raises the question of whether and in what circumstances it is wrong to spend money in exchange for intimacy. Many people believe that sexual intercourse should not be commodified. But it is not clear why this applies solely to sexual intercourse and does not extend to all other sexual activities. There might not exist an objective standard to separate what should be commodified from what should not.[246] Furthermore, viewing prostitution as a violation of human dignity only leads to further discrimination and stigma against sex workers.[247] If it remains illegal, they will suffer serious negative consequences. In this sense, criminalizing prostitution simply ends in the deprivation of their human dignity, in the name of saving the human dignity of all women.

Many feminists prefer the Nordic model. The punishment of customers, its most important element, appears on its face to be appropriate, but it might not work as expected.[248] The Nordic experience shows that enforcing the punishment of customers is very difficult and filled with loopholes. Nor does it appear to wipe out the demand.[249] Moreover, when the purchase is illegal, sex workers cannot provide their services openly and are forced to work behind closed doors and in unsafe areas. Fearing the possibility of arrest, their customers will be reluctant to share information about themselves, making it difficult for sex workers to determine which ones are dangerous. As a result, their chances of becoming crime victims greatly increase. As long as customers are punished, sex workers will not be safe.[250] Moreover, so long as prostitution remains illegal, they are technically committing a crime, even if they will not be punished for it. Sex workers therefore will still face serious negative consequences.[251]

Amnesty International recently adopted a resolution to legalize prostitution.[252] In light of serious discrimination against sex workers, it proposed to "repeal existing laws and refrain from introducing new laws that criminalize or penalize directly or in practice the consensual exchange of sexual services between adults for remuneration." Many people supported this proposal.[253] However, many disappointed feminists condemned it,[254] reflecting the opposition to legalizing prostitution.

In Japan, providing sexual intercourse for payment and patronizing it are both illegal, but there is no criminal punishment. This is a clear example of criminalization without punishment. Most Japanese academics and experts support the status quo. Nevertheless, prostitution is available almost everywhere, and sex workers are calling for its total legalization. Japanese feminists generally prefer the Nordic model and urge the government to impose criminal punishment on customers; prostitution would remain illegal and sex workers would still not be penalized.[255] Furthermore, many feminists want to expand the scope of prohibited activities to include all kinds of sexual services beyond sexual intercourse.[256] Reflecting the divide in academic and expert opinions worldwide, there are similar arguments for and against Japan's prostitution ban without criminal punishment in Japan.

Reconsidering the Constitutionality of the Prostitution Ban

Despite the multitude of views on prostitution, very few people have asked whether one has a constitutional right to engage in it. Nor, if such a right does exist, have they asked whether its restriction can be constitutionally justified.[257] Therefore, it is necessary to ask whether prostitution is a constitutionally protected right in the first place. Those who favour a ban typically insist that it is not.[258] Nonetheless, if the Constitution protects sexual freedom, including whether, with whom, and how to have sex, the fact that sex can be accompanied by payment is immaterial. As long as it is consensual, it should be included as a sexual freedom. Excluding it from the scope of sexual freedom makes no sense. Even if the ban on prostitution carries no criminal punishment, it is surely an infringement of this constitutional right. Given this, it would need to be justified, just as other restrictions on sexual freedom need to be justified.

Conservative people would defend the prostitution prohibition on the grounds of morality and public safety. But as discussed above, morality is not legitimate grounds to restrict sexual autonomy. The relationship between prostitution and public safety is dubious since prostitution can be offered in a brothel or a room, and its likelihood of causing a public disturbance is slim. Prostitution services might attract unsavoury individuals or organizations whose intent is to take advantage of sex workers and thus disturb public safety. But they should be punished, and there is no need to forbid prostitution altogether.

As mentioned earlier, those who defend the ban argue that it should remain prohibited because most sex workers are forced into the industry and cannot exercise their right to sexual freedom.[259] However, to paint all sex workers with this brush is probably a generalization. Some choose to partake in sex work and exercise their own rational judgment in making that decision. If this is accepted, it is difficult to suggest that all sex workers are forced to serve as prostitutes or that they had no choice.

It is both a necessary and a legitimate goal of government to ensure that no one is forced into prostitution. Sex work is permissible only if it is voluntary; no one should be forced into it to pay off debts or for advance payment. It is also necessary to ensure that sex workers have total freedom to exit the profession whenever they choose and that they can refuse a customer. However, a total prohibition on prostitution cannot be justified as a means to eradicate coercion and pressure on women to become involved in it. Women should possess the freedom to choose what type of work they do.

It is tempting to argue that prostitution and human or sex trafficking are inherently related, making a ban on the former essential in wiping out the latter. It is true that the popularity of prostitution does encourage trafficking,[260] and some data do suggest that the risk of sex trafficking could increase if prostitution were legalized.[261] The difficulty with this argument is that not all prostitutes are forced or coerced into the work. Although trafficking is a very serious problem, and the government should do everything possible to stamp it out,[262] the best strategy is for the government to stand up and enforce a ban on trafficking. For those who truly choose sex work, a complete prohibition on prostitution merely hinders their ability to earn a living. The ban is for the benefit of other women who might be forced or coerced into the industry. Therefore, we need to determine whether, with the intent of protecting vulnerable women, we can legitimately restrict the rights of those who willingly opt for sex work. Given that other less drastic alternatives may be available, this step may not be justifiable.

Furthermore, prohibiting prostitution for the sake of all women is paternalistic – women are deprived of their freedom for their own benefit. It may be true that many women do need such protection. But once we justify it, simultaneously asserting that women should be granted the constitutional right to sexual autonomy becomes rather difficult. If a woman is not permitted to exercise this right in connection with prostitution, how can we expect her ever to do so? If this occurs, we might end up denying the constitutional right to sexual autonomy for all women.

Moreover, one problem with this argument is that it ignores the existence of current active sex workers. As noted above, the ban or criminalization of prostitution has had significant negative effects on the lives of sex workers. The argument thus ends up justifying the prevention of future sex workers at the sacrifice of current ones.

Some people argue that prostitution allows men to exploit women, thus giving the impression that women are merely objects, a belief that can lead to violence and sex crimes against them.[263] Although sexual discrimination is obviously unacceptable, it is also wrong to accuse sex workers of allowing or facilitating it. It is doubtful whether a prohibition on sex work can be justified in the name of eradicating sexual discrimination.

It is understandable that many people oppose prostitution on the grounds that it violates human dignity.[264] It is also understandable that they see some conduct, including that of a sexual nature, as exempt from commodification. Yet, when it comes to explaining why, their arguments may be less persuasive. Moreover, when it comes to determining what activities lie beyond the pale, the arguments immediately run into serious problems. Even in the United States, the definition of prostitution varies significantly from state to state. Some states describe it as "an act of sexual penetration" or sexual intercourse, whereas others include fellatio, cunnilingus, assisted masturbation, or "physical contact of [a] person's clothed or unclothed genitals, pubic area, buttocks, [or] if such person be a female, breast." Moreover, some states omit certain acts from their definitions, including self-masturbation where there is no physical contact between parties; sado-masochistic acts such as "foot licking, spanking, domination and submission" where no other sexual activity is involved; and sexually suggestive acts where no other sexual activity is involved, such as sucking on someone's finger.[265] When human dignity is brought into the equation, drawing a clear line between what is banned and what is not becomes a challenge.

Also, many occupations, especially in the world of entertainment, involve a generous dose of sex appeal. When someone becomes a pop singer or musician, an actress, a dancer (except perhaps for those who dance nude), or a model (except perhaps for those who pose nude), no one suggests that the sexual aspects of the job violate human dignity, at least not so far. And of course, no one objects to paying a fee to watch them perform, at least so far. Frankly, it is impossible to say what forms of conduct are essential to human dignity and thus must not be commodified.[266]

In the end, it is questionable whether a total ban on prostitution could be justified in light of the Constitution, even if the sex workers are not subject to criminal punishment. As long as prostitution remains illegal, they will face serious consequences, and as long as customers are punished, they will be in serious danger.[267]

Moreover, the proposal to expand the definition of prostitution to include activities that go beyond sex in the narrow sense is questionable. Surely, as long as the government is allowed to keep the prostitution ban, it could be argued that prostitution should also encompass sex in the broader sense, which includes oral and anal intercourse, as well as lesbian sex. But if the ban itself is questionable, the expansion would surely not be justified. Further, expansion to include sex in the broadest sense is similarly questionable. In light of the justification to prohibit prostitution, it is apparently too broad to forbid all these activities. Broader sexual activities, including ones that might stimulate sexual desires, are not included in constitutionally protected sexual autonomy. Therefore, there might not be any constitutional objection to disallowing them. But in practice, such a measure would be utterly unworkable since the activities that might arouse sexual desire are virtually numberless, and it is impossible to draw a reasonable line. Even though there is no constitutional right to engage in them, any arbitrary and discriminatory ban will violate the equality right and would be unconstitutional.

Lessons from the Comfort Women System

In this regard, it is important to learn from the comfort women system employed by the Japanese military in China during the Second World War. At that time, Japan invaded China and other Asian countries, stationing a huge number of Japanese soldiers there. To satisfy their sexual needs and to prevent them from having non-consensual sex with local women, the Japanese military established the comfort women system.[268] A huge number of women, perhaps as many as 200,000, were installed in comfort women stations, mostly run by private operators with the cooperation of the military. The exact form and extent of this cooperation remains unclear because no documentary evidence survives to corroborate testimonies from the participants themselves.[269] Apparently, the military did check their health and ensured that there was no risk of transmissible disease.

Opinions on how to categorize these women remain sharply divided: some term them "sex slaves," whereas others see them simply as prostitutes.[270] Most appear to have been Japanese, though it cannot be denied that many were Korean. All had fixed-term service contracts with the operators. Their participation was supposed to be voluntary, and many Japanese women were recruited to work in Asia. No hard evidence suggests that the government, the military, or the police systematically used physical force to round up or kidnap them and send them to comfort stations. But many were recruited because of their poverty and lack of good jobs. Many were probably tricked by brokers or pressured into participating by family or society. In that sense, it is undeniable that they were "practically forced" to serve as comfort women.

It must be noted, however, that many Japanese women were also practically forced to serve as prostitutes at home because many were in a sense "sold" by their family due to extreme poverty in rural areas. Refusing to engage in the work or running away would violate the contract, thereby forcing the woman and her family to return the huge lump sum they had already received, intolerable to imagine. They were thus virtually forced to offer sexual services during the term of their contract. It must be also remembered that the Japanese government established similar kinds of systems for the Allied soldiers who occupied Japan after the war.[271] Unfortunately, there was no notion that women possessed sexual autonomy or that forcing or tricking them to accept this work was unacceptable. Government involvement in these systems makes them all the more troublesome. Whether directly or indirectly, the government played a role in practically forcing women into these services.

These experiences demonstrate the integral importance of the right to sexual autonomy and the necessity of excluding government interference with that right. However, the lessons provided by the comfort women system do not lead to the conclusion that prostitution should be proscribed altogether.

The Future of the Prostitution Ban

Despite being sustained by academics and experts, the Japanese ban on prostitution seems never to have been strictly enforced or widely obeyed. It has been largely ignored in many entertainment business facilities, and the number of persons arrested for violating the Prostitution Prevention Act is far lower than the actual estimated number of those who escape arrest.[272] The number of sex workers sent to rehabilitation centres after being convicted for solicitation dropped dramatically,[273] and women's shelters, which were designed for women who were in danger of engaging in prostitution, now accept many other women who need help and assistance, including victims of domestic violence.[274]

Indeed, many people are calling for a radical revision of the Prostitution Prevention Act, which is extremely outdated and out of touch with reality and social development. Critics of the act demand that it stops treating sex workers as criminals and instead structures the legal system to offer service and protection to women in need. However, the Gender Equality Bureau of the Cabinet Office (GEB), which is charged with accomplishing gender equality, takes an anti-prostitution stance: in its opinion, prostitution is an affront to the human dignity of both the sex worker and the customer. As such, it should be eradicated. Further, the GEB has vowed to strengthen its efforts to prevent prostitution, to bolster its campaign against it, to offer assistance to sex workers to become self-dependent, and to rehabilitate arrested sex workers.[275] Given this, the Japanese government does not appear to be interested in helping sex workers do their jobs in safe conditions that are free from abuse.[276] In light of its stated commitment to eliminating prostitution, it is highly unlikely that the government will legalize it.[277]

Rape: The Right Not to Be Forced to Have Sex

3

Everyone should have the right to refuse sex, which is why rape and sexual assault are illegal all over the world. But when it comes to this subject, Japan's criminal justice system is riddled with shortcomings and flaws.[1] The right not to be forced to have sex is protected by the Constitution, which should impel the government to punish those who violate it. Any failure in this regard is an unconstitutional infringement of the right to refuse sex. Despite recent attempts to protect victims of sex crimes and to enhance punishments for such crimes, Japan's rape law remains inadequate.

The Criminal Justice System for Sex Crimes in Japan

Rape and Sexual Assault Law in the Criminal Code
The Japanese Criminal Code, originally enacted in 1880 and substantially renewed in 1907, covers sexual offences. The substantial requirements of these sex crimes remained unchanged until amendments were made in 2017.

Before that year, article 176 of the code stipulated that

> a person who, through assault or intimidation, commits a forcible obscene act upon another man or woman of not less than thirteen

years of age shall be punished by imprisonment with labour for not less than six months but not more than ten years. The same shall apply to a person who commits a forcible obscene act upon another man or woman under thirteen years of age.[2]

This prohibition was arguably equivalent to bans on sexual assault. Although a forcible obscene act was defined as involving "assault or intimidation," merely touching an intimate part of the body without consent could qualify.[3] Infliction of psychological pain could also be assault.[4] Moreover, sexual intent was not required to constitute a forcible obscene act if the conduct at issue were sexual in nature.[5]

Further, before the 2017 amendments, article 177 of the Criminal Code banned "rape," stating that

> a person who, through assault or intimidation, forcibly raped a female person of not less than thirteen years of age commits the crime of rape and shall be punished by imprisonment with labour for a definite term of not less than three years. The same shall apply to a person who commits sexual intercourse with a female person under thirteen years of age.[6]

Article 178(1) of the Criminal Code also disallowed "quasi-forcible obscene acts" or quasi-sexual assault by providing that "a person who commits an obscene act upon another person by taking advantage of loss of consciousness or inability to resist, or by causing a loss of consciousness or inability to resist, shall be punished in the same manner as prescribed for in article 176."[7] Before 2017, article 178(2) also banned "quasi-rape," stipulating that "a person who forcibly raped a female person by taking advantage of a loss of consciousness or inability to resist, or by causing a loss of consciousness or inability to resist, shall be punished in the same matter as prescribed in [article 177]."[8] Article 178-2 imposed an enhanced penalty on "gang rape," providing that "when two or more persons jointly commit the crimes prescribed under article 177 or paragraph (2) of the previous article [article 178], they shall be punished by imprisonment with labour for a definite term of not less than four years."[9]

Unsuccessful attempts at committing these crimes were subject to the same punishment as successful ones.[10] Before 2017, public prosecution of the offences from article 176 through to article 178 required a criminal complaint from the victim. Exceptions to this rule were forcible obscene acts proscribed under article 176, quasi-forcible obscene acts proscribed under article 178(1), or attempts at the same committed jointly by two or more persons at the scene of the crime.[11] Therefore, if two or more assailants perpetrated a forcible obscene act, a quasi-obscene act, or a gang rape, a prosecutor could file a charge without a complaint from the victim.[12]

Furthermore, anyone who committed or attempted to commit a forcible obscene act or a quasi-forcible obscene act and thereby caused the death or injury of the victim would be imprisoned with labour for an indefinite term or for a definite term of not less than three years.[13] Before 2017, when a person committed or attempted to commit rape or quasi-rape and thereby caused the death or injury of a female person, he or she would be imprisoned with labour for an indefinite term or for a definite term of not less than five years.[14] Additionally, before 2017, the punishment for committing or attempting to commit a gang rape and thereby causing the death or injury of a female person was imprisonment with labour for an indefinite term or for a definite term of not less than six years.[15] If rape were accompanied by robbery, the punishment was life imprisonment or a definite term of not less than seven years.[16]

The Criminal Code prohibits several other sex-related crimes. For example, public obscene acts (public indecency),[17] abduction for the purpose of an obscene act,[18] purchase of a person for an obscene act,[19] and transportation of a person abducted or sold for the purpose of an obscene act[20] are all specifically prohibited.[21] On the other hand, as discussed in the previous chapter, prostitution comes under the Prostitution Prevention Act,[22] but no criminal punishment is imposed on either prostitutes or their customers.[23]

Other Sex-Related Crimes
Moreover, in addition to the Criminal Code, certain special statutes proscribe other sex-related crimes. Aside from the Prostitution Prevention Act, the most important of these is the Child Prostitution Prohibition

Act.[24] Under this legislation, a "child" is anyone under the age of eighteen.[25] It prohibits "procuring child prostitution," which is "having sexual intercourse et al. (sexual intercourse or any conduct similar to sexual intercourse) with a child, or, with the purpose of satisfying one's sexual curiosity, touching genital organs et al. (meaning genital organs, anus, or nipples) of a child or having a child touch one's own genital organs et al. in return for giving or promising remuneration."[26] It prohibits "any sexual exploitation or sexual abuse of a child,"[27] and imposes imprisonment with labour for up to five years or a fine of up to 3 million (roughly US$22,000) (if we use the exchange rate at the time of writing, which was JPY 1 to US$0.0075).[28]

Child welfare legislation also forbids indecent acts committed against children. For instance, the Child Welfare Act bans anyone from making a child perform any conduct that is sexually indecent.[29] The Child Abuse Prevention Act also prohibits inflicting obscene acts on a child or making a child perform obscene acts, which it classifies as child abuse.[30]

Moreover, all local governments have anti-nuisance ordinances that apply to behaviour in public places. The Tokyo Metropolitan Government's anti-nuisance ordinance,[31] for instance, disallows acts that cause "the other person to feel embarrassment or forces another person to feel anxiety without a legitimate reason." It lists "touching another person's body through an outfit such as clothes or directly in public places or on public transportation."[32] Sexual touching on public transportation (a serious social problem) could be chargeable under this clause or as a forcible obscene act under the Criminal Code. There is a separate ban on photographing undergarments or body parts that are normally covered by clothing in "places where a person normally stays undressed partly or wholly such as living places, restroom, bath or dressing rooms," and in "places of transportation used by an unspecified number of persons or many persons such as public places, public transportation, schools, offices or taxies."[33]

Most local youth protection ordinances also disallow indecent sexual conduct toward young people. The Tokyo Metropolitan Government's ordinance[34] defines "youth" as anyone under age eighteen[35] and bans sexual intercourse and analogous conduct with them.[36] Therefore, although having sexual intercourse with someone older than thirteen and younger than eighteen may not qualify as rape if assault or intimidation are not involved, it could violate these local ordinances, and perpetrators could thus face criminal punishment.[37]

Requirements for the Punishment of Rape

Rape is commonly seen as the most serious sex crime, and a rapist often incurs the harshest punishment. But, in Japan before 2017, as discussed above, only sexual intercourse with a girl under the age of thirteen or forcible sexual intercourse with a girl or woman not less than thirteen, combined with "assault or intimidation," constituted rape.[38] This provision was largely based on that of the French Criminal Code.[39] Its original purpose was to protect the chastity of a woman as a property interest of her father or husband, from a patriarchal perspective,[40] but it was eventually viewed as protecting the sexual freedom of women.[41] Nevertheless, despite all the reforms up to 2017, it had several critical shortcomings.[42]

Before 2017, "rape" meant "sexual intercourse ... committed when a part of the man's penis was inserted into the woman's vagina regardless of whether there was ejaculation or resulting pregnancy."[43] Therefore, only a woman could be subject to rape,[44] and no other sexual conduct, such as forcible oral intercourse, anal intercourse, or the insertion of fingers or any object into the vagina, qualified as rape.[45]

For the additional elements required under the rape provision, "assault" referred to the use of physical force and "intimidation" to verbal threats. The requirement of "assault or intimidation" meant that some method must have been employed that made it "very hard for the victim to resist."[46] The method did not have to extend so far as to make the victim incapable of resistance. It was sufficient if it made it impossible or very hard for her to resist, given her age, sex, ordinary behaviour, and past experiences, or given the time, environment, location, or other circumstances of the crime.[47] Thus, if the victim were unable to resist or if resistance were very difficult, the sexual intercourse could qualify as rape. Even though the SCOJ has insisted that the degree of assault or intimidation must have been sufficient to make it difficult to resist, lower courts have loosely interpreted this requirement to find most instances of forced sexual assault involving sexual intercourse to be rape.[48] Moreover, if the victim were unconscious or incapacitated, sexual intercourse was deemed to be quasi-rape.[49] In other words, Japanese law focused on the circumstances that made it impossible to give consent or very difficult to resist instead of concentrating on the existence of consent. It was only when a female victim not less than the age of thirteen could easily have resisted or escaped but did not do so that courts might find that there was no assault or intimidation.[50] Nevertheless, exactly what kinds of physical force or intimidation were required to secure a conviction for rape was never clearly specified, and there was a perception among the public that physical resistance was required on the part of the woman in order to secure a conviction of rape.

On the other hand, if an assailant had sexual intercourse with a girl under the age of thirteen that did not involve assault or intimidation that was still considered rape even if she consented. This is statutory rape.

Before 2017, prosecutors required a criminal complaint from the victim in order to file a prosecution for rape. This rule was designed to respect the wishes of the victim. The minimum punishment for rape was imprisonment with labour for no less than three years. The maximum punishment was imprisonment for twenty years in cases where the attacker was charged only with rape, or thirty years if he committed other crimes at the same time. If two or more people participated in a rape, the minimum sentence was imprisonment for four years. If the rape resulted in the death or injury of the victim, the sentence increased to a minimum of five years, and the maximum could be incarceration with labour for an indefinite term.[51] The limitation period for a prosecutor to file a rape charge was normally ten years, but it increased to thirty if the victim died as a result of the incident.[52] As we will see, many people complained that the punishment for sex crimes was too lenient.

Hardships for Rape Victims

Filing a Crime Report and a Criminal Complaint
In Japan, the number of reported rapes reached its peak in 1964, with 6,857 cases. Since then, the number has been in decline, with 1,250 cases in 2014.[53] Thus, the incidence of reported rape was roughly 1.9 per 100,000 women.[54] The number of forcible obscene acts peaked in 2003 (10,029 cases) but declined thereafter to 7,400 in 2014.[55]

It is a well-known fact, however, that sex-related crimes are extremely underreported to police.[56] Most victims are women, who often fear the negative consequences of revealing what has happened to them. In many instances, they have been targeted by a relative or an acquaintance, which makes them especially reluctant to come forward. They often feel that they themselves did something wrong and are thus not entirely free from blame. Perhaps they should have exercised more caution. Maybe they somehow provoked the assailant. Blaming rape victims for their supposed carelessness or provocation remains common today, as many victims have discovered.

If a woman does report being raped, she may encounter an upsetting reaction from the police. Indeed, in the past, there was no serious concern for crime victims in general, and especially not for victims of sex crimes. They were treated merely as the initiators of criminal investigations. Rape victims thus had to recount the events to police officers, sometimes multiple times. They endured the probing eyes of officers and had to answer sensitive and sometimes embarrassing questions. They were forced to relive the experience through questioning and investigation. Police officers, predominantly male, were often insensitive to the injury and humiliation involved, were commonly skeptical from the outset, and sometimes denied the allegations made by victims. They often showed little concern for the feelings of victims when they tasked doctors with verifying injuries. Nor were they willing to protect victims from repeated assault in the future.

Many victims also reported that the police did not make a concerted effort to catch their attacker.[57] In many cases, accusations ended up in a "he said, she said" situation and ultimately went nowhere. Many victims also knew that prosecutors might be reluctant to file charges.[58] Even if the perpetrator were arrested and brought before a court, many victims fear that their names would be recorded in writs of prosecution and read out in court. In this situation, there is no legal way of preventing the media or anyone in attendance from revealing their identities to the public.

The conviction rate in Japan is quite high.[59] Defendants are overwhelmingly likely to be found guilty if prosecuted. But, as we will see, even when this occurs, courts may suspend the sentence and the perpetrator may avoid going to jail.[60] Moreover, even if he is incarcerated, length of the imprisonment sentence is generally very short, and the assailant can often be quickly released.[61] Victims are aware of this too.

Fortunately for the victims of sex crimes, police do not release their names unless they were killed. And although there is no legal ban, the media do not reveal their identity.[62] Victims do not have to worry that eager journalists may hound them or contact their family or friends for comment. But preventing the spread of rumours is difficult, and victims may nonetheless fear that their identity could be revealed if they go to the police or end up in court.

In light of all this, rape victims are often very reluctant to go to the police and have their victimization reported.[63]

Obtaining Justice via the Criminal Process
Obtaining justice through the criminal process is another hurdle for victims of sex crimes. The Constitution of Japan mandates that any member of the public can attend a trial except when "a court unanimously determines publicity to be dangerous to public order or morals."[64] Therefore, a court could choose to hold a closed trial in sex crime cases where this criterion is met. However, courts have proven unwilling to do this, and trials typically remain open to the public. Victims must therefore appear in open court to provide their testimony as to the identity of the assailant, their relationship with him, and the details of the assault. They will relive the experience of rape and will be questioned by defence attorneys. Since there are no shield laws or any restrictions on evidence that can be introduced, defence attorneys can ask all kinds of questions that are apparently relevant, even in connection with the victims' sex life. This is an embarrassing and humiliating experience for many victims.

The barriers to conviction are quite high. As discussed above, before 2017, rape was defined solely as forcible sexual intercourse with a woman who was not under age thirteen. The scope for punishment was therefore very narrow. Other forcible sex acts did not qualify as rape (although they could be classed as forcible obscene acts). To constitute rape, sexual intercourse must also be accompanied by "assault or intimidation." If this involved physical violence or a weapon, prosecutors could find it easier to prove this requirement. Yet, some decisions also suggested that the use of physical force or threats must be sufficiently grave as to overcome physical resistance. This requirement raised a serious challenge, especially when the assailant deceived the victim or took advantage of a position of power to coerce sex. Courts interpreted this requirement quite broadly so as to allow a conviction if the attacker made a victim feel that there was no other alternative to engaging in sex.[65] If she were fully intoxicated or if her assailant used a drug to render her unconscious, this would constitute quasi-rape, whose punishment remained the same as for rape. However, prosecutors could have difficulty filing a charge where a victim was highly but not fully intoxicated, unconscious, or incapacitated, or where the police could not ascertain that the assailant had forced or tricked her to drink to incapacitation or that she lost consciousness because of drink or drugs.[66]

This approach differs from that of other countries. For instance, Canada radically reformed its Criminal Code sex crime provisions in 1983. The revisions abolished the distinction between rape and indecent assault, merging them into the single offence of sexual assault.[67] The word "rape" was dropped because it inflicted traumatic associations on victims. Any sexual assault without consent is a crime, and prosecutors are not required to prove that assault or intimidation occurred. Therefore, they must prove only that a victim did not consent to sex, evidence that does not need to be corroborated.[68] In other words, mere testimony from a victim could be sufficient to secure a conviction.

Moreover, in Japan, a prosecutor must prove that the accused intended to commit rape. If the woman consented to sex, his conduct would not be illegal. Further, if he had a mistaken but honest belief that she had consented, there would be no intent to commit rape and he could not be held liable. The prosecutor thus needs to prove that there was no consent and that the defendant knew it. This requirement can present a challenge.[69] When an accused insists that consent was given, the court will assess the factual basis for his belief. If the facts correspond to his claims, the court will determine whether he could reasonably infer consent. Therefore, even if he asserts that consent had been given, the court could reject his defence if there is no factual foundation for his belief or if inferring consent on the basis of the facts was unreasonable. This approach also differs markedly from that of other countries. In Canada, for example, affirmative consent is required.[70] To claim a belief in consent, the accused must point to evidence that the victim agreed through words or actions, not just that he or she failed to object or resist. Moreover, reasonable steps must be taken to confirm the existence of consent.[71]

Given this, it is not easy for a rape victim in Japan to persuade prosecutors to file charges and to obtain a conviction in court.[72] If the assailant alleges that sex was consensual, the prosecutor might consider the likelihood of successfully rebutting this allegation and decide to drop the charges.[73] Furthermore, the accused could potentially sue the victim for defamation. Thus, simply by filing a report and going to court, victims could be subject to condemnation, vilification, and harassment.[74]

Even when a perpetrator is convicted, as mentioned above, if the court chooses imprisonment for a period of not more than three years, the sentence could possibly be suspended.[75] If that occurs, a convicted assailant can avoid incarceration entirely. Moreover, the minimum sentence for rape was imprisonment with labour for three years. There was no ostensible maximum (although since it has to be a definite term of imprisonment, as explained above, the maximum was thus limited to twenty years, as opposed to no maximum for indefinite term sentences). In Canada, the sexual assault of an adult is punishable by a maximum of ten years in jail, with no fixed minimum. Thus, the penalty for rape would seem to be harsher in Japan. But many have criticized it, pointing out that most convictions for rape carry much shorter sentence and, in comparison with other punishments, such as the minimum five-year sentence for robbery, it is too lenient.[76]

The Path to Reform

Increasing Criticisms

All of these difficulties provoked serious criticism. In response, the government gradually accepted the necessity of reform. In 2004, the Gender Equality Bureau (GEB) issued a report that outlined an agenda and necessary countermeasures against sexual violence toward women.[77] It called for a lengthening of prison terms for rape; strict enforcement of rape provisions and child welfare provisions against the sexual abuse of children; criminal punishment for voyeurism; strict enforcement against unwanted sexual touching; and for it to be made clear that infliction of psychological pain could constitute assault.[78] It also urged better care for and respect toward victims of sex crimes by improving police interviewing and evidence collection, allowing a support person to accompany the victim during their testimony in courtroom, shielding victims during testimony or permitting them to use a video link, further upgrading of counselling and information provided at police and prosecutors' offices, and augmenting the number of both female police officers and experts providing care.[79]

Even so, the international community was not impressed by the situation in Japan. In its concluding remarks of 2008, the UN Human Rights Committee expressed concern that the definition of rape in article 177 of the Criminal Code applied only to actual sexual intercourse between men and women and required victims to resist the attack. The committee criticized the fact that rape and other sex crimes could not be prosecuted basically without a complaint filed by the victim.[80] It voiced concern over reports that perpetrators of sexual violence frequently escaped punishment or received light sentences and that judges often unduly focused on the sexual past of victims and required them to prove that they had resisted. The committee highlighted the lack of doctors and nurses with specialized training in sexual violence, as well as the minimal support from non-government organizations in providing such training.[81]

The committee thus pressed Japan to broaden the scope of the article 177 definition of rape and to ensure that incest, sexual abuse other than sexual intercourse, and the rape of men were classed as serious criminal offences. It suggested that Japan remove the burden on victims to prove they had resisted and to prosecute rape and other crimes of sexual violence ex officio.[82] It called for the introduction of mandatory gender-sensitive training on sexual violence for judges, prosecutors, police, and prison officers.[83] Voicing concern about the age of sexual consent, which was thirteen for both boys and girls,[84] it urged Japan to raise it, with a view to protecting the normal development of children and to prevent their abuse.[85]

Respect for the Victims of Sex Crimes

Over the years, the Japanese government has gradually displayed increasing concern for victims of crime, especially those of sex crimes.[86] First, in 1980, the Diet passed the Crime Victims Support Benefit Act, which was the first step in its protection measures for victims.[87] After calls for more robust initiatives, the Diet passed the Crime Victims Protection Act in 2000,[88] mandating the protection of victims during criminal trials and allowing them to participate in trials. Then, in 2004, the Diet passed the Crime Victims Fundamental Act,[89] clarifying its own duties as well as those of local governments, mandating the adoption of a victim protection plan, and declaring basic protection policies for crime victims. The Crime Victims Protection Fundamental Plan was subsequently adopted.[90]

In 1996, the National Police Agency (NPA), which manages and supervises all local police organizations, adopted the Crime Victim Protection Guideline and committed to greater concern for the victims of crime. With the enactment of the Crime Victims Fundamental Act and the adoption of the Crime Victims Protection Fundamental Plan, the NPA submitted a bill to revise the Crime Victims Support Benefit Act and increased benefits to victims in 2008. With the adoption of the Second Fundamental Plan, the NPA revised the Crime Victims Protection Guideline to the Crime Victims Support Guideline. Finally, with the adoption of the Third Fundamental Plan, the NPA adopted the Crime Victims Support Fundamental Plan in 2016.[91]

On the basis of these guidelines and fundamental plans, the police now offer various services to crime victims, including those of sex crimes.[92] The police prepared an information manual for victims, instituted a system to inform them of the progress of their criminal investigation as well as any final decisions, and opened a one-stop centre for them to obtain support.[93] During interviewing, officers are mandated to treat victims with care and respect, and to provide sympathetic support for filing a report or a complaint.[94] In respecting the privacy of victims, police officers do not use marked patrol cars, and uniformed officers are not sent to their residences.[95] The local police will send officers to ensure the safety of victims, provide advice, and receive requests or complaints.[96] The police now have counsellors for victims, and they work in unison with private counsellors or support groups. They also provide victim supporters and upgraded meeting spaces to help victims feel more comfortable in speaking with officers.[97]

The prosecutors' office also hired support staff, provided a victims hotline for questions and consultation, and initiated a notification program designed to supply updated information on the progress of criminal proceedings.[98] When prosecutors decide not to file charges, all the records and evidence are not open to the public, but the prosecutor can disclose information to victims.[99] If they are dissatisfied, they can file a complaint with the Prosecution Review Board, a kind of grand jury consisting of citizen representatives, to review the decision.[100] In the past, the Board's decisions were not binding, but now if it concludes that the prosecutor should have filed a charge and if this is confirmed a second time, a judge must appoint an attorney to file charges as an appointed prosecutor. This allows suspects to be charged even if the prosecutors were reluctant to do so.

During a criminal trial, the court may decide not to reveal the identity of a victim.[101] If it takes this step, the prosecutor, defence attorney, and the defendant must not disclose it during the proceedings. The prosecutor reads the writ of prosecution without naming the victim. The prosecutor can ask the defence attorney not to reveal the identity to others, including the defendant, and can provide the defence attorney with information about the victim on the condition that the identity be kept secret, even from the defendant, or can even refuse to name the victim if it is necessary.[102]

When victims testify in open court, they can ask to be accompanied by a support person, to be hidden from view, or to testify from a separate room via video link.[103] They are now given priority for trial attendance and may ask the court through the prosecutor to participate in the criminal process.[104] If permitted, they can sit alongside the prosecutor, question witnesses and the accused, and state their final opinion following the final argument of the prosecutor and immediately before the defence counsel delivers his or her final arguments.[105] They may also ask for attorneys to participate on their behalf, and if they cannot afford a lawyer, they will be provided with a government-appointed attorney.[106] They may also request access to (and copies of) trial transcripts.[107]

When the defendant and victim reach a civil settlement, the victims may ask the court to incorporate it into the trial transcript, thus making it valid as a court order.[108] In certain serious cases, the victim may ask the court to issue an order against the defendant for damages.[109] After a conviction, the same court holds hearings (limited principally to four) and on the basis of evidence produced during the criminal trial decides the civil liability of the defendant. If a defendant challenges this order, the proceeding will return to a standard civil litigation proceeding, but the civil court can consider all evidence produced during the criminal trial. Victims are also entitled to be notified about the treatment of the defendant in prison and about his release. If it is necessary to avoid further damage or injury, they can ask the prosecutor for pre-release notification and can participate in the release hearing after the sentence has been served.[110] They may ask for the return of any items that were used as evidence and can attend the destruction of evidence.[111] They may also ask for access to court records upon the conclusion of the case.[112]

A Reconsideration of the Sex Crime Provisions

In addition, the government gradually questioned the substantive requirements for rape and other sex crimes, as well as their punishment. The GEB's 2004 report, "Agenda and Countermeasures against Sexual Violence toward Women," prompted the Diet to lengthen imprisonment time for rape and to add new provisions on gang rape and gang rape resulting in death or injury.[113]

In 2010, the Third Gender Equality Fundamental Plan declared the reconsideration of punishment for sex crimes, including dropping the complaint requirement and increasing prison terms.[114] In 2012, the GEB published a report on the re-examination of sex crimes in Japan.[115] The report recommended the imposition of much harsher punishment, removing the complaint requirement, raising the age of consent, deleting the "assault or intimidation" requirement, shifting the burden of proof to the defendant, criminalizing rape against men, and increasing prison terms.[116]

In 2014, under the leadership of Prime Minister Shinzo Abe, the justice minister revealed her strong commitment to the 2012 GEB reconsiderations,[117] and the Ministry of Justice (MOJ) established a study group of academics and professionals to make recommendations. In August 2015, the group issued a report,[118] showing majority support for several amendments to the Criminal Code.[119] In October 2015, the justice minister solicited official recommendations from the Legislative Council, which then created an outline draft of the amendments to sexual crimes in the Criminal Code.[120] In 2017, this led to the submission of a radical reform bill and the enactment of multiple amendments to the Criminal Code.

Improving Justice for Sexual Offences

Treating Victims with Respect

First, the government took many steps to protect victims of sex crimes during the criminal process. As a result, the police, the prosecutors' office, and courts all contribute to significantly enhanced protection for them.

Via a common speed dial, victims may directly contact the police for a consultation call.[121] The police also offer counselling,[122] and they have further expanded their support services.[123] In prefectural headquarters, sex crime investigation supervisors manage investigations, and the number of sex crime investigation experts has risen, as has the number of female officers in each police station, who collect evidence and accompany victims to hospitals. In addition, the evidence collection process has been made less traumatic for victims by providing alternative clothing or using dolls to ascertain the details of the crime (in the past, the victim was asked to re-enact it, with actual police officers taking the part of the assailant). Police also provide support funding for related medical bills and for prescription medication to prevent pregnancy.

Victims may also take advantage of various protective measures during the criminal procedure. Protecting their identity could be especially beneficial for them.[124] The same is true for being accompanied by a support person during the trial, being shielded from view, or testifying in a separate room via video link. They may participate or ask their attorneys – even government-appointed ones – to participate on their behalf, question witnesses or the defendant, or make a final statement at trial. If they wish for harsh punishment, the statement provides an opportunity to express that desire to the court. They can also ask for damage orders during the trial, allowing judges to order damages once it is over.

Indeed, an increasing number of victims are participating in rape trials. In 2014, 129 did so. Twenty-eight questioned witnesses, 62 questioned the accused, and 89 made concluding remarks and expressed their wishes regarding sentencing.[125] Fifty-eight asked to be shielded from view, 28 were accompanied by support persons, and 120 asked for specific assistance from their attorney.[126] Moreover, among the 264 applications for damage orders by crime victims in 2014, 38 came from victims of rape.[127] Here too, an increasing number of rape victims are asking for damage orders.

Furthermore, the introduction of a "citizen judge" system has brought significant changes to rape trials. Responding to calls for more citizen participation in the criminal process, the government introduced this system, whereby six randomly chosen citizens sit with three professional judges to participate in conviction and sentencing for serious criminal cases.[128] In fact, the citizen judge trial is mandatory for serious crimes. If rape results in the death or injury of the victim, such a trial is required. Thus, under the new system a number of rape trials are heard by citizen judges. As it turns out, they have a tendency to choose much longer jail sentences than is the norm for bench trials in sex crime cases.[129]

Enhancing Criminal Punishment for Sex Crimes
The 2017 amendments to the Criminal Code also significantly amplified punishment for sex crimes.

First, in connection with forcible obscene conduct, the article 176 definition of the victim as a "man or woman" was replaced with a "person."[130] There was no change as to the other elements of the crime. The change in wording may not seem especially momentous, but it nonetheless applies criminal punishment for forcible obscene conduct to anyone.

Second, the rape provision in article 177 was redefined:

> a person who had sexual intercourse, anal intercourse or oral intercourse (hereinafter cited as "sexual intercourse et al.") through assault or intimidation against another person of not less than thirteen years of age shall be punished for a crime of sexual intercourse et al. with definite term of imprisonment with labour for not less than five years. The same shall be applied to a person who had sexual intercourse et al. with another person under thirteen years of age.[131]

This amendment widened the definition of victims to "anyone," rather than female persons only, and it expanded the list of banned acts, adding oral and anal intercourse to vaginal penetration by a penis. Further, punishment was increased to a minimum five-year sentence, up from three years, raising the minimum sentence to at least the same level as for robbery. This made it extremely difficult to obtain a suspended sentence because only terms of not more than three years in jail are eligible for this. Thus, convicted defendants will be more likely to go to prison.

As a result of these changes, although the crime of a quasi-forcible obscene act remained unchanged,[132] the quasi-rape provision was revised to become the quasi-sexual intercourse et al. provision.[133] The special provision for gang rape was thereby abolished, and anyone who commits forcible sexual intercourse et al., regardless of the number of perpetrators, is now subject to a minimum term of five years in jail.

Third, a new crime – an "obscene act or sexual intercourse et al. by guardians" – was added to the code. According to article 179, "a person who commits an obscene act against another person under eighteen years of age by taking advantage of his or her influence as a guardian to that person" shall be punished just as under article 176.[134] And "a person who had sexual intercourse et al. against another person under eighteen years of age, taking advantage of his or her influence as a guardian of that person," shall be punished just as under article 177.[135] In other words, there was no requirement that assault or intimidation be involved.

Failed attempts at committing all these crimes were also criminalized, just as before.[136]

Fourth, the criminal complaint requirement was removed. Prosecutors could lay charges without a complaint from the victim.

Fifth, the enhanced punishment of imprisonment with labour for an indefinite term or a term of not less than six months and not more than ten years is now imposed for a forcible obscene act (article 76), quasi-forcible obscene act (article 178(1)), or an obscene act by guardians (article 179(1)); and imprisonment for an indefinite term or a term of not less than three years is imposed for any attempt of such crimes that "thereby caused the death or injury to that person" (article 181(1)). [137] Imprisonment with labour for a definite term of not less than five years is now imposed for forcible sexual intercourse et al. (article 177), quasi-forcible sexual intercourse et al. (article 178(2)), or sexual intercourse et al. by guardians (article 179(2)), and imprisonment for an indefinite term or a term of not less than six years is imposed for any attempt of such crimes that caused death or injury to that person (article 181(2)). [138]

The amendments took effect on July 13, 2017.

The Right to Refuse Sex and the Punishment for Rape

The Government
As we saw in Chapter 1, the Constitution protects sexual autonomy, which includes the right to have sex but also not to be forced to have sex. Thus, criminal punishment of persons who force someone to have non-consensual sex is appropriate.

However, constitutional protection normally precludes government interference with rights and liberties of the citizens. In most countries, constitutional rights and freedoms protect citizens against unreasonable government actions. If the government passed a statute that forced the public to have sex without consent or if government officials forced people to have sex under the law or by government order, that would be an unconstitutional infringement of the right not to be forced to have sex. But no one has any constitutional rights against fellow citizens. The Constitution is binding solely on the government and the exercise of government powers. Therefore, a rapist is not infringing the constitutional rights of the victim. On the other hand, if criminal punishment for rape is insufficient, victims could be left unprotected. The failure of the government to provide sufficient protection could be seen as an unconstitutional violation of the right to sexual autonomy.

The Sufficiency of Protection: Procedural Protection for Victims
The changes brought about in 2017 certainly represented an improvement for the victims of sex crimes. Yet, many hurdles remain.

Female police officers, for example, are still extremely thin on the ground.[139] The government needs to increase their numbers. The extent to which all police officers actually do treat victims with greater respect and care may be questioned as well. Moreover, rape kits are available in only a limited number of hospitals, and the victim must go through the police to gain access to them (an officer, female if available, may escort the victim to the hospital for a free rape kit examination and treatment).[140] The numbers of rape crisis centres (one-stop facilities for victims) are critically limited, and the non-profit organizations that are supposed to provide help to victims are underfunded and understaffed. Overall, help and support for victims are woefully inadequate.

The Sufficiency of Protection: Enhanced Punishment
The 2017 amendments to the Criminal Code also amplified the punishment for sex crimes, a major advance. Nevertheless, shortcomings do persist, and it is questionable whether the chances of obtaining justice through the criminal process are greatly improved.

In this respect, it is important to point out that the 2017 amendments did not incorporate all the proposed measures discussed thus far.[141] Many were left behind, and whether the amendments themselves were appropriate or sufficient is debatable.

First, the amendments did not move sex crimes from the Criminal Code section on "crimes against social welfare" to the section on "crimes against individual life and liberty." This failure manifestly demonstrates the insensitivity of legislators with regard to the moral implications of sex crimes. Feminist scholars have thus criticized the revisions as unsatisfactory because they are still grounded in the underlying patriarchal ideology that a woman is a property interest of her father and/or husband and that her chastity must therefore be safeguarded.[142] Although the rape provision is now interpreted as protecting the sexual autonomy of a woman, the fact remains that it is still situated in the section on crimes against social welfare.[143]

Second, although the scope of criminalized conduct was expanded, the offence of forcible sexual intercourse et al. still requires penile penetration. As a result, lesbian sex or penetration with anything that is not a penis do not fall under this heading. The amendment reflects a special emphasis on sexual intercourse, as distinguished from other sexual conduct that might be equally violent and harmful.[144] If the offence of forcible sexual intercourse et al. is designed to protect the sexual autonomy of a victim, further expansion may be needed.[145]

Third, forcible sexual intercourse et al. still involves the use of "assault or intimidation." Courts have found that this requirement is satisfied when a victim was powerless to resist out of fear or was coerced. It is, therefore, a misunderstanding that it could prevent a finding of rape even where the victim said "no" or gave no consent. In most circumstances where consent was absent or forced, the court could find the existence of assault or intimidation and convict the accused of rape. Some criminal law experts who participated in the 2014 study group that led to the 2017 amendments thus opposed the removal of this requirement as it was already loosely construed and because in almost all rape cases, there was virtually no barrier to a finding that assault or intimidation had occurred.[146] They feared that, if it were deleted, the accused could be convicted even if the judge were not convinced that the alleged victim had not consented. Some opposed the adoption of a consent-based rule because the presence or absence of consent is much harder to prove than the existence of assault or intimidation.[147] If prosecutors were required to prove that no consent had been given, working a rape case would become onerous, discouraging prosecution and thus leaving many victims without justice.[148] But there is ambiguity surrounding the satisfaction of the assault or intimidation requirement, and any sexual intercourse et al without consent should definitely be regarded as forced sexual intercourse et al.[149] It is thus certainly arguable that Japan should follow Canada and require affirmative consent to justify sexual intercourse et al.[150]

Many also argued that the Criminal Code should be amended to make it clear that non-consensual sex with a spouse came under the offence of forced sexual intercourse et al., but this proposal was not adopted. The offence is thought to include spousal rape as a matter of interpretation,[151] so there may be no obvious need for additional clarification. However, it could be beneficial, especially as virtually no one is convicted for spousal rape in Japan.[152]

Furthermore, although punishment was amplified for guardians who commit forcible sexual intercourse et al. against a young person, no such provision captured other relationships with a young person in which power is unequal. This would apply to employers, teachers, coaches, directors, producers, and many more. Adult victims in a similar unbalanced situation were not provided for protection either.[153] Anyone who capitalizes on a position of authority to have sex with a young person or an adult should be subject to the special category of punishment without assault or intimidation.

Under the old provision, sexual intercourse with a girl under the age of thirteen was automatically classed as rape. Under the current provision, sexual intercourse et al. with a person under thirteen is automatically deemed forcible sexual intercourse et al. However, given that thirteen is still the age of consent in Japan, a thirteen-year-old can consent to sexual intercourse et al., and punishment is possible only when it is accompanied by assault or intimidation. Although international criticism urged the Japanese government to raise the age of consent, it declined to do so. As noted above, criminal punishment under the Child Welfare Act and local youth protection ordinances is possible, but the age of consent could be raised to protect children.[154]

In addition, despite the increased protection for victims during the criminal process, evidence regarding their sexual history can still be used in court. As a result, defence attorneys are free to introduce such evidence to undermine arguments that a victim was terrified due to lack of sexual experience.[155] Moreover, since the finding of assault or intimidation depends on age, ordinary behaviour, or past experience, the prosecutor must sometimes prove that the victim was a virgin or had very limited experience of sex. In these circumstances, the victim is forced to disclose her sexual experiences. As this simply discourages victims from coming forward, Japan should consider limiting the introduction of sexual history during trials.

Finally, a proposal to abolish the time limit for filing a prosecution was not adopted.[156] It is true that evidence may be lost over time, but in light of the seriousness of the crime and its traumatic impact, it is worthwhile to reconsider whether the statute of limitations should be removed, as is the case for homicide.[157]

Clearly, the shortcomings listed above demonstrate that many reforms may still need to be introduced in Japanese law.

Radical Reforms May Not Bring Significant Change
It can be questioned, however, whether revising the clauses in a statute is enough to alter societal attitudes. As mentioned, Canada radically reformed its rape provisions in 1983, a step that was praised as bringing major improvements. Nevertheless, now that almost four decades have gone by, one may ask whether these reforms have actually made much difference.[158]

For example, the number of self-reported incidents of sexual assault in Canada has not substantially changed since 1983.[159] More than 90 percent of sexual assaults are never reported,[160] and the police still dismiss a significant number of allegations as unfounded.[161] In 2014, Statistics Canada listed the most common reasons for the failure to report: the crime was minor, so reporting it was not worthwhile (71 percent); the incident was a private or personal matter and was handled informally (67 percent); and finally, no one was harmed (63 percent).[162] Furthermore, a higher proportion stated that they did not report the incident because they did not want others to learn of it and because they feared that reporting would bring shame and embarrassment to their family.[163] The reforms implemented to avoid using the word "rape" and to integrate it into sexual assault have apparently not made it easier for victims to come forward. In addition, prosecutors are very reluctant to file prosecutions.[164] During trial, a victim's sexual history cannot be introduced as evidence, but many cases nonetheless turn on the issue of her credibility.[165]

As a result, the conviction rate for sexual assault is very low.[166] Moreover, almost all cases are tilted toward the least severe category of sexual assault, and the accused, even if convicted, is likely to receive a very lenient sentence.[167] This is believed to be a reflection of prosecutors' tendency to file charges under offences where it is easier to obtain a conviction even where there may have been a more violent or aggravated sexual assault.[168] Given this, most victims will not obtain the justice they seek through the criminal process.[169]

Many feel a sense of responsibility for their assault and fear embarrassment and shame from society, family, and friends. They anticipate that their interviews with police and subsequent trial testimony will be major ordeals. They also know that their attacker has an excellent chance of walking out the courtroom door as a free man. It is therefore natural that many choose not to file reports with the police.

Some commentators wonder whether this situation is partly a result of the 1983 reforms. Victims are now called complainants, and rape is now called sexual assault, a category that can range from sexual touching to forcible sexual intercourse. The change in wording may make the crime appear less severe and less traumatic, thus contributing to the lighter sentences.[170] In other words, the reform might have trivialized rape.

Whatever the case, the Canadian situation has not greatly improved.[171] Over the years, the rate of sex crimes has remained fairly stable, even as the rate of violent crimes in general has declined.[172] Sexual double standards for men and women are still in place, victims are still blamed for their own misfortunes, and many rape myths still flourish in the Canadian justice system.[173] All of this leads to the realization that much more than a mere reform of the criminal justice system is needed to change society.

Reconsidering the Forced Sexual Intercourse Provision

The same seems to be true in Japan, where five cases after the 2017 reform revealed that victims of forced sexual intercourse were still not receiving sufficient protection.[174] In all five, the court handed down very controversial acquittals. These judgments were given at the Fukuoka District Court, Kurume Branch, on March 12 (the Kurume case);[175] the Shizuoka District Court, Hamamatsu Branch, on March 19 (Hamamatsu case);[176] the Nagoya District Court, Okazaki Branch, on March 26 (the Okazaki case);[177] and the Shizuoka District Court on March 28 (Shizuoka case).[178] Furthermore, the Fukuoka District Court acquitted the defendant on July 18, 2019 (Fukuoka case).[179] In all these cases, the courts cast doubt on whether the defendant's conduct satisfied the requirements for rape or forced sexual intercourse et al. They thus cast serious doubt on the appropriateness of the rape and forcible sexual intercourse et al. provision.

In the Kurume case, the defendant was charged with quasi-rape for having sex with the victim, who was completely intoxicated. He was acquitted because he believed that she had consented and had not realized that she was unable to give consent, although the court found that she was so drunk as to be incapable of resisting him. In the Hamamatsu case, the defendant was charged with forcible sexual intercourse et al. resulting in injury. He picked up the victim at midnight, as she left a convenience store, tried to have oral sex with her, and ejaculated on the ground beside her. The prosecutor alleged that she was very panicked and incapable of resisting. The court agreed, but it acquitted the defendant because he could have believed that her lack of refusal signified consent. It also doubted whether he intended to force her, especially since he discontinued the sexual encounter when he realized that she was refusing.

In the Okazaki case, a father was charged with quasi-forcible sexual intercourse et al. with his nineteen-year-old daughter for forcing her to have sex twice: once in his office and once in a hotel room. The court agreed that non-consensual sex had occurred. It was revealed that he had molested and assaulted her since she was in junior high school and continued to molest her for several years. The court cast doubt on the prosecutor's argument that she was incapable of giving consent because of the long-lasting sexual molestation and assault, and the defendant was acquitted. In the Shizuoka case, a father was charged with forcible sexual intercourse et al. with his daughter (who was twelve at the time). She also alleged that he had assaulted her almost three times a week for over two years, since she was in fifth grade. But the family of seven lived in a small house, and the girl always shared a bedroom with a younger sister. She claimed that she said "no" to her father many times and called for her sisters. However, the court found her testimony highly unreliable since the house was very small, the sound proofing was poor, and the room in which she and her sister slept was adjacent to her parents' room, and yet no one ever noticed the assault despite its frequency. Finally, in the Fukuoka case, the defendant had sex with his adopted fourteen-year-old daughter who had intellectual disabilities. He was charged with forced sexual intercourse et al. with a person who was under guardianship. The court questioned the reliability of her testimony and acquitted him.

The Hamamatsu and Fukuoka cases were concerned with whether sexual intercourse had in fact occurred, but the three other cases involved the undisputed fact that it had. They all presented the issue of intent and ultimately questioned whether the defendant had intended to commit forcible sexual intercourse et al. However, all were highly controversial and were condemned by most feminists. They were all considered likely to be reversed on appeal when they were appealed (all but one such case was appealed).

Indeed, in the Kurume case, the Fukuoka High Court reversed the acquittal of the District Court and convicted the defendant.[180] The court found that he knew of the victim's condition and that his belief that she gave consent was unreasonable. It sentenced him to imprisonment with labour for four years. In the Okazaki case, the Nagoya High Court also reversed the acquittal of the District Court and convicted the defendant.[181] It agreed that the victim was suffering from long-standing molestation and assault by her father and was incapable of resisting him, thus sentencing him to imprisonment with labour for ten years, as requested by the prosecutor.[182] Also in the Fukuoka case, the Fukuoka High Court held that the District Court failed to evaluate the reliability of the victim's testimony in light of her age, degree of disability, and the impact of the abuse, thus reversing the acquittal and sending the case back to the District Court.[183] Finally, in the Shizuoka case, the Tokyo High Court reversed the acquittal of the District Court. The defendant father was convicted and sentenced to imprisonment with labour for seven years.[184] The Tokyo High Court held that the testimony of the alleged victim was more convincing than that of the defendant and rejected the District Court finding by asserting that its reliability could not be denied simply because other family members had failed to notice the assault. These judgments are much more in line with the predominant understanding of the crime of rape and forced sexual intercourse et al. by other courts. The SCOJ affirmed the Fukuoka High Court's decision in the Fukuoka case, dismissed the defendant's appeal in the Okazaki case,[185] and dismissed the final appeal from the father in the Shizuoka case.[186] Apparently, the SCOJ is much more willing to convict an assailant in cases of rape and forced sexual intercourse et al. than some lower courts.

It is now incorrect to believe that unless a defendant uses some type of physical force or unless a victim is totally incapable of saying no, resisting, or escaping, there can be no conviction. However, as manifested by these lower court decisions, the assault and intimidation requirement can be construed to deny forcible sexual intercourse et al. or criminal intent. Given this, the revised provision on forcible sexual intercourse et al. is still insufficient in protecting victims.

Difficulties Ahead

I Just Didn't Do It

In response to the unsatisfactory impact of rape law reforms, a growing number of feminist groups have advocated for acceptance of the accusations of all sexual assault victims. Taking this step presents, however, a difficult challenge in light of the need to protect the rights of the accused.

It is undoubtedly necessary to change the suspicion that can greet the allegations and testimonies of rape victims. It is obviously wrong to assume that they will be little more than a tissue of lies. On the other hand, anyone can tell a falsehood, omit certain information, or refuse to disclose all the relevant facts. Blindly accepting an accusation without question could have a devastating impact on the life of a suspect, and thus determining its reliability is essential in all instances. Cases of sexual touching can vividly demonstrate this danger.

Sexual touching is a vexing social problem in the overcrowded commuter trains and buses of Japan. Many women and girls have been targeted, but catching the perpetrator can be difficult. In response, rail and bus companies, the police, and prosecutors adopted the policy of charging everyone who was accused of it. The companies immediately call the police regardless of the available evidence. Solely on the basis of victim testimony, police can arrest and detain a suspect for up to twenty-two days, subjecting him to repeated interrogation without sufficient access to a lawyer. If he confesses, a summary conviction will be made available, and he could get out of detention. If he persists in denying the charges, the police can hold him for the full twenty-two days before sending him to a prosecutor. The prosecutor would then file charges based solely on the victim's testimony. In other words, even if a suspect denies any wrongdoing, he can be arrested, detained, interrogated without the meaningful aid of a lawyer for as long as twenty-two days, and then be prosecuted. Because the conviction rate is so high, being charged is virtually synonymous with being convicted.

Since sexual touching often occurs on crowded commuter trains or buses, accurately identifying the attacker can be a challenge, and everyone is so crammed together that the contact is sometimes unintentional. Often, there are no witnesses and no physical evidence to prove that touching occurred or to link it to any particular suspect. Therefore, innocent passengers are at risk of being misidentified or accused of intentional touching when the contact was inadvertent.

The 2007 film *I Just Didn't Do It*,[187] by award-winning director Masayuki Suo, vividly depicts the perils of this situation. Riding on a packed commuter train on his way to a job interview, the young protagonist is accused of sexual touching by a junior high school student. Although he truthfully denies the charge, he is arrested and eventually goes to trial. As the film illustrates, the practice of police and prosecutors in sexual touching cases had a profound impact on the life of the accused. In this case, his name is released upon arrest and the alleged crime becomes public knowledge. During the detention period, most suspects lose their jobs, as well as the support of family and friends. As the conviction rate is so high, the chances of acquittal are extremely slim. The victim's testimony trumps all doubts and concerns, and a suspect is treated as guilty on that basis alone. Essentially, his life could be destroyed simply because someone points a finger.

Many defence attorneys felt that this went too far. Finally, in one of these sexual touching cases, the SCOJ set aside a conviction and acquitted the defendant.[188] In this case, a university professor was accused of touching a young girl on a commuter train and was prosecuted for a forcible obscene act. Although he repeatedly denied the charges, he was convicted by the Tokyo District Court and sentenced to one year and ten months imprisonment with labour without suspension. The Tokyo High Court sustained the judgment. However, in an extremely rare move, the SCOJ reversed the conviction, and he was acquitted. It pointed out that there was no objective physical evidence to corroborate the victim's testimony. She had accused the professor of inserting his fingers into her underwear, but there was no trace of fibres on his fingers. Further, the SCOJ doubted the credibility of her testimony. She said that she had stepped out of the train but had returned to him, where the touching allegedly continued, and there was nothing to show that she had tried to avoid him, even though their encounter ostensibly lasted for quite some time. Once the train reached its destination, her behaviour changed: she grabbed his tie, raised her voice, and handed him over to station officials. The court deemed this conduct to be unnatural. It called for more careful factfinding, especially when the only available evidence is victim testimony.

Indeed, the SCOJ acquitted the defendant in a rape case after both lower courts convicted him.[189] In this case, a woman claimed that he had threatened to kill her if she did not follow him down a street. According to her, he led her to a nearby building where he raped her. His semen was left on her coat. Later, he promised to pay another woman for a "hand job" but left without giving her the money and was subsequently questioned by a police officer. His semen was then identified as a match to that on the coat of the alleged rape victim. As a result, he was prosecuted and convicted by both lower courts. Although the SCOJ had dismissed the defendant's initial legal appeal, it nevertheless reviewed the facts of the case ex officio and concluded that the courts had made grave errors in factfinding. Ultimately, it acquitted the defendent. There was no hard evidence that assault, intimidation, or sexual intercourse had occurred. The only evidence was the victim's allegations. The SCOJ held that in such a case, credibility must be carefully assessed. The lower courts had found her allegations sufficiently credible, but the SCOJ was not convinced. First, with respect to assault or intimidation, she claimed that he grabbed her arms and threatened to kill her if she did not come with him. But this took place in a public street full of pedestrians, the police station was located nearby, and potential sources of help were available. Nevertheless, once he released her, she simply followed him and did not ask for aid. Moreover, immediately prior to the alleged rape, a uniformed security guard walked by. The guard did not notice anything suspicious, and again she did not ask for assistance. The SCOJ therefore questioned the existence of intimidation. As for whether sexual intercourse occurred, the SCOJ raised questions about her allegation that she was raped while standing despite a considerable height difference and pointed out that no semen was found in her vagina, no injury was found, that the torn stocking she claimed to have thrown away at a nearby convenience store was not located, and that there was no evidence to corroborate her claim that she bought new stockings at that store. Furthermore, the defendant had a habit of soliciting passing women for hand jobs for payment, and he retained many smartphone videos of those encounters. Apparently, no other women had lodged similar complaints of being raped by him. As a result, the SCOJ questioned whether forcible sexual intercourse actually had taken place. It concluded that the factfinding of the lower courts was utterly unreasonable and that a reasonable doubt remained as to whether the defendant had committed the offence. Finding that there was no sufficient proof for his alleged crime, the SCOJ reversed the conviction and, once again in a very rare move, acquitted him.

It is true that the decisions of the SCOJ provoked scathing criticisms by some feminist scholars for the failure to believe the victims and for ignoring the difficulty of running away.[190] It is undeniable that in certain circumstances victims cannot say no, try to get away, or ask for help. Judges are aware of this and should take care to examine the specific circumstances. But at the same time, it is incorrect to assume that women can never say no, attempt to escape, or ask for aid. Such an assumption comes close to denying their capacity to control their own sexual freedom.

Moreover, at least one woman conspired with her boyfriend and attempted to extort money from a man by falsely accusing him of sexual touching. She testified that he had touched her on the train, and her boyfriend corroborated her story to the police. They noticed inconsistencies between the two accounts, and eventually she confessed that the accusation was fabricated. Her boyfriend, the orchestrator of the plan, was later convicted for false accusations and was sentenced to imprisonment with labour for five-and-a-half years.[191] This case provides a good reminder that not all victim testimonies are credible and that corroborating evidence or consistency with established facts is necessary.

In another case, a man who was convicted of rape and forcible obscene acts involving a teenage girl was sentenced to imprisonment for twelve years but was released after serving six when she admitted that she had lied. After she revealed this, the prosecutor took a second look at the case and found that a doctor's note had recorded no traces of sexual assault, but the police had made no effort to acquire it, and thus it was never introduced as evidence and never examined by the court. The prosecutor ultimately pursued a retrial, and the accused was acquitted.[192] He sought damages against the government for negligence on the part of police, prosecutor, and judge (the police had not carefully investigated the evidence, the original prosecutor denied the existence of any medical records although the mother testified that she had taken the girl to a doctor, and the judge denied an application for further inquiries, including a call to obtain the mother's testimony).[193]

It is true that such miscarriages of justice are incredibly rare, especially in comparison with the many instances in which victims of rape and sex crimes do not obtain justice via the criminal process. It is therefore important to improve the system for victims. But this does not justify ignoring the procedural protection that is to be accorded to suspects and defendants or the presumption that a person is innocent until proven guilty.[194]

Moreover, everyone has sexual freedom, and no one should be punished for engaging in consensual sex. To impose criminal punishment, a prosecutor must prove that there was no consent. The court needs to ensure that the claim of the alleged victim is reasonable.[195]

The Possible Presumption of Guilt

Although many people have criticized the Japanese sex crimes provision as outdated, it is not clear whether this was in fact the case. It is true that the rape provision, after being introduced in 1907, was not substantially changed until 2017, but that does not necessarily make it outdated. France and Germany also require an element of force to secure a rape conviction.[196] In the United States, many states such as Virginia still require some type of force as a requirement for rape.[197] Like Japan, these jurisdictions focus on coercion rather than the non-existence of consent.

Moreover, it is not clear whether requiring a prosecutor to prove either coercion or the lack of consent would be the best approach for victims. Establishing lack of consent would typically be challenging for prosecutors, since there would normally be no witnesses or corroborating evidence. Which of the two options would work best for prosecutors or be better for victims cannot easily be determined.[198]

One could argue that the requirement to provide corroboration should be scrapped, as in Canada, where a defendant can ostensibly be convicted solely on the basis of victim testimony. But, in reality, the Canadian police, prosecutors, and courts are very reluctant to convict a defendant without any corroborating evidence. Moreover, if the outcome of the trial hinges solely on the victim's testimony, her credibility naturally becomes the focal point. In other words, she herself is essentially put on trial. If her testimony is found to be unreliable or implausible, the defendant will typically be acquitted.[199] It is not clear whether it is best to focus on her allegations rather than his conduct.

Japanese society is commonly depicted as highly sexualized, given that pornography is widely available and a plethora of adult entertainment facilities sell some form of sexual service.[200] Some pornography depicts rape or other sexual contact in which women enjoy being forced.[201] Many girls and women have experienced sexual touching and groping on public transportation,[202] and many have been harassed and targeted by sexually inappropriate conduct at work.[203] Moreover, Japanese girls are taught to be modest and submissive from an early age.[204] They are not socialized to talk about sex, let alone give explicit consent to it, and are raised to value perseverance and sacrifice as virtues. Because assertiveness is not part of their socialization, they can have difficulty in saying no to sex or in seeking justice even when they are raped. The very small number of reported cases may be a good indication of the difficulty of coming forward in Japan.[205]

Furthermore, as Catherine Burns reminds us in *Sexual Violence and the Law in Japan*, general assumptions about what is normal reveal the dominant understandings of gender and sexual relationships, providing a normative image of what is not permissible.[206] In that sense, law is not merely a passive reflector of dominant social values and conventions, but also a producer of a particular kind of knowledge and a particular image of gendered sexual relationships. Japanese society is premised on the assumption that the male is an active subject who has desires and the female is a passive object of those desires. This presumption implies a tolerance of sexual violence. Therefore, forcible sex without consent from the woman may itself not necessarily be viewed as impermissible.

But, because Japanese society is so highly sexualized, should we simply presume that anyone who is accused of a sex crime must be guilty? Should any accusation be accepted as true? Given that this would constitute a total denial of due process for the defendant, taking such a stance would probably be too extreme.

The Future of the Rape and Sexual Assault Law
In such a male-dominated society, what should the government do to secure the right not to be forced to have sex?

Because the Constitution protects freedom of thought and expression, we cannot punish people for either holding or expressing opinions that many find offensive or distasteful. But to change permissible conduct, it might be better to redefine sexual intercourse without consent as rape or forcible sexual intercourse et al. It may be best for the law to presume that if assault or intimidation occurred, consent was not given, thus shifting the burden of proof to the accused to demonstrate that it was. Under this framework, failing to take reasonable steps to obtain consent could qualify as proof of the intent to commit rape or forcible sexual intercourse.

However, as the Constitution also protects the right to have sex, no one should be punished for having consensual sex. The difficult issue here is whether the government can force anyone to prove that sex was consensual rather than allowing a victim to prove that it was not. The former option may be best for victims. It may not be sufficient that a defendant simply believed there was consent. He would need to provide evidence that it existed. However, such a system imposes punishment for defendants who cannot prove that consent was given, even when it was. This might be somewhat questionable. But at least, if a prosecutor can prove that consent was not given or that assault or intimidation were used, this should be enough to impose criminal punishment without leaving room for a defendant to claim a belief in consent.

The Japanese government should revisit these issues and reconsider the operation of the sexual assault criminal justice system.[207] The necessity of retaining the assault or intimidation requirement should be seriously assessed, and the feasibility and desirability of switching to an affirmative consent requirement should be scrutinized. The assault and intimidation requirement is sometimes interpreted to mean that a victim was physically restrained and thus could not resist or escape, but this is out of step with the reality of most sexual assaults. The legislature should allow prosecutors to prove that victims did not consent. If they can prove it, that would be sufficient. However, proving lack of consent is often difficult since defendants normally claim that consent was given. Prosecutors should also be allowed to prove that the defendant used force or intimidation. If this is achieved, that should be regarded as an irreversible presumption that there was no consent. Assault and intimidation do not necessarily involve the use of physical force. If a victim is too frightened to refuse sex, fight back, or run away, that should be enough to constitute the use of assault and intimidation. Prosecutors could thus obtain a conviction if they could prove that consent did not exist or that the assailant used force or intimidation. Although this change alone would be unlikely to alter societal attitudes immediately, it could represent a steppingstone toward broader societal change.

Defendants often claim that they believed consent was given. Even now, courts can review this belief and convict a defendant if they find it unreasonable. Forced sexual intercourse et al. requires criminal intent, and it may be questioned whether the government could impose punishment in situations where a defendant erroneously believed that consent existed. But the defence cannot rely on the fact that the alleged victim didn't say no, resist, or attempt to escape to prove the existence of consent. There is no room for implied consent. It must be explicitly expressed.

If a victim were deeply intoxicated, unconscious, or otherwise incapable of consenting, that should be sufficient to convict an attacker. The term "quasi-forcible sexual intercourse et al." is confusing since it essentially equates with forcible sexual intercourse et al. without consent. Moreover, the victim doesn't have to be blind drunk or completely incapacitated. If she were unable to understand what was happening and to appreciate the implications of having sex, that should be sufficient to justify a conviction. The Diet should revise the language to clarify the much lower threshold to satisfy elements of the crime of sexual intercourse et al. without consent.

The legislature needs to clearly spell out all of these terms in the forcible sexual intercourse et al. provision. Otherwise, the government will fail to protect the right not to be forced to have sex.

Childbirth: The Right to Have a Child

4

Sex can lead to pregnancy and, ultimately, to childbirth. For many centuries, humans could reproduce in no other way. Having children is seen as an individual freedom, and governments have typically not attempted to restrict it, though some have castrated sex offenders, sterilized persons with mental disabilities, or limited the number of children a couple can have. None of this occurs in present-day Japan, but in the past individuals with serious mental illnesses or an intellectual handicap could be sterilized. However, the present family system could have an impact on the right to have a child. This raises the important question of whether the right to become a parent should be accepted as a constitutional right and whether restrictions can be justified.

Moreover, infertility has significantly increased in Japan,[1] and many couples are struggling with this problem. Due to recent technological developments, it is now possible for women to become pregnant via the use of assisted reproductive technology (ART) or medically assisted reproduction (MAR) (or ART/MAR).[2] For a couple who cannot have a child through sex, it is imperative to access these technologies. However, though there are few legal restrictions, they must surmount two significant obstacles. First, access may be limited by government regulation and other barriers, and the technology may not be easily available for many couples. Second, the law of parentage has not caught up with developments in technology. It does not provide sufficient incentives to encourage people to use ART/MAR.

These issues raise the very important question of whether individuals have a right of access to ART/MAR and what kind of limitations could be justified. They also raise the question as to whether the constitutional right to have a child or to become a parent should include the right to be treated as a parent-in-law and how the law of parentage needs to be created or revised.

The Right to Have a Child

The Right to Have a Child and the Constitution
As discussed above, articles 13 and 24 of the Constitution of Japan should be interpreted as protecting sexual autonomy, which should include the right to become a parent. Having children is a deeply personal decision, and many people see it as an opportunity to raise the next generation, which will inherit and sustain their culture and history. Therefore, every individual should have a constitutional right to become a parent by having sex with a consenting partner.[3] Of course, no one has the right to force a partner to have sex or to have a child. Becoming a parent needs to be strictly consensual.[4] Moreover, the right to become a parent could be viewed as part of the right to create a family.[5] Indeed, various international human rights conventions now protect the right to have a family,[6] which can include the right to become a parent.

If becoming a parent is accepted as a constitutional right, any legislation or government measures to restrict it must be constitutionally examined and justified. Since this right is so personal and so important in a liberal democracy, any limitation needs to be justified under strict scrutiny. In other words, it must be justified as a narrowly tailored means to accomplish compelling government interests.

The Castration of Sex Offenders
Some jurisdictions have legalized compulsory castration for certain serious offenders. For instance, before it was struck down in 1942, the Oklahoma Habitual Criminal Sterilization Act defined a "habitual criminal" as a person who, having already been convicted two or more

times in any American state for crimes "amounting to felonies involving moral turpitude," was later convicted of such a felony in Oklahoma and sentenced to incarceration in that state. Under the act, the attorney general could file a state court proceeding for a judgment that the person would be rendered sterile. If the court or jury found that the individual was a habitual criminal who "may be rendered sexually sterile without detriment to his or her general health," sterilization could proceed: a male offender was given a vasectomy and a female offender was given a salpingectomy. In 1942, the Supreme Court of the United States (SCOTUS) struck down this statute in *Skinner v Oklahoma* as a violation of the equal protection clause of the Fourteenth Amendment.

As the SCOTUS stated, "this case touches a sensitive and important area of human rights. Oklahoma deprives certain individuals of a right which is basic to the perpetuation of a race – the right to have offspring." The SCOTUS pointed out that under this statute some criminals who were charged with crimes of the same nature and were punishable in the same manner could be castrated, whereas others could not. It thus questioned whether there was any persuasive explanation for this difference. The SCOTUS emphasized,

> We are dealing here with legislation which involves one of the basic civil rights of man. Marriage and procreation are fundamental to the very existence and survival of the race. The power to sterilize, if exercised, may have subtle, far-reaching and devastating effects. In evil or reckless hands it can cause races or types which are inimical to the dominant group to wither and disappear. There is no redemption for the individual whom the law touches. Any experiment which the State conducts is to his irreparable injury. He is forever deprived of a basic liberty.

It continued:

> When the law lays an unequal hand on those who have committed intrinsically the same quality of offense and sterilizes one and not the other, it has made as an invidious a discrimination as if it had selected a particular race or nationality for oppressive treatment ... We

have not the slightest basis for inferring that that line has any significance in eugenics nor that the inheritability of criminal traits follows the neat legal distinctions which the law has marked between those two offenses ... The equal protection clause would indeed be a formula of empty words if such conspicuously artificial lines could be drawn.[7]

As a result, the statute was struck down as unconstitutional. This holding is quite understandable as the line between the persons who could be castrated and those who could not was ambiguous and lacking adequate explanation. This suggests that the statute targeted poor, violent criminals rather than their white-collar counterparts and that it selected for Black people or persons of colour.

Certain American states have mandatory surgical or chemical castration of sex offenders.[8] In both California and Florida, statutes provide for mandatory injections of Depo Provera for repeat sex offenders, as well as discretionary injections for first-time offenders. Depo Provera is an FDA-approved birth control drug. Often called "chemical castration," it is meant to quell the sex drive by lowering testosterone levels. Men who take it lose their sex drive but do not become physically sterile. For instance, section 645 of the California Penal Code provides that

(a) Any person guilty of a first conviction of any offense specified in subdivision (c), where the victim has not attained 13 years of age, *may*, upon parole, undergo medroxyprogesterone acetate treatment or its chemical equivalent, in addition to any other punishment prescribed for that offense or any other provision of law, at the discretion of the court.

(b) Any person guilty of a second conviction of any offense specified in subdivision (c), where the victim has not attained 13 years of age, *shall*, upon parole, undergo medroxyprogesterone acetate treatment or its chemical equivalent, in addition to any other punishment prescribed for that offense or any other provision of law ...

(d) The parolee shall begin medroxyprogesterone acetate treatment one week prior to his or her release from confinement in the state prison or other institution and shall continue treatments until the

Department of Corrections demonstrates to the Board of Prison Terms that this treatment is no longer necessary.
(e) If a person voluntarily undergoes a permanent, surgical alternative to hormonal chemical treatments for sex offenders, he or she shall not be subject to this section.[9]

Section 794.0235 of Florida Statutes on Crimes also provides for discretionary as well as compulsory administration of medroxyprogesterone acetate to persons convicted of sexual battery.[10] Therefore, in both states, the court has the discretion or obligation to order chemical castration, and a defendant apparently cannot refuse it. As recently as 2019, Alabama also introduced mandatory chemical castration for certain sex offenders, becoming the seventh state to allow or require it.[11]

In several jurisdictions, sex offenders may be offered chemical castration as an alternative to further incarceration. In some American states, agreement to it may be a formal condition of parole or release, whereas in others, refusal to cooperate may increase the likelihood of further jail time though no formal link is made between the two.[12] In these states, offenders technically have the freedom to choose. In Texas, only voluntary surgical castration is allowed, not chemical castration.[13]

Other countries, such as Poland, have a mandatory castration system for sex offenders.[14] Some countries, such as the Czech Republic, allow castration as a means to reduce jail time or as a condition for probation.[15] Germany permits chemical castration for sex offenders upon consent for reducing their jail sentence.[16] The South Korean government accepts chemical castration for certain sex offenders.[17]

It is highly questionable whether such mandatory measures, especially involving surgical castration, can be justified.[18] The government could potentially claim that they will eliminate recidivism and protect public safety. It is true that sex crimes have a very high recidivism rate, and no one doubts that some individuals are addicted to sex and are thus likely to reoffend. However, whether someone will do so can never be predicted with absolute certainty. Moreover, since sex is such an integral part of being human, it is doubtful that compulsory castration of any type can ever be justified. Its damage or harm to an offender is likely to be excessive. There is also a gender equality issue: under such a statute, men are far more likely than women to be castrated.[19]

If it is offered as a choice, there might be some support for it.[20] However, in situations where agreeing to it could reduce the period of incarceration or qualify an offender for parole, it is doubtful that consent is truly voluntary. Informed consent must be provided without any pressure.[21]

Some commentators attempt to defend this system by arguing that castration will increase the future autonomy of offenders.[22] But even if this claim were accurate, the measure is unlikely to be justified if it is not accompanied by true voluntary consent. If an individual possesses a constitutional right to have sex, any restriction on this right must be justified by real consent or by a compelling government interest. Promoting the autonomy of offenders would not count as a legitimate government interest, let alone a compelling one.[23]

The Sterilization of Persons with Disabilities

Japan does not practise mandatory castration of sex offenders, but in the past it did allow the compulsory sterilization of mentally ill patients and intellectually handicapped persons. The Eugenic Protection Act, passed in 1948, was intended to "prevent the birth of inferior off-springs from the perspective of eugenics."[24] It permitted the use of a "surgical operation to sterilize by removing the reproductive glands."[25] If a patient and his or her spouse (including a common law spouse) consented, a physician could proceed with the surgery. If the spouse were unknown or unavailable, consent from the patient alone was sufficient. Sterilization was permitted when

1. the patient or spouse has hereditary mental illness, hereditary mental retardedness, hereditary mental abnormality, hereditary sick character, hereditary physical disease, or hereditary deformity and is capable of transmitting these to offspring,
2. family relatives of the patient or spouse within the four family-degree have hereditary mental illness, hereditary mental retardedness, hereditary mental abnormality, hereditary sick character, hereditary physical disease, or hereditary deformity and are capable of transmitting these to offspring,

3. the patient or spouse is suffering from leprosy and is capable of transmitting it to offspring,
4. pregnancy or childbirth is capable of endangering the life of the mother's body, or
5. has more than several children and additional childbirth could lower her health.[26]

However, sterilization was not always voluntary. If a physician felt that it was necessary to prevent the transmission of any of the conditions listed above, he or she could apply to the local eugenic protection commission to allow sterilization without getting consent from the patient.[27] If the commission approved the application, it notified the patient and the physician who was designated to operate.[28] If there were no objection or when the order was finalized, the physician performed the surgery,[29] and the government paid all the costs.[30]

As a result, the mentally ill and the intellectually disabled could be sterilized without their consent. Compulsory sterilization continued until the Eugenic Protection Act was replaced with the current Mother's Body Protection Act in 1996. It was reported that 24,911 people were sterilized under this provision before 1996.[31]

The provision was carried over from the National Eugenics Act of 1940, which was modelled after the infamous Nazi Law for the Prevention of Hereditarily Diseased Offspring, enacted in 1933 and taking effect in 1934.[32] With the intent of purifying the German gene pool and thus securing the master race, it allowed the compulsory sterilization of listed patients who were seen as genetically inferior. Included were individuals with a congenital mental deficiency, schizophrenia, epilepsy, hereditary deafness and blindness, "any severe hereditary deformity," and alcoholism. People who were seen as outsiders – criminals, prostitutes, misanthropists, or even those who didn't conform to social norms and were therefore considered "problematic" – were sterilized.[33] Nazi Germany was not the first or the only jurisdiction to introduce compulsory sterilization of persons with disabilities. Indeed, many American states have done the same.[34]

Twenty years after the Eugenic Protection Act was abolished in Japan, persons who had been involuntarily sterilized under its provisions finally filed a suit demanding damage awards from the government. In response, the Sendai District Court held that compulsory sterilization was unconstitutional.[35] Finding that the right to have a child was protected by the Constitution, it held that such compulsory sterilization was highly unreasonable. Nevertheless, it dismissed the damage claim, holding that the statute of limitations had already expired (in tort law, the statute of limitations is typically three years from the time when the victim learns of the damage and perpetrators and, more generally, it also runs out after twenty years from the time of damage). The court also concluded that the government was not negligent in failing to repeal the law much sooner. In 2019, the government passed a statute granting compensation to everyone who was compulsorily sterilized under the Eugenic Protection Act.[36]

Intended to prevent the reproduction of persons with inferior genes, the Eugenic Protection Act is completely unjustifiable. It is impossible to prove whether anyone possesses either superior or inferior genes. Apologists attempted to justify the statute by claiming that it could prevent the transmission of hereditary diseases or the birth of disabled children. Yet, everyone has a right to be born, and everyone should have a right to give birth, even if a hereditary disease or disability could quite possibly be transmitted. No government should be allowed to stop the birth of a person who has a disease or a disability. Further, these types of laws contribute to stigmatizing disabled persons; obviously, the law would work to inflict social stigma on them.

Some might argue that sterilization is justifiable when it is a paternalist measure to protect vulnerable persons who could be sexually exploited and forced to have children. Some individuals may not be capable of understanding the meaning of sex or of refusing it. Thus, they may easily be tricked into sexual intercourse and could become pregnant. When they give birth to children, however, they may not be capable of providing child care. As a result, they may need some form of paternalistic restriction for their own welfare, which is why they defend the practice of sterilization. But compulsory sterilization is far too excessive. Surgical sterilization permanently divests individuals of their right to reproduce. It is hard to justify such a deprivation by claiming that it is for their own good. Moreover, even though the government may be obliged to care for any disabled child that such a person may produce, this is neither a legitimate nor a compelling justification for compulsory sterilization.

Limitations on the Number of Children

Some countries have limited the number of children a couple can have. For instance, the Chinese government imposed a one-child policy for many years.[37] Although the policy may have contributed to economic growth,[38] and may have improved the status of women,[39] it took a heavy toll on women, children, and society in other ways.

To implement the policy, many women were forced to have abortions or to be sterilized.[40] A couple who violated it could be subject to a hefty fine, and officially registering the birth of a second child entailed serious risks for them. As a result, countless numbers of children were not registered. Sometimes called "ghost children," they had no official registration and were thus not eligible for government services.[41] Moreover, because many families preferred to have boys, female fetuses were often aborted, with the result that male babies greatly outnumbered female ones.[42] This created large problems for the government when it realized that the policy had backfired. Perceiving the necessity of increasing the number of birth, it found a significant shortage of women who could reproduce. The fertility rate is far below the replacement level.[43] The one-child policy is now widely seen as a catastrophe for China.

The policy was dropped in 2016, after which the government encouraged couples to have an additional child, thus pursuing a two-child policy.[44] In 2021, it increased the count to three.[45] However, recovering from the deep drop in the fertility rate and increasing the number of children, especially girls, has been very difficult and may prove impossible.[46]

From a constitutional perspective, limiting the number of children someone can have is an infringement of the right to become a parent. Whereas imposing criminal punishment for having additional children is more dire than imposing a fine, the right is nonetheless infringed.

The purpose of the one-child policy was to secure sufficient food and well-being for everyone and to promote economic development. However, such policies raise the most important question addressed in this book, which is whether sexual autonomy could ever be restricted in service of government population policies. As revealed in the final chapter, the answer is definitely no. In obtaining its goals, the government could try exchanging the stick for the carrot. For example, it could encourage couples to limit the number of children, for example, by limiting the subsidies it allocates to those who have too many children. It could also facilitate and promote family planning by allowing the wide dissemination of contraceptives and abortion pills or by providing greater access to abortion clinics. But it should not be allowed to use either criminal or economic sanctions to achieve its ends.

Difficulties in Getting Pregnant and Giving Birth

In Japan, the family law system could have a significant practical impact on the right to have a child. As mentioned, the assignment of sex at the time of birth and the extreme reluctance to depart from this norm prevents many transgender people from changing sex or gender, precluding legal marriage for them. As a result, they are discouraged from bearing children. Because bigamy is illegal, some persons cannot remarry, despite the fact that the previous marriage relationship is totally broken down, thus thwarting childbirth as well. The requirement that everyone in a family must share the same surname also forces some couples away from marriage, again discouraging childbirth. Since same-sex marriage is not legal in Japan, homosexual couples are unable to marry, and they too are discouraged from becoming parents.

This is partly the result of a long-standing and strong social prejudice and discrimination against children who are born out of wedlock.[47] In the past, family law permitted legal discrimination against illegitimate children by limiting their inheritance to half of what legitimate children received.[48] Although this was eventually struck down by the SCOJ,[49] the family registration system still distinguishes between legitimate and illegitimate children, and people retain a very strong prejudice against the latter. As a result, many women have little desire to become unwed mothers.

Even if there is no explicit legal restriction on the right to have a child, these systems impose serious practical difficulties for many couples in their attempts to reproduce. If we accept sexual autonomy as a constitutional mandate, these barriers need to be assessed. Sexual autonomy should include the right to determine one's sexual or gender identity, the shared surname requirement should be abandoned, and getting a divorce should be much easier, even if one partner disagrees. Same-sex marriage needs to be accepted. These changes would help many couples to reproduce. Moreover, the government needs to increase the protection of illegitimate children by prohibiting discrimination against them.

Access to ART/MAR

The Development of ART/MAR

The advent of ART/MAR has raised some very important issues with respect to the right to become a parent. Infertility is a significant problem in Japan. It is reported that 10 percent of couples that want to have a baby are infertile.[50] Approximately 470,000 patients were receiving treatment for infertility in 2002.[51] In response, ART/MAR has rapidly developed. One common treatment option is artificial insemination, where sperm is placed directly into a woman's uterus to increase the chance of conception. Artificial insemination allows her egg to be inseminated not only by her spouse's sperm (AIH, artificial insemination using the husband's semen), but also by a donor's sperm (AID, artificial insemination using donor semen). A second option is in vitro fertilization (IVF), where the egg is extracted and fertilized by sperm in a laboratory, creating an embryo which is then placed in the woman's uterus. IVF can unite a wife's egg with her husband's sperm, but it can also use a donor egg. It is also possible to create an embryo using a donor egg and sperm, and then to transfer it to the intended mother's uterus. Directly injecting sperm into an egg (intra-cytoplasmic sperm injection, ICSI) or extracting it from the husband's testicles (testicular sperm extraction, TESE) allows a woman to become pregnant from a partner who may be impotent. Freezing technology also enables the preservation of sperm, eggs, and embryos, which permits IVF to occur long after the extraction or fertilization. New screening technologies have also rapidly improved the success rate of ART/MAR by determining any genetic predispositions in the embryo or fetus that might interfere with typical development before birth.

Finally, the practice of surrogacy – where a woman conceives and carries a child expressly for the purpose of surrendering it to an individual or couple – has also become a common option. Surrogacy involves the use of an egg from the surrogate mother and sperm from the intended father, or the egg and sperm of both intended parents, or the egg of the intended mother and sperm from a donor, or even egg and sperm from donors. If the intended parents supply both egg and sperm, they will have a complete biological relationship with the baby. If the surrogate uses her own egg and the intended father's sperm or the intended mother's egg and donor sperm, the couple will have a partial biological relationship with the baby. If they provide neither sperm nor egg, they will have no biological relationship with the baby. Unless the surrogate mother uses her own egg to create the embryo, she too will have no biological relationship with the baby.

Problems in Accessing ART/MAR

Although Japan prohibits human cloning,[52] it has no laws to control the use of ART/MAR (even after the enactment of the The Medically Assisted Reproduction Act in 2020, discussed below, which does not contain legal restrictions on ART/MAR).[53] The situation is somewhat similar in the United States,[54] but it differs sharply from that in Europe, where countries generally have more restrictions on the use of ART/MAR.[55] On the whole, the decision on whether and how to use ART/MAR is left to patients and their physicians in Japan. However, the rules established by the leading self-regulating medical association have created significant barriers to access.

The Japan Society of Obstetrics and Gynecology (JSOG),[56] a public non-profit organization, is the most prestigious academic association of obstetricians and gynecologists in Japan. Membership in the JSOG is voluntary, but being affiliated with it is very important for practitioners. With the development of ART/MAR, the JSOG established a Code of Ethics for its members and regulates the use of ART/MAR through various guidelines. Although the guidelines are not legally binding, they do critically influence the use of ART/MAR throughout Japan.

For instance, the JSOG Code of Ethics allows both the AIH and AID forms of artificial insemination but limits their use to circumstances where no alternatives are available or where the mother or the child will be gravely endangered if another method were used.[57] Initially, the Code of Ethics also restricted AIH or AID to legally married couples, who were obliged to supply an official copy of the family register as proof of marriage. Although the JSOG has offered AIH to common law couples in recent years, it still limits AID to married couples.[58] This presents a significant barrier to couples who are not legally married. The same is true for single women. Although the JSOG requirements have been somewhat relaxed, they could impede access to artificial insemination.

Furthermore, the JSOG Code of Ethics permits the use of IVF only if conception by any other method is virtually impossible and IVF would be beneficial for the pregnancy. The code also prohibits the use of donor sperm and donor eggs for IVF: it is reserved for legally married couples, using his sperm and her eggs.[59] Finally, the JSOG also prohibits surrogacy.[60]

In 2000, an expert committee of the Ministry of Health, Labour and Welfare (MHLW) published a report, which revealed that the ministry would be willing to permit IVF that used donor sperm, eggs, and embryos in truly exceptional cases.[61] In 2003, the same committee proposed that the government allow the use of donor gametes and embryos.[62] The Ministry of Justice (MOJ) subsequently started drafting special legislation concerning parental relationships for children who were produced by the new reproductive technologies.[63] It advised the JSOG to wait until the statute was passed before beginning to use donor gametes or embryos.[64] However, the MHLW eventually abandoned the idea of enacting legislation to allow the use of donor gametes and embryos, and the MOJ did not submit its bill on parentage to the Diet. As a result, the use of donor eggs, sperm, and embryos never became permissible, and the JSOG has simply continued not to provide IVF using donor gametes.

With the gradual call for liberalization, the JSOG no longer requires that a couple be legally married or that they provide an official copy of their marriage registration before they can use IVF.[65] But although the JSOG has abandoned this legal marriage requirement, it still limits the use of IVF to those couples in a marriage-like relationship, such as a common law relationship. In addition, IVF must use only the mother's egg and her husband's sperm, thus precluding transferring an embryo that was created by a donor egg and donor sperm.[66]

The guidelines imposed by the JSOG Code of Ethics are quite restrictive, preventing many couples from accessing various fertility treatments. In response to a call for more flexibility in the use of ART/MAR, the Japanese Society for Reproductive Medicine (JSRM) came to attract broader public attention.[67] A voluntary association, the JSRM consists of ART/MAR experts and is more flexible and responsive to the plight of infertile couples than the JSOG, sanctioning IVF with the use of donor eggs.[68] Furthermore, though the JSRM does not officially approve of surrogacy, it does not explicitly prohibit it either, thus leaving some potential room for it in the future.[69]

The members of medical associations do not always adhere to their guidelines. Because the guidelines are regulated by professionals, there are no legal sanctions when they are violated.[70] Some JSOG members, for example, have breached its Code of Ethics.[71] Practically speaking, this means that some people may access ART/MAR that is not officially accepted by the JSOG. Furthermore, the Japanese Institution for Standardizing Assisted Reproductive Technology (JISART) – an organization for ART institutions meant to assist in achieving and maintaining high standards in infertility management by implementing quality management systems – has adopted guidelines allowing IVF procedures using donor gametes,[72] subject to application approval.[73] Thus, though the JSOG does not sanction the technology, some children have been born through IVF using donor gametes (against the advice of the MHLW). However, as the JSOG is the most prestigious medical association in Japan and its affiliation is viewed as vital for all gynecologists, not many fertility doctors are willing to violate its Code of Ethics. It is unknown how many people have resorted to using IVF with donor eggs or surrogacy, or how many children have been born as a result of these not officially accepted means.

Going Abroad to Have a Baby

As a result of the stringent guidelines and the difficulties of accessing ART/MAR,[74] as well as the practical age limitation for women who can receive it,[75] an increasing number of Japanese people are travelling abroad to obtain it. Some jurisdictions, such as Nevada, have accepted foreign patients and will provide them with ART/MAR at a hospital or clinic. At present, it is unknown exactly how many people travel abroad to obtain ART/MAR, but in Japan the number is reported to be significantly increasing.[76]

After receiving ART/MAR abroad, a Japanese couple will generally return home. In the case of artificial insemination or IVF, there is nothing to indicate the method via which the woman became pregnant. If she gives birth in Japan, as we will see later, the presumption of paternity will be applicable to her husband, and the couple can register the child as their own.

When a couple uses a surrogate abroad, they often stay in her country until she gives birth and will then start legal proceedings to declare their parenthood. If the country or state recognizes surrogate motherhood, it will record the couple as the legal parents of the child. When they return to Japan, they are required to register the baby's birth. If its foreign birth certificate indicates that the wife is the mother, she will be recorded as its legal mother. If, however, questions arise as to who gave birth or when it is known that a surrogate was involved, the couple will face challenges because Japanese law views the birth mother as the legal mother. In instances of surrogacy, it will not accept paperwork from a foreign country that lists the wife as the legal mother. But if there are no suspicions about surrogacy, municipal offices tend to register the child without question. As a result, it is highly likely that at least some Japanese children were birthed by a surrogate mother, not the woman whose name appears on their registration.

The Difficulties of ART/MAR

In 2018, 454,893 women used IVF and gave birth to 56,978 babies in Japan. The total number of babies born that year was 918,400, meaning that 1 in 16 was conceived through IVF.[77] This is a significant increase, which clearly shows that access to ART/MAR has become an integral part of reproduction in Japan.

However, obtaining ART/MAR in not always a simple matter.[78] It is expensive, perhaps prohibitively so for some couples. Each IVF cycle, for example, costs anywhere between JPY 320,000 (roughly US$2,400) and JPY 380,000 (about US$2,800).[79] The success rate is less than 20 percent.[80] Many couples try IVF several times before conception is achieved, requiring a huge outlay of money. Moreover, before 2020, IVF was not covered by Japan's national health insurance. Although the government did view physical and functional infertility as a disease, it did not see infertility in general in this way. It did provide some financial subsidies to couples who use IVF, but depending on their age, these were limited to either three or no more than six times. None was sufficient to cover the costs.[81] The government had been reluctant, however, to extend national health insurance coverage to all fertility treatments and to pay all the costs. Although the government finally decided to apply the national health insurance to infertility in 2020,[82] the cost of infertility treatment is still a huge concern for many couples facing infertility.

Furthermore, a woman who uses IVF must visit the hospital or the clinic over ten times throughout the process (for testing, receiving hormone shots, egg growth, extracting eggs, and for implanting the embryo into the uterus). If she holds a paying job, she must be absent from work each time, creating additional hardships for working women. Many women feel that the government's special subsidy is not enough and demand sufficient paid leave from the workplace when using IVF. The government has not been willing to mandate employers to provide this.

Access to ART/MAR, the Constitution, and Legislation

Since every individual has a constitutional right to become a parent, this should also entail the use of technological assistance as required. In other words, the individual should be granted a constitutional right to access ART/MAR.

Even if Japan were to explicitly recognize a constitutional right to become a parent, some might argue that this should extend solely to natural birth. In that case, access to ART/MAR would not be constitutionally protected. But what is natural birth? Does hormone injection to stimulate pregnancy result in a natural birth? Does giving birth in a hospital with the help of a doctor constitute a natural birth? What about a Caesarean section? It is simply impossible to say definitively what qualifies as a natural birth, which makes it equally impossible to say that only natural births should be protected by the Constitution. It makes most sense to understand the right as granting persons the freedom to choose whatever method or technology they want to assist them in reproduction.

Viewed in this light, any restrictions on the right to access ART/MAR need to be constitutionally justified. If their purpose is to secure the safety of the fetus and to protect the life and health of the mother, they are warranted. However, they must always be narrowly tailored to secure these compelling government interests.

Moreover, the government should not allow medical professions to unreasonably restrict access to ART/MAR. In light of the absence of laws regulating ART/MAR in Japan, appropriate legislation should be enacted to secure right of access to ART/MAR and to remove all practical barriers to its access (the Medically Assisted Reproduction Act of 2020, as discussed below, does not guarantee such rights). Such a statute should declare that everyone has a constitutional right to access ART/MAR. It would also need to clarify the circumstances in which ART/MAR would be restricted. Some of the JSOG guidelines are questionable. For example, it is unclear why ART/MAR should be limited to married couples (or those in a marriage-like relationship, such as common law couples). It is also unclear why ART/MAR must be a means of last resort. So long as the procedure is safe and the parties consent, there is no reason why a couple should be made to try all other alternatives before moving on to ART/MAR.

Limitations forbidding the use of donor gametes should also be questioned. As long as the safety of everyone involved is secured and all parties consent, there may be no reason to exclude it. It is understandable that doctors may be concerned about identifying the legal father should a couple opt for ART/MAR using donated sperm, as the law of parentage is not yet settled and there are no clear legislative guidelines. Yet, there is no reason to force such couples to delay until the law of parentage is clarified by legislation. At present, it is unclear whether and when the government will take this step, and it is unreasonable to force couples to wait any longer.

The exclusion of surrogacy may also be questioned. Those who argue against its legitimization are concerned about the potential exploitation of women, who could be treated as baby-making machines. On the other hand, if a surrogate gives consent, the procedure is safe, and there are sufficient guarantees that the intended parents will receive the newborn, there may be no compelling reasons to reject surrogacy. To forestall the possibility that it might lead to the commercialization of human reproduction, the government can limit the surrogacy fee to cover the actual costs involved. But there is no need to ban surrogacy altogether.

At present, because no legislation regulates the use of ART/MAR, it is unknown whether any of these practices would be constitutionally valid. The government will first need to enact legislation clarifying the conditions and requirements for the use of ART/MAR. At that point, it will be possible to discuss whether they could be justified in light of the constitutional guarantee of the right to have a child or to become a parent.

The Medically Assisted Reproduction Act of 2020, finally enacted after the long cry for clarification for ART/MAR, lays the groundwork for the use of the ART/MAR.[83] It declares four fundamental principles:[84]

1. Medically assisted reproduction needs to be provided as infertility treatment to make sure that it is appropriate in accordance with physical as well as mental conditions of the persons provided and to protect the health of the women who will be thereby pregnant and deliver the children,
2. Medically assisted reproduction needs to be implemented by providing necessary and adequate explanation and securing the full understanding of parties involved and their consent,
3. Collection, management, and treatment of sperm or egg need to be handled by securing its safety, and
4. Necessary care needs to be provided to children born by medically assisted reproduction to make sure that they can be born and grow up physically and mentally healthy.[85]

Under the terms of the act, the government must establish and implement a comprehensive policy to secure the proper provision of MAR, based on the four principles listed above.[86] It must also pay attention to life ethics or ethics of life and seek public understanding.[87] Physicians and other medical professionals are to provide good quality and appropriate MAR based on the fundamental principles.[88] Through public announcements and education, the government must inform the public on infertility treatment, with respect to pregnancy and childbirth.[89]

Further, it should establish necessary counselling services for persons who plan to use or are using MAR and for children who are born via this technology.[90] The government is tasked with implementing the necessary legislative measures to provide appropriate MAR in accordance with the provisions of the act.[91]

The Medically Assisted Reproduction Act is the first major legislative attempt to provide for ART/MAR. But it is merely a declaration of fundamental principles, and it leaves the specifics to further consideration, which is to be completed within two years. These would include how to regulate both MAR and the supply of sperm, eggs, and embryos, as well as establishing a system for storage, management, and disclosure of information on suppliers of sperm or eggs and on children born via MAR.[92] However, in light of the long history of discussions on regulating ART/MAR, it is highly questionable whether the government can come up with a detailed draft of proper regulations. Until the specific rules and regulations on ART/MAR are introduced, the fact remains that there is still no legal regulation on ART/MAR. Furthermore, the Medically Assisted Reproduction Act makes no provision for grounding the statute in the constitutional right to reproduce and to access ART/MAR. It simply plans to regulate it as if it were merely another medical service regulation.

The Cabinet's decision to apply the national health insurance to infertility treatment in 2020, including IVF,[93] is surely good news for many couples, who would otherwise be forced to spend huge sums on treatment. However, commentators have expressed apprehension about the limitations that the government has imposed on access.[94] We must wait and see how well the plan works.

The Law of Parentage

The Basic Framework of the Law of Parentage
The second barrier to ART/MAR is the law of parentage, which is not designed to facilitate its use.[95] In Japan, family relationships are recorded in the family registration system.[96] Every Japanese citizen is required by law to be listed in a family register. These collect information on the family unit, including couples in a legal marriage and their unmarried

children.[97] The first person listed in the register – "first person listed" – is the husband or wife whose surname the couple adopted after their marriage.[98] Although spouses must share the same surname, it does not matter which one is chosen. In reality, however, it is usually the husband's name, with the result that he will be listed first in the register.[99]

When a child is born, he or she must be added to the family register as soon as the parents submit his or her birth registration application to their local municipal office.[100] If the child is born in wedlock, it is deemed "legitimate." The notification of birth must be filed by either the mother or father within fourteen days of the birth,[101] and the child is added to their register.[102] The presumption of paternity, as explained later, will play a critical role in deciding who is to be regarded as the father.

Conversely, if a baby is born out of wedlock, the mother must file the notification of birth within fourteen days,[103] and the child will be added to her register.[104] If she is listed in her parents' register, a new one will be created for her, and the child will be added to it.[105] The father's name will be left blank. If he chooses, he can filiate the child – declare that it is his.[106] If he does so, the fact of filiation is recorded on the mother's register, and his name and place of register is added. His register is similarly revised to add the fact of filiation together with the name of the mother, place of her registry, and name of the child. He is then regarded as the legal father, but the child remains on the mother's register, and the fact of illegitimacy is not changed by the fact of filiation.

Childbirth and the Law of Parentage

The Japanese law of parentage would seem to be relatively simple and straightforward. [107] But in reality, it is filled with ambiguities.

Although the Japanese Civil Code does not explicitly state who should be a child's legal mother,[108] it has ordinarily been presumed to be she who gave birth to a baby.[109] Generally, maternity is easy to establish because the child's birth certificate, issued by the physician or midwife who delivered the baby, is submitted at the same time as the birth registration application,[110] apart for some exceptional cases.[111]

On the other hand, determining the legal father can sometimes be challenging. Article 772(1) of the Civil Code stipulates that when a child is conceived by a woman during marriage, her husband is presumed to be the father.[112] Article 772(2) also states that if a child is born after two hundred days of the formation of a marriage, it is presumed to have been conceived in wedlock.[113] When a child is born within three hundred days of a divorce or the dissolution of the marriage, it is presumed to have been conceived during the marriage.[114] These legal presumptions can be overturned only in court. A child covered by any one of them is called "a child covered by the presumption."

This presumption system sometimes causes difficulties. For instance, a child born to a married woman is registered as that of her husband, regardless of whether he actually is the biological father. If a birth registration application lists a father who is not the husband, the municipal office will not accept it. If the husband knows or discovers that he is not the father, he can challenge paternity.[115] To do so, he must bring a suit against the child or the mother[116] within one year of learning of the birth.[117] However, if he admits paternity, he cannot subsequently deny it.[118] These laws are meant to settle questions regarding the paternity of the child as early as possible. Thus, if more than a year elapses between the birth and the husband's discovery that he is not the father, he has no legal recourse to challenge paternity.[119]

What kind of recourse is available to a woman whose husband is not the father of her child? For instance, if she is still legally married but has separated from her husband and now lives with a new partner, she might want him to be registered as the father. In this case, she would need to register the baby as her husband's child and then ask him to deny his paternity. Only after he does so in court can she register her child as the offspring of her new partner.

When a child is born within two hundred days of its parents' marriage, such as when they marry after the woman discovers that she is pregnant, the presumption of paternity is technically inapplicable. However, the Great Court of Judicature, the predecessor to the SCOJ, held that in such circumstances, the child should be treated as legitimate,[120] and the municipal office can accept a birth registration application, listing her husband as the father unless the mother indicates otherwise. In other words, although the legal presumption of paternity is inapplicable, a practical presumption of paternity applies when a baby is born to a married couple. The child in this situation is called a "child not covered by the presumption."

When a baby is born less than three hundred days after its parents divorce, the ex-husband is legally regarded as the father. The mother must file birth registration application listing him as the father. If he is not the biological father, she will then be faced with the same difficulties as described above: after filing the application, she must ask him to deny paternity.

What happens if a woman gives birth within three hundred days of her divorce but after two hundred days of her remarriage? The legal presumptions of paternity would be in conflict. In such a case, paternity must be decided by a court in a paternity suit.[121] To prevent such a situation from occurring, the Civil Code used to prohibit women from remarrying within six months of their divorce.[122] However, the SCOJ decided that this waiting period was too long and reduced it to a hundred days. It held that the mandatory waiting period could be justified to ensure the legal presumption of paternity in the interest of the child.[123] As a result, the Civil Code was amended to require a newly divorced woman to wait one hundred days before she remarried.[124] Since the municipal office will not accept an application to register a marriage if this requirement has not been observed, this situation is unlikely to unfold as such.

It is evident that the rules on parentage are often unclear, and in many circumstances a couple must figure out who should be the legal mother and who should be the legal father.

Adoption

In Japan, any adult can adopt a child.[125] The only limitation is that one cannot adopt one's ascendant or anyone older than oneself.[126] When adoptive parents are married, both are required to adopt the child at the same time.[127] If the child is under fifteen years old, his or her legal representatives (basically legal parents) must give consent.[128] Leave from the family court is also required.[129]

If the notification of adoption is legal, the municipal office will accept it,[130] and the name of the adoptive parents will be added to the family register of the child, with a note recording the adoption.[131] The child will also be added to the register of its new parents, including the date of adoption, the names of the natural parents, and their family registry address.[132]

The child is regarded as the legitimate offspring of the adoptive parents,[133] sharing their family name.[134] However, it maintains a relationship with its original legal parents because adoption does not change familial status between children and their natural parents.[135]

On the other hand, adoption is not popular in Japan.[136] When it does occur, it commonly involves the adoption of adults rather than children.[137] Owners of corporations adopt an adult, typically male, as their successor. One reason for the rarity of child adoption is the strong preference for a blood tie between parents and children; many people simply don't want to adopt a child who is not related to them. Another reason is the long-standing and serious prejudice against adopted children: mothers are often reluctant to surrender a newborn for adoption because they know that the child will often encounter discrimination.

Past Attempts to Adjust the Law of Parentage

Despite significant changes in social attitudes since the 1896 enactment of the Japanese Civil Code, the legislature has not revised the provisions on parentage to reflect these developments. However, it has made some attempts to adjust the parentage registration system to make it align with reality. For example, when a child is born less than three hundred days after a divorce, the MOJ has started to allow the mother to file the birth registration application without listing her ex-husband as the father if she can produce a note from her physician indicating that she conceived the baby after separation.[138] Although this change essentially modifies the statutory language on the presumption of paternity in the Civil Code, the MOJ has been reluctant to actually amend the basic provision of the legal presumptions of paternity.

The SCOJ has also altered the law of parentage so that it better reflects social reality. It has recognized that the legal presumptions of paternity present difficulties for couples in certain circumstances. For example, if, one year after the birth of a child, a husband discovers that the child is not his, he has no legal recourse under the Civil Code to deny paternity. However, after the Second World War, the SCOJ started to recognize unwritten suits to confirm the absence of parental relationships in certain circumstances. It can then confirm the absence of a parental relationship when it is patently obvious that the husband could not have fathered the child, because they were separated or estranged or because they lived far apart at the time of conception.[139] This would apply when the husband was deployed abroad for military service or when he was incarcerated. In such circumstances, the SCOJ simply rejects the presumption of paternity and allows a man who is not the husband to be registered as the father. A child in this situation is called a "child excluded from the presumption" (notice the difference between a "child not covered by the presumption" and a "child excluded from the presumption").

This is an unusual development, as the Civil Code allows a husband to deny paternity and requires him to file suit only within one year of learning of the birth of the child. The statute is clear that, after one year, paternity must be respected. However, the SCOJ essentially rewrote this provision. A suit to confirm the absence of a parental relationship can be filed by any interested party, including a husband himself, and there is no statute of limitations. Thus, even if one year has passed since a husband learned of the child's birth, any interested party can challenge the presumption of paternity.

Moreover, although the presumption is technically applied under the Civil Code, the SCOJ has also come to reject it when parties have been separated for over two and a half years and have had no sexual relationship during that time.[140] Furthermore, it also allows the family courts to accept applications for mediation prior to a child's birth to confirm the absence of a parental relationship and to allow the mother to challenge the presumption of paternity. If a husband or ex-husband is not cooperative, the family court can convert the application to an application for recognition of paternity and can allow the biological father to prove his paternity. This solution offers families more flexibility under the rigid Civil Code system. Although, in the absence of clear, objective circumstances, the SCOJ has been reluctant to overturn the presumption of paternity,[141] these changes further allow acceptance of a parental relationship in accordance with social reality.

The SCOJ has also invoked the abuse of rights doctrine, enshrined as a primary principle of the Civil Code,[142] to preclude challenges from interested parties to deny a long-established parental relationship. For example, because of prejudicial attitudes toward adopted children, some people evade the official adoption procedure by unlawfully registering children as their own offspring. Thus, a woman may register her daughter's child as her own, or an older sister may do the same for a younger one. In such cases, there is technically no legal parental relationship between the registering parent and the child.[143] The child may not know, however, whom his or her true parents are and may be unaware of the false registration. As a result, the SCOJ refused to allow a suit for confirmation of the absence of a parental relationship filed by a woman who had unlawfully registered a child,[144] as well as by other members of the family,[145] to wipe out the long-established parental relationship between the child and a parent. The SCOJ held that denying the parental relationship would seriously affect the child, who was not responsible for the false registration or the relationship built by others and that such a claim constituted an abuse of rights. As a result, although the parents were not the legal parents of the child, no one was allowed to challenge this fact in court, leaving the false registration with no possibility of correction.

Thus, the law of parentage is outdated and out of touch with reality. Due to various adjustments and the development of unwritten rules, it has become overly complicated for anyone who tries to use this area of the law.

ART/MAR and the Law of Parentage

The development of ART/MAR further aggravated the ambiguous law of parentage and the gap between law and practice. Thanks to ART/MAR, a woman can give birth to a baby who is not her biological child. The various permutations of surrogacy – with the egg and sperm of both intended parents, with the surrogate's egg and the intended father's sperm, or with a donor egg and donor sperm – make nailing down the definition of "mother" and "father" even more challenging.

These developments further complicated the decision on who should be the mother and who should be the father, as stipulated by the law of parentage. Despite calls for clarification, however, the Diet has been reluctant to enact special legislation defining legal parentage for children who are conceived through ART/MAR.[146] As a result, the burden has fallen on the courts to determine parentage under the established framework.

Who Is the Legal Mother?

What happens when a surrogate gives birth to a baby who is not her biological child? Who, then, should be regarded as the legal mother? In Japan, surrogacy is generally not accepted, but some children have nonetheless been born through it.[147] Increasing numbers of couples are travelling abroad for the purpose of seeking a surrogate.

This occurred in the case of Aki Mukai, a Japanese TV personality who had had her uterus removed due to cervical cancer. To protect her eggs from the subsequent radiation therapy, she underwent an operation to push her ovaries into her chest cavity. Thus, though she could not bear children in the usual way, she retained viable eggs. She and her husband then drafted a surrogacy contract with a woman in Nevada, where surrogacy is legal. Using Mukai's eggs and her husband's sperm, the surrogate gave birth to twins. After a Nevada court recognized them as Mukai's children, the state issued birth certificates naming her as the legal mother and her husband as the legal father. When the couple submitted these to the municipal office back in Japan, it refused to accept the application to register the children. The couple were told that the woman who gives birth should be the person who should register as the legal mother. The SCOJ agreed, rejecting the couple's argument that the twins should be treated as their legal children.[148] According to the SCOJ, if a judgment of a foreign court is to be recognized in Japan, it must conform to "public policy and good morals." Parental relationships are a matter of public policy and good morals. Therefore, if a foreign judgment recognizes a parental relationship that is not legally recognized in Japan, it will be viewed as contrary to public policy and good morals. In Japan, because the legal mother is defined as she who gave birth to the child, the Nevada court judgment had no legal force. Thus, despite the fact that the surrogate had no biological relationship to the twins and no intention of raising them, whereas Mukai had a biological relationship and every intention of raising them, the SCOJ held that she was not their legal mother.

Mukai's case suggests that when a woman gives birth, she will be perceived as the legal mother regardless of whether she and the baby have a biological relationship. A surrogate mother would need to put the child up for adoption, and the intended parents would have to adopt the baby and add him or her to their family register.[149]

Generally, the adoption is noted on the register.[150] However, because of concerns about possible prejudice against adopted children, the Diet has created a special adoption procedure.[151] Unlike the regular procedure, where the fact of adoption is added to the register and the relationship between the child and its biological parents is not severed, the special adoption procedure treats the adopted child as the "natural child" of its adoptive parents.[152] In addition, the parental relationship between the child and the biological parents is terminated.[153] Due to the SCOJ decision in Mukai's case, intended parents are forced to follow this special adoption procedure, even if they have an immediate blood tie with the child.[154]

Although the SCOJ decision did not make things easier for anyone who wanted to have a child through surrogacy, it did provide some measure of certainty for a woman who opts for IVF using her own egg and donor sperm. Although the resulting child is not biologically related to her husband, she will nonetheless be regarded as its legal mother so long as she gives birth to it. Moreover, if she gave birth to a child using IVF with a donor egg, the SCOJ will probably view her as the legal mother, even though she has no biological relationship with the baby.[155]

Who Is the Legal Father? ART/MAR and Donor Sperm

When it comes to who should be regarded as the legal father, the situation becomes much more complex. Artificial insemination and IVF using donor sperm now allow couples to have a baby who will have no biological relationship with one of the parents.[156] For instance, when a married woman becomes pregnant through artificial insemination using donor sperm (AID), she will be the legal mother as long as she herself gave birth to the child. Her husband is presumed to be the legal father. Therefore, if he agrees to be the father prior to the birth, he will have no difficulty in registering the child as his.[157] Neither parent is permitted to deny parentage once they have given consent or agreed to be the parent.[158] Such a situation could occur when a couple separates after the mother becomes pregnant through AID.

In some instances, married couples use ART/MAR with donor sperm because the husband cannot father a child. This situation can arise when he is transgender. Although same-sex marriage is not legal in Japan, transgender people are now allowed to have sex reassignment surgery and to change their sex on the family register.[159] Afterward, they can marry a partner who is the same sex as they were assigned at birth. In one controversial SCOJ case, a transgender male, registered as female at birth, legally changed his sex to male and married a woman. She conceived via AID and gave birth to a baby. When the couple attempted to register the child, the municipal office refused to recognize the husband as the legal father, because he was not physically capable of impregnating his wife. As a result, the "father" column on the register was left blank. The couple applied to the court for permission to correct this. The SCOJ held that individuals who have been allowed to legally change their sex to male should be legally treated as male. Such a man should be allowed to marry a woman, and he should be entitled to enjoy the same legal presumption of paternity.[160] Thus, in such cases, the municipal office cannot refuse to identify the husband as the father simply because he could not impregnate his wife. This can be considered a blessing for some 2SLGBTQ+ couples.

Who Is the Legal Father? ART/MAR and a Deceased Husband

What happens when a woman gives birth to a child conceived through ART/MAR using frozen sperm from her deceased husband? Even without ART/MAR, a couple can conceive a baby who is born after the death of the husband. Under the Civil Code, if a baby is born fewer than three hundred days after the husband's death, the presumption of paternity applies and he will be treated as the legal father. However, when ART/MAR was added to the mix, the SCOJ refused to recognize a parental relationship between the child and the deceased husband.[161]

In this instance, a married couple was trying to have a child using ART/MAR. The husband had leukemia and was scheduled to receive a bone marrow transplant, followed by radiation therapy. Aware of its debilitating effects, they froze his sperm. Before the transplant, he asked her to use it if he passed away and expressed the same desire to various relatives. They decided to try IVF with the sperm, but he died before the operation occurred. The wife nevertheless went ahead with the plan, obtaining the consent of his parents. The doctor who performed the IVF did not realize that the husband was dead. A suit was filed by the mother in the name of the child against the public prosecutor, asking for filiation after the father's death.

The SCOJ held that the Japanese legal rule on parentage did not anticipate a paternal relationship between a child born via ART/MAR and a father who had predeceased the birth. Such a child, the SCOJ held, could not be subject to parental rights of the deceased father. It could not claim child support from him or inherit a portion of his estate. Therefore, a parental relationship could not be accepted. As a result, it would need to be created and decided by the legislature. The SCOJ concluded that, in the absence of such legislative measures, this form of family relationship could not be accepted in court. In such situations, the child has no legal father.

There have been no cases in Japan concerning a woman impregnated by sperm collected from her husband after his death (postmortem sperm collection). Since the JSOG limits IVF to married couples, a doctor is unlikely to provide it. If it were to occur, however, the SCOJ would probably reach the same conclusion as in the case above, where sperm was gathered before the husband died.

Who Is the Legal Father? ART/MAR without His Consent

What happens when a married couple is separated, but the wife uses the husband's frozen sperm without obtaining his consent? Normally, such a situation would not arise, because fertility doctors must ask for specific consent before using ART/MAR. In one case, however, the doctor was somehow led to believe that the husband had consented and administered the procedure, after which the wife became pregnant and gave birth. When the husband challenged his paternity by filing a suit to confirm the absence of a parental relationship, the lower court rejected his claim, and the SCOJ eventually dismissed his appeal.[162] This couple consisted of a foreign husband and a Japanese wife, who were married in 2004 and started infertility treatments in 2009 after having embryos frozen. Using IVF with a frozen embryo, they had a boy in 2011. Then, their relationship deteriorated and they separated in 2013. Thereafter, without obtaining her husband's consent, the wife had the doctor perform the IVF procedure with another frozen embryo and had a baby girl in 2015. The couple were divorced in 2016. The ex-husband then filed a suit to confirm the absence of a parental relationship, insisting that he had not given advance consent.

Although ART/MAR requires advance consent from both parties, the Nara Family Court held that the legal presumption of paternity should apply in the absence of clear, objective circumstances that precluded any possibility of the couple having a sexual relationship. In this case, the court held that, although the couple were separated, they did go on a trip together, which signalled that the marriage had not irretrievably broken down. The court found that the legal presumption of paternity was applicable and that the ex-husband should be regarded as the legal father.

The judgment in this case is somewhat ambiguous and has left the door open to the denial of a parental relationship where advance consent to ART/MAR is not given and if a sexual relationship between the parties is not possible. If there is any indication that a sexual relationship is possible, even if the couple have separated, the judgment is consistent with the traditional position of the SCOJ. Had the court found that a parental relationship should be granted even though consent was lacking and there was no evidence of the possibility of a sexual relationship, that would have been a new development in Japan.[163]

Who Is the Legal Father? Lesbian Parents and ART/MAR

If a child is born to a lesbian couple, one of whom is transgender and who supplied the frozen sperm used for conception, who is the legal father? The birth mother is the legal mother. Her partner, who was born male, was diagnosed with a sexual identity disorder, underwent sex reassignment surgery, and legally changed sex to female, according to the statute. Given this, both partners are legally women. Since Japanese law does not accept same-sex marriage, they are not legally married. Therefore, their baby is the illegitimate child of the birth mother. Both partners cannot register as its legal mother, because the birth registration accepts only one mother and one father. The transgender partner and the child have a biological relationship. Nevertheless, she was not treated as the father, because the couple were not legally married. Her attempt to filiate the child was also rejected since she is now legally a woman. Is there any way to accept a transgender woman who wants to be treated as a father?

The Tokyo District Court denied the application of filiation filed by the mother of a child against a transgender woman who is the child's biological father.[164] The court admitted that a biological relationship did exist. But the transgender partner did not give birth to the child, so she could not be its mother. And because the Civil Code assumes that a husband must be male, she could not be its father either. As a result, the parental relationship between the child and the biological father was not accepted.

Reforming the Law of Parentage

The Constitutional Right to Be Treated as a Parent

Obviously, as shown above, the Japanese law of parentage is not well equipped to deal with ART/MAR. Sometimes, it is unclear and sometimes it produces a result that couples who use ART/MAR did not anticipate. Therefore, it needs to be reformed.

What should this entail? First, it is imperative to consider the interests of those who wish to become parents. It needs to be accepted that the Constitution protects the right to have a child or to be a parent, that this includes the right to access ART/MAR, and that parties who use it should be granted the status of legal parents. Once this is in place, it could be argued that refusing to grant the status of legal parentage to anyone who uses ART/MAR is an infringement on his or her constitutional rights.[165]

In the United States, the 1989 case of *Michael H. v Gerald D.* involved a man who had fathered a child with his married lover. He filed an action to establish his paternity, invoking the right to privacy as protected under the due process clause of the Constitution. The SCOTUS rejected his claim because the right to be accepted as the legal father of a child born in an adulterous relationship and raised by the adulterous wife and her husband could not find support in the traditional conception of privacy.[166] Nevertheless, the issue of accepting a biological father as a legal father still remains compelling. Individuals have a legitimate interest to be recognized as a parent, even when a child is the result of adultery.

The child also has a legitimate and compelling interest to know and have a meaningful relationship with its biological father if they so wish. Denying the possibility of granting legal status to the biological father is therefore not justified.

Indeed, some American states have already demonstrated the means to create a much more flexible family relationship. At common law, there is a presumption of paternity favouring the husband of the birth mother when a child is born during a marriage.[167] At one time, the presumption was so strong that it was almost irrefutable.[168] It could be overcome only by strong evidence that the husband was sterile or did not have contact with his wife during the crucial period of conception. The types of evidence that the court could consider were extremely limited.[169] Over time, however, this presumption eroded. An increasing number of husbands have challenged the presumption of paternity through litigation, and courts have struggled to respond.[170] As a result, state legislatures have been forced to enact statutes to regulate parentage to accommodate the conflicting interests of husband, wife, and child.

In California, for example, when a woman gives birth, she will be recognized as the legal mother.[171] Her name will be recorded in the birth certificate issued by a hospital, doctor, or midwife. However, surrogacy contracts are valid in California, and when one exists and when it grants the status of parent to a client couple, they will be recognized as the legal parents.[172]

Also in California, if parents are married when a baby is born, there is a conclusive presumption that they are its legal parents.[173] Thus, the husband is presumed to be the legal father. Furthermore, anyone who "receives the child into his or her home and openly holds out the child as his or her natural child" is presumed to be the legal parent.[174] There is also a conclusive presumption of paternity for the husband when he and his wife are cohabiting.[175] When this presumption is applied and the father wishes to deny paternity, he must file a suit.[176] Only in exceptional circumstances, such as when DNA testing reveals that he is not the biological father, can he disestablish paternity.[177]

A mother, on the other hand, can include the name of the father on a child's birth certificate if she wishes. There is no requirement that he must be the biological father or that she must obtain his consent. If he voluntarily accepts parentage, he can sign a declaration of paternity at the hospital.[178] His name will be added to the birth certificate issued by the hospital. If this occurs and he later denies paternity, the wife does not have to go to court to certify her husband's paternity. The father can also accept paternity afterward, but his declaration must be signed at a public agency or witnessed by a notary public. It must also be filed with a local public agency. If it is properly filed, it will have the same effect as a court order.[179] If the father denies paternity, the mother can ask a child support agency to go to court to summon him to undergo DNA testing, or she can file a petition with the court to establish a parental relationship.[180] If the DNA testing shows that he is the biological father, the court will issue an order to treat him as the father. If the DNA testing shows that he is not, the suit will be dismissed.[181]

Once a declaration of paternity has been signed and filed, rescinding or altering paternity is very difficult. If a man wishes to do so, he must file a declaration of paternity rescission form at the local government office within sixty days of signing the declaration of paternity.[182] He can also go to court to set aside the paternity declaration within two years of the child's birth by proving via a blood and genetic test that he is not the biological father or by showing that he signed the declaration as a result of fraud or duress.[183] Once paternity is established by the court order, challenging it thereafter becomes extremely difficult.[184]

California has also updated its family code to include a presumption of parentage for children who are born through ART/MAR. Generally, when a mother uses donor sperm, her partner, not the donor, is regarded as the legal father.[185] It must also be noted, however, that the California Family Code does not preclude a child from having more than two parents,[186] and courts can recognize more than two in certain circumstances.[187]

Moreover, same-sex couples are not required to use the words "husband" and "wife." California also discarded the distinction between "mother" and "father," opting instead for "mother" and "other parent."[188] Thus, California shows how the law of parentage can be adjusted to match the development of ART/MAR and to accept more flexible rules.

The Best Interests of the Child

The right to have children and to be treated as a parent is not absolute. There may be compelling state interests that warrant overriding it. One of the most compelling would be to protect the best interests of the child.

In 1994, Japan ratified the United Nations Convention on the Rights of the Child,[189] which states that the best interests of the child shall be a primary consideration in regulating parental relationships.[190] A restriction on a person's right to have a child or to be treated as a parent would therefore be justified if its purpose were to secure the best interests of the child.

The possibility of such restrictions is well indicated in contexts where courts are faced with the right to create a family relationship. In rejecting the argument that it is impermissible to accept any waiting period for women to remarry after divorce, the SCOJ has already held that the presumption of paternity and the quick establishment of a parental relationship is vital, even though it forces women to wait for one hundred days before they can remarry.[191] Some have criticized this holding, pointing out that paternity can easily be established by DNA testing and that a waiting period is therefore unnecessary. Whereas this may be true, the issue is that Japanese law does not anticipate that DNA testing will supply proof of paternity before the birth registration application is submitted or the possibility that the DNA testing result could subsequently change the listing of the legal father. According to the SCOJ, the best interests of the child mandate women to wait the hundred days in order to clarify legal paternity through the presumption of paternity. Although this conclusion is controversial, it indicates that, in some cases, the best interests of the child may be a critical factor in determining the existence of a parental relationship. Even if the right to be treated as a parent is to be constitutionally protected, introducing restrictions that are in the best interests of the child is justifiable.

Finding the Right Balance

The question then comes down to finding an appropriate balance between the constitutional right to be treated as a parent and the best interests of the child. In considering this question, it is important to note that Japanese law does not currently recognize the existence of a constitutional right to have a child. Nor are the presumption of paternity and decisions regarding parental relationships intended to serve the best interests of the child. Indeed, the current rules of parentage have no guiding principles: they do not prioritize either the wishes of the parents or the best interests of the child.

Although many people prioritize biological relationships when accepting the status of a parent, the law of parentage now recognizes the importance of legal marriage and the existence of a parental relationship where people adopt a child with whom they have no blood tie. The biological relationship is not the guiding principle. The development of ART/MAR created further confusion and uncertainty surrounding determinations of parentage. Nevertheless, the Diet was not willing to revise the law of parentage to accord with the changing landscape of family relationships or to fit the use of ART/MAR. The Japanese courts have simply introduced some fixes and modifications of the rules to adjust to the social reality. It is seriously doubtful that the rules maintain a proper balance between two competing interests: the autonomy rights of the parent and the best interests of the child.

There are four possible approaches to determining parentage: prioritizing the biological relationship; prioritizing the wishes of the parents; giving broad discretion to their wishes but limiting this based on the best interests of the child; and prioritizing the best interests of the child. The traditional approach is the first one: prioritizing the biological relationship. Under this approach, in the absence of a blood tie, the parental relationship could be created only through adoption. It would not be accepted without a biological relationship, and the legal status would change based only on the biological relationship. The second approach respects the autonomy of the parents. It allows them to choose who will be a parent based on the biological relationship, or on their wishes, without any kind of limitation. The third approach is similar to the second, except that it limits their choice, which will be modified if it conflicts with the best interests of the child. The fourth approach grants priority to the best interests of the child. For children, it is of utmost importance to be supported and cared for by parents, regardless of whether any biological relationship exists. It is not necessary to have two parents, but two might be better. Then, the determination of parentage can be decided by considering who would serve the best interests of the child. In light of the examinations so far, the best and only justifiable approach is the third one.

Treating the birth mother as the legal mother would benefit a woman who uses ART/MAR and who does not have a biological relationship with the baby. As in California, if a woman gives birth through ART/MAR, she should be regarded as the legal mother, regardless of whether the egg is her own or that of a donor.[192] Yet, if she uses a surrogate, she would be deprived of legal motherhood, even if the baby is biologically related to her. It is doubtful whether such a deprivation could be justified as being in its best interests.[193] In California, where surrogacy is legal, the surrogacy contract can assign the status of legal mother to the intended mother. This is not the case in Japan, where legal presumptions of parenthood cannot be modified through a contract. Although surrogacy contracts are not banned, they are simply not respected. Forcing an intended mother to follow the special adoption procedure even when she is biologically related to the child is unreasonable.[194] It would be better to recognize her as the legal mother.[195]

A husband should also be regarded as the legal father of a child conceived through the use of donor sperm. As long as he agrees to the procedure and both parents are willing to raise the child, recognizing him as the legal father would be in the best interests of the child.[196] Even in situations where he has no clear intent to become a father, if he is married to the birth mother and could possibly have had a sexual relationship with her when the baby was conceived, it is not unreasonable to presume that he would be its legal father.

The legal presumption that the husband is the father is reasonable in the absence of clear, objective evidence that a marriage-like relationship no longer existed or that a sexual relationship was impossible. It is important for a child to have a legal father, and the relationship should not be changed easily. Therefore, the legal presumption may not be overcome after a very short period of time. Even if the law does not allow a husband to deny paternity by invoking the results of a DNA test after that short period, such a rule should not be struck down as unconstitutional, because it ensures the best interests of the child.

When the biological father differs from the legal father, it is necessary to decide who shall be accorded the status of father. The current rule is grounded in the assumption that there can be only one. But if a child has both a biological and a legal father, the court could potentially allow that it has more than two parents. Its interests may be best served by granting both men equal status or by granting secondary status to one of the fathers. If it were to take this step, the court must carefully balance the interests of the child with those of the adults.

Perhaps the most difficult scenario would be that in which, without obtaining her husband's consent, a wife uses his frozen sperm or a frozen embryo to produce a child. Even if the couple were separated, the legal presumption of paternity would prevail unless he could prove that the marital relationship no longer existed and that a sexual relationship was impossible.[197] Because a child should have a legal father to the extent possible, he should be recognized as its legal father even though he did not consent.[198]

The legislature needs to revise the Civil Code law of parentage to conform to the approach outlined above. Leaving these matters unaddressed, without any attempt to examine the law of parentage despite the development of ART/MAR, is simply unconstitutional.[199] Moreover, it may be time to consider whether the labels of "father" and "mother" need to be retained. As in California, it may be better to opt for "mother" and "other partner" or, if same-sex marriage is accepted, both mothers or fathers. Or it may be better to leave the choice up to the parties themselves.

The Medically Assisted Reproduction Act of 2020, finally enacted, only partially clarified the law of parentage for children who were born through ART/MAR. The act declares that "a woman who became pregnant and gave birth to a child born using another woman's eggs or embryos using another woman's eggs through medically assisted reproduction should be regarded as the legal mother."[200] It also declares that, despite the provisions in article 774 of the Civil Code, the "husband is not allowed to deny the legitimacy of a child when his wife became pregnant using the sperm of other men than him through medically assisted reproduction."[201]

The act merely confirms what is already widely accepted and fails to solve the complicated issues that emerge in the law of parentage. The legislature remains unwilling to ground this law on the constitutional right to have a child or to become a parent while simultaneously securing the best interests of the child. It should do better.[202]

Abortion: The Right Not to Be Forced to Have a Child

5

The flip side of the right to have a child is the right not to be forced to have one. Being pregnant and bringing a fetus to term should be an individual choice for every woman. This freedom is a necessary corollary of the freedom to choose whether to have a child. It includes the right to prevent or to terminate a pregnancy via contraceptives or an abortion.

When a woman has sex, there is almost always a possibility that she could become pregnant. This might be a hoped-for outcome, but it may also be unexpected or unwanted. In Japan, the use of contraceptives has been tightly regulated, but they are becoming increasingly available. Nevertheless, due to long-standing concerns over safety, the pill is not popular. The most common choices are condoms or withdrawal, which often prove unreliable. Thus, many women find themselves in the unenviable position of having to rely on their partner to ensure that they don't get pregnant – to use the condom properly or to withdraw before ejaculation. Should such methods fail, as is often the case, they must then make the difficult decision of whether to give birth or have an abortion.

Under the Criminal Code, "abortion" is technically unlawful in Japan.[1] But when legitimate reasons exist, the Mother's Body Protection Act permits the "artificial termination of pregnancy" (ATP), which is practically the same as the induced abortion banned by the Criminal

Code.[2] In actuality, all abortions are virtually legally free if they occur during the early stage of pregnancy.[3] As a result, there has been little discussion around the adequacy of the tight contraceptive restrictions or the permissibility of abortion. However, the gap between legal text and actual practice, as well as the total reliance on a merciful exercise of discretion by government officials rather than the rule of law, is troubling. Furthermore, concern is growing over the dignity of the fetus and allowing ATP for discriminatory purposes, not officially accepted as lawful. Given this, the government could potentially reconsider its abortion policy, enforcing the statutes or revising them to limit access to ATP, especially in light of the low birthrate and declining number of children. If this were to occur, the right to abortion and the limits of this right would become a central issue.

The History of Abortion Regulations

A Brief History of the Abortion Ban

Abortion was not prohibited in Japan until the modern period. In fact, during the long centuries before the Meiji Restoration of 1868, abortion and infanticide were rather popular means of reducing the number of children.[4] Because they were so common, the Edo government feared that the farming population would be too small to sustain rice production and thus support its revenue.[5] It finally prohibited the abandonment of babies in 1690 and infanticide in 1767, as well as restricting abortion.[6] However, the bans were never strictly enforced in rural areas, with the result that they were ineffective.[7]

After the Meiji Restoration, the government concentrated on building a wealthy country and a strong military. To bolster the ranks of the military, it promoted childbirth, especially of male babies. In service of this, it immediately issued a declaration to ban abortion by midwives, and it enacted the Abortion Prohibition Order in 1869, incorporating it into the first Criminal Code in 1880.[8] The ban was carried over into the current Criminal Code of 1907.[9] As a result of these measures, abortion was illegal before the end of the Second World War. The government also tried to enforce the ban quite aggressively for some time.[10]

However, as it rushed to mobilize during the war effort, the government became concerned about the fitness of men for combat. Following the Nazi precedent, it passed the National Eugenics Act in 1940,[11] whose purpose was to prevent the increase of persons with hereditary diseases and to encourage the birth of those who could become healthy soldiers.[12] It thus authorized the sterilization of individuals who had a certain listed hereditary disease, based on an application from the patients themselves or from their mental institution.[13] It also allowed induced abortion when a doctor obtained a second opinion from another doctor and notified the appropriate authority.[14] This was meant to terminate the pregnancy of parents whose genes were seen as inferior while simultaneously precluding any other abortions, especially of healthy babies.

Changes after the Second World War
The Criminal Code ban on abortion and the National Eugenics Act's lawful termination of undesirable pregnancies continued even after the end of the war. However, during that period of chaos, illegal abortions appear to have been conducted quite openly. There are reports that at a clinic in Futsukaichi, Fukuoka Prefecture, doctors performed illegal abortions for women who had been raped on their journey back from China.[15] Moreover, food was in extremely short supply at the time, and families could not afford the luxury of having yet another mouth to feed. If they wished to survive, abortion was their only option.[16] Unsurprisingly, the Japanese government turned a blind eye to these illegal practices.

In 1948, the government passed the Eugenic Protection Act, the first abortion law to be introduced after the war.[17] Triggered by the food shortages and by serious concerns about an unexpected spike in population growth,[18] it incorporated the eugenicist policy of the National Eugenics Act and authorized ATP. Its stated purpose was to prevent the birth of "improper" offspring and to protect the life and health of pregnant women.[19] It provided for sterilization and ATP, which was defined as the "artificial discharge of an unborn child and its appendages out of its mother's body in a period when the unborn child cannot survive outside the mother's body."[20] Under the act, doctors who were designated by their local physicians' associations could perform ATP, with the consent of the woman and her husband. The act listed five categories of women who qualified for the procedure:

1. A person who herself or her spouse has mental illness, mental retardation, psychopathy, hereditary physical disease or hereditary deformity;
2. A person who herself or her spouse has a relative within the fourth degree that has hereditary mental illness, hereditary mental retardation, hereditary psychopathy, hereditary physical disease or hereditary deformity;
3. A person who herself or her spouse is suffering from leprosy;
4. A person for whom the continuation of pregnancy or delivery may significantly harm her physical health due to bodily or economic reasons; or
5. A person who was raped with an assault or intimidation or who could neither resist nor refuse and became pregnant.[21]

The first two clauses served the eugenicist agenda. Targeted by the third clause, leprosy is not hereditary, but it was included for reasons of social protection.[22] The fourth clause was intended to protect mothers. Its reference to "economic reasons" was added in 1949, immediately after the enactment of the statute.[23] The fifth clause was added on compassionate grounds to allow victims of rape and quasi-rape to obtain ATP.[24]

However, over time growing numbers of people expressed concern about the rapid decline in the birthrate. During the 1960s, some members of the ruling Liberal Democratic Party (LDP) demanded that the Eugenic Protection Act be amended to make it more difficult to get ATP, hoping that this step would correct the drop in childbirth.[25] The conservative religious group Seicho-no-ie condemned abortion and supported this call.[26] Yet, no amendment was implemented. In 1972, an amendment bill was introduced into the Diet that removed economic reasons as grounds for ATP.[27] Women's groups rallied in opposition to the bill, insisting that women had the right to decide whether to have a child. They were joined by the designated doctors who provided ATP, as they feared the loss of important revenue.[28] As a result, the bill was never passed. This scenario was repeated in the 1980s, and that amendment too was never realized.[29]

In 1995, however, groups supporting persons with disabilities demanded that the word "Eugenic" be removed from the title of the act and that it be revised to disallow ATP conducted because a fetus had disabilities.[30] In 1996, the title was changed from the Eugenic Protection Act to the Mother's Body Protection Act,[31] eugenicist perspectives were deleted, and clauses that allowed ATP due to eugenic reasons were removed.[32]

The Current Framework of Abortion Regulation

The Legal Framework

Under the Criminal Code, "when a pregnant woman causes her own abortion by drugs or any other means, imprisonment with labour for not more than one year shall be imposed."[33] Abortion is defined by courts as "artificially separating the fetus from the mother's body before the natural birth period."[34] Also under the Criminal Code,

> a person who, at the request of a woman or with her consent, causes her abortion, shall be punished by imprisonment with labour for not more than two years. If the person thereby causes death or injury of the woman, the person shall be punished by imprisonment with labour for not less than three months but not more than five years.[35]

If a physician, midwife, pharmacist, or pharmaceutical distributor causes the abortion, the punishment is imprisonment with labour for not less than three months but not more than five years. If the mother dies or is injured, the penalty will be increased to not less than six months but not more than seven years.[36] Therefore, both the woman who asks for the abortion and the medical professional who provides it will be subject to criminal punishment.

The punishment is much more severe when the woman does not give consent for an abortion. As the Criminal Code explains, "a person who, without request of the woman or her consent, causes her abortion shall be punished by imprisonment with labour for not less than six months but not more than seven years."[37] Failed attempts are also subject to penalty.[38] Anyone who performs abortion without consent and thereby causes the death or injury of the woman "shall be dealt with by the punishment prescribed for either the crimes of injury or the preceding article, whichever is greater."[39]

Criminal abortion is thus often categorized as either with or without consent. The former is subdivided into self-administered abortion, abortion by non-professionals, and abortion by medical professionals.[40] However, even when the woman has given consent, the fetus, obviously, has not, because the fetus is not regarded as a human being who is capable of giving consent. So the question of consent does not apply to the fetus, and from its standpoint, therefore, all abortions are without consent.[41] In other words, the fetus will always be a victim and the mother will always be an assailant, even when she agrees to the abortion.[42] As a result, the legal interest protected by abortion bans is primarily that of the fetus.[43] Since the definition of abortion does not include killing a fetus, merely removing it from the mother's body can be punished since removal is capable of causing its death.[44]

On the other hand, the Mother's Body Protection Act defines ATP as an "artificial discharge of an unborn child and its appendages out of its mother's body in a period when the unborn child cannot survive outside the mother's body."[45] This is nothing but an induced abortion. And the act allows certain doctors to perform ATP in certain circumstances:

> A doctor designated by a local medical association, a public interest incorporated association established for the area of a prefecture (hereinafter referred to as a "designated doctor"), may perform an ATP on a person who falls under any of the following items after obtaining consent from the relevant person and her spouse:
>
> (i) A person for whom the continuation of pregnancy or delivery may significantly harm her physical health due to bodily or economic reasons; or
> (ii) A person who was raped accompanied with assault or intimidation or at a time when she could neither resist nor refuse and became pregnant.[46]

If the spouse is unknown, cannot express an intention, or is dead, his consent is obviously not necessary.[47] Every month, doctors who perform ATP must report the number of procedures to the local governor.[48]

Designated doctors who provide ATP are seen as engaging in "lawful professional conduct," which is legal under the Criminal Code.[49] They will be excused from the crime of professional abortion.[50] Although the act does not grant immunity to the mother who obtains ATP, the criminal punishment under the Criminal Code will not apply to her if she does so lawfully.[51]

Therefore, on the face of the statute, ATP is permissible only when either pregnancy or delivery could significantly harm the mother's physical health "due to bodily or economic reasons" or when she was "raped accompanied with assault or intimidation or at a time when she could neither resist nor refuse and became pregnant." Moreover, the consent of a husband is essential.

Even when these requirements are not satisfied, an abortion can be performed under certain circumstances. For example, though the time limit may have expired, any doctor can provide it if it is necessary to save the mother's life.[52]

Abortion in Practice

As specified by the Ministry of Health, Labour and Welfare (MHLW) in 1990, ATP can be performed within the first twenty-one weeks of pregnancy.[53] When this was first implemented in 1953, the cut-off was twenty-eight weeks, but as medical knowledge and technology improved, it was dropped to twenty-four in 1976 and then to twenty-one, which is the earliest limit, and the individual doctor makes the ultimate decision on viability in every case.[54] This is thus merely a guideline. In reality, however, no doctor is willing to perform ATP after twenty-one weeks.[55]

ATP is performed through a surgical method, either by extraction or by vacuum aspiration during early pregnancy, up to eleven weeks.[56] It is relatively safe and not burdensome (sometimes it takes only one day), although a follow-up appointment is usually required. ATP due to economic reasons is not covered by the national health insurance system.[57] It can cost up to JPY 250,000 (US$1,800).[58] ATP between twelve and twenty-one weeks involves an induced delivery.[59] It is riskier and can be more burdensome and expensive for women.[60]

Very few people are charged with criminal abortion in Japan. In 2015, two cases were reported to the police and only one person was arrested.[61] It is unclear how many cases actually proceeded to a conviction and what kind of conduct was charged as abortion.[62]

The number of ATP peaked in 1955, with 1,170,000. After that, it gradually dropped, reaching 182,000 in 2014.[63] The ratio of ATP per 1,000 women was 50.2 in 1955 and 6.9 in 2014.[64] The total number further declined to 176,388 in 2015, 168,015 in 2016, and 161,741 in 2018.[65] The ratio of ATP per 1,000 women was 6.8 in 2015, 6.5 in 2016, and 6.4 in 2018.[66] In 2001, women between the ages of twenty and twenty-four accounted for the largest portion (24.2 percent), followed by those between twenty-five and twenty-nine (21.3 percent) and those between thirty and thirty-four (18.5 percent).[67] Women who were under twenty, however, figured relatively significantly as well (13.6 percent).[68]

It is well known that reported figures are highly unreliable.[69] Although doctors who provide ATP are obligated to report it, many can be rather careless in this respect. Since the operation is not covered by health insurance, there is no government subsidy and thus no incentive for a doctor to go through the complicated reporting procedure. If the woman prefers confidentiality, doctors are inclined to respect her wishes.

However, according to one statistic, 54.0 percent of ATP occurred before seven weeks, followed by 39.6 percent between eight and eleven weeks.[70] Only 1.21 percent took place during the twentieth and the twenty-first week.[71] These statistics show that almost all ATP are done during the early stages of pregnancy.[72]

There are no statistics on how many ATP were conducted due to health reasons or reasons of economic hardship. One survey revealed that 99.8 percent were justified due to possible harm to the woman, whereas pregnancy due to rape accompanied with assault or intimidation was cited in only 0.15 percent of all ATP.[73] A 2016 survey showed that married couples wanted to have an average of 2.33 children, whereas the number they presently had was 1.68. Their main reason for not having more was concern over the cost of raising a child.[74] A survey of teenagers who had ATP gave a breakdown of their reasons for choosing it: being unable to raise a child due to low income (67.7 percent), being too young (63.7 percent), being unmarried (46.3 percent), lacking confidence in their ability to raise a child (44.2 percent), feeling that having a child would interfere with their education (38.7 percent), and being urged to do so by parents (27.3 percent).[75] These two surveys show that the reasons for seeking ATP were totally unrelated to the eligibility criteria in the statute and that economic difficulty was the most important factor in the decision.

How, then, can one convert economic difficulty into a significant harm to the health of the mother and thus a justifiable reason for ATP? The answer is obvious. If having a baby will impose financial hardships on a woman, she will need to acquire additional income, which means she will have to work more hours or find a better-paying job. She could ask her family for monetary aid but might not necessarily receive it. She will have to hire a nanny or find a daycare, which could be costly, and this will force her to work more to cover the expense. All of this could potentially damage her health. This is true even when she is married. When she makes such a claim, a doctor could and would see it as satisfying the requirement for ATP. Thus, economic difficulty is easily converted into possible damage to the health of the mother. Neither the woman nor her partner must back up their assertion of economic difficulty by supplying official paperwork that documents their income or financial situation. They do not need to prove that family support will not be forthcoming. Therefore, when a woman asks for ATP, doctors will accede for whatever reason she might give.[76] As a result, ATP is virtually freely available before twenty-two weeks, although technically it is permitted only for the listed legitimate reasons.[77]

Moreover, no one checks the identity of the husband or whether he actually has given consent. In this situation, there is no specific criminal punishment for forging or falsifying his agreement. As long as a signature and a personal stamp appear on the consent form, ATP can proceed. Furthermore, consent from the spouse is not necessary if he is unknown, cannot express an intention, or has died. In these cases, the woman has no need to lie or resort to forgery. Nor does she need to provide documentary proof that he cannot consent. The doctors can simply accept her word.[78]

When a pregnant woman is unmarried, doubt can sometimes arise over who should give consent for an abortion. In practice, most doctors demand that the biological father must agree (if he is a minor, his parents must also consent). But since the MHLW has insisted that in cases where a woman is not married, her consent is sufficient,[79] permission from a biological father is rather merely obtained but is not a legal requirement.

In 2016, the United Nations Committee on the Elimination of Discrimination against Women recommended that Japan

(a) Amend the [Criminal] Code and [Mother's Body] Protection Act to ensure the legalization of abortion not only in cases of threats to the life and/or health of a pregnant woman but also in all cases of rape, irrespective of the use of violence, threat against or resistance by the victim, incest and serious foetal impairment and decriminalise abortion in all other cases, [and]
(b) Revise the [Mother's Body] Protection Act in order to remove the requirement of spousal consent for pregnant women to obtain an abortion; and ensure that where abortion is sought on the ground of serious foetal impairment, the free and informed consent of the pregnant woman is obtained.[80]

But satisfying these recommendations would merely be a matter of form, as, in practice, there is no limitation on the reasons for seeking ATP, and the spousal consent requirement is almost totally meaningless.

Abortion Law and Birth Control Policy

Sex Education
As stated above, 161,741 Japanese women had ATP in 2018, and the ratio of abortions per thousand women was 6.4.[81] This figure is substantially higher in other countries: it was 11.7 in the United States, 13.1 in the United Kingdom, 14.5 in France, and 17.7 in Sweden. Germany scored a bit lower, with 5.7.[82] Yet the fact that 161,741 women went through an abortion in one year means that there are many unwanted pregnancies in Japan. This is a good indicator that birth control policies need improvement.

First, sex education is inadequate and often inappropriate. A 2011 study found that throughout the three grades of junior high school, an average of only 9.19 hours was allocated to the subject. With respect to knowledge on sexuality, the average correct response rate from students was as low as 34.5 percent for boys and 39.4 percent for girls, with many answering "I don't know."[83]

A 2010 survey showed that only 59.3 percent of students in the first grade of senior high knew that withdrawal was not a reliable contraception method.[84] No wonder that approximately two thousand high school students per year become pregnant.[85] Even at the college and university level, one survey revealed that only about half of sexually active students always used some form of birth control, 40 percent sometimes did, and 6 to 10 percent never did.[86]

Problematic Contraception Methods
Second, in Japan, the most popular contraception method is the condom (82.0 percent), followed by withdrawal (19.5 percent).[87] Although the condom provides good protection against sexually transmitted diseases, it is highly unreliable as a contraceptive, with a failure rate of 18 percent. Withdrawal is notorious for its ineffectiveness.[88] The dependence on these two methods may explain why there are so many unwanted pregnancies in Japan.

On the other hand, the pill is not popular, though it is widely used in other countries. The government delayed approving it for decades, granting official sanction only in 1999.[89] It insisted that the dosage was calibrated for European and American women, which meant that it might be too strong for Japanese women, who are typically much smaller. It was also concerned about possible side effects, so it demanded further studies on the topic.[90] The pill did initially contain high levels of estrogen and progestin, and various side effects did occur, so this concern might have been justified. Once low-dosage pills become standard and there were no reported harms, however, the government changed its approach, contending that the pill must be disallowed because its use would encourage people to abandon the condom, thus facilitating the spread of HIV and other sexually transmitted diseases.[91] Many advocates of the pill criticized this recalcitrance.[92] Even after the pill was approved, it was accessible only by prescription,[93] and many women remain apprehensive about possible side effects. Moreover, remembering to take the daily dosage can be burdensome, and cost remains a factor.[94] These are the primary reasons why only 4.2 percent of Japanese women opt for the pill.[95]

Morning-After and Abortion Pills

Third, Japanese women have little ability to avoid pregnancy after sex. The morning-after pill, or emergency contraception pill, levonorgestrel or NorLevo, is designed to prevent pregnancy after sex. It requires a doctor's prescription and cannot be purchased at a pharmacy as an over-the-counter drug.[96] Nor is it covered by the national health insurance.[97] Since it must be taken within seventy-two hours after sex, women could potentially have difficulty in obtaining it.[98] It is a relief for women that the morning-after pill is now available by online prescription after COVID-19.[99]

The abortion pill, Mifepristone or RU486, has not yet been approved and cannot be obtained even from a doctor.[100] This drug is an abortifacient, and thus it is illegal under the Criminal Code. Using it without a doctor's prescription is a violation of the conditions for ATP, as governed by the Mother's Body Protection Act. A woman who takes it, perhaps obtaining it by importing it from overseas, could be punished under article 212 of the Criminal Code, which prohibits her from causing her own abortion.

Given all the above, Japanese women have very little choice but to choose ATP – abortion – if they wish to avoid childbirth.[101] As such, abortion has become the primary method of birth control in Japan.[102]

Abortion and Government Aid

Like various other countries, Japan has a public national health insurance system. It applies to all illness and injury, and it covers most costs of medical treatment: basically, patients pay 30 percent of costs, but there is also an exemption for poor families. In and of themselves, neither pregnancy nor childbirth are illnesses or injuries, and therefore they are not covered by this scheme. However, the system does provide a grant to support childbirth.[103] Of course, any complications or medical emergencies associated with pregnancy or birth are covered by insurance. This is also true of medically necessary abortions. On the other hand, if an abortion is not medically necessary, the woman will pay for it, including the diagnosis, the procedure, and the after-care. Unlike childbirth, it is not eligible for government support.

The Abortion Ban without Enforcement

The Japanese Abortion Policy in Comparative Perspective

The stance on abortion differs from country to country.[104] Some have very strict bans.[105] Poland is probably the most restrictive country in Europe. According to its Family Planning, Human Embryo Protection and Conditions of Permissibility of Abortion Act of 7 January 1993,[106] "the right to life shall be subject to protection, including in the prenatal phase, to the extent provided in the Act."[107] This statute permits abortion only in very limited circumstances and only after a very demanding procedure is followed:

1. A termination of pregnancy may be performed only by a doctor, when:
   (1) The pregnancy poses a threat to the life or health of the pregnant woman,
   (2) Prenatal examinations or other medical conditions indicate that there is a high probability of a severe and irreversible fetal defect or incurable illness that threatens the fetus's life,
   (3) The are reasons to suspect that the pregnancy is a result of an unlawful act,
   (4) (repealed).
2. In the cases referred to in paragraph 1(2), the termination of pregnancy shall be permissible until the fetus is capable of living independently outside the body of the pregnant woman; in the cases referred to in paragraphs 1(3) or 1(4), if not more than 12 weeks have elapsed since the beginning of the pregnancy.
3. In the cases referred to in paragraphs 1(1) point 1(2), the termination of the pregnancy shall be performed by a doctor at a hospital.

4. The written consent of woman is necessary to terminate the pregnancy ...
5. A doctor, other than the one who terminates the pregnancy, ascertains that the circumstances referred to in paragraphs 1(1) and 1(2) have occurred, unless the pregnancy is a direct threat to the woman's life. The circumstances referred to in paragraph 1(3), shall be ascertained by the public prosecutor.[108]

On October 22, 2020, however, the Constitutional Tribunal of Poland held that abortion could not be justified when a fetus had a severe defect or a life-threatening illness, thus striking down this provision of the act.[109] The public was outraged by the decision and the willingness of the government to enforce it, thus disallowing the most common reason for seeking an abortion in Poland.[110]

Some jurisdictions have adopted a very liberal stance toward abortion. For example, as section 125.05 of the New York Penal Law states,

The following definitions are applicable to this article:

1. "Person," when referring to the victim of a homicide, means a human being who has been born and is alive.
2. "Abortional act" means an act committed upon or with respect to a female, whether by another person or by the female herself, whether she is pregnant or not, whether directly upon her body or by the administering, taking or prescription of drugs or in any other manner, with intent to cause a miscarriage of such female.
3. "Justifiable abortional act." An abortional act is justifiable when committed upon a female with her consent by a duly licensed physician acting (a) under a reasonable belief that such is necessary to preserve her life, or (b) within twenty-four weeks from the commencement of her pregnancy. A pregnant female's commission of an abortional act upon herself is justifiable when she acts upon the advice of a duly licensed physician (1) that such act is necessary to preserve her life, or (2) within twenty-four weeks from the commencement of her pregnancy. The submission by a female to an abortional act is justifiable when she believes that it is being

committed by a duly licensed physician, acting under a reasonable belief that such act is necessary to preserve her life, or, within twenty-four weeks from the commencement of her pregnancy.[111]

Thus, a woman is free to seek or implement an abortion during the first twenty-four weeks. As we will see, this statute was enacted before *Roe v Wade*,[112] a 1973 Supreme Court of the United States (SCOTUS) decision that banned the state from prohibiting abortion during the first trimester. New York's stance on abortion was far more permissive than that of other states. In 2019, with *Roe*, it further expanded the scope of abortion by passing the Reproductive Health Act,[113] which solidified its liberal stance toward abortion. Section 2599-AA of the act declares as follows:

The legislature finds that comprehensive reproductive health care is a fundamental component of every individual's health, privacy and equality. Therefore, it is the policy of the state that:

1. Every individual has the fundamental right to choose or refuse contraception or sterilization.
2. Every individual who becomes pregnant has the fundamental right to choose to carry the pregnancy to term, to give birth to a child, or to have an abortion, pursuant to this article.
3. The state shall not discriminate against, deny, or interfere with the exercise of the rights set forth in this section in the regulation or provision of benefits, facilities, services or information.[114]

It also states,

1. A health care practitioner licensed, certified, or authorized under title eight of the education law, acting within his or her lawful scope of practice, may perform an abortion when, according to the practitioner's reasonable and good faith professional judgment based on the facts of the patient's case: the patient is within twenty-four weeks from the commencement of pregnancy, or there is an absence of fetal viability, or the abortion is necessary to protect the patient's life or health.

2. This article shall be construed and applied consistent with and subject to applicable laws and applicable and authorized regulations governing health care procedures.[115]

The act thereby removed the crime of abortion from the penal law, except for section 125.05(1).[116] It was a significant change, since all health care practitioners, not only licensed physicians, could now provide an abortion. It also extended the period when an abortion could occur without having to give a reason, moving from the first trimester, as indicated in *Roe*, to twenty-four weeks, which practically speaking, means before the third trimester.

Many countries opt for the middle ground, imposing certain restrictions but leaving some freedoms. Germany, for instance, allows fairly broad room for abortion. First, section 218 of the German Criminal Code flatly bans it:

(1) Whoever terminates a pregnancy incurs a penalty of imprisonment for a term not exceeding three years or a fine. Acts whose effects occur before nidation is completed are not deemed to be a termination of pregnancy within the meaning of this statute.
(2) In especially serious cases, the penalty is imprisonment for a term of between six months and five years. An especially serious case typically occurs where the offender
   1. acts against the will of the pregnant woman or
   2. recklessly places the pregnant woman in danger of death or at risk of serious damage to health.
(3) If the act is committed by the pregnant woman, the penalty is imprisonment for a term not exceeding one year or a fine.
(4) The attempt is punishable. The pregnant woman is not liable for attempt.[117]

Yet, section 218a of the code grants fairly broad exemptions from punishment:

(1) The elements of the offence under section 218 are not deemed fulfilled if

1. the pregnant woman requests the termination of pregnancy and demonstrates to the physician by producing the certificate referred to in section 219(2) sentence 2 that she obtained counselling at least three days prior to the procedure,
2. the termination is performed by a physician and
3. no more than 12 weeks have elapsed since conception.

(2) A termination which is performed by a physician with the consent of the pregnant woman is not unlawful if, considering the pregnant woman's present and future circumstances, the termination is medically necessary to avert a danger to the life of or the danger of grave impairment to the pregnant woman's physical or mental health and if the danger cannot be averted in another manner which is reasonable for her to accept.

(3) The conditions of subsection (2) are also deemed fulfilled with regard to a termination performed by a physician with the consent of the pregnant woman if, according to medical opinion, an unlawful act under sections 176 to 178 has been committed against the pregnant woman, there are cogent reasons to support the assumption that the pregnancy was caused by the act and no more than 12 weeks have elapsed since conception.

(4) The pregnant woman does not incur the penalty specified in section 218 if the termination was performed by a physician after counselling (section 219) and no more than 22 weeks have elapsed since conception. The court may dispense with imposing a penalty pursuant to section 218 if the pregnant woman was in exceptional distress at the time of the procedure.[118]

As we will see,[119] this was a compromise reached after the Federal Constitutional Court of Germany held that an earlier attempt to liberalize the abortion ban was unconstitutional.

Canada also prohibited all abortions before 1969, but section 287 of the Criminal Code eventually allowed for some exceptions:

287 (1) Every one who, with intent to procure the miscarriage of a female person, whether or not she is pregnant, uses any means for the purpose of carrying out his intention is guilty of an indictable offence and liable to imprisonment for life.

(2) Every female person who, being pregnant, with intent to procure her own miscarriage, uses any means or permits any means to be used for the purpose of carrying out her intention is guilty of an indictable offence and liable to imprisonment for a term not exceeding two years ...
(4) Subsections (1) and (2) do not apply to
(a) a qualified medical practitioner, other than a member of a therapeutic abortion committee for any hospital, who in good faith uses in an accredited or approved hospital any means for the purpose of carrying out his intention to procure the miscarriage of a female person, or
(b) a female person who, being pregnant, permits a qualified medical practitioner to use in an accredited or approved hospital any means for the purpose of carrying out her intention to procure her own miscarriage, if, before the use of those means, the therapeutic abortion committee for that accredited or approved hospital, by a majority of the members of the committee and at a meeting of the committee at which the case of the female person has been reviewed,
(c) [a therapeutic abortion committee or approved hospital] has by certificate in writing stated that in its opinion the continuation of the pregnancy of the female person would or would be likely to endanger her life or health, and
(d) [a therapeutic abortion committee or approved hospital] has caused a copy of that certificate to be given to the qualified medical practitioner.[120]

Yet, as discussed further below, the Supreme Court of Canada (SCOC) struck down section 287 since the time-consuming procedures outlined in the exemption forced women to wait for a substantial period, causing further health risks due to the later abortion and thus infringing the right to security of the person.[121] Since the legislature failed to revise the clause, Canada no longer had any ban on abortion. In 2019, Parliament officially repealed it.

Viewed from this comparative perspective, the Japanese approach to abortion is unique. Most countries that forbid it list certain exceptions to the ban in their criminal or penal codes. Only a few do not, Japan among them. Of course, a doctor who performs an abortion could contend that he or she was engaging in "lawful professional conduct," which is legal under the Criminal Code, but the woman cannot avail herself of this defence. On the other hand, the Mother's Body Protection Act allows ATP – abortion – under certain limited circumstances. Its provisions are roughly in line with those of many other countries, which permit abortion only when the life or health of the mother could be endangered or when the pregnancy is the result of rape. The inclusion of "economic reasons" is unusual and could be controversial. As we saw, this is a legacy of the Eugenic Protection Act of 1948, which attempted to cope with severe food shortages and a sudden spike in births. Yet, apparently, it does provide limited leeway for doctors to provide an abortion during the early phase of pregnancy.

Nevertheless, in practice, early abortion is virtually free for the asking in Japan: designated doctors never question or verify a woman's reason for seeking one. Even if the reason is somewhat unclear or confusing, most doctors are kind enough to convert it into legitimate grounds for ATP. If the abortion does not satisfy the strict requirements of the Mother's Body Protection Act, the woman who asks for it and the doctor who performs it are technically violating the Criminal Code. However, they are highly unlikely to be arrested, charged, or convicted for their actions.

The Gap between Legal Text and Practice

As long as abortion remains so freely available, there may not be much to complain about, which probably explains why the abortion ban has prompted so little discussion in Japan.

However, the huge gap that exists between the text of the statute and actual practice is problematic from the perspective of the rule of law. Criminal statutes need to be unambiguous. If they are not, they could potentially violate the mandate of due process under article 31 of the Constitution of Japan.[122] The abortion ban in the Criminal Code is almost meaningless in practice, and therefore, serious questions could be raised as to its constitutionality. Moreover, the ATP requirements in the Mother's Body Protection Act, which are supposed to define the legal exceptions from the general ban on abortion, have been construed quite differently from what is reasonably inferred from the provisions themselves. This too raises the question of constitutionality.

Furthermore, whether to enforce these statutes is left entirely to the discretion of government officials. Prosecutors make the decision of whether to file charges for violations of the Criminal Code, and the MHLW chooses whether to bring a disciplinary action against a physician. So long as they are reluctant to enforce the ban as it is written, women will possess some practical freedom. But it springs from the merciful exercise of discretion by government officials.

The gap between text and practice exists in other areas of Japanese society. Moreover, since Japanese society and culture often emphasize appearance while leaving actual practice less constricted, it may be said that this gap is "culturally consistent and understandable" from the Japanese standpoint.[123] Furthermore, the approach to abortion may be seen as serving "a hortatory purpose; it does not condone disrespect for the sanctity of prenatal life; it admonishes that abortion is a serious matter, allowable only in very special circumstances." Meanwhile, the law, as applied, largely leaves the abortion decision up to the persons who are most immediately concerned, allowing them "to bend, stretch, finesse, even disregard the values articulated in the written law, but it does not allow them to gloat over it or claim social justification for doing so."[124] This approach could also be seen as enabling society to demonstrate respect for conflicting sets of values and to balance social interests with the private desire of the pregnant woman, denying in principle that abortion is purely a private matter but leaving the decision itself to the private choice of the woman.[125]

Nevertheless, such a huge discrepancy between legal text and actual practice denies the expectation expressed in written law and affords room for conduct that is banned under it. If written law does little more than pay lip service to an ideal, only to be undermined by contrary practice, it is nothing but a cover. It is doubtful that such a situation can be justified.

In addition, the semantic sleight of hand that masks the cover-up is intriguing. Abortion is illegal, but the artificial termination of pregnancy is not, despite the fact that they are the same thing. Ultimately, by reserving "abortion" for the Criminal Code and "artificial termination of pregnancy" for the Mother's Body Protection Act, Japanese law gives the impression that somehow there is no conflict or contradiction between them.

Rights for Women and Government Policy

Moreover, abortion is not a legally guaranteed right in Japan. Under the Mother's Body Protection Act, its availability is entirely at the discretion of the designated doctor. The woman does not have a right to demand it. Abortion is provided as a medical service, and therefore at least theoretically, is available only under certain conditions and only as supplied by certain qualified medical professionals. If the request for ATP is denied, there is no legal recourse to seek redress.

Determining the timeframe in which an abortion is permissible is also left to the MHLW. As mentioned, the Eugenic Protection Act initially authorized ATP before the twenty-eight-week mark of pregnancy, but this was later reduced to before twenty-four weeks and is now set at before twenty-two weeks.[126] The MHLW can decide the viability without any limitations, and it makes this determination simply by issuing a notification. This is highly questionable.

Furthermore, the availability of abortion has been heavily influenced by government population policy and more broadly by the economic considerations of society.[127] As discussed earlier, when the government felt the need to increase the population, it restricted abortion. When it felt the need to limit the population, it made abortion much easier to get. This means that obtaining an abortion depends on the priorities of the government and the economic and population policies of the moment. Given this, the status of abortion in Japan is fragile.[128]

Practical Difficulties

In addition, though abortion is so freely granted in Japan, various hurdles may impede its attainment, which raises serious questions about its accessibility. In Japan, there is no family doctor system (everyone can go directly to a specialist, even in large hospitals), and though there are some exceptions, licensed physicians can operate at clinics or hospitals with any specialty (there is no general family practice and no legal limitations on the areas in which a doctor can practice). As a result, a woman who wants an abortion will need to start with a gynecologist. For many, this will be a new experience, prompted solely by the unhappy discovery that they are pregnant. Visiting a gynecologist can be somewhat fraught, since anyone who learns of it could see it as a clear indication of pregnancy or as evidence that the woman is seeking ATP, which is especially devastating for those in rural areas.

Moreover, becoming a gynecologist does not automatically qualify a doctor to perform ATP, and the requirements listed in the Mother's Body Protection Act are rather demanding.[129] As a result, the number of designated doctors who can provide it is limited. In one case, two doctors who worked in a gynecology hospital performed ATP without designation, resulting in the death of a pregnant woman. They were arrested and sent to the prosecutor for performing a professional abortion.[130] Both were licensed physicians, but they may nevertheless face criminal punishment.

Facilities that can offer ATP are also regulated by the Mother's Body Protection Act. Basically, they must possess hospital equipment and be capable of caring for hospitalized patients.[131] Of course, this requirement was added to cover patients who develop complications after the procedure. But because of it, outpatient clinics are practically prohibited from providing ATP. This limits the number of facilities that can.[132]

Although the location of designated doctors and approved facilities is not published, it is a fair guess that most tend to cluster in cities.[133] Given this, many women who live in rural areas may have difficulty in getting access to them.

As mentioned, ATP for economic reasons is not covered by the national health insurance system, which means that the patient pays the cost.[134] The amount will vary, but it can be a serious barrier. And there is no government support to offset it.

Furthermore, many women who have had ATP retain feelings of guilt.[135] They often feel sorry for the unborn fetus because they could not bring it to life. This guilty conscience resulted in the custom of commemorating unborn babies by creating a baby Buddha or engaging in *mizuko kuyō*, a ritual involving prayers for their safety and happiness.[136] Many women also want to hide the fact that they resorted to ATP. Although it is lawful and nothing to be ashamed of, many nonetheless feel a sense of shame.[137]

All of this can make ATP difficult. It is virtually free in practice, but the decision is not a simple one and the service may not be easily accessible.

The Future of the Abortion Ban

The Rapid Decline of the Birthrate

The future of abortion in Japan is uncertain. Seicho-no-ie, the conservative religious group that encouraged the government to restrict it, has now grown into the Nippon Kaigi (Japan Conference), a very powerful right-wing think-tank with strong ties to former prime minister Shinzo Abe and other nationalist LDP politicians.[138] Yet, there is a more compelling impetus for the government to reconsider its abortion policy: the serious decline in the birthrate.

As we will examine more closely in Chapter 6, the birthrate is rapidly declining in Japan, which will cause various social problems in future. The government has thus been forced to promote childbirth. One way of achieving this could involve placing limits on abortion, especially ATP for economic reasons. For example, Seiko Noda, who was the LDP general council chairperson in 2013, once suggested that the huge number of ATP needed to be reconsidered as a countermeasure to the dropping birthrate.[139] Some criticized her remark as a call to ban ATP performed for economic reasons.[140] Evidently, her intent was to encourage adoption or the creation of an economic measure to alleviate the financial burden of raising children.[141] Even so, in its efforts to bolster the childbirth, the government could easily be tempted to eliminate economic reasons as a justification for ATP.

Of course, there are many ways of promoting childbirth. As we will see, the government has already provided a financial incentive in the shape of a grant, hoping to make having an additional child a bit easier. However, this measure has not had a significant impact.

Facilitating adoption is perhaps another option, which involves both encouranging women to give up a baby for adoption rather than having an abortion, as well as encouraging the general public to adopt more.[142] As noted earlier, it is not common in Japan, and there is widespread prejudice against adopted children. As a result, many women are reluctant to surrender their babies, and few families will take them. The government has introduced many legal reforms to conceal the fact of adoption, including the special adoption procedure discussed in Chapter 4,[143] but there is a limit on what it can do. Currently, there is no ban on discriminating against an adopted child. The government should streamline the adoption process, making it easier to surrender babies and for families to take them (subject of course to tight regulation of eligibility and ongoing supervision).[144] But it should also introduce civil rights legislation or human rights legislation to prohibit unreasonable discrimination, including against an adopted child. Since it has done none of this, naturally the number of adopted children has not risen significantly.

In any event, whether these measures actually could increase childbirth is somewhat unclear. If the government needs to adopt more efficient and effective measures to promote it, it should probably concentrate on changing society as a whole, which is a much more challenging task. This is a reason why some people focus on the quick fix of tightening the eligibility for ATP.

The Dignity of the Fetus

Moreover, there is growing concern over the dignity of the fetus. The current Criminal Code ban on abortion is grounded in the belief that the fetus is not a person who deserves to be protected as a human and that it becomes a person once it is born.[145] Nevertheless, the code forbids abortion on the premise that the fetus has a legal interest that is separate from the mother's and that it deserves to be protected against termination.[146] Thus, it could be seen as a potential human.

But its legal status presents somewhat complicated questions. The Civil Code provides that a person acquires legal rights upon birth,[147] but it regards the fetus as already having some rights, such as for the purpose of inheritance[148] and the right to seek damage awards.[149] However, there is a complicated issue with respect to criminal law. Since the killing of a "person" is homicide,[150] killing a pregnant woman could constitute homicide of the mother but not of the fetus. Nevertheless, when a newborn died because its mother had been poisoned at a chemical factory, the case went before the Supreme Court of Japan (SCOJ). Viewing the fetus as a part of her body, the SCOJ held that the poisoning of the mother was an injury to the fetus as well, thus upholding the punishment of the factory managers, who were charged with professional negligence causing an injury that resulted in the death of the fetus.[151] This ruling aroused fierce controversy over the adequacy of accepting an injury to a fetus as a justification for criminal punishment.[152]

Constitutional academics have been somewhat ambivalent on whether a fetus is a person in the constitutional sense. In the United States, the SCOTUS once ruled in *Roe* that it was not.[153] Even so, it held that the states have a compelling interest to protect the potential life of a fetus after it reaches viability – once it becomes capable of surviving outside of the uterus.

The SCOTUS however came to reject this viability criteria and came to accept that the state could have a legitimate interest in protecting the prenatal life of the fetus in *Dobbs v Jackson Women's Health Organization*.[154] It looks like the SCOTUS now denies that the Constitution defines when the life begins or when the fetus's prenatal life deserves to be protected by the States as humans.

On the other hand, the Federal Constitutional Court of Germany (FCCG) held that the fetus is entitled to human dignity as protected by the Basic Law.[155] It added that the government has a constitutional duty to protect its life even against the mother by using criminal law.[156]

In Japan, some commentators argue that a fetus deserves to be protected as a person from the moment of conception.[157] They criticize the arbitrary distinction between a fetus and a person upon birth.[158] They also reject viability as a critical criterion to distinguish a fetus from a person as being scientifically ambivalent and lacking in objectivity.[159] As a result, they contend that a fetus should be viewed as a person immediately upon conception and then try to accommodate this right against the right of the mother to have an abortion.[160] This view could accept ATP but might question its permissibility in certain instances, especially when it is requested for economic reasons.[161]

A growing concern over human dignity and the potential life of the fetus may thus force the legislature to rethink the status of the fetus and the whole abortion scheme.

Discriminatory Abortions
Furthermore, the permissive abortion practice in Japan has provoked concern, especially when a disabled fetus is involved. The Eugenic Protection Act encouraged aborting such a fetus. But disabled persons banded

together, insisted that it could not be justified, and demanded that it be discontinued.[162] As a result, ATP for genetic reasons was removed from the list. In actuality, however, it remains quite common, though the original eugenicist impetus no longer applies, and criticism of this practice is intensifying.[163]

This issue has become more serious with the widespread use of non-invasive prenatal testing (NIPT) or non-invasive prenatal genetic testing.[164] Before its advent, genetic abnormalities in a fetus could be confirmed solely via amniocentesis, but because this involves collecting fluid from the uterus and is thus invasive, women often chose to forego it. By contrast, NIPT consists of a simple blood test, and many women have opted for it. Concerned with its accuracy and the tough choices that women must sometimes make after learning of their results, the MHLW, together with five concerned associations, published guidelines to limit its availability to certified testing institutions and to certain categories of patients. It also mandated that they receive professional counselling.[165] Yet, growing numbers of gynecologists began to use foreign testing organizations rather than the MHLW-certified equivalents and also offered NIPT without counselling.[166] In response, the Japan Society of Obstetrics and Gynecology (JSOG) decided to permit a much larger number of gynecologists to use NIPT, though with some restrictions.[167] This decision heightened concerns since 96.5 percent of women who learned via NIPT that their fetus could potentially have a genetic abnormality and who then tested positive through amniocentesis chose abortion.[168]

Furthermore, if a woman really does have the right to reproduce, should she not be allowed to choose the sex of the baby? In some instances, there are good medical reasons for this, such as when she has a hereditary disease that is most likely to manifest in a certain sex. However, non-medical reasons could raise serious questions about sexual discrimination. NIPT can show the genetic abnormalities of the fetus during pregnancy. Moreover, the pre-implantation genetic testing, or pre-implantation genetic diagnosis (PGD), which tests embryos for abnormal chromosomes before they are transferred to the uterus, can offer other information on genetics of the embryos, including the gender. So far, the JSOG has allowed NIPT as well as PGD only for medical reasons.[169] But there is nothing to prevent a pregnant woman from asking for ATP because of the sex of the fetus, and some Japanese companies do use foreign testing institutions to provide NIPT testing, apparently to allow for ATP based on the sex of the fetus.[170] The wide availability of sex-selective ATP prompts concern that a couple could potentially abort female fetuses until they finally conceive a boy, or select an embryo with a male gene for IVF, resulting in an extreme imbalance between men and women.[171]

All of this may lead ultimately to the question of whether women should be allowed to have a baby that suits their preferences. If they do have an unfettered right to abortion, the leap to the right to have whatever baby they choose may not be very great. Then, with the spectre of the designer baby looming on the horizon, we need to decide where to draw the line.

If society does not accept the termination of a pregnancy because a fetus has a disability or is of the wrong sex, the government should enforce the Mother's Body Protection Act to preclude abortion for discriminatory reasons. The legislature may need to clearly prohibit these practices through the statute rather than simply leaving the decision to the judgment of doctors.[172]

Abortion and the Right Not to Be Forced to Have a Child

The Constitutional Right to Abortion: A Comparative Perspective
In light of the uncertain future, it is essential to go back to the foundation for decisions on abortion. We need to start from a place where sexual autonomy is protected by the Constitution and confirm that it includes the right to have a child as well as the right not to be forced to have one. The right to abortion is precisely the latter. Regardless of why she is pregnant, a woman should not be forced to give birth. In this sense, we need to start from the premise that she has a constitutional right to abortion.

Although the permissible scope of abortion is a contentious matter throughout the world, surprisingly it is mostly debated in the legislative and political process, not in terms of constitutional law. However, the United States, Canada, and Germany have raised serious constitutional questions regarding the permissibility of the abortion ban. And all three countries ended up adopting quite different approaches under their

Constitutions. The differences in these countries show the path that Japan could have followed.

The United States inherited the British common law system, which permitted abortion only before the baby quickened (began to move). However, during the colonial period and after the War of Independence, it was relatively free.[173] Gradually, with the development of medical knowledge and medical professions, increasing numbers of states banned it. By the 1880s, the criminal code or penal code of virtually every American state disallowed abortion, unless there were a compelling reason to save the life (and health) of the mother.[174] During the 1960s, however, with the surge in women's liberation movements, some states liberalized it.[175] Some went on to remove criminal punishment during early pregnancy. But others were more reluctant to change.

In 1973, the SCOTUS in *Roe v Wade* struck down the abortion ban in the Texas Penal Code,[176] which prohibited abortion unless it were necessary to save the life of the mother.[177] Although the Constitution does not explicitly guarantee the right to abortion, the SCOTUS held that it was included in the "liberty" protected under the Fourteenth Amendment, which protects such liberty against unreasonable deprivation and infringement without due process of law.[178] The SCOTUS did not accept the argument of the plaintiff that the right to abortion was absolute, leaving no room for government regulation.[179] However, it held that the right was a "fundamental right" that could not be restricted, under strict scrutiny, unless the restriction served compelling government interests and was narrowly tailored to serve them alone.[180] The SCOTUS found two possible state interests to regulate abortion: first, the protection of the life and safety of the pregnant woman and, second, the protection of the fetus as a possible human being.[181] It thereby rejected the argument that a fetus becomes a human at conception and deserves to be protected as such.[182] Under the Constitution, the SCOTUS held, a fetus becomes a person only after birth, at which point it qualifies for protection. However, the court admitted that states have a legitimate interest in securing the potential life of the fetus.[183] It held that the two interests became "compelling" at different stages in the pregnancy.[184] The first, protecting the life and health of the woman, becomes compelling only after the first trimester, since abortion is safe before this juncture is reached, and the woman and her doctor can freely determine whether it is appropriate.[185] After the first trimester, the state can regulate abortion to the extent necessary to protect the life and health of a mother.[186] The second state interest in protecting the potential life of the fetus becomes compelling only after the fetus becomes viable, capable of independent survival.[187] Once that occurs, the state can prohibit abortion if it wishes.[188] In *Roe*, the SCOTUS suggested that the fetus could become viable between the twenty-four to twenty-eight weeks.[189] It thus struck down the Texas ban, as it was overbroad.[190]

The *Roe* decision is a continuation of the developing SCOTUS jurisprudence on the right to privacy. In 1965, the SCOTUS in *Griswold v Connecticut* struck down a legislative ban on the use of contraceptives as unconstitutional.[191] Although it reasoned that an individual has a privacy interest and the right to use contraceptives at home was included in the privacy right, it was reluctant to invoke the due process clause directly. However, it did so in *Roe* to protect the right to abortion by deeming it to be a privacy right.

This decision triggered a series of SCOTUS rulings that questioned various state restrictions on abortion.[192] Although strongly welcomed by advocates for abortion (who became known as "pro-choice"), *Roe* was condemned by its critics (later known as "pro-life"). As a result, abortion became the single-most controversial constitutional issue during the 1970s and 1980s, and it has become one of the most contentious topics in the United States.[193]

In 1992, amid increasing demands from conservatives that *Roe* be reversed, the SCOTUS ruled in *Planned Parenthood of Southeastern Pennsylvania v Casey* that it accepted the basic holding of *Roe* because it was a well-established precedent.[194] In taking this step, it confirmed that the right to abortion was constitutional.[195] Nevertheless, the court no longer believed that it was also a fundamental right, which would automatically trigger strict scrutiny for its restriction. Instead, the SCOTUS allowed state regulation unless it imposed an "undue burden" on a woman who sought an abortion, thus abandoning strict scrutiny and the strict trimester framework.[196] As a result, the SCOTUS came to accord less protection for the right to abortion.[197] Encouraged, a growing number of states introduced various limitations on abortion, hoping that they would be sustained by the SCOTUS.[198] A woman's right to abortion came to be quite tightly regulated in many American states.[199]

In 2021, however, the SCOTUS first upheld the Texas abortion law in *Whole Women's Health v Jackson*,[200] which prohibited physicians from "knowingly perform[ing] or induc[ing] an abortion on a pregnant woman if the physician detected a fetal heartbeat for the unborn child" unless a medical emergency prevents compliance. Instead of imposing criminal punishment, the law directed enforcement through "private civil actions" culminating in injunctions and statutory damages awards against those who perform or assist prohibited abortions. The SCOTUS did not find any of the state officials, including Attorney General, has any enforcement power and thus rejected the pre-enforcement suit.

Then, in 2022, in *Dobbs*,[201] the SCOTUS finally came to accept the error in the *Roe* holding and reversed it entirely. Now, the SCOTUS declares that the right to have an abortion is not constitutionally protected, and the issue of abortion should be left to the people and their representatives. As we saw in the Chapter 1, the SCOTUS now focuses exclusively on the history to see whether a particular unenumerated right can be accepted as a part of the liberty protected by the Due Process Clause of the Fourteenth Amendment. Reviewing the history of abortion regulation in the United States,[202] the SCOTUS now found that in the common law abortion is a crime at least after "quickening." In the United Kingdom, indeed, abortion was a crime and, although a pre-quickening abortion was not itself considered homicide, it does not follow that abortion was permissible in common law – much less that abortion was a legal right. The historical record in the United States is similar. However, during the nineteenth century, the vast majority of states enacted statutes criminalizing abortion at all stages of pregnancy. By 1868, the year the Fourteenth Amendment was ratified, three-quarters of the states, or twenty-eight out of thirty-seven, had enacted statutes making abortion a crime even if it was performed before quickening. Of the nine states that had not yet criminalized abortion at all stages, all but one did so by 1910. By the end of the 1950s, according to the *Roe* court's own count, statutes in all but four states and the District of Columbia prohibited abortion "however and whenever performed, unless done to save or preserve the life of the mother." At the time *Roe* was decided, a substantial majority – thirty States – still prohibited abortion at all stages except to save the life of the mother. And though *Roe* discerned a "trend toward liberalization" in about "one- third of the States," those states still criminalized some abortions and regulated them more stringently than *Roe* would allow. The SCOTUS thus concluded that "[t]he inescapable conclusion is that a right to abortion is not deeply rooted in the Nation's history and traditions. On the contrary, an unbroken tradition of prohibiting abortion on pain of criminal punishment persisted from the earliest days of the common law until 1973."

Therefore, the *Dobbs* case reversed *Roe* and *Casey*, which confirmed it, and return back the decision to the state legislatures. At the time of writing, abortion is banned in at least eight states as laws restricting the procedure take effect following the Supreme Court's decision to overturn *Roe v Wade*. Another four states now ban abortion after six weeks of pregnancy, before most women know they are pregnant.[203] It is expected that roughly the half of all states will introduce a total ban or the most restrictive abortion regulations.

In Canada, the Criminal Code banned abortion except when a committee in an accredited hospital found it to be necessary.[204] In *R. v Morgentaler*, the Supreme Court of Canada (SCOC) struck down this prohibition.[205] The plaintiff invoked *Roe*, yet the SCOC refused to follow the example of the SCOTUS and announce a constitutional right of privacy, including the right to abortion.[206] Nevertheless, it found that the exemption included in the Criminal Code was too narrow and too hard to satisfy. Days could pass before the hospital committee granted permission for the abortion, diminishing its safety and thus infringing the woman's right to security of the person.[207] Since all the requirements were not justified, the SCOC concluded that the abortion ban in the Criminal Code was unconstitutional.[208] Although it never indicated that it wished to preclude abortion regulations altogether, the legislature failed to enact revisions, thus making the abortion ban invalid. Thereafter, in Canada, there was no criminal ban on abortion.[209] And it was finally removed from the Criminal Code in 2019.

On the other hand, the German Basic Law, which is the Constitution for Germany, prioritized human dignity in its first article and thereby made it a supreme constitutional value.[210] Although abortion was once prohibited in Germany, the legislature of West Germany legalized early abortion during the 1960s and 1970s. Upon receiving a request for review, the FCCG held the legalization of abortion to be unconstitutional in 1975.[211] It concluded that the fetus was entitled to enjoy human dignity and that the government had a constitutional duty to protect its dignity even against the mother.[212] Although there could be various ways to protect the fetus, the FCCG held that in this case the legislature was constitutionally mandated to prohibit abortion by criminal punishment since the fetus had no power to defend itself.[213] If abortion were necessary to avert a danger to the life of the mother or the serious impairment of her health, it should be lawful. But other than that, the legislature should not be allowed to permit it.[214] Where legitimate reasons existed for an abortion, the FCCG agreed that the legislature could refrain from imposing punishment on women.[215] Nevertheless, it concluded that the legislature should not be allowed to make abortion lawful.[216]

After the unification of East and West Germany, the legislature was forced to reconcile two Criminal Codes. That of East Germany was more liberal toward early abortion, so the legislature hit on a compromise. This too was struck down by the FCCG, which confirmed its original decision.[217] In the end, the unified German legislature managed to revise the Criminal Code and come up with a workable compromise.[218]

The Constitutional Right to Abortion Must Be Accepted
This brief survey shows that the constitutional approach to abortion can be significantly varied. However, as stated initially, if sexual autonomy is to be protected by the Constitution, it should include freedom of choice in matters of childbirth. In turn, that freedom should include not only the right to have a child but also not to have one. The latter should include the right to use contraceptives and to access abortion.

It is true that the constitutional right not to be forced to have a child is not officially recognized worldwide. The right to an abortion was squarely recognized by the SCOTUS in *Roe* in the United States, but now *Roe* has been reversed. The SCC, while striking down the Canadian abortion ban, did not accept the right to an abortion explicitly. The FCCG, while allowing the state to legalize certain abortions and to refrain from imposing criminal punishments on pregnant mothers under certain circumstances, did not make it clear whether the woman had a constitutional right to an abortion. Nevertheless, the right not to be forced to have a child, including the right to an abortion, is an essential part of sexual autonomy and needs to be squarely recognized as a constitutional right.

Although there is no prohibition on contraceptive medication and devices in Japan, drugs and medical devices must be approved by the MHLW. As mentioned, the government dragged its feet for many years before finally approving the pill. This could potentially be seen as an unconstitutional infringement of the right to prevent pregnancy. However, if the unwillingness were based on sound medical reasons, the claim about unconstitutionality would probably fail. On the other hand, if the delay were rooted in an unwillingness to provide women with a choice or a belief that the pill would encourage promiscuity, the argument about unconstitutionality would have a better chance of succeeding.

The pill cannot be obtained in Japan without a prescription, and many women feel uncomfortable in using it. Challenging the prescription requirement as an unconstitutional infringement of a woman's right to use contraceptives could at least be possible. If the requirement is grounded in a medical concern, it would probably be sustained. However, the pill has proven safe and reliable worldwide, so it seems there is no legitimate reason to require a prescription in Japan.[219]

Should all contraception be available free of charge to all women? Does the Constitution mandate the government to provide it for free? Probably not. The government is not required to manufacture or obtain birth control medication or devices and distribute them free of cost. As long as their price remains reasonable, these tasks could justifiably be left to the market. However, if the price becomes too high, one could argue that women are being prevented from accessing birth control, and the government should be obliged to step in.

Moreover, the current situation, in which health insurance covers the pill for medical reasons but not contraception, is questionable. Since the Constitution protects the right not to be forced to have a child, using a contraceptive should come under that heading. Then, it could be argued that exempting the pill for contraception from the insurance scheme while covering it for other medical reasons (such as the treatment of illness) is highly unreasonable.

For its part, the abortion situation is more complicated than the situation involving contraceptives. In Japan, feminists have been somewhat ambivalent about the right to abortion.[220] Although they oppose the Criminal Code ban and the limitations on ATP in the Mother's Body Protection Act, they typically frame their arguments in terms of "freedom of abortion" or "reproductive freedom," not as the "right to abortion."[221] This springs largely from their reluctance to assert the right to abort a disabled fetus as a constitutional right, thereby leaving themselves open to accusations of condoning discrimination against disabled persons.[222] As a result, they chose to present the issue as one of freedom from government interference: the government has no right to determine whether a pregnant woman can or cannot ask for an abortion.

But this choice is also partly due to the moral dilemma that many women experience when they terminate a pregnancy. As we saw above, they can feel guilty for taking this step.[223] Although legally speaking, they are free to do so, the sense of culpability may persist. This situation is all the more distressing given the inadequacy of contraception in Japan and the fact that abortion is often the only available method of birth control. The sense of guilt makes it difficult to assert that a fetus is only part of a woman's body, that it does not deserve to be protected as a potential life, or that the woman has a constitutional right to obtain an abortion and will not face any responsibility if she does.[224]

Therefore, many Japanese feminists, while opposing the Criminal Code ban, are still reluctant to invoke the Constitution as a justification for ATP, especially discriminatory ATP.[225] This has made their arguments somewhat weaker than those of their American sisters. Japanese women have opposed attempts to limit access to ATP, sometimes successfully, but they have refrained from structuring their arguments in terms of constitutional rights.[226]

Although their hesitancy is understandable, there are appropriate times to advance this argument, especially given that the government currently feels such a strong need to increase the birthrate. Indeed, scholars who study constitutional matters accept such a constitutional right as a right to pursue happiness,[227] which is protected under article 13 of the Constitution of Japan.[228] Moreover, article 24 of the Constitution features a special provision on family, mandating that family law must be based on individual dignity and the essential equality of both sexes.[229] This provision could be interpreted as protecting the constitutional right to create a family by allowing a couple to marry and define their own relationship, including whether and how to have children.[230] In other words, the constitutional right to abortion is already well accepted by constitutional academics. As a result, it is not such a leap for feminists to accept such a constitutional right as well.[231]

Should we follow the example of the FCCG and assert that a fetus becomes a human being at conception and that it is entitled to receive human dignity? Or should we follow the SCOTUS in *Roe* and conclude that the fetus is not constitutionally a person who possesses constitutionally protected rights but that the states could have a compelling interest to protect the potential life after it's deemed viable? Or should we follow *Dobbs* in rejecting the argument that the Constitution does not allow the people and the states to decide when personhood starts and admit that the state has a legitimate interest in protecting all prenatal life at all stages of pregnancy? This question is very difficult to answer, but an embryo may not necessarily be securely anchored in the uterus and therefore is not always capable of growth, although many people may see the moment of conception as magical. Moreover, miscarriages do commonly occur. In that sense, the fetus is still a potential life and not a person. The legislature should be allowed to protect this potential life by, for instance, enabling the fetus to inherit the estate of a parent who dies before its birth. The government should also be allowed to impose criminal punishment for killing a fetus. However, when the mother decides to terminate a pregnancy, she is exercising her constitutional right and should not be subject to punishment for doing so on the basis that human life starts from the time of conception and that any destruction of such prenatal life should not be allowed.

Permissible Restrictions on Abortion

Even when we accept that the right to abortion should be constitutionally protected, it is not absolute and is subject to necessary and minimum regulations. We need to ensure, however, that they truly are legitimate regulations and that they can be justified.[232]

As we saw, *Roe* accepted two state interests to regulate on abortion: the state interest to protect the health and safety of pregnant mothers and the state interest to protect the potential life of the fetus. *Roe* thus allowed abortion regulation after the second trimester when the abortion could be considered dangerous for women and banned abortions after the fetus became viable except to save the life of the mother. The trimester system adopted by *Roe* was later abandoned by *Casey*, and it was replaced by the "undue burden" test. And now *Dobbs* has totally reversed *Roe* and *Casey*. In *Dobbs*, the SCOTUS explicitly rejects the reliance on the viability of the fetus to draw the line[233] and applies the regular rationality review on the permissibility of abortion regulation during all stages of pregnancy. It sustained the Mississippi abortion regulation based on several legitimate state interests as rational: "respect for and preservation of prenatal life at all stages of development ... the protection of maternal health and safety; the elimination of particularly gruesome or barbaric medical procedures; the preservation of the integrity of the medical profession; the mitigation of fetal pain; and the prevention of discrimination on the basis of race, sex, or disability."[234] The SCOTUS also rejects the "undue burden" test as well.[235]

Nevertheless, the risk of miscarriage is especially higher in the early stages of pregnancy, and the abortion procedure is relatively safe during early stages of pregnancy. In this regard, it does make sense to make a distinction based on the different stages of pregnancy. If we could view the right to an abortion as an integral part of the right of sexual autonomy, then any restriction on it would need to be justified not just as a rational means to accomplish some legitimate interests, but as an essential and necessary measure to achieve legitimate compelling interests.

Viewed from this perspective, the Japan Criminal Code's blanket ban on abortion is hardly justifiable, even though in practice the procedure is freely available during early pregnancy. Since it is a matter of the constitutional rights of a woman, prohibiting it and threatening her with criminal punishment is utterly unconstitutional. We cannot just leave this issue as a practical freedom despite the theoretical illegality.[236]

Moreover, the Mother's Body Act allows ATP only in limited circumstances, although, in practice, it is virtually unimpeded during early pregnancy. There is no legitimate interest to restrict lawful ATP during the early stage. In addition, the mandate that ATP can be performed only by a designated doctor in a designated facility is too restrictive. Furthermore, the current situation in which the termination of pregnancy must always involve surgery is unreasonable and unjustified. The government should be constitutionally mandated to approve the abortion pill, and all licensed physicians should be allowed to use it.[237] In the end, the best course would be to make the drug easily available in pharmacies without a prescription and at reasonable prices (if there are risks in the use of the abortion pill, the drugstore may be required to keep the product behind the counter, and its pharmacist may be obliged to provide full information about its risks to anyone who purchases it or to mandate that customers take it in the presence of the pharmacist).

Only with respect to a late abortion, which can be risky and needs special surgical skill, should the government be permitted to introduce regulations to protect the life and health of the pregnant woman. Also, once the fetus becomes viable, the government should be allowed to prohibit an abortion for the sake of its potential life. However, this should not enable the government to decide when a lawful ATP should be allowed and when it is no longer permitted. If viability is a critical issue, that decision is best left to medical professionals, not to bureaucrats at the MHLW. The current practice, in which the ministry determines the timeframe for ATPs, is hardly justifiable. Also, the government should not be allowed to impose punishment when a late abortion must be performed to save the life and health of the mother. Presently, it is lawful as an emergency action. But there is no explicit exemption in the Criminal Code or the Mother's Body Protection Act. It is imperative for the legislature to specifically exempt such cases from criminal punishment.

Does the government have a constitutional obligation to provide free abortion in all cases? As for contraceptives, it might be difficult to establish that the answer is yes. But since the right to abortion is a constitutional right, the government should at least include all abortions in the national health insurance scheme. Presently, it covers only medically necessary ATP, leaving all others to be paid for by the woman, a distinction that is unreasonable. Forcing women to shoulder the financial burden of the procedure is an infringement of their constitutional right to seek an abortion.

Abortion regulation in Japan requires radical change in order to survive constitutional scrutiny.

Sex, Childbirth, and the Government: Sexual Freedom, Freedom of Choice, and Population Policy

6

In Japan, the population is rapidly aging, whereas the birthrate is dropping. Hoping to increase childbirth, the government has generated various policies, which prompt a number of questions: Will they work? How will they affect sexual autonomy, can that impact be justified, and what are the limits? Are there alternatives?

In the past, the government regulated abortion mostly as a method of population control. As mentioned, however, this was strongly opposed, and, for now, it is unlikely to receive much support. Moreover, regulating abortion cannot radically increase the number of births, which is the goal. The government must come up with a new comprehensive plan to encourage population growth, one that is based on sexual autonomy and that necessitates sweeping changes to society. This will be a difficult task, but if it is not attempted, the government will not solve the present problem.

Rapid Aging and a Declining Birthrate

An Aging Population and Declining Childbirth

Japan is facing a difficult challenge: an aging society and a dropping birthrate. Although this is not unique to Japan, the problem is particularly pressing because Japan has an unprecedented proportion of seniors and one of the lowest birthrates in the world.[1]

The number of births has diminished for several decades. Although a baby boom occurred immediately after the Second World War, births have trended downward ever since.[2] After some fluctuations, the drop was constant from 1973 onward. For comparison, 2,678,792 children were born in 1947, whereas there were only 865,239 in 2019.[3] This pattern corresponds to a decline in the number of marriages. There were 934,170 marriages in 1947 but only 599,007 in 2019.[4] The total fertility rate (TFR), meaning the average number of children that would be born to a woman over her lifetime, was 4.54 in 1947 but only 1.36 in 2019.[5] It is estimated that if a population is to be maintained, its TFR must be 2.1.[6] Japan's TFR dropped below 2.1 in 1974 and has been declining ever since, which means that Japan is not producing enough children to replace its population. According to the 2015 national census, the total population in Japan was 127,094,745, a loss of 1,074,953 from the previous census of 2010.[7] The statistics indicate that the group between age sixty-five and sixty-nine, the first baby boomers, and the group between forty and forty-four, the second baby boomers, babies born to the first boomers, showed a significant increase, but that the population constantly declines after them.[8]

Further, Japanese society is rapidly aging. The estimated total population for 2019 was set at 126,170,000, among which 35,890,000 were seniors over age sixty-five, or 28.4 percent of the population.[9] By contrast, seniors accounted for only 5 percent of the population in 1950, but their numbers have steadily increased.[10] Projected statistics assume that the overall population will continue to decrease, reaching 99,7240,000 in 2053 and 88,080,000 in 2065. The percentage of seniors is estimated to rise to 33.3 in 2036 and 38.4 in 2065.[11] In other words, 1 in 3.0 people in Japan will be seniors in 2036, and 1 in 2.6 will be in 2065.[12] In 2065, seniors who are older than seventy-five are expected to account for 25.5 percent of the population.[13]

Japan currently has the highest percentage of seniors in the world,[14] and it also has one of the lowest fertility rates.[15]

Problems

Rapid aging and the declining birthrate have had a significant impact on Japanese society. For example, the size of the workforce has contracted. In 1990, individuals of working age (fifteen to sixty-four) made up 70 percent of the population, a figure that declined to 63 in 2015 and is expected to reach 52 in 2050.[16] Many businesses are already struggling to find enough staff to stay afloat. With the shrinking number of children, the working age population is estimated to drop below 70,000,000 in 2029 and to 45,290,000 by 2065.[17] As the situation progresses, Japanese companies will find it increasingly difficult to acquire sufficient staff and thus sustain the economy.

Further, the smaller population will inevitably reduce tax revenue for the government.[18] In an effort to cope, it will take the obvious step of pulling back on spending. Yet, the growing cohort of seniors will require increasing amounts of social security and medical assistance, as well as various other infrastructure. As a result, the government will very probably find itself on the horns of an unpleasant dilemma: whether to raise taxes or cut down on spending for seniors. Neither option is likely to be popular with the public, which could be damaging to the government.

This issue is perhaps most acute in connection with health care. It is well known that seniors are much more vulnerable than anyone else to illness and injury, necessitating huge medical spending. In Japan, every resident must contribute to the national health insurance fund.[19] As health care became increasingly expensive, the government had to adjust the payment level for the insurance, with the result that every patient now pays 30 percent of his or her health care costs. In other words, the mandatory insurance covers only 70 percent. In the past, the government covered all the medical costs of seniors. Nevertheless, the cost exceeded the insurance premium payment, necessitating the government subsidy. Anticipating that the cohort of elderly seniors would continue to expand, the government struggled to cope and finally decided to charge seniors a portion of the bill and to introduce special health insurance coverage for the elderly. Now, people over the age of seventy-five are categorized as elderly seniors and will pay 10 percent of the cost to see a doctor, whereas those between seventy and seventy-four will pay 20 percent as seniors.[20] The fund to cover all medical costs is maintained by a premium paid by residents or employees (28.3 percent) and employers (20.1 percent), government assistance (38.1 percent), and patients' own expenses (12.7 percent), with the government shouldering 25.9 percent of all spending in 2010.[21] The increase in the cost of care for elderly seniors and the need for support forced the government to spend huge amounts of tax money. The total medical cost in 2017 was JPY 43.7 trillion (roughly $US320 billion), 7.87 percent of GDP. Of this, the government paid JPY 10.8 trillion (about US$80 billion) (25.3 percent).[22] Obviously, as the population ages, the government's financial burden will become significantly heavier.

Further, in addition to medical spending, there is a pressing need to cover the cost of care for the elderly, such as building and maintaining group homes or care facilities, staffing them with medical professionals and care workers, or providing home care, all with some government assistance. This form of spending is rapidly increasing as well. Part of it is covered by health insurance,[23] but care for healthy seniors necessitates a different system. Traditionally, looking after seniors was a private matter, handled by families, and the younger generation had a duty to take care of the older one.[24] In the distant past, this may have made sense, since several generations of a family commonly lived together. However, once the nuclear family of parents and unmarried children became the norm, many seniors found themselves living alone. Children and grandchildren who live far away cannot look after them. As a result, the government introduced the mandatory elderly care insurance system for every resident in 1997.[25] Essentially, all residents over the age of forty are required to pay a premium to set up a fund for elder care, to which the government contributes as well.[26] When they themselves become old enough to require care, the fund covers most of the cost.[27]

All of this is expensive. In 2000, the total cost of care for seniors was only JPY 3.6 trillion (roughly $US27 billion). By 2016, it had jumped to JPY 10.4 trillion (about $US78 billion).[28] In 2000, 2.1 million seniors required care; in 2015, the figure had risen to 6.0 million. As their numbers are projected to expand from 33.0 million in 2015 to 36.6 million in 2025 and the total annual cost of their care is expected to be between JPY 18 and 21 trillion (roughly $US100 to $150 billion) in 2025.[29] The government will have to find some way of paying this bill.

Furthermore, the declining birthrate and shrinking workforce will have an immediate impact on the pension system. In the past, employees paid into a pension scheme that would cover their living expenses once they retired.[30] In fact, the system is cross-generational – contributions made by the current workforce fund the lives of people who have already retired. This arrangement is widely adopted elsewhere in the world, but with the dramatic increase of seniors and the declining number of workers, it will obviously become top-heavy – and unsustainable – at some point in the not very distant future.

In 1950, there was 1 senior per 12.1 working age individuals (from ages fifteen to sixty-five) in Japan; by 2015, the ratio had plummeted to 1 per only 2.3.[31] It is predicted to drop to 1 per 1.3 in 2065.[32] This means that in 2065 almost one employed person must support one senior, making the current system entirely unfeasible.

The total pension payout for 2019 was JPY 22.2 trillion (roughly US$160 billion). Of this, JPY 13.0 trillion (about US$97 billion) came from the government old-age pension scheme, and JPY 9.0 trillion (approximately US$67 billion) came from company pensions. The amount of payment was supposed to cover 61.7 percent of the average monthly salary of a male worker, which is JPY 357,000 (some US$2,700). It is a bit difficult to predict how much the government will need to pay to support the pension system. This will be determined by many variables, including how well the economy fares, whether salaries rise or fall, and whether the birthrate increases or decreases. The future estimated payments and coverage could be different depending on these variables–but something between JPY 25.0 and 19.9 trillion (roughly US$187 to $150 billion), covering 54.3 and 51.3 percent of the average salary in 2040, and something between JPY 32.7 and 18.8 trillion (about US$245 to $140 billion), covering 46.1 percent of the average salary in 2060.[33] Since the government shoulders half of this spending, it should be ready to disburse additional funds to address seniors' pensions in the future. In an effort to reform the system, it reduced the amount of pension payments and moved the starting age for payments from sixty to sixty-five. Currently, it estimates that it will be able to pay a pension of at least 50 percent of the average income made by a male worker before retirement, but many doubt that this is sustainable. Further delaying the age threshold for receiving pension payments, reducing the amount of the payment, and increasing the contribution to the plan have all been floated as possible solutions. Moreover, many people question whether the pension payment will provide a decent standard of living for retirees.[34]

Some countries have baseline public support systems for seniors, guaranteeing a minimum income to every senior. In Japan, this is provided by the welfare system. If, despite their best efforts, seniors cannot make ends meet, the government will add a welfare payment that is sufficient to secure a healthy and meaningful life.[35] Recipients are not expected to seek employment. Topping up the old-age pension cheque with a welfare stipend increases government expenditures.[36]

All of these measures necessitate an ever-increasing outlay on social security. In 2020, the budget allocation for social security was JPY 35.2 trillion (roughly US$260 billion), consuming 28.3 percent of the total general budget, which was JPY 126.8 trillion (about US$950 billion).[37] Social security expenses will probably expand to between JPY 140.2 and 140.6 trillion (approximately US$1 trillion) in 2025 and to a further JPY 188.2 to 190.0 trillion (about US$1.4 trillion) in 2040.[38]

The Diet has relied on government bonds to collect the necessary funds to cover its ever-increasing social security disbursement.[39] In 2020, only two-thirds of the total general budget of JPY 102.7 trillion (roughly US$770 billion) was covered by tax revenue, and 31.7 percent (JPY 32.6 trillion, about US$244 billion) relied on government bonds.[40] But since Japan's national debt has already reached JPY 932 trillion (about US$7 trillion),[41] which is close to 250 percent of its GDP and the highest among developed countries,[42] it is questionable whether relying on bonds will be enough to pay the bills. Clearly, the government must come up with a solution to the problem of a rapidly aging population combined with a declining birthrate. The clock is ticking. The government does not have the luxury of waiting for some miracle to fix this dilemma.

Increasing the Birthrate: Promoting Marriage and Childbirth

Past Government Measures
In 2003, feeling pressured to find a way of enlarging the birthrate, the government passed the Fundamental Act on Declining Childbirth

Countermeasures.[43] The Declining Childbirth Countermeasures Council, headed by the prime minister and consisting of appointed Cabinet members, was created to promote various measures adopted under the act. In 2007, the government established a state minister in charge of the declining birthrate. This is an ad hoc appointment established inside the Cabinet Office without clear statutory authorization, and it is up to the prime minister to maintain it. Since 2007, the prime ministers have continued this appointment. The Child and Child Raising Headquarters was founded in the Cabinet Office to implement various countermeasures.[44]

In 2014, the government compiled a Declining Childbirth Whitepaper, the most recent version of which was published in 2020.[45] The 2020 whitepaper summarized the current state of the birthrate, reviewed past countermeasures, and introduced the "New Outline of Declining Birthrate Countermeasures."[46]

As a guideline for government policies to implement various countermeasures adopted under the Fundamental Act, the outline had already been published in 2004, 2010, and 2015. The 2020 version appeared within the shocking context that the number of births had dipped to below 900,000 and the TFR had dropped to 1.36. Despite the significant impact of COVID-19, the government hoped to raise the TFR to 1.8.[47] To accomplish this, it emphasized marriage support, support for getting pregnant and giving birth, better working conditions for both men and women to reconcile work with child raising, social support for child raising offered through local communities, and financial aid for families with many children.

In short, it has attempted to promote marriage and childbirth.

Past Government Measures: Promotion of Marriage
Most young people probably expect to get married and raise a family at some point in their lives. However, the difficulty of meeting a suitable partner, a sense that there is no rush, insufficient monetary resources, and a desire to concentrate on work are among the primary reasons that delay or prevent marriage.[48] Aware of these barriers, the government has attempted to address them.

First, it is well known that economic instability and low wages are a significant impediment to marriage. The increasing numbers of informal workers (those lacking permanent positions) are poorly paid and will thus have difficulty in getting married.[49] Hoping to improve both their stability and wages through providing more permanent, full-time jobs, the government attempted to aid them in finding employment, provided work opportunities for "freeters" (who don't have regular or consistent work but who hop from job to job depending on availability and convenience), and facilitated jobs for new graduates. For instance, under the Labour Contract Act, it launched an initiative in which contractual employees who had held the same job for more than five years through renewals of their contract could ask to occupy the position on a permanent basis.[50] However, many employers scuttled this scheme by terminating the contract or refusing to renew it before the five-year deadline approached. The government was thus forced to issue specific instructions to prevent them from doing this. It also guaranteed part-time and fixed-term workers the same wage as permanent ones and enabled them to become permanent employees under the Improvement of Employment Management of Part-Time and Fixed-Term Workers Act.[51] However, it was merely providing administrative guidance and consultation services. In 2018, this statute was amended by the Act concerning the Adjustment of Relevant Acts to Promote the Way of Work Reform.[52] To enable fairness regardless of employment type, the amended act now provides for the elimination of discriminatory treatment and intensifies the employer's obligation to provide more fulsome explanations regarding the treatment of workers. It created an administrative alternative dispute resolution (ADR) procedure for settling disputes between employee and employer together with protection by the Dispatch Workers Act.[53]

It also supported various attempts by local governments and chambers of commerce to encourage marriage, such as supplying information through various means or hosting conferences. In addition, it funds matchmaking systems created by local governments and hosts various conferences that promote marriage. This kind of matchmaking is important because many young people cite difficulties in finding an appropriate partner as the prime reason for being single. The matchmaking will give them an opportunity to meet and find partners.

Further, the government implemented a "newlywed support program," partially funding local government efforts to help financially challenged newlyweds start their lives together, such as covering the cost of rent or moving.[54] This is an attempt to alleviate the financial burden of getting married and to promote moving into a new house after marriage. If the couple receive a wedding present in the shape of money from their parents or grandparents, the government will waive the donation tax.[55]

The government has established certain programs for youth to get them thinking about marriage and childbirth. High school students are given a "life planning" guide under the government Revitalization Plan.[56] This guide is an encouragement for young students to think about the future, including marriage and children.

Past Government Measures: Supporting Childbirth and Child Raising

In 1977, married couples felt that the ideal number of children was 2.61. But, as of 2015, this figure had declined to 2.32.[57] Evidently, married couples have chosen to welcome a smaller number of offspring. Moreover, the estimated number of children that they actually did have declined from 2.17 in 1977 to 2.01 in 2015.[58] The serious drop in the TFR is a culmination of the declining number of both marriages and births. The biggest reason for the fewer number of children is cost.[59] However, many couples want to have children but are infertile.[60]

To encourage the growth of families, the government founded the Comprehensive Child Raising Family Support Centre under the Mother and Child Health Protection Act[61] and the Children, Families and Pregnant Mothers Continuing Support Act.[62] The centre provides an "after-birth care program" and "pre-birth and post-birth support programs." The government also arranges medical checks for pregnant mothers, which are paid for through public funds.

The government tries to prevent the harassment of female workers due to pregnancy or childbirth and to provide for maternity protection under the Labour Standards Act, which prohibits dangerous work during pregnancy and guarantees pre-birth and after-birth leaves. A one-time subsidy of JPY 420,000 (roughly US$3,200) is available for mothers who give birth, although childbirth itself is not covered by the national health insurance system. Female workers who take pre-birth and after-birth leave will be exempt from paying social security premiums during that time. The government has attempted to help hospitals and family clinics by bolstering the number of gynecologists who specialize in pregnancy and childbirth.[63] It supported an increase in midwives and tried to increase the ranks of emergency and intensive-care medical professionals and medical facilities in cases of complications or for children who require intensive care.

Moreover, government support is available for infertility treatment and childbirth. Couples who spend large sums on treatments are eligible for a government subsidy to offset some of the cost. Further, as mentioned above, national health insurance has been extended to infertility treatments and ART/MAR.

Families whose income is under a certain amount receive child benefits from the government.[64] For instance, if a family has two children under age three and an income of less than JPY 9.6 million (roughly US$72,000), it will receive a monthly grant of JPY 15,000 (approximately US$112). If the children are between three and twelve, the grant will be JPY 10,000 (about US$75). If there are three or more children, it will be JPY 15,000 (about US$112). If the children are in junior high school, the grant is JPY 10,000 (roughly US$75). Families who supersede the income cut-off will be granted a flat JPY 5,000 (roughly US$37) per month. Additionally, the government has attempted to support kindergarten and childcare facility charges. It subsidizes the construction of homes that accommodate three generations and provides funding to grandparents to find a nearby house so that they can babysit their grandchildren. The government facilitates the provision of public housing geared for young families by providing support through the local government.

Further, it assists single parents by mandating local governments to prioritize the admittance of their children at daycare centres. If the parent cannot pick up and take care of the children, it provides helpers, offers financial consultation services, and promotes the opportunity to gather together or provide support. It aids single parents in securing better and more stable jobs, and it provides a child support benefit and single parent welfare loans. It has intensified child abuse prevention measures, especially for abuse that occurs in families.

The government promotes extra social support for children who are in its care and who typically are no longer a state responsibility once they turn eighteen.[65] For the benefit of future employers, it allows the head of the care facility to provide a personal guarantee for these children,[66] and it subsidizes their rent and offers loans for living expenses. If they are enrolled in post-secondary education, they can stay in the facility until age twenty-two, and children who were placed in foster families can also remain there until age twenty-two if necessary.

The government also allows grandparents to fund their grandchildren's education without charging a donation tax.

It passed the Fundamental Act for Persons with a Disability in 1970,[67] and the Fourth Fundamental Plan for Persons with a Disability was adopted in 2018.[68] This plan emphasizes that children with disabilities must receive the same educational opportunities as all other children, though simultaneously tailored to their needs. In 2013, the government passed the Act on the Elimination of Discrimination against Persons with Disability.[69]

Finally, the government has tried to increase the number of childcare facilities and to provide opportunities for working parents to enrol their children in them. This is essential because many working mothers struggle to find a daycare spot for their children. Moreover, most of the public approved facilities have no vacancies, and only unapproved private facilities have the occasional opening. The government promised to wipe out the waiting lists, but it still has a long way to go before it reaches this goal.[70]

No Prospect of Success

Perhaps over time, the initiatives outlined above may bear fruit. So far, however, they have not achieved a great deal. The number of marriages has continued its downward trend. In 2018, 586,481 people tied the knot, and the marriage rate was the lowest it had ever been at 4.7 per 1,000 persons. In 2019, the number increased slightly to 598,965 and the rate also rose to 4.8. Even so, it was roughly half of the 1,099,984 marriages in 1972, the highest number, when the rate was over 16.0 per 1,000 persons.[71] The birthrate too has constantly dropped, reaching its nadir in 2005 at 1.26, rebounding slightly to 1.45 in 2015, but declining again ever since. In 2018, it was 1.42, and in 2019 it was 1.36.[72]

Of course, all of this was easy to predict. Since marriage requires a strong commitment and necessitates all kinds of work – such as preparations for the wedding and making arrangements for living together – people will naturally feel hesitant about embarking on it. The expense involved naturally makes young couples feel unready. The arranged marriage, once very popular in Japan, is now quite rare. People need to find appropriate partners, and many complain that they are very difficult to locate. Dating is also hard because many people put in long hours at work simply to survive. Many thus complain that they have no time for dating. Even when couples are romantically involved, they often prefer to live together rather than getting married. It is no wonder that many people do not opt for matrimony.

Women still face tremendous obstacles in having and raising children. For working women, asking for maternity leave is not easy. Childcare facilities are limited, and many women are frustrated by the difficulty of finding a vacancy. Many struggle with the dual responsibilities of raising a child and holding down a job. Nor has the expense diminished. It is therefore unsurprising that many women choose to remain childless or to refrain from increasing the number of children they already have.

The government needs to reconsider whether its marriage and childbirth policies have any possibility of success.

Increasing the Population: Accepting More Immigrants

Japan's Immigration Policy
Another measure that could be used to increase the population is to accept more immigrants. Some countries, such as Canada, have offset their declining population and birthrate by taking in a huge number of immigrants.[73] This might be a viable choice for Japan as well.

Japan has allowed foreign residents to work in certain circumstances. For instance, permanent residents and foreign spouses of Japanese citizens have been allowed to work without any restrictions, and some foreign professionals, such as university professors or researchers, were gradually accepted as well. But this cohort is quite small. With the population decrease, the number of Japanese workers is rapidly shrinking. Since very few people will happily accept a challenging job that pays poorly, some employers have encountered a serious labour shortage. It is no wonder that a growing number of people are calling for a significant increase in immigrants.

In the past, Japan has not accepted unskilled immigrants. Tourists are permitted to visit the country for ninety days without a visa, but foreigners who wish to work there must have a specific visa corresponding to specific job classifications.[74] There is no general unskilled foreign worker visa, and Japan has accepted only professionals who have job security.[75] As a consequence, there are no unskilled foreign workers who can fill the void created by the lack of Japanese workers.

Moreover, Japan has been notoriously reluctant to take in refugees. Its acceptance ratio is the lowest among developed countries.[76] In 2019, for instance, it accepted only 81 of the 10,375 refugees who applied for entry: of them, 44 came under the protected refugee status and 37 were granted a stay based on humanitarian grounds.[77]

Admitting Limited Numbers of Foreign Workers

Faced with the critical shortage of workers, the Japanese government has accepted a limited number of foreign workers. Some are individuals of Japanese descent who are admitted to work for Japanese companies. Many Japanese people immigrated to South American countries in the past, especially Brazil, but during the 1980s that country experienced serious economic hardships, whereas the Japanese economy was booming, which prompted many Japanese Brazilians to come to Japan for work. In 1990, the government decided to accept foreigners with Japanese ancestry, spouses of second-generation Japanese descent, and their children (third-generation Japanese) as "settled foreigners."[78] This included Brazilians of Japanese descent. In 1990, 46,429 of them came to Japan, a number that later increased to 119,333.[79] Although they appear not to have been the primary target of the "settled foreigners" policy, they benefitted most greatly from it.[80]

A second solution would be to accept more foreign students, a measure that the government has been promoting. As of May 1, 2019, there were 312,214 foreign students studying in Japanese educational systems.[81] If they are permitted to work, they can take a part-time job for up to twenty-eight hours a week (eight hours a day and forty hours a week during extended holidays). But the job must not interfere with their studies, and working in the sex entertainment industry is barred to them.[82]

A third possible alternative is the acceptance of foreign trainees. Japanese companies have practised this for a long time, but only after the government officially accepted it in 1993 as a separate system did trainees become a significant portion of the foreign worker cohort. Various issues in the system led to the passage of the Job Trainee Act in 2016,[83] which introduced tighter controls over the acceptance system. Under this system, a company can accept foreign trainees from its subsidiaries, affiliated companies, or non-profit management corporations, and if the correct permit is obtained the trainees can be assigned to an affiliate company in Japan.[84] The purpose of the system is to promote a technology transfer between Japan and developing countries by training foreign workers and sending them back home. It was not intended to correct the domestic labour shortage. However, many companies have taken advantage of the system, importing a large number of foreign workers by passing them off as trainees, paying them poorly, and offering no job security.

In 2014, the government also decided to accept a limited number of care worker candidates from the Philippines, Vietnam, and Indonesia. After a period of training, they could challenge the government exam to become nurses or care workers in Japan.[85] Japan entered into an economic partnership agreement with the three countries. After entering the country, the candidates take a six-month Japanese language course, receive practical training (three years for nurses and four years for care workers), and can then sit the exam. A total of 6,400 have been accepted. This program was not meant to offset the labour shortage in care fields, but many foreigners came to Japan to become nurses or care workers and have remained there.[86]

In the end, however, none of these measures were intended to offset the labour shortage. As a result, there is a major limitation on using foreign workers to fill the void, and calls for more robust measures have intensified. Moreover, these systems were badly exploited by smugglers and brokers who recruited foreign workers and sent them to Japan, arranging their trips at a hefty charge, often via a loan, thus making it impossible for many to escape their control. Many came to Japan mainly for work as trainees or students.[87]

In 2019, some 1.66 million foreign workers were employed in Japan,[88] and more than half of the 2.93 million foreigners who visited the country stayed for over ninety days.[89] Still, many claim that their numbers are not sufficient to correct the labour shortage in Japan.

Moreover, permitting foreign families to immigrate to Japan might be seen as a good strategy due to the assumption that many foreign workers tend to have large families with numerous children. Taking this course could significantly boost the number of children in Japan and the total number of the population as well.

The Increased Acceptance of Foreign Workers

In 2018, the Japanese government finally modified its policy and began to accept unskilled foreign workers. The Immigration Control Act was amended to create an additional legal status to permit a stay in Japan through two means: specified skill 1 status and specified skill 2 status.[90] The former allows foreign workers to be employed in a specified field where labour is extremely sparse. They must also possess substantial knowledge and experience in their field, which includes health care, construction, shipbuilding, hotels, restaurants, farming, and others. Their Japanese language and professional skills are tested, and if their status is renewed, they can work in Japan for up to five years. They cannot be accompanied by family and are expected to return home once they finish their work.

If, however, they accumulate enough experience, they can challenge the specified skill 2 status examination. If they pass, they can work in Japan with a renewal for an indefinite period and, if permitted, can be joined by their family.[91] However, the specific fields are limited to construction and shipbuilding. As a result, most foreign workers accepted under the new status level will be returning home. Nevertheless, the companies for which they work must conclude labour contracts with them that satisfy legal requirements, provide equal pay, and furnish support for them. Up to 350,000 foreign workers are expected to be admitted during the next five years.

Still, the government remains unwilling to accept immigrants, which means that, so far, virtually all foreign workers are expected to go home and are not supposed to settle in Japan.

Immigration: An Unwelcome Solution

The government reluctance to admit immigrants could be rooted in traditional Japanese culture, which concentrates on community harmony, mutual respect, and cooperation, with a strong push toward homogeneity. Outliers or vocal critics are unwelcome. Everyone is supposed to look and act the same. This marked preference for uniformity and homogeneity is both a strength and a fundamental shortcoming. Foreigners, who are often called *gaijin* (outsiders), are often treated differently from everyone else and can encounter discrimination and disadvantages. Japanese society is not welcoming to immigrants. All foreigners are expected to adjust their philosophy and attitudes to accord with Japanese norms.[92] In order to accept an increased number of foreign workers, Japanese people and Japanese society must radically rethink their mindset.[93]

But there is a broader concern regarding the acceptance of foreign workers: its implications for other aspects of society and administration. For instance, since many workers would bring their families with them or could create new ones in Japan, the educational system would need to accommodate them. There would be an urgent demand for Japanese language classes and remedial or supplementary education, which would oblige the government to train and hire the requisite number of Japanese language teachers. Translators would also need to be hired.

Furthermore, bringing in large numbers of foreign workers would necessitate important changes in the health care, welfare, and pension systems. For example, everyone who lives in Japan for more than ninety days, including foreigners, must pay health insurance premiums, which entitles them to receive government-subsidized health care. Hospitals and doctors are obliged to treat any patient who asks for medical attention. When tourists are badly injured or become seriously ill, they are often rushed to hospital, regardless of whether they have health insurance. Many do not. Some fail to pay back the cost of their care, leaving hospitals and doctors on the hook for their medical expenses. If Japan is to accept a huge number of foreign workers, the government must come up with a better system to guarantee that everyone is insured. The current welfare system is intended to provide a baseline standard of living to Japanese citizens living in Japan. Although the government has provided discretionary welfare payments to foreigners, it should reconsider the entire system if it officially accepts large numbers of immigrants. All of these changes will necessitate further tax spending, which will come ultimately from the wallets of taxpayers.[94]

In the past, since the government had not accepted unskilled foreign workers, Japan's expatriate population remained fairly small. In 2019, of the 2.93 million foreigners who remained in the country for longer than ninety-day stays, 312,000 were special permanent visa holders (mostly resident Koreans), 793,000 were regular permanent visa holders, 410,000 were trainees, and 345,000 were students. Other professionals totaled 271,000.[95] This number is far smaller than in other countries.[96] Nevertheless, many local governments have encountered extreme challenges in accepting them. If the central government opens the door to unskilled foreign workers, it must find a way to accommodate its traditional system and administrative philosophy to the incomers.

With the expansion of the expatriate population in Japan, an increasing number of local governments have shown a willingness to incorporate multiculturalism into their policies regarding resident foreigners. The central government expressed an interest as well. Yet, social conservatives fiercely opposed this move, as did the conservative members of the ruling Liberal Democratic Party, prompting the government to back down. Its recently published documents contain no mention of multiculturalism. It is doubtful, therefore, that the Japanese people and their government will manage to embrace a philosophy of accepting immigrants, especially as long as the Liberal Democratic Party remains in power.

Another consideration is that foreign workers are often vulnerable to exploitation. Even when Japan admitted very few, some unscrupulous individuals took advantage of loopholes and brought a number of foreign workers into the country. For instance, many Filipina women, who ostensibly came in as entertainers, ended up working in the sex industry. The brokers who recruited them and helped them come to Japan took away their passports and practically forced them to enter the sex trade. Many foreigners were accepted as trainees, only to be exploited and deprived of their rights in the name of training. Housed in unhealthy and overcrowded apartments, they were forced to work full-time but were paid extremely low wages for their work as trainees.

Many young foreigners were accepted as students and were allowed to work with some limitations. In reality, however, these "students" were not studying; rather, they were spending most of their time working. They were an easy target for exploitation since they could be poorly paid. Thus, further acceptance of foreign workers might produce a bifurcated structure: one stream for domestic workers and one for foreign workers. The latter involves much harsher employment conditions, far lower remuneration, and a greater probability of exploitation.[97] Moreover, foreign workers are vulnerable to economic fluctuations and will have a greater chance of losing their jobs if the economy takes a downturn. This is particularly challenging, as foreign workers who lose a job will have difficulty in obtaining a new one.[98]

Unless the government is willing to make the necessary changes to accommodate a huge influx of foreigners, it simply cannot admit them. Moreover, if their acceptance is grounded largely in the hope that they will raise the birthrate, this seems somewhat unjust. Even though many foreign workers might bring more children into the country, this policy may simply offload the birthrate problem onto foreign women. Tasking them with extricating Japan from its present predicament is unfair.

The Population Policy Reconsidered

What Are Possible Solutions?

Given that the various government measures to encourage marriage and childbirth have had so little success, and that Japan is unlikely to open its arms to immigrants, what is the Diet to do? Perhaps the answer lies in finding better ways of promoting childbirth.

One possible path is the use of force – mandating everyone to reproduce. But no government that valued its political future would choose this option. Besides, it is a direct infringement of the right to sexual autonomy. It is true that the Japanese government has never officially accepted sexual autonomy as a constitutional right. Nor has it ever questioned the legitimacy of using a population policy to achieve its ends. Thus, it might simply be refraining from imposing force due to political and policy considerations, not constitutional ones. Therefore, at least as far as the Constitution is concerned, it might not perceive any impediment to introducing some kinds of force in hopes of achieving its goal. For now, however, it obviously has no interest in taking this path, as it would risk stirring up opposition. After all, increasing the birthrate surely necessitates cooperation from the public. Given this, it is no wonder that the Declining Childbirth Whitepaper, a signature manifestation of the government countermeasures against the falling birthrate, does not discuss the use of force.

Nevertheless, the government promotion of marriage and childbirth could have an indirect impact on the right of the public to exercise sexual autonomy. So far, the government has concentrated on incentivizing people to comply with its wishes by providing financial help for couples to get married and have children, preferably as many as possible. There are no government disincentives for not complying – for not getting married and not having children. Indeed, given that so many individuals have refrained from marriage and have no plans either to marry or have children, the government pressure to do otherwise does not seem particularly strong. However, Japanese people know that government endorsements and promotions can sometimes trigger serious pressure on individuals who choose instead to follow their own path. It is hoped that the government emphasis on marriage and childbirth will never become so strong that individuals who do not wish to get married or have children feel compelled to do so.

Moreover, as mentioned, efforts have been made to disallow economic reasons for artificial termination of pregnancy (ATP), the most often cited grounds for requesting an abortion.[99] Women's groups and the doctors who were designated to perform ATP successfully opposed this step. The removal of economic reasons would have directly infringed the rights of women not to give birth and would had forced many to provide a medical diagnosis that the pregnancy and childbirth could endanger their life and health, which is not an easy choice for many women. This requirement is a flagrant violation of the Constitution, as it does not allow women to make their own choices.

Furthermore, some commentators have called for the introduction of a new "tax for being single," which would apply only to individuals who remain unmarried after reaching a certain age.[100] This scheme is based on the presumption that if you have children, they will contribute to the economy and will support you in your old age. But if you have no children, you will need to rely on the government. The proposal thus aims to recoup some of the extra spending that the government must allocate to unmarried seniors.

The idea of imposing differential tax burdens on certain people is nothing new. Even now, individuals are taxed at differing rates, depending on how much money they make, whether they are married, or whether they have dependent children. The formula is decided by highly political policy considerations. However, single people already face a higher tax burden than their married counterparts because they are ineligible for the spousal tax break.[101] If the couple also have a dependent child, they receive another tax break. As a result, the tax burden on a married person with a child is lighter than for a single person. Imposing additional taxes on being single could be a further blow for many people who cannot have children or who have no wish for them, a choice every individual is entitled to make under the Constitution.

In Search of a New Sexual Autonomy Perspective

From our examination, it is apparent that the government needs to start from the constitutional premise that every individual has sexual autonomy: the right to have sex and the right to have a child. This extends to the right not to be forced to have sex and not to be forced to have a child. Therefore, the government cannot and should not force anyone to have sex or to have children. This applies to marriage as well. Under the current Constitution, family law regarding marriage must be grounded in individual dignity and the essential equality between the sexes.[102] The right to get married is also a constitutional right, which includes the right not to be forced to marry, which should apply to everyone. The government is therefore precluded from forcing people into matrimony.[103]

Could the government be allowed to restrict sexual autonomy for the sake of its population policy? We have already seen that sexual autonomy, as an essential element of personal development and democracy, needs to be protected by courts as a right that demands strict scrutiny for its restriction. Prevention of harm or injury to others is a legitimate government objective, as is the protection of the life and safety of the individual concerned. However, population policy promotes the general welfare of the community and is not a measure to protect the rights of the public. Therefore, a population policy should never be accepted as a legitimate goal to restrict sexual autonomy.

There is no doubt that population policies are very important for any government.[104] If there are too many people, reducing population growth might be necessary to secure sufficient food and resources for everyone. If there are too few people to sustain or develop the economy and society, increasing the population and thus the workforce might be necessary to achieve the same ends. The question is whether such an important policy goal should and could be accepted as a justification for restricting the constitutional right of sexual autonomy. Given that this right is essential to personal development and to facilitating a democracy, the answer should be no.

Various Possible Measures to Increase Childbirth

Surely, in addition to the measures it has tried so far, the government can explore new ways of increasing childbirth.

First, however, it is important to provide full protection to sexual autonomy before thinking about how to raise the birthrate. In other words, the starting point for all discussion should be the acknowledgment that the right to sexual autonomy is a constitutional right that needs to be constitutionally protected. This is imperative since people will not be willing to engage in sex, give birth, or raise a child without the full assurance that their sexual autonomy will be protected. For instance, removing the Criminal Code ban on abortion and radically changing the Mother's Body Protection Act to allow women to have total discretion on whether to have an abortion would be a good start. The government should also enable them to avoid unwanted pregnancy more efficiently. This can be achieved by providing birth control more freely and publicizing its effectiveness and safety. Making the pill and the morning-after pill available over the counter at an inexpensive price would help women freely make decisions surrounding whether to have children. Finally, making it easier to access abortion would protect women's sexual autonomy. The current limitation – that an abortion must be surgical and that it must be performed by a designated gynecologist – is utterly meaningless. The abortion pill needs to be approved and should be sold at any drugstore or pharmacy, without prescription. By providing women with more confidence that an unwanted pregnancy is preventable, they can have sex without anxiety.[105]

Moreover, although there is no strictly legal regulation on access to ART/MAR, obtaining it can be very difficult. The absence of a statute that guarantees the right of access to ART/MAR critically narrows the possibility of getting medical help to reproduce. The government needs to enact a statute guaranteeing access and prohibiting doctors, hospitals, and medical associations from imposing unreasonable restrictions. Furthermore, ART/MAR is extremely expensive, especially IVF. As a result, many couples who try it are overwhelmed by the financial burden. Some never attempt it, because it is beyond their means. The recent government announcement that the national health insurance system would cover infertility treatment, including IVF, is good news for many couples who are struggling to pay for it. However, it is still unclear to what extent their concerns will be alleviated. It is best that the government allows a maximum coverage from national health insurance to pay for ART/MAR, including the costs of all examinations and advanced technology, and that it permits any woman who wants a child to access this coverage.

Additionally, the law of parentage needs to be re-examined. Inflexible and outdated, it cannot respond appropriately to ART/MAR. It needs radical revision to allow a couple who wish to have a child to become parents and to guarantee the maximum welfare of the child. The legal relationship between child and parent should be clarified, and a child born via ART/MAR may need to have multiple parents. This would also require a major change in the understanding of what it means to be a family.

For working women, another hurdle to accessing ART/MRT is the significant time commitment involved. Often, they must visit the clinic more than ten times, resulting in repeated absences from work, something that is very difficult to achieve without an understanding employer. The government found that very few private companies had a system to accommodate female staff who were receiving infertility treatment, such as providing special leaves or flexible hours, moving them from permanent to part-time positions, or offering special subsidies.[106] Many employers are reluctant to allow staff to skip work for multiple infertility treatments, and as a result, 16 percent of women who had tried or were trying ART/MRT were forced to quit their jobs.[107] Many complained of the difficulty of keeping their job while receiving the treatment. Many wanted their employers to establish a paid infertility leave, allow them to work flexible hours, temporarily transfer them to a part-time position, or provide special financial subsidies.[108]

Also, working women face extreme difficulties in giving birth and raising a child. A female employee is legally entitled to six weeks of leave before her due date and a further eight weeks after the baby is born.[109] Both parents are also legally entitled to take leave until the child reaches age one.[110] The Equal Employment Opportunity Act (EEOA), which obligates employers to implement measures against sexual harassment, recently mandated them to introduce necessary labour management measures to prevent harms in the workplace based on speech or conduct surrounding pregnancy or childbirth.[111] The EEOA also prohibits employers from firing or imposing disadvantages on female employees because of pregnancy or childbirth.[112] Furthermore, under the Labour Standards Act, female staff who have applied for leave due to serious hardships during their menstural periods must not be forced to work.

The Diet also mandated the government, employers, and employees to implement measures to prevent speech or conduct that is inconsistent with preventing harassment of female workers because of pregnancy or childbirth.[113] Evidently, the government believes that this step will bar employers from engaging in speech or conduct that prevents or discourages pregnancy or that discriminates on the basis of pregnancy or childbirth.[114] For instance, this would presumably apply in situations where a superior complains that granting maternity leave would force co-workers to pick up the slack or makes other statements that somehow discourage female employees from having children. But it is not clear whether this would be sufficient. Moreover, even though male partners can also ask for childcare leave, not many do.[115] As a result, working women face additional hardships in taking care of their children. There is an urgent need to further protect them.

The Need to Reform Japanese Society

To provide confidence and security to women who choose to have children, however, much more needs to be changed. Frankly speaking, a radical revision of Japanese society is urgently needed.

Childcare facilities, especially for infants and small babies, are limited in number, and finding a space in a publicly supported daycare is very difficult.[116] Many women struggle with this problem. Some can rely on their parents for help, but many others cannot. Moreover, childcare facilities often have serious limitations on service, forcing mothers to leave the office to pick up their children when they close. Most do not accept children when they are sick. Therefore, whenever a child is unwell, the mother must skip work. Providing sufficient childcare for all infants and babies is vital for the promotion of childbirth.

In addition, the workplace environment for female employees must be fundamentally improved. The government has already taken some steps in this direction, especially for working women.[117] It wants to cut down on working hours.[118] It hopes to introduce more flexible hours, especially for female workers who need to raise children, to create a proper balance between work and childcare.[119] It introduced measures that require equal treatment of staff, regardless of whether they work on a permanent full-time basis or as part-timers.[120] Yet, all these reforms require a fundamental shift in the work environment and have yet to demonstrate whether they will accomplish significant change. If they do, female employees would feel a great deal more comfortable with having a child while working. These kinds of measures are especially important now since 70 percent of women aged between 15 to 64 are working.[121]

Moreover, Japanese men are notorious for putting in long hours at the office and carrying a heavy workload, which means that many are simply not at home,[122] leaving their wives to handle the household chores and look after the children.[123] Most women will be working as well.[124] Unsurprisingly, they often feel that juggling paid employment with the 24/7 task of child raising is simply beyond their capacity. It is vital that both men and women work fewer hours a week to allow them to better share the duties of child raising and housework. To achieve this, it is simply not enough to ban workplace discrimination and harassment regarding pregnancy and childbirth. It is not enough to offer maternity leave before and after birth and to provide unpaid childcare leave for both mothers and fathers. Many workers are reluctant to apply for this type of leave, because their absence will place a burden on their colleagues. It is therefore imperative that absolute maximum working hours be set without exception so that all employees can spend time at home with their families. And, without exception, both mothers and fathers must automatically receive paid childcare leave. To accomplish this goal, the government should impose criminal punishment on any company that fails to comply.

Many families are also worried about the financial costs of having children. Public school is free, but parents often prefer that their children attend a pricey private school. They will want to provide various extracurricular activities such as music lessons or involvement in sport. If the children are to be accepted by the most prestigious schools, they will need to attend a cram school. These offer supplementary education, starting from kindergarten, elementary school, junior high school, high school, and ultimately to university. All of this comes at a cost, and the bills can quickly pile up.[125]

All parents wish to provide the best opportunity for their children to be happy and successful, but the enormous price tag puts this beyond the reach of many. The government child benefits cover only a tiny fraction of the cost. If the government is serious about promoting childbirth, it must significantly lower the cost of raising a child or support the family by providing substantial benefits.

Unless the government can alleviate all the burdens discussed above, women will naturally feel reluctant to have children. Even when they do have one child, the difficulties of raising it will probably discourage them from having another. The government needs to find a better way to diminish the burdens on women rather than simply providing subsidies that are too small to have much impact.

Moreover, it is also vital to face the more deeply daunting task of motivating people to have sex. It is well known that Japanese people are extremely uneager to engage in sex.[126] In 2020, the Japan Family Planning Association surveyed young people in their twenties, revealing that 39.0 percent of the men and 26.7 percent of the women had never had a sexual experience. Among those who had, only roughly 18.0 percent of both male and female respondents reported having sex more than twice a week, and 17.9 percent of the men and 16.3 percent of the women had not had sex during the past year.[127] In 2015, among unmarried people, 69.8 percent of men and 59.1 percent of women had no regular sexual partner of the opposite sex, a slight increase from 61.4 percent and 49.5 percent respectively in 2010.[128] Apparently, having sex with someone is not a popular pastime in Japan.[129] Moreover, 51.9 percent of marriages are sexless, a gradual increase from 47.2 percent in 2010.[130] This clearly shows that, even among married couples, the disinclination to engage in sex remains strong.[131] This is very interesting, given the popularity of the sex industry and the fact that Japan is often accused of being overly sexualized. But to increase the number of children, the government needs to promote sex and childbirth.

There has been some speculation as to why Japanese people are reluctant to have sex. Many have pointed out that long hours on the job and the stress caused by overworking are major factors in discouraging young people from making an effort to date and have sex. Working style reform and the reduction of working hours would definitely be necessary to change the root cause of apathy for sex. It is vital for Japanese people to discover that they will be much happier if they can just enjoy life and sex, rather than worrying about their job, work, and future.

The Need for a Major Change in Government Policy
All of these necessary changes to society must be accompanied by a drastic rethinking of government policies regarding sex, childbirth, and family. Although the government has made various attempts to encourage childbirth, it appears to be trapped in traditional conceptions surrounding sex, birth, and family.

The traditional attitude toward sex, especially for young women, is that women should know nothing about sex and should never initiate it. They should be passive and modest, trusting men to take the lead in the bedroom, and should remain chaste until their wedding day. Therefore, the government never believed that promoting sex regardless of marriage was essential. It saw sex as essentially restricted to marriage. Probably, this needs to be changed, and the government should at least make it easier to get married.[132]

Furthermore, the traditional belief is that being born to a loving and well-established married couple is best for a child and that being born out of wedlock is undesirable.[133] As a result, anyone who is not married is ineligible for ART/MAR.

This tradition-based assumption is not justified. It is vital to grant full sexual autonomy to women and to guarantee that it will be fully protected. The government also needs to accept and promote childbirth by enabling whoever wishes to have a child through consensual sex or by using ART/MAR. It should also ensure that all children will be raised with ample government and community support.

Diversifying Family: The Acceptance of the 2SLGBTQ+ Community

Moreover, the government should be ready to accept more diverse forms of family. So far, it has concentrated on promoting marriage as traditionally defined: the exclusive union of one man and one woman. It has thus excluded same-sex marriage. It also rarely permits transgender individuals to change their registered legal sex as either male or female. As a result, transgender couples wanting to get married face many hurdles. For example, a transgender woman who is still legally categorized as a man can marry a woman but not a man. If she is diagnosed as having a sexual identity disorder and receives sex reassignment surgery, she can change her legal sex under certain conditions. If she does so, only then can she marry a man. The same requirements are true for transgender men. It is absurd that the government is so reluctant to accept such diverse forms of family.

This limitation has a significant implication for the use of ART/MAR, which only heterosexual couples in a marriage-like relationship can access. In the past, ART/MAR was reserved solely for legally married couples, and though the requirement was loosened, a marriage-like relationship is still necessary. This means that a single woman is ineligible for ART/MAR. The same is true for a gay or lesbian couple, as their relationship cannot be marriage-like.

There is no reason to bar single women or homosexual couples from obtaining infertility treatments or ART/MAR. Furthermore, the permissible and available ART/MAR technology needs to be liberalized. IVF doesn't have to be the means of last resort, and women should be allowed and encouraged to use it if they wish. If a woman is forced to try other fertility treatments first, time will pass, and her chances of conceiving will diminish as she ages, making the success rate of IVF much smaller. The sooner the better, and a woman should consult with her physician and start IVF when appropriate. Moreover, surrogacy should be legalized. Although the government might be allowed to regulate the commercial sale and purchase of surrogacy, there is no legitimate reason to ban it. Then, heterosexual couples as well as homosexual couples who cannot have children on their own can arrange for a surrogate to bear their children.

All of this brings into question the government's strict adherence to the traditional, heteronormative conception of family. As mentioned, there is no criminal ban on atypical sex in Japan. As a result, sex between 2SLGBTQ+ people is not subject to penalty. Although prostitution is prohibited, it is narrowly defined to include only "sexual intercourse." Therefore, the applicability of this ban to 2SLGBTQ+ people can be questioned. But as it is not effectively enforced anyway, they have nothing to worry about on this score. On the other hand, many 2SLGBTQ+ people do not come under the Criminal Code reference to "sexual intercourse et al.," because this is restricted solely to the penile penetration of a vagina, mouth, or anus. These excluded people must rely upon the ban on forcible obscene acts – sexual assault – if they are coerced into sexual activities. There is nothing to prevent 2SLGBTQ+ individuals from having children, but as we saw, their chances of accessing ART/MAR are very limited. Nor are they banned from using contraceptives or access to abortion. As mentioned, though a husband must consent to ATP, this requirement is not strictly enforced. Thus, practically, 2SLGBTQ+ people have nothing to worry about in this context either.

However, they do encounter all sorts of problems. There is no such thing as a legal marriage or even a common law marriage between 2SLGBTQ+ partners.[134] This results in various disadvantages for them: an 2SLGBTQ+ individual cannot be treated as a legal spouse, cannot be a legal heir, cannot enjoy tax breaks as a spouse, and so forth. Moreover, prejudice and discrimination against 2SLGBTQ+ people are abundant. Nevertheless, the government has been rather reluctant to secure equality for them.[135]

Such an exclusive stance against the 2SLGBTQ+ community, probably rooted in the traditional sense of family, is no longer justifiable.[136] Sexual freedom should include the right to legally change one's sex or gender identity, and it encompasses all kinds of atypical sex and the creation of intimate personal relationships. A sexual orientation or identity that differs from the mainstream needs to be accepted as a permissible choice.

Now is the time to accept 2SLGBTQ+ people and more diverse forms of family, especially if the government wants to enlarge the birthrate. The acceptance of various forms of family will surely contribute to the increase of marriage and will consequently encourage more people to have children.

Conclusion

Although sex has been regarded as a freedom that is available to everyone, many restrictions have been placed on this freedom. But it is rare to find any constitutional examination of whether one has the right to decide and change sex or gender identity, whether sexual freedom is constitutionally protected, and whether the restrictions at issue can be justified. Although individuals possess the freedom not to be forced to have sex, the rape and sexual assault laws that protect it differ widely throughout the world. Yet, we will find no discussion of whether the punishment for rape is constitutionally justified and whether it is sufficient to protect the freedom not to be forced to have sex.

In most countries, the freedom to have a child is generally respected, though some try to restrict it. Moreover, because of worsening infertility, access to ART/MAR has become vital. But many countries have introduced obstacles for access. Nevertheless, it is rare to find any examination of whether this is an infringement of the constitutional right to sexual autonomy and whether it can be justified. Further, the freedom not to be forced to have a child entails the right to use contraceptives and to have an abortion. Many countries variously limit this freedom. Although this has been challenged as unconstitutional in some countries, all discussions of contraceptives and abortion tend to focus on policy and legislative issues.

This book argues that the absence of constitutional concern for sex and childbirth is not beneficial and that they must be examined as constitutional issues. Moreover, the book is premised on the idea that the issues need to be approached in light of "sexual autonomy," which ought to be protected by the Constitution.

This critical reflection on the need to examine all issues of sex and childbirth in terms of sexual autonomy is all the more important because many countries are now beset with declining birthrates and a rapidly aging population. In their search for solutions, governments will take the obvious step of trying to increase childbirth, an initiative that will necessarily implicate the serious concern of sexual autonomy. Whatever solutions they choose must of necessity protect it.

Concentrating on Japan, this book examined the freedoms to have sex or not to have it and the freedoms to have a child or not to have one. All of these issues were examined from the perspective of sexual autonomy under the Constitution of Japan. This book found that the Constitution provides ample support for sexual autonomy and critically examined various restrictions on it.

Other countries can learn a great deal from Japan's experience. It is vital to acknowledge sexual autonomy as a constitutional right and to grant constitutional protection to sexual freedom and the freedom of choice on childbirth. If these are taken as givens, we must then question the denial of the right to determine one's own sex or gender identity and any restriction on the right to have sex. Moreover, in granting constitutional protection to the right not to be forced to have sex, we must question the constitutionality of rape and sexual assault bans. By accepting constitutional protection of the right to have a child, we must question various limitations on that right and on the right of access to ART/MAR. Furthermore, by accepting constitutional protection of the right not be forced to have a child, we must question the constitutionality of regulating contraception and forbidding abortion. Finally, when we accept sexual autonomy as a constitutional right, we must question whether it could justifiably be circumscribed in the service of government population policies and must find the best way of increasing the birthrate without resorting to restrictions on sexual autonomy.

Many countries are grappling with the problem of a rapidly aging population and a declining birthrate, but because Japan has the highest percentage of seniors in the world and one of the lowest fertility rates, it is in many ways the canary in the coal mine. As such, it can provide valuable lessons on how best to proceed.

Caselaw, Legislation, and Treaties

Caselaw

Canada
Canada (Attorney General) v Bedford, [2013] 3 SCR 1101
R. v Ewanchuk, [1999] 1 SCR 330
R. v J.A., [2011] 2 SCR 440
R. v Labaye, [2005] 3 SCR 728
R. v Morgentaler, [1988] 1 SCR 30
R. v Oakes, [1986] 1 SCR 103
RJR-MacDonald Inc. v Canada (Attorney General), [1995] 3 SCR 199

Germany
BVerfGE 39, 1
BVerfGE 88, 203

Japan
Daishinin [Great Court of Judicature], October 19, 1909 (Meiji 42), 15 Keiroku 1420
Daishinin [Great Court of Judicature], December 8, 1911 (Meiji 44), 17 Keiroku 2183
Daishinin [Great Court of Judicature], November 19, 1913, 19 Daishinin hanketsuroku 1255
Daishinin [Great Court of Judicature], December 13, 1919, 25 Keiroku 1367

Daishinin [Great Court of Judicature], December 1, 1925, 4:12 Keishu 741
Daishinin [Great Court of Judicature], January 23, 1940, 19:5 Minshu 54
Daishinin [Great Court of Judicature], September 20, 1940, 19:18 Minshu 1596
Fukuoka chihō saibansho, Kurume Shibu [Fukuoka DC, Kurume Branch], March 12, 2019, unreported
Fukuoka chihō saibansho [Fukuoka DC], July 18, 2019, unreported
Fukuoka kōtō saibansho [Fukuoka HC], August 31, 1966, 19:5 Kokei 575
Fukuoka kōtō saibansho [Fukuoka HC], February 5, 2020, unreported
Fukuoka kōtō saibansho [Fukuoka HC], March 11, 2020, unreported
Hiroshima chihō saibansho [Hiroshima DC], March 26, 1969, 235 Hanrei Times 285
Hiroshima chihō saibansho [Hiroshima DC], January 16, 2003, 1131 Hanrei Times 131
Hiroshima kōtō saibansho, Matsue Shibu [Hiroshima HC, Matsue Branch], June 18, 1987, 1234 Hanrei jihō 154
Hiroshima kōtō saibansho [Hiroshima HC], November 20, 1978, 922 Hanrei jihō 111
Maebashi chihō saibansho [Maebashi DC], February 7, 2003, courts database, http://www.courts.go.jp/app/hanrei_jp/detail4?id=6320
Nagoya chihō saibansho, Okazaki shibu [Nagoya DC, Okazaki Branch], March 26, 2019, unreported
Nagoya kōtō saibansho [Nagoya HC], March 12, 2020, unreported
Nara katei saibansho [Nara FC], December 15, 2007, unreported
Niigata chihō saibansho [Niigata DC], December 10, 2015, unreported
Osaka chihō saibansho [Osaka DC], March 12, 1971, 267 Hanrei Times 376
Osaka chihō saibansho [Osaka DC], March 27, 1972, 283 Hanrei Times 332
Osaka chihō saibansho [Osaka DC], October 24, 2008, courts database, http://www.courts.go.jp/app/hanrei_jp/detail4?id=37008
Osaka chihō saibansho [Osaka DC], January 8, 2019, unreported
Osaka chihō saibansho [Osaka DC], June 20, 2022, unreported
Osaka katei saibansho [Osaka FC], November 28, 2019, unreported
Osaka kōtō saibansho [Osaka HC], June 19, 2007, unreported
Osaka kōtō saibansho [Osaka HC], April 26, 2018, unreported
Saikō saibansho [SCOJ], 3rd petty bench, May 10, 1949, 3:6 Keishu 711
Saikō saibansho [SCOJ], 1st petty bench, August 18, 1949, 13 Shukei 307
Saikō saibansho [SCOJ], 3rd petty bench, February 19, 1952, 6:2 Minshu 110
Saikō saibansho [SCOJ], 2nd petty bench, October 3, 1952, 6:9 Minshu 753
Saikō saibansho [SCOJ], grand bench, June 24, 1953, 7:6 Keishu 1366
Saikō saibansho [SCOJ], 2nd petty bench, June 6, 1958, 126 Shukei 171
Saikō saibansho [SCOJ], 2nd petty bench, April 27, 1962, 16:7 Minshu 1247
Saikō saibansho [SCOJ], 1st petty bench, May 29, 1969, 23:6 Minshu 1064
Saikō saibansho [SCOJ], grand bench, December 12, 1973, 27:11 Minshu 1536

Saikō saibansho [SCOJ], grand bench, October 23, 1985, 39:6 Keishu 413
Saikō saibansho [SCOJ], grand bench, September 2, 1987, 41:6 Minshu 1423
Saikō saibansho [SCOJ], 3rd petty bench, January 19, 1988, 42:1 Keishu 1
Saikō saibansho [SCOJ], 2nd petty bench, August 31, 1998, 189 Shumin 497
Saikō saibansho [SCOJ], 2nd petty bench, August 31, 1998, 189 Shumin 437
Saikō saibansho [SCOJ], 2nd petty bench, March 29, 2005, 59:2 Keishu 54
Saikō saibansho [SCOJ], 2nd petty bench, July 7, 2006, 220 Shumin 673
Saikō saibansho [SCOJ], 2nd petty bench, July 7, 2006, 60:6 Minshu 2307
Saikō saibansho [SCOJ], 2nd petty bench, September 4, 2006, 60:7 Minshu 2563
Saikō saibansho [SCOJ], 2nd petty bench, March 23, 2007, 61:2 Minshu 619
Saikō saibansho [SCOJ], 3rd petty bench, April 14, 2009, 63:4 Keishu 331
Saikō saibansho [SCOJ], 2nd petty bench, July 25, 2011, 304 Shumin 139
Saikō saibansho [SCOJ], grand bench, September 4, 2013, 67:6 Minshu 1320
Saikō saibansho [SCOJ], 3rd petty bench, December 10, 2013, 67:9 Minshu 1847
Saikō saibansho [SCOJ], 1st petty bench, July 17, 2014, 247 Shumin 79
Saikō saibansho [SCOJ], grand bench, December 16, 2015, 69:8 Minshu 2427
Saikō saibansho [SCOJ], grand bench, December 16, 2015, 69:8 Minshu 2586
Saikō saibansho [SCOJ], grand bench, November 29, 2017, 71:9 Keishu 467
Saikō saibansho [SCOJ], 2nd petty bench, April 8, 2018, unreported
Saikō saibansho [SCOJ], 2nd petty bench, June 5, 2019, unreported
Saikō saibansho [SCOJ], 3rd petty bench, September 11, 2020, unreported
Saikō saibansho [SCOJ], 3rd petty bench, November 4, 2020, unreported
Saikō saibansho [SCOJ], 3rd petty bench, November 6, 2020, unreported
Sapporo chihō saibansho [Sapporo DC], March 17, 2021, https://www.courts.go.jp/app/hanrei_jp/detail4?id=90200
Sendai chihō saibansho [Sendai DC], May 28, 2019, unreported
Shizuoka chihō saibansho [Shizuoka DC], March 28, 2019, unreported
Shizuoka chihō saibansho, Hamamatsu shibu [Shizuoka DC, Hamamatsu Branch], March 19, 2019, unreported
Tokyo chihō saibansho [Tokyo DC], August 10, 1979, 947 Hanrei jihō 122
Tokyo chihō saibansho [Tokyo DC], April 15, 1987, 1304 Hanrei jihō 147
Tokyo chihō saibansho [Tokyo DC], December 16, 1994, 1562 Hanrei jihō 141
Tokyo chihō saibansho [Tokyo DC], August 9, 2010, unreported
Tokyo chihō saibansho [Tokyo DC], December 18, 2019, unreported
Tokyo kōtō saibansho [Tokyo HC], September 16, 1998, 51:3 Kateisaibansho geppo [Kagetsu] 165
Tokyo kōtō saibansho [Tokyo HC], January 24, 2014, unreported
Tokyo kōtō saibansho [Tokyo HC], November 11, 2016, unreported
Tokyo kōtō saibansho [Tokyo HC], December 21, 2020, unreported
Tokyo kōtō saibansho [Tokyo HC], May 27, 2021, unreported
Urawa chihō saibansho [Urawa DC], October 3, 1989, 1337 Hanrei jihō 150

United States
Bowers v Hardwick, 478 U.S. 186 (1986)
Carey v Population Services Int'l, 431 U.S. 678 (1977)
City of Akron v Akron Center for Reproductive Health, 462 U.S. 416 (1983)
Colautti v Franklin, 439 U.S. 379 (1979)
Dobbs v Jackson Women's Health Organization, 597 U.S. – (2022)
Doe v Bolton, 410 U.S. 179 (1973)
Eisenstadt v Baird, 405 U.S. 438 (1972)
Erotic Service Provider Legal, Education & Research Project v Gascon, 881 F.3d 792 (9th Cir. 2018)
Gonzales v Carhart, 550 U.S. 124 (2007)
Griswold v Connecticut, 381 U.S. 479 (1965)
Harris v McRae, 448 U.S. 297 (1980)
Johnson v Calvert, 851 P. 2d 776 (Cal. 1993)
June Medical Services v Russo, 591 U.S. – (2020)
Lawrence v Texas, 539 U.S. 558 (2003)
Maher v Roe, 432 U.S. 464 (1977)
Michael H. v Gerald D., 491 U.S. 110 (1989)
Obergefell v Hodges, 576 U.S. – (2015)
Planned Parenthood of Southeastern Pa. v Casey, 505 U.S. 833 (1992)
Planned Parenthood v Casey, 505 U.S. 833 (1992)
Planned Parenthood v Danforth, 428 U.S. 52 (1976)
Roe v Wade, 410 U.S. 113 (1973)
Romer v Evans, 517 U.S. 620 (1996)
Skinner v Oklahoma, 316 U.S. 535 (1942)
Stenberg v Carhart, 530 U.S. 914 (2000)
Thornburgh v American College of Obstetricians and Gynecologists, 476 U.S. 747 (1986)
Troxel v Granville, 530 U.S. 57 (2000)
United States v Carolene Products Company, 304 U.S. 144 (1938)
Warren v Commonwealth, No. 2086-17-3, 2019 WL 189386 (Va. Ct. App. January 15, 2019)
Webster v Reproductive Health Services, 492 U.S. 490 (1989)
Whole Woman's Health v Hellerstedt, 579 U.S. – (2016)
Whole Women's Health v Jackson, 595 U.S. – (2021)

Legislation

Canada
Canadian Charter of Rights and Freedoms, 1982
Criminal Code of Canada, R.S.C., 1985, c. C-46

France
French Penal Code, 1994

Germany
German Basic Law, 1949
German Criminal Code, 1871
German Prostitution Act, 2001

Japan
Baishun boushihō [Prostitution Prevention Act], law no. 118 of 1956
Boshi hokenhō [Mother and Child Health Protection Act], law no. 141 of 1965
Botai hogohō [Mother's Body Protection Act], law no. 156 of 1948
Buke shohatto [Law for the Military House] (1615)
Dainihon teikoku kenpō [Constitution of the Empire of Japan], promulgated in 1889 (Meiji Constitution)
Fujin hodouinhō [Women's Rehabilitation Centre Act], law no. 17 of 1958
Fujo ni inkō wo saseta monotō no shobatsu nikansuru chokurei [Imperial Order on Punishment of Persons Who Force Women to Perform Prostitution], imperial order no. 9 of 1947
Fukuokaken seishounen kenzen ikusei jourei [Fukuoka Prefecture Youth Protection Ordinance], Fukuoka ordinance no. 46 of 1995
Fuzoku eigyōtō no kisei oyobi gyoumu no tekiseikatō nikansuru hōritsu [Act on Regulation of Entertainment Business and Its Proper Administration], law no. 122 of 1948 (Entertainment Business Regulation Act)
Gaikokujin no ginō jisshuu no tekiseina jisshi oyobi ginō jisshusei no hogo nikansuru hōritsu [Act on Proper Implementation of the Foreign Trainee System and on the Protection of Trainees], law no. 89 of 2016
Goseibai shikimoku [Formulary of Adjudications], originally enacted in 1232
Hansen byō mondai no kaiketsu no sokushin nikansuru hōritsu [Act on Facilitation of the Solution to Leprosy Problems], law no. 28 of 1996
Hanzai higaishatō kihonhō [Crime Victims Fundamental Act], law no. 161 of 2004
Hanzai higaishatō kyuuhukin no shikyutō niyoru hanzai higaishatō no shien nikansuru hōritsu [Crime Victims Support Benefit Act], law no. 36 of 1980
Hanzai higaishatō no kenri rieki no hogo wo hakarutame no keijitetsuduki nihuzuisuru sochi nikansuru hōritsu [Act concerning Measures with Respect to Criminal Procedure to Protect the Rights and Interests of Crime Victims], law no. 75 of 2000 (Crime Victims Protection Act)
Hatarakikata kaikaku wo suishin surutame no kanren hōritsu no seibi hōritsu: [Act concerning the Adjustment of Relevant Acts to Promote the Way of Work Reform], law no. 71 of 2018 (Way of Work Reform Act)

Hito nikansuru clone gijutsutō no kisei ni kansuru hōritsu [Act on Regulation of the Use of Cloning Technology in Humans], law no. 146 of 2000

Ikuji kyugyou, kaigo kyugyotō ikuji matawa kazokukaigo wo okonau roudousha no hukushi ni kansuru hōritsu [Infant Care and Elder Care Leave Act], law no. 76 of 1991

Internet isei shoukai jigyou wo riyoushite jidō wo yuin-suru koui no kiseitō nikansuru hōritsu [Act on Regulation of Enticing Children Using an Internet Dating Service], law no. 83 of 2003 (Dating Service Regulation Act)

Jidō gyakutai no boushitō nikansuru hōritsu [Child Abuse Prevention Act], law no. 82 of 2000

Jidō hukushihō [Child Welfare Act], law no. 164 of 1947

Jidō hukushihōtō no ichibuwo kaiseisuru hōritsu [Act to Amend Parts of the Child Welfare Act], law no. 63 of 2016

Jidō kaishun, jidō porn ni kakawaru kouitō no kisei oyobi shobatsu narabini jidō no hogotō nikansuru hōritsu [Act on Regulation and Punishment of Persons Who Had Become Customers of Child Prostitution and Child Porn and the Protection of Children], law no. 52 of 1999 (Child Prostitution Prohibition Act)

Jidō teatehō [Child Benefit Act], law no. 73 of 1971

Josei no shokugyou seikatsu niokeru katsuyaku no suishin nikansuru hōritsu [Act on Promotion of Women's Professional Life], law no. 64 of 2015

Josei no shokugyou seikatsu niokeru katsuyaku no suishin nikansuru hōritsutō no ichibu wo kaiseisuru hōritsu [Act to Amend Parts of the Act on Promotion of Women's Professional Life], law no. 24 of 2019

Kaigo hokenhō [Elderly Care Insurance Act], law no. 123 of 2007

Keihō [Criminal Code], law no. 47 of 1907

Keihō [Old Criminal Code], dajokan hukoku no. 36 of 1880, replaced by the 1907 Criminal Code

Keihō no ichibu wo kaisei suru hōritsu [Act to Amend Parts of the Criminal Code], law no. 67 of 2022

Keiji soshohō [Code of Criminal Procedure], law no. 131 of 1948

Keisatsu hanzai shobatsurei [Police Offences Punishment Regulation], regulation no. 16 of the Ministry of Internal Affairs of 1908

Kokumin yuseihō [National Eugenics Act], law no. 107 of 1940

Kon-nan na mondai wo kakaeru josei no shien nikansuru hōritsu [Act concerning Support for Struggling Women], law no. 52 of 2022

Kosekihō [Old Family Registration Act], dajokan hukoku no. 170 of 1871

Kosekihō [Family Registration Act], law no. 224 of 1947

Koyou no bunya niokeru danjo no kintō na kikai oyobi taigu no kakuhotō nikansuru hōritsu [Act to Secure the Equal Employment Opportunity and Equal Treatment in the Employment Fields], law no. 113 of 1972 (Equal Employment Opportunity Act – EEOA)

Kujikata osadamegaki [Law of Tokugawa Military Government], 1742

Kyu yusei hogohō nimotoduku yusei shujutsutō wo uketamono nitaisuru ichijikin no shikyu nikansuru hōritsu [Act on Payment of One-Time Benefit for

Those Who Received Sterilization under the Former Eugenic Protection Act], law no. 14 of 2019
Minpō [Civil Code], 1896
Nihonkoku kenpō [Constitution of Japan], 1946
Rai yobohō [Leprosy Prevention Act], law no. 214 of 1953 (repealed in 1996)
Roudou keiyakuhō [Labour Contract Act], law no. 128 of 2007
Roudou kijunhō [Labour Standards Act], law no. 49 of 1947
Roudou seisaku no sogoutekina suishin narabini roudousha no koyōno antei oyobi shokugyou seikatsu no juujitu ni kansuru hōritsu [Act concerning Comprehensive Promotion of Labour Policies and Implementation of Stable Employment of Employees and Fulfillment of Work Life], law no. 132 of 1966
Roudousha haken jigyō no tekiseina un-ei no kakuho oyobi haken roudousha no hogotō nikansuru hōritsu [Act to Secure the Fair Administration of Worker Dispatch Business and the Protection of Dispatch Workers], law no. 88 of 1985 (Dispatch Workers Act)
Seidouitsusei shougaisha no seibetsu no toriatsukai no tokurei wo sadmeru hōritsu [Act to Provide Special Treatment of Sex for Sexual Identity Disorder Patients], law no. 111 of 2003
Seiiku katei niarumono oyobi sono hogosha narabini ninsanpu ni taisi hitsuyouna seiiku iryou wo kiremenaku teikyō surutame no sesaku no sougoutekina suishin nikansuru hōritsu [Act on Comprehensive Promotion of Various Measures to Provide Necessary Support without Disruption to Children, Families, and Pregnant Mothers], law no. 104 of 2018
Seikatsu hogohō [Welfare Assistance Act], law no. 144 of 1950
Shiji seiteki gazoukiroku no teikyotō niyoru higai no boushi nikansuru hōritsu [Act on Prevention of Damages Resulting from Distribution of Private Sexual Visual Images], law no. 126 of 2014 (Revenge Porn Prevention Act)
Shogeigi torishimari kisoku [Regulation to Control Playing Girls], regulation no. 44 of the Ministry of Internal Affairs of 1900
Shotokuzeihō [Income Tax Act], law no. 33 of 1965
Shougai wo riyu tosuru sabetsu no kaishouno suishin nikansuru hōritsu [Act on the Elimination of Discrimination Based on Disability], law no. 65 of 2013
Shougaisha kihonhō [Fundamental Act for Persons with a Disability], law no. 84 of 1970
Shoushika shakai taisaku kihonhō [Fundamental Act on Declining Childbirth Countermeasures], law no. 133 of 2003.
Shutsu nyukoku kanri oyobi nanmin ninteihō [Immigration Control and Refugee Approval Act], law no. 319 of 1951 (Immigration Control Act)
Shutsu nyukoku kanri oyobi nanmin ninteihō oyobi houmushō secchihō no ichibu wo kaiseisuru hōritsu [Act to Amend Parts of the Immigration Control and Refugee Recognition Act and Ministry of Justice Establishment Act], law no. 102 of 2018

Shuugin giin senkyohō [House of Representatives Members Election Act], law no. 3 of 1889

Tanjikan roudousha oyobi yukikoyou roudousha no koyoukanri no kaizentō nikansuru hōritsu [Act concerning the Improvement of Employment Management of Part-Time Workers and Fixed-Term Workers], law no. 76 of 2003 (Part-Time Workers Act)

Tokyoto koushu ni ichijirushiku meiwaku wo kakeru bouryokuteki huryo kouitō no boushi nikansuru jourei [Tokyo Metropolitan Government Ordinance on Prevention of Violent Nuisance Acts That Causes Extreme Annoyance to the Public], Tokyo Metropolitan Government ordinance no. 103 of 1962 (Tokyo Anti-Nuisance Ordinance)

Tokyoto seishounen no kenzen na ikusei nikansuru jōrei [Tokyo Metropolitan Government Ordinance on Healthy Upbringing of Youth], Tokyo Metropolitan Government ordinance no. 181 of 1964 (Tokyo Youth Protection Ordinance)

Yusei hogohō [Eugenic Protection Act], law no. 156 of 1948 (renamed Botai hogohō)

Yusei hogohō no ichibu wo kaiseisuru hōritsu [Act to Amend Parts of the Eugenic Protection Act], law no. 216 of 1949

Yusei hogohō no ichibuwo kaiseisuru hōritsu [Act to Amend Parts of the Eugenic Protection Act], law no. 141 of 1952

New Zealand
Prostitution Reform Act, 2003

Sweden
Swedish Criminal Code, 1962

United Kingdom
U.K. Sexual Offences Act, 2003

United States
Arizona Revised Statutes
California Family Code
California Penal Code
Code of Virginia
Colorado Revised Statutes
Connecticut General Statutes
Delaware Code
Florida Statutes
Georgia Code

Idaho Statutes
Kentucky Revised Statutes
New Mexico Stat. Anno.
New York Consolidated Laws
Revised Codes of Washington
Texas Government Code
Texas Penal Code

United Nations Treaties
Convention on the Rights of the Child, 1989
International Covenant on Civil and Political Rights, 1966
International Covenant on Economic, Social and Cultural Rights, 1966
Universal Declaration of Human Rights, 1948

Notes

Introduction

1 For histories of Japan, see George Sansom, *A History of Japan to 1334* (Redwood City, CA: Stanford University Press, 1958); Kenneth Henshall, *A History of Japan*, 3rd ed. (London: Palgrave Macmillan, 2012); Brett L. Walker, *Concise History of Japan* (Cambridge, UK: Cambridge University Press, 2015).

2 George Sansom, *A History or Japan, 1334–1615* (Redwood City, CA: Stanford University Press, 1961); George Sansom, *A History of Japan, 1615 to 1867* (Redwood City, CA: Stanford University Press, 1963); Marius B. Jansen, *The Making of Modern Japan* (Cambridge, Mass.: Belknap Press, 2002); Andrew Gordon, *A Modern History of Japan: From Tokugawa Times to the Present*, 4th ed. (Oxford: Oxford University Press, 2019).

3 Harold G. Wren, "The Legal System of Pre-Western Japan," 20 Hastings L.J. 217 at 232–33 (1968); Dan F. Henderson, "Far Eastern Section, Some Aspects of Tokugawa Law," 27 Wash. L. Rev. & St. B.J. 83 at 104–5 (1952).

4 Wren, *supra* note 3 at 232.

5 Henderson, *supra* note 3 at 100.

6 Henderson points out that, "as a general characteristic, this is one of the most striking – that in the whole system of criminal and civil law the individual has no legal existence as such or except as he is a part of a group, family ... village or class." Ibid., at 105.

7 Donald Keene, *Emperor of Japan: Meiji and His World, 1852–1912* (New York: Columbia University Press, 2005); Anne Walthall and M. Williams Steele, *Politics and Society in Japan's Meiji Restoration: A Brief History with Documents* (Boston/New York: Bedford/St. Martin's, 2016); W.G. Beasley, *The Meiji Restoration* (Redwood City, CA: Stanford University Press, 2018).

8 Elise K. Tipton, *Modern Japan: A Social and Political History*, 3rd ed. (London and New York: Routledge, 2017); Mark Ravina, *To Stand with the Nations of the World: Japan's Meiji Restoration in World History* (Oxford: Oxford University Press, 2017).
9 Dainihon teikoku kenpō [Constitution of the Empire of Japan], 1889, art. 1, art. 4.
10 Ibid., chapter II (rights and duties of subjects).
11 Ibid., art. 29 (protecting liberty of speech "within the limits of law").
12 Shigenori Matsui, "The Constitution and the Family in Japan," in *Japanese Family Law in Comparative Perspective*, ed. Harry N. Scheiber and Laurent Mayali (Berkeley, CA: Robbins Collection, 2009), 33–60; Shigenori Matsui, "'Never Had a Choice and Have No Power to Alter': Illegitimate Children and the Supreme Court of Japan," 44 Ga. J. Int'l & Comp. L. 577 (2016).
13 For the lead-up to the enactment of this Constitution, see Theodore McNelly, *The Origins of Japan's Democratic Constitution* (New York and Oxford: University Press of America, 2000); Ray A. Moore and Donald L. Robinson, *Partners for Democracy: Crafting the New Japanese State under MacArthur* (Oxford: Oxford University Press, 2002). See also John W. Dower, *Embracing Defeat: Japan in the Wake of World War II* (New York: W.W. Norton, 2000).
14 Nihonkoku kenpō [Constitution of Japan], 1946.
15 Ibid., preamble and art. 1.
16 Ibid., art. 1, art. 4.
17 Ibid., art. 11.
18 Ibid., art. 13.
19 Ibid., art. 14(1).
20 Ibid., art. 24.
21 Ibid., art. 97.
22 For the conservative nature of Japanese society, see Ruth Benedict, *The Chrysanthemum and the Sword: Patterns of Japanese Culture* (Boston: Houghton Mifflin, 1946); Ross Mouer and Yoshio Sugimoto, *Images of Japanese Society* (London: KPI, 1986); Yoshio Sugimoto, *An Introduction to Japanese Society* (Cambridge, UK: Cambridge University Press, 1997). It must be noted that an increasing number of researchers have detected a gradual rise of individualism in Japan. Yohtaro Takano and Eiko Osaka, "Comparing Japan and the United States on Individualism/Collectivism: A Follow-Up Review," A21:4 Asian J. Social Psychology 301 (2018).
23 Cabinet Office, *Reiwa 3-nen koureikashakai hakusho* [Aging Society Whitepaper, 2021], https://www8.cao.go.jp/kourei/whitepaper/w-2021/zenbun/pdf/1s1s_01.pdf.
24 Ibid.
25 United Nations, Department of Economic and Social Affairs, "World Population Ageing 2019: Highlights," 12, https://www.un.org/en/development/desa/population/publications/pdf/ageing/WorldPopulationAgeing2019-Highlights.pdf.
26 Aging Society Whitepaper, 2021, *supra* note 23.
27 Ibid.

28 World Population Review, Birth Rate by Country in 2022, https://worldpopulationreview.com/country-rankings/birth-rate-by-country (ranking Japan as the country with fourth lowest birth rate in the world); The 20 countries with the lowest fertility rates in 2021, Statista, https://www.statista.com/statistics/268083/countries-with-the-lowest-fertility-rates/ (ranking Japan as country with the 11th lowest fertility rate).
29 Aging Society Whitepaper, 2021, *supra* note 23.
30 Ibid.

Chapter 1: Sexual Autonomy

1 "Sex" usually refers to "a set of biological attributes in humans and animals. It is primarily associated with physical and physiological features including chromosomes, gene expression, hormone levels and function, and reproductive/sexual anatomy," whereas "gender" usually refers to "socially constructed roles, behaviours, expressions and identities." "What Is Gender? What Is Sex?" Canadian Institutes of Health Research, https://cihr-irsc.gc.ca/e/48642.html. See also United Kingdom Office for National Statistics, "What Is the Difference between Sex and Gender?" February 21, 2019, https://www.ons.gov.uk/economy/environmentalaccounts/articles/whatisthedifferencebetweensexandgender/2019-02-21. "Transgender" or trans is an umbrella term for people whose gender identity differs from the sex assigned to them at birth. But some prefer the word "transsexual," especially for people who receive sex reassignment surgery and hormone therapy to physically change their sex. Therefore, I use "decide on or change sex or gender" to refer to an individual's right to determine sexual or gender identity.
2 Geoffrey R. Stone, *Sex and the Constitution: Sex, Religion, and Law from America's Origins to the Twenty-First Century* (New York and London: Liveright, 2017).
3 *Constitution of the United States,* Fourteenth Amendment, s 1.
4 *Skinner v Oklahoma,* 316 U.S. 535 (1942) (acknowledging the right to procreate as "one of the basic civil rights of man," the court invalidated an Oklahoma statute that required the sterilization of habitual criminals because it violated the equal protection clause of the Fourteenth Amendment).
5 *Griswold v Connecticut,* 381 U.S. 479 (1965) (right of a married couple to use contraceptives); *Eisenstadt v Baird,* 405 U.S. 438 (1972) (right of an unmarried couple to access contraceptives); *Carey v Population Services Int'l,* 431 U.S. 678 (1977) (right of access to contraceptives for minors).
6 *Roe v Wade,* 410 U.S. 113 (1973) (right to an abortion), now overruled by *Dobbs v Jackson Women's Health Organization,* 597 U.S. – (2022).
7 *Bowers v Hardwick,* 478 U.S. 186 (1986).
8 *Lawrence v Texas,* 539 U.S. 558 (2003).
9 *Obergefell v Hodges,* 576 U.S. 644 (2015).
10 Ibid.
11 Ibid.

12 *Lawrence v Texas, supra* note 8 at 566–67.
13 *Obergefell v Hodges, supra* note 9.
14 *Lawrence v Texas, supra* note 8 at 572 (emphasis added).
15 Ibid., at 578 (emphasis added).
16 Ibid.
17 *Planned Parenthood v Casey*, 505 U.S. 833 (1992).
18 *Dobbs v Jackson Women's Health Organization, supra* note 6 at –.
19 Ibid., at –.
20 Ibid., at –.
21 Ibid., at –.
22 Ibid., at –.
23 Ibid., at –.
24 Ibid., at –.
25 Ibid., at –.
26 The SCOTUS emphasized the seriousness of the error in the precedent. "*Roe* was also egregiously wrong and deeply damaging. For reasons already explained, *Roe*'s constitutional analysis was far outside the bounds of any reasonable interpretation of the various constitutional provisions to which it vaguely pointed.

   Roe was on a collision course with the Constitution from the day it was decided, *Casey* perpetuated its errors, and those errors do not concern some arcane corner of the law of little importance to the American people. Rather, wielding nothing but "raw judicial power," ... the Court usurped the power to address a question of profound moral and social importance that the Constitution unequivocally leaves for the people ... Together, *Roe* and *Casey* represent an error that cannot be allowed to stand." Ibid., at –.
27 Ibid., at – (Breyer, J, Sotomayor, J & Kagan, J, dissenting). Justice Thomas indeed emphasizes the necessity of reconsidering the whole substantive due process jurisprudence, including a right to contraception, right to private consensual sexual acts, and the right to same-sex marriage. Ibid., at – (Thomas, J, concurring).
28 "*Roe*'s defenders characterize the abortion right as similar to the rights recognized in past decisions involving matters such as intimate sexual relations, contraception, and marriage, but abortion is fundamentally different, as both *Roe* and *Casey* acknowledged, because it destroys what those decisions called 'fetal life' and what the law now before us describes as an 'unborn human being.'" Ibid., at –.
29 Ibid., at – ("And to ensure that our decision is not misunderstood or mischaracterized, we emphasize that our decision concerns the constitutional right to abortion and no other right. Nothing in this opinion should be understood to cast doubt on precedents that do not concern abortion").
30 The SCOTUS appears to admit this. Ibid., at –.
31 Responding to the argument that, because same-sex couples cannot procreate, allowing them to marry is not required, the SCOTUS stated, "That is not to say the right to marry is less meaningful for those who do not or cannot have children.

An ability, desire, or promise to procreate is not and has not been a prerequisite for an invalid marriage in any State. In light of precedent protecting the right of a married couple not to procreate, it cannot be said the Court or the States have conditioned the right to marry on the capacity or commitment to procreate. The constitutional marriage right has many aspects, of which childbearing is only one." *Obergefell v Hodges*, supra note 9 at –. Marriage is not necessarily connected with procreation. Sex and marriage are also not necessarily linked. Nevertheless, sex was once the only means of procreation and still remains the primary one, although people should be allowed to enjoy sex without procreation.

32 Nihonkoku kenpō [Constitution of Japan], 1946.
33 Ibid., art. 41 (the Diet shall be the highest organ of state power and shall be the sole law-making organ of the state).
34 Ibid., art. 76 (judicial power is vested in a Supreme Court and in such inferior courts as are established by law).
35 Ibid., art. 81 (the Supreme Court is the court of last resort, with the power to determine the constitutionality of any law, order, regulation, or official act).
36 Since the Constitution is binding only on the government, I will focus on government restriction of this constitutional right. Saikō saibansho [SCOJ], grand bench, December 12, 1973, 27:11 Minshu 1536 (Mitsubishi Plastic Corporation case). But it must be remembered that the protection of sexual autonomy is very important in social and private contexts as well.
37 The Japanese version of the right to due process is given in article 31 of the Constitution, which stipulates that "no person shall be deprived of life or liberty, nor shall any other criminal penalty be imposed, except according to procedure established by law." Constitution of Japan, *supra* note 32 art. 31. Indeed, many academics argue that article 31 is comparable to the Fourteenth Amendment of the Constitution of the United States, as a due process clause that also protects substantive due process, prohibiting government infringement of "liberty" without reasonable grounds or disproportionately.
38 Ibid., art. 13.
39 Nobuyoshi Ashibe, with Kazuyuki Takahashi, *Kenpō* [Constitution], 7th ed. (Tokyo: Iwanami shoten, 2019), 121, 128; Kōji Sato, *Nihonkoku kenpōron* [Constitution of Japan], 2nd ed. (Tokyo: Seibundo, 2020), 196–99, 212.
40 Ashibe, *supra* note 39 at 128; Sato, *supra* note 39 at 212, 214–16.
41 Constitution of Japan, *supra* note 32 art. 24.
42 Shigenori Matsui, *Nihonkoku kenpō* [Constitution of Japan], 3rd ed. (Tokyo: Yuhikaku, 2007), 547; Hideki Shibutani, *Kenpō* [Constitution], 3rd ed. (Tokyo: Yuhikaku, 2017), 467.
43 Matsui, *supra* note 42 at 549; Shibutani, *supra* note 42 at 467.
44 Of course, this right applies to everyone. There is no legitimate reason that protection from rape or sexual assault should apply solely to women. Matsui, *supra* note 42 at 382.

45 *Roe v Wade*, supra note 6.
46 *Whole Woman's Health v Hellerstedt*, 579 U.S. (2016); *Planned Parenthood v Casey*, 505 U.S. 833 (1992). See also *June Medical Services v Russo*, 591 U.S. (2020).
47 *Dobbs v Jackson Women's Health Organization*, supra note 6. The SCOTUS thus rejected the constitutional challenge against the Mississippi law that prohibited the abortion if the probable gestational age of the fetus has been determined to be greater than fifteen (15) weeks except in a medical emergency or in the case of a severe fetal abnormality.
48 *R. v Oakes*, [1986] 1 SCR 103; Dieter Grimm, "Proportionality in Canadian and German Constitutional Jurisprudence," 57:2 U. Toronto L.J. 383 (2007).
49 *R. v Oakes*, supra note 48.
50 *RJR-MacDonald Inc. v Canada (Attorney General)*, [1995] 3 SCR 199.
51 Shigenori Matsui, "Judicial Review of Restrictions on Constitutional Rights in Japan: Highly Ad Hoc, Contextualized and Deferential," in *Proportionality in Asia*, ed. Po Jen Yap (Cambridge: Cambridge University Press, 2020), at 140.
52 *Romer v Evans*, 517 U.S. 620 (1996). In striking down the ban on sodomy between homosexual couples, *Lawrence* was not clear on what standard of review was applied. But at least, the SCOTUS indicated that the ban was hardly justifiable even under the rationality standard.
53 *United States v Carolene Products Company*, 304 U.S. 144 (1938).
54 See Stone, *supra* note 2.
55 *R. v Labaye*, [2005] 3 SCR 728 at [14] (emphasis added).
56 Ibid., at [28].
57 Ibid., at [29] (emphasis in original).
58 Ibid., at [36].
59 Ibid., at [37] (emphasis added).
60 On the other hand, the government interest in prohibiting sexual behaviour because it could potentially predispose "others to anti-social conduct" could be questionable. The publication of obscene material is often forbidden on the grounds that it plays a role in the increase of sex crimes, but it is debatable whether this is accurate. Moreover, the possibility of "predisposing" others is utterly ambiguous, and it is questionable how the courts can decide whether any given conduct could predispose anyone to a particular conduct. Furthermore, the SCOC is talking about "anti-social" behaviour, not breaking the law. It is indeed doubtful whether the government should be allowed to ban conduct that might simply lead to anti-social behaviour rather than to transgressing the law.

Chapter 2: Sexual Freedom
1 Geoffrey R. Stone, *Sex and the Constitution: Sex, Religion, and Law from America's Origins to the Twenty-First Century* (New York and London: Liveright, 2017).
2 Buke shohatto [Law for the Military House] (1615).

3 Goseibai shikimoku [Formulary of Adjudications], originally enacted in 1232. Updated several times, this was regarded as being a law for samurai warriors.
4 Kujikata osadamegaki [Law of Tokugawa Military Government], 1742; Yoshio Nagai, *Edono seijijo* [Sex and Crime during the Edo Period] (Tokyo: Best Sellers, 2016); Sabine Frühstück, *Colonizing Sex: Sexology and Social Control in Modern Japan* (Berkeley, CA: University of California Press, 2003). In addition, there once was a ban on sodomy. Keikanritsu [Sodomy Ban], 1872.
5 Nagai, *supra* note 4 at 6. See also Yoshio Nagai, *Edo no Mi-tsu* [Adultery during the Edo Period] (Tokyo: Gakken shinsho, 2010). Because these crimes were seen as embarrassing or shameful, few people reported them, with the result that the punishments were rarely enforced.
6 Keihō [Old Criminal Code], dajokan hukoku no. 36 of 1880, replaced by the 1907 Criminal Code.
7 Minpō [Civil Code], 1896.
8 Keihō [Criminal Code], 1907.
9 See generally, Hiroshi Oda, *Japanese Law*, 3rd ed. (Oxford: Oxford University Press, 2011); Curtis Milhaupt, J. Ramseyer, and Mark West, *The Japanese Legal System*, 2nd ed. (St. Paul, MN: Foundation Press, 2012).
10 Kosekihō [Old Family Registration Act], dajokan hukoku no. 170 of 1871.
11 Shugin gi-in senkyohō [House of Representatives Members Election Act], law no. 3 of 1889, art. 6(1).
12 See, for example, Civil Code, supra note 7 art. 14–18 (married women could not manage property without permission from their husbands); art. 788 (marrying woman entered into the house of her husband). Moreover, the previous Nationality Act granted the Japanese nationality automatically to a child of Japanese father, but not to a child of Japanese mother. Kokusekihō [Nationality Act], law no. 66 of 1899, art. 1.
13 Old Criminal Code, *supra* note 6 art. 346.
14 Ibid., art. 347.
15 Ibid., art. 348.
16 Ibid., art. 349.
17 Ibid., art. 351.
18 Ibid., art. 353.
19 Dainihon teikoku kenpō [Constitution of the Empire of Japan], promulgated in 1889 (Meiji Constitution).
20 Ibid., preamble, art. 1, art. 4.
21 Ibid., art. 2.
22 His person was sacred and inviolable. Ibid., art. 3.
23 Ibid., arts. 22–29 (rights of subjects).
24 For instance, ibid., art. 29 (protecting freedom of speech within the confines of the law).

25 Richard J. Samuels, *Rich Nation, Strong Army: National Security and the Technological Transformation of Japan* (Ithaca, CT: Cornell University Press, 1996).
26 Bill Mihalopoulos, *Sex in Japan's Globalization, 1870–1930; Prostitutes, Emigration and Nation-Building* (Abingdon and New York: Routledge, 2016); Susan L. Burns, *Gender and Law in the Japanese Imperium* (Honolulu, HI: University of Hawai'i Press, 2015).
27 Civil Code, *supra* note 7 part 4 (family law) and part 5 (succession law), added in 1898.
28 Article 732(1) of the Civil Code defined "house" as "family members of the housemaster who are living within the house and their spouses." The housemaster and all members of the house were required to take the house name as their surname. Ibid., art. 746. The family register was organized according to house name, listing the housemaster and his family.
29 Ibid., art. 737(1). Anyone who did not obey the housemaster's decision regarding residence or did not obtain his approval for marriage could be kicked out of the house. Ibid., art. 749, 750. The putative successor to an estate could not enter another house or create one of his own. Ibid., art. 744.
30 Ibid., art. 749.
31 Ibid., art. 750. However, marriage without approval of the housemaster was not invalid, and he could evict girls only within one year of it. Ibid. Nevertheless, parents had the power to approve the marriage of their offspring until the age of thirty for sons and twenty-five for daughters. They could also annul a marriage if it were performed without their approval. Ibid., art. 772(1).
32 Ibid., art. 747.
33 Miyoko Tsujimura, "Women's Rights in Law and Praxis: The Significance of Three Statistics from Politics, the Household, and Labor," in *Five Decades of Constitutionalism in Japanese Society*, ed. Yoichi Higuchi (Tokyo: University of Tokyo Press, 2000), 156; Shigenori Matsui, "The Constitution and the Family in Japan," in *Japanese Family Law in Comparative Perspective*, ed. Harry N. Schreiber and Laurent Mayali (Berkeley, CA: Robbins Collection, 2009), 33.
34 Shugin gi-in senkyohō, *supra* note 11 art. 6(1) (granting the franchise only to Japanese male subjects over the age of twenty-five who paid a certain amount of tax).
35 Civil Code, *supra* note 7 art. 801 (a husband was supposed to manage his wife's property).
36 Ibid., art. 970.
37 For a general overview, see Shigenori Matsui, *Constitution of Japan: A Contextual Analysis* (Oxford: Hart, 2011), 153.
38 Nihonkoku kenpō [Constitution of Japan], 1946, art. 11.
39 Ibid., art. 97.
40 Ibid., preamble and art. 1.

41 Ibid., art. 98 ("This Constitution shall be the supreme law of the nation and no law, ordinance, imperial rescript or other act of government, or part thereof, contrary to the provisions hereof, shall have legal force or validity").
42 Ibid., art. 81 ("The Supreme Court is the court of last resort with the power to determine the constitutionality of any law, order, regulation or official act").
43 *Lawrence v Texas*, 539 U.S. 558 (2003).
44 Ibid., art. 13.
45 Ibid., art. 24.
46 Tsujimura, *supra* note 35; Matsui, *supra* note 35.
47 For histories of the enactment of the Constitution, see Shōichi Koseki, *The Birth of Japan's Postwar Constitution* (New York/Abingdon: Perseus, 1998); Ray A. Moore and Donald L. Robinson, *Partners for Democracy: Crafting the New Japanese State under MacArthur* (Oxford: Oxford University Press, 2002).
48 Beate Sirota Gordon, *The Only Woman in the Room: A Memoir of Japan, Human Rights and the Arts* (Chicago/London: University of Chicago Press, 1997); Elise Meyer, "Walking the Beate: How One American Woman Helped Change Japanese Marriage Law Forever," Law School International Immersion Program Papers, No. 13 (2016), https://chicagounbound.uchicago.edu/cgi/viewcontent.cgi?article=1036 &context=international_immersion_program_papers.
49 Civil Code, *supra* note 7 art. 2.
50 Kosekihō [Family Registration Act], law no. 224 of 1947, art. 6. The family register was compiled according to the "first person listed." Ibid., art. 9. This is the spouse whose surname the couple adopted upon marriage. Ibid., art. 14.
51 Civil Code, *supra* note 7 art. 731. Now it was amended to allow both men and women to get married at the age of eighteen. Ibid.
52 Ibid., art. 737.
53 Ibid., art. 750.
54 Ibid., art. 752 (husband and wife must live together, cooperate, and help each other).
55 Ibid., art. 890 (spouse), art. 887 and art. 900 (children). With respect to inheritance, illegitimate children could expect to receive only half of the share granted to legitimate children right after the Second World War. Yet, this discrimination was ultimately struck down by the SCOJ. Saikō saibansho [SCOJ], grand bench, September 4, 2013, 67:6 Minshu 1320. See Shigenori Matsui, "'Never Had a Choice and Have No Power to Alter': Illegitimate Children and the Supreme Court of Japan," 44 Ga. J. Int'l & Comp. L. 577 (2016). It is now amended to allow all children, legitimate or illegitimate, to secure equal entitlement to the estate.
56 Criminal Code, *supra* note 8 art. 177 (rape, or after 2017, "forcible sexual intercourse et al.," i.e., forcible sexual intercourse, anal intercourse or oral intercourse) and art. 176 (forcible obscene acts).

57 Ibid., art. 177 (before the 2017 amendment). Now, forcible sexual intercourse et al. with anyone under the age of thirteen is a crime.
58 Baishun boushihō [Prostitution Prevention Act], law no. 118 of 1956, art. 3.
59 Criminal Code, *supra* note 8 art. 183 (deleted in 1947).
60 Jidō kaishun, jidō porn ni kakawaru kouitō no kisei oyobi shobatsu narabini jidō no hogotō nikansuru hōritsu [Act on Regulation and Punishment of Persons Who Had Become Customers of Child Prostitution and Child Porn and Protection of Children], law no. 52 of 1999, art. 2(3), art. 4 (Child Prostitution Prohibition Act).
61 Fukuokaken seishounen kenzen ikusei jourei [Fukuoka Prefecture Youth Protection Ordinance], Fukuoka ordinance no. 46 of 1995, art. 31 (prohibiting indecent sexual conduct or obscene conduct with youth). The ordinances often use the ambiguous phrase "indecent sexual conduct" without providing any definition. But everyone agrees that at least sexual intercourse is included. On the other hand, the Tokyo Youth Protection Ordinance bans sexual intercourse or conduct that is analogous to it. Tokyoto seishounen no kenzen na ikusei nikansuru jōrei [Ordinance on Healthy Upbringing of Youth], Tokyo ordinance no. 181 of 1964, art. 18–6 (Tokyo Youth Protection Ordinance) (prohibiting sexual intercourse and analogous conduct). If the offender is a minor, the criminal punishment is not applied. Ibid., art. 30.
62 Jidō hukushihō [Child Welfare Act], law no. 164 of 1947, art. 34(1).
63 Jidō gyakutai no boushitō nikansuru hōritsu [Child Abuse Prevention Act], law no. 82 of 2000, art. 3.
64 Ibid., art. 2 (prohibiting obscene conduct against a child or making a child perform obscene conduct).
65 Family Registration Act, *supra* note 50 art. 49(1). Although the Family Registration Act lists only the family relationship between a parent and a child to be included in the regitry, the government has maintained the custom of differentiating "firstborn boy," "secondborn boy," or "thirdborn boy" or "firstborn girl," "secondborn girl," or "thirdborn girl." As a result, whether a child is male or female is apparent from the registry.
66 Ibid., art. 49(2).
67 Seidouitsusei shougaisha no seibetsu no toriatsukai no tokurei wo sadmeru hōritsu [Act to Provide Special Treatment of Sex for Sexual Identity Disorder Patients], law no. 111 of 2003.
68 Saikō saibansho [SCOJ], grand bench, June 24, 1953, 7:6 Keishu 1366.
69 When the rape provision was radically revised in 2017, it protected both women and men. Criminal Code, *supra* note 8 art. 177 (after the 2017 amendment).
70 Saikō saibansho [SCOJ], grand bench, October 23, 1985, 39:6 Keishu 413 (holding that the ban on indecent sexual conduct under the local youth protection ordinance "should not be interpreted to mean all sexual conducts toward youth but should be interpreted only to mean sexual intercourse or sexual intercourse analogous conducts with improper means such as enticing, intimidating, deceiving or

embarrassing the youth or sexual intercourse or sexual intercourse analogous conduct that is viewed nothing other than the conduct to treat the youth merely to satisfy the sexual desires").

71 Criminal Code, *supra* note 8 art. 177 (before the 2017 amendment).
72 Ibid., art. 177 (after the 2017 amendment).
73 Prostitution Prevention Act, *supra* note 58 art. 2 (defining prostitution as sexual intercourse for payment or the promise of payment).
74 Child Prostitution Prohibition Act, *supra* note 60 art. 2(2).
75 Child Welfare Act, *supra* note 62 art. 34.
76 Child Abuse Prevention Act, *supra* note 63 art. 2.
77 Tokyo Youth Protection Ordinance, *supra* note 61 art. 18–6.
78 Yukiko Tsunoda, *Sei to hōritu* [Sex and Law] (Tokyo: Iwanami shoten, 2013), 216–18; Hiroshi Nakasatomi, "Post-gender ki no josei no seibaibai" [Prostitution and Buying Prostitution of Women in the Post-gender Period], 59:2 Tokyo daigaku shakai kagaku kenkyu 39 (2007), https://jww.iss.u-tokyo.ac.jp/jss/pdf/jss5802_039069.pdf.
79 Furthermore, Japanese revenge porn legislation bans the unconsented distribution of "private sexual visual images" by telecommunication and defines such images as follows (since revenge porn legislation bans unconsented disclosure of intimate image, mostly intimate sexual images, it would show which sexual conduct needs to be protected against unwanted disclosure);

1   a person – the image could be focused on a particular person, usually the ex-partner – engaged in sexual intercourse or conduct that is analogous to it,
2   another person touching his or her genitals, anus, or nipples, or a person touching the genitals, anus, or nipples of another person to excite or stimulate desire, or
3   a naked or partially undressed person exposing or emphasizing the sexual parts of the body (genitals or nearby area, buttocks, or breasts) to excite or stimulate desire.

Shiji seiteki gazoukiroku no teikyotō niyoru higai no boushi nikansuru hōritsu [Act on Prevention of Damages Resulting from Distribution of Private Sexual Visual Images], law no. 126 of 2014 (Revenge Porn Prevention Act). These definitions give us somewhat different understanding of what should be regarded as private sexual conduct.

80 See *supra* note 67. At the time it was passed, one needed to be over the age of twenty but the provision was later amended when the majority age of the Civil Code was amended.
81 Criminal Code, *supra* note 8 art. 177.
82 Kokusekihō [Nationality Act], law no. 147 of 1950, art. 2 (before 1984).
83 For the purpose of official identification, an official copy of the local residence registration is more frequently used. Japan has two different registration systems:

one is family registration that records all family relationships of all Japanese citizens and the other one is local residence registration that records all personal information on local residents, regardless of nationality. In order to prove their identity, public authority and financial institutions require the official copy of the local residence registration and not an official copy of the family registration, which contains far more sensitive and intimate information. However, the passport requires the official copy of the family registration (which was created based on the family registration). It distinguishes between male and female. Japanese passports also still make the distinction between male (M) and female (F), although drivers' licences do not.

84 The SCOJ recently upheld the constitutionality of the requirement that a person who asks to change his or her registry listing must not be the parent of a minor. Saikō saibansho [SCOJ], 3rd petty bench, November 30, 2021, https://www.courts.go.jp/app/files/hanrei_jp/733/090733_hanrei.pdf.

85 In Canada, citizens are now allowed to indicate their sexual identity as "M: male," "F: female," or "X: other gender" on their passport. They can ask for a change of sexual identity for passport and other travel documents. Government of Canada, Choose or update the gender identifier on your passport or travel document, https://www.canada.ca/en/immigration-refugees-citizenship/services/canadian-passports/change-sex.html. See also U.S. Department of State, "Issuance of the First U.S. Passport with an X Gender Marker," press release, October 27, 2021, https://www.state.gov/issuance-of-the-first-u-s-passport-with-an-x-gender-marker/.

86 *Lawrence v Texas, supra* note 43.
87 *Griswold v Connecticut*, 381 U.S. 479 (1965).
88 Ibid., at 485.
89 *Lawrence v Texas*, supra note 43 at 567 (emphasis added).
90 Ibid., at 577–78, quoting Bowers, 478 U.S., at 216 (Stewart, J., dissenting).
91 Ibid., at 578 (emphasis added).
92 *New York Consolidated Laws, Penal*, s 130.25 (rape in the third degree), s 130.30 (rape in the second degree), s 130.35 (sexual intercourse with forcible compulsion: rape in the first degree) (*New York Penal Law*).
93 For instance, in New York, anyone who engages in sexual intercourse, oral sex, or anal sex without the consent of the partner is guilty of "sexual misconduct." Ibid., s 130.20. Anyone who engages in oral or anal sex with a person who is incapable of consenting or with anyone under age seventeen commits a "criminal sexual act," s 130.40 (sexual criminal act in the third degree), s 130.45 (criminal sexual act in the second degree), s 139.50 (criminal sexual act in the first degree). Under s 130.52, "forcible touching" applies to situations in which a person intentionally, and for no legitimate purpose, forcibly touches the sexual or other intimate parts of another person for the purpose of degrading or abusing such person; or for the purpose of gratifying the actor's sexual desire; or subjects another person to sexual contact for the purpose of gratifying the actor's sexual desire and with the intent

to degrade or abuse the person. "Sexual abuse," ss 130.55 to 130.65, occurs when a person subjects another person to sexual contact without the latter's consent. And "aggravated sexual abuse," ss 130.65-a to 130.70, occurs when a person inserts a foreign object in the vagina, urethra, penis, rectum, or anus of another person without the consent.

94 New York Penal Law, s 230.00 and s 130.00; Tom DeFranco and Rebecca Stellato, "Prostitution and Sex Work," 14 Geo. J. Gender & L. 553 at 558–59 (2013).
95 *California Penal Code*, s 647(j)(4).
96 *Arizona Revised Statutes*, s 13-1425D.6, citing s 11-811D.18 (a) and (b).
97 *Delaware Code*, s 11-1335(a)(9).
98 Ibid.
99 Carmen M. Cusack, *Laws Relating to Sex, Pregnancy, and Infancy* (New York: Palgrave Macmillan, 2015).
100 Criminal Code, *supra* note 8 art. 174. Until recently, the Criminal Code distinguished between imprisonment with labour and simple confinement. The former, which was generally imposed for more serious and heinous crimes, carried the mandatory obligation to work as part of punishment, whereas confinement was merely incarceration in prison. In a recent amendment to the Criminal Code, the Diet merged both sentences into imprisonment without labour. Keihōtō no ichibuwo kaiseisuru hōritsu [Act to Amend Part of the Criminal Code], law no. 67 of 2022. This integration will take effect within three years of promulgation.
101 *Colorado Revised Statutes*, s 18-7-301 (explicitly bans acts of sexual intercourse in a public place as indecency); *Connecticut General Statutes*, s 53a-186 (explicitly bans sexual intercourse in a public place as public indecency); *Georgia Code*, s 16-6-8 (same).
102 *New York Penal Law*, s 245.00 (public lewdness), s 245.01 (public exposure).
103 Cusack, *supra* note 99.
104 *R. v J.A.*, [2011] 2 SCR 440.
105 Ibid., at [3].
106 Ibid., at [43].
107 *R. v Labaye*, [2005] 3 SCR 728.
108 *Criminal Code of Canada*, R.S.C., 1985, c. C-46, s 210(1).
109 *Idaho Statutes*, s 18-6603.
110 *New York Penal Law*, s 255.17; *Idaho Statutes*, s 18-6601.
111 Criminal Code, *supra* note 8 art. 183 (deleted in 1947).
112 Tsujimura, *supra* note 33.
113 Civil Code, *supra* note 7 art. 770.
114 In 2015, the Constitutional Court of South Korea struck down the criminal ban on adultery. Choe Sang-Hun, "Adultery Is No Longer an Affair of the State in South Korea," *New York Times* (February 26, 2015), https://www.nytimes.com/2015/02/27/world/asia/south-korea-strikes-down-adultery-law.html.
115 *New York Penal Law*, s 255.25, s 255.26, s 255.27; *Code of Virginia*, s 18.2-361B.

116 Criminal Code, *supra* note 8 art. 179.
117 However, an incestuous relationship could be an obstacle to marriage. Close relatives are precluded from marriage, even if there is no blood tie and even if the family relationship has ended. Civil Code, *supra* note 7 art. 734.
118 *Bowers v Hardwick*, 478 U.S. 186 (1986). *Georgia Code*, s 16-6-2, provided for an offence of sodomy "when he or she performs or submits to any sexual act involving the sex organs of one person and the mouth or anus of another." This clause still remains in the code.
119 The case involved s 21.06 of the Texas Penal Code, which stated that "a person commits an offense if he engages in deviate sexual intercourse with another individual of the same sex." This clause remains in the code, even though *Lawrence* struck it down as unconstitutional.
120 For instance, *Kentucky Revised Statutes*, KRS #510.100.
121 As mentioned above, oral or anal intercourse that involves assault or intimidation is illegal, regardless of whether it is heterosexual or homosexual. Consensual oral and anal sex is not banned. However, there once was a sodomy ban. *Supra* note 4.
122 *New York Penal Law*, s 130.20 (sexual misconduct).
123 *Revised Codes of Washington*, RCW 9A.44.105.
124 *Florida Statutes*, XLVI 872.06.
125 *New York Penal Law*, s 130.20 (sexual misconduct).
126 *Code of Virginia*, s 18.2-361.
127 Emily Malhiot, "Chapter 86: Nevada Finally Outlaws Bestiality," 49 U. Pac. L. Rev. 555 (2018).
128 Sangeeta Singg, "Health Risks of Zoophilia/Bestiality," 1:1 J. Bio. & Med. Sci. (2017), https://www.researchgate.net/publication/317057166_Health_Risks_of_ZoophiliaBestiality.
129 *Warren v Commonwealth*, No. 2086-17-3, 2019 WL 189386 (Va. Ct. App. January 15, 2019).
130 See *supra* notes 65–67.
131 Civil Code, *supra* note 7 art. 732.
132 Ibid., art. 763.
133 Ibid., art. 770.
134 Saikō saibansho [SCOJ], 3rd petty bench, February 19, 1952, 6:2 Minshu 110.
135 Statement of Justice Minister, Press Interview, September 20, 2019, https://www.moj.go.jp/hisho/kouhou/hisho08_01165.html – replaced it.
136 Civil Code, *supra* note 7 art. 750.
137 See *supra* notes 47–48.
138 Saikō saibansho [SCOJ], grand bench, December 16, 2015, 69:8 Minshu 2586. This judgment was confirmed by Saikō saibansho [SCOJ], grand bench, June 23, 2021, unreported, https://www.courts.go.jp/app/files/hanrei_jp/412/090412_hanrei.pdf.
139 Moreover, the widespread prejudice against unwed mothers and illegitimate children makes single women wary of becoming pregnant, a possibility that might

cool their enthusiasm for sex. There is surely a need to ban discrimination based on marital status or illegitimacy.
140 *New York Penal Law*, s 130.25 (rape in the first degree), s 130.96 (predatory sexual conduct against a child).
141 U.K. *Sexual Offences Act*, 2003, s 5 (rape of a child under thirteen).
142 *New York Penal Law*, s 230.04 (patronizing a prostitute in the third degree), s 230.06 (patronizing a prostitute in the first degree); *New Mexico Stat. Anno.*, s 30-6A-4 (sexual exploitation of children by prostitution).
143 Criminal Code, *supra* note 8 art. 177 (imprisonment with labour for a definite term of no less than five years for having sexual intercourse et al. with a person under the age of thirteen).
144 See Child Prostitution Prohibition Act, *supra* note 62 art. 2(2). The punishment is imprisonment with labour for up to five years. When anyone has sexual intercourse with a child under the age of thirteen or uses assault or intimidation to have sexual intercourse with a child under the age of eighteen, the Criminal Code's ban on forcible sexual intercourse et al. will be applied. When anyone patronizes a child and engages in other sexual activities with a child under the age of eighteen, either the Criminal Code ban on forcible obscene act et al. or the Child Prostitution Prohibition Act could be applied.
145 See *supra* note 61.
146 SCOJ, grand bench, October 23, 1985, *supra* note 70.
147 Civil Code, *supra* note 7 art. 731. However, the recent amendment changed the legal age for marriage to eighteen both both male and female. Therefore, anyone age eighteen or older, who is eligible for marriage, will not be violating the local ordinance any more. But it is surely conceivable that a couple could have sex before marriage.
148 *Criminal Code of Canada*, *supra* note 108 ss 150.1(2) and 150.1(2.1).
149 Ibid., s 150.1(1). Consent from anyone sixteen or older can be a defence. Ibid.
150 Miho Mitsunari, "Nihon niokeru baibaishun no rekishi" [History of Prostitution in Japan], Gender History, https://ch-gender.jp/wp/?page_id=189.
151 Janet R. Goodwin, *Selling Songs and Smiles: The Sex Trade in Heian and Kamakura Japan* (Honolulu: University of Hawai'i Press, 2007).
152 Mitsunari, *supra* note 150.
153 Ibid.
154 Ibid. A typical contract between the business manager and the parents stipulated a fixed term, mandating girls and women to stay at the designated place and to provide services as obliged. Girls aged seven or eight would serve until the age of twenty-eight, violating the contract was subject to penalties, and parents received an advance payment. Ibid.
155 Ibid.
156 Ann Marie L. Davis, *Imagining Prostitution in Modern Japan, 1850–1913* (Lanham/Boulder/New York/London: Lexington Books, 2019).

157 Mitsunari, *supra* note 150; Geishogi kaihōrei [Emancipation Order for Playing Girls], Dajokan hukoku no. 295 of 1872.
158 Shogeigi torishimari kisoku [Regulation to Control Playing Girls], regulation no. 44 of the Ministry of Internal Affairs of 1900.
159 Keisatsu hanzai shobatsurei [Police Offences Punishment Regulation], regulation no. 16 of the Ministry of Internal Affairs of 1908.
160 Many brothels were transformed into rental room providers with a licence, which allowed each prostitute to rent a room for prostitution, but the manager turned a blind eye. The contract between prostitutes and the manager did not differ from previous fixed-term contracts, with advance payment. Mitsunari, *supra* note 150. See also Davis, *supra* note 156; Amy Stanley, *Selling Women: Prostitution, Markets, and the Household in Early Modern Japan* (Berkeley, CA: University of California Press, 2012).
161 John Lie, "The State as Pimp: Prostitution and the Patriarchal State in Japan in the 1940s," 38:2 *Sociological Quarterly* 251 (1997).
162 Mark McLelland, *Love, Sex, and Democracy in Japan during the American Occupation* (New York: Palgrave Macmillan, 2012).
163 Fujo ni inkō wo saseta monotō no shobatsu nikansuru chokurei [Imperial Order on Punishment of Persons Who Force Women to Perform Prostitution], imperial order no. 9 of 1947.
164 Prostitution Prevention Act, *supra* note 58.
165 Livia Gershon, "The Battle to Keep Prostitution Legal in 1950s Japan," JSTOR Daily, September 21, 2015, https://daily.jstor.org/battle-to-legalize-prostitution-in-1950s-japan; G.G. Rowley, "Prostitutes against the Prostitution Prevention Act of 1956," 23 U.S.-Japan Women's Journal 39 (2002), https://www.jstor.org/stable/42772190?mag=battle-to-legalize-prostitution-in-1950s-japan.
166 Holly Sanders, *Indentured Servitude and the Abolition of Prostitution in Postwar Japan; USJP Occasional Paper 06–11* (Cambridge, MA: Harvard University, 2006); Minoru Yokoyama, "Analysis of Prostitution in Japan," 19:1 Int'l J. of Comparative and Applied Criminal Justice 47 (1995); Minoru Yokoyama, "Emergence of Anti-Prostitution Law in Japan – Analysis from Sociology of Criminal Law," 17:2 Int'l J. of Comparative and Applied Criminal Justice 211 (1993).
167 Prostitution Prevention Act, *supra* note 58 art. 1.
168 Ibid., art. 2.
169 Ibid., art. 3.
170 Mari Kanagawa, "Kon-nichiteki baishun no hōkisei" [Legal Regulation of Modern Prostitution], 11 Ryukoku daigaku daigakuin hougakukenkyu 23 (2009).
171 Prevention Act, *supra* note 58 art. 5.
172 Ibid., art. 6.
173 Ibid., art. 7.
174 Ibid., art. 8.
175 Ibid., art. 9.

176 Ibid., art. 10.
177 Ibid., art. 11.
178 Ibid., art. 12.
179 Ibid., art. 13.
180 Ibid., art. 17. The protection order to send these prostitutes to rehabilitation centres can be applied for only six months. Ibid., art. 18.
181 Ibid., art. 34(1).
182 Ibid., art. 36.
183 Fuzoku eigyōtō no kisei oyobi gyoumu no tekiseikatō nikansuru hōritsu [Act on Regulation of Entertainment Business and Its Proper Administration], law no. 122 of 1948 (Entertainment Business Regulation Act).
184 Ibid., art. 2(1).
185 Ibid., art. 2(3).
186 Ibid., art. 2(5).
187 Ibid., art. 2(6).
188 Ibid., art. 2(7).
189 Ibid., art. 2(8).
190 Ibid., art. 2(9) and (10).
191 Ibid., art. 3(1). This act also applies to pachinko parlours, mahjong parlours, and slot machine or game centres that do not provide sexual services.
192 Ibid., art. 12 to art. 18–2.
193 Ibid., art. 22.
194 Ibid., art. 27.
195 For detailed examinations of the sex industry in Japan, see Atsuhiko Nakamura, *Nihon no huzokujō* [Sex Workers in Japan] (Tokyo: Shinchosha, 2014); Atsuhiko Nakamura, *Nihon no seihuzoku* [Sex Industry in Japan] (Tokyo: Mediax, 2016); Shingo Sakatsume, *Seihuzoku no ibitsu na genba* [Ugly Current Situation of the Sex Industry] (Tokyo: Chikuma shobo, 2016); Shingo Sakatsume, *Karada wo uru kanojotachi no jijō* [Why These Women Are Prostituting] (Tokyo: Chikuma shobo, 2018); Hanako Montgomery, "How Japan's Secretive 'Soapland' Brothels Operate," *Vice* (October 20, 2020), https://www.vice.com/en/article/z3vb7j/how-japans-secretive-soapland-brothels-operate; Yokoyama, "Analysis of Prostitution," *supra* note 166; Tenica Peterfreund, "Japan's Prostitution Prevention Law: The Case of the Missing Geisha," Law School Student Scholarship 57 (2010) https://scholarship.shu.edu/student_scholarship/57; Charlie Campbell, "The Sexual Exploitation of Young Girls in Japan Is 'on the Increase,' an Expert Says," *Time* (October 29, 2019), https://time.com/5712746/japan-sex-trafficking-prostitution/.
196 The Dispatch Worker Act, which regulates companies that send out employees to work, mandates that the companies must ensure that the work obeys all laws and is appropriate. Roudousha haken jigyō no tekiseina un-ei no kakuho oyobi haken roudousha no hogotō nikansuru hōritsu [Act to Secure the Fair Administration of Worker Dispatch Business and the Protection of Dispatch Workers], law no. 88

of 1985, art. 31 (Dispatch Workers Act). A company that forces a dispatched workers to offer sexual intercourse is thus violating this act. Moreover, a company that sends out an employee for "harmful work from public health or public morality" is liable for criminal punishment. Ibid., art. 58.

197 Under article 7 of the Dating Service Regulation Act, operators are required to register their dating websites. Article 7 of the act prohibits them from the following:

1 enticing a child to become a partner in sexual intercourse or conduct analogous to it, touching the sexual organs, anus, or nipple of others, or letting other persons touch his or her own sexual organs,
2 enticing a person (except for a child) to become a partner to sexual intercourse involving the child,
3 enticing a child to go on a date with another person of the opposite sex (excluding the sexual intercourse) by indicating that he or she will be providing compensation,
4 enticing a child to go on a date with another person of the opposite sex by indicating he or she will be compensated, or
5 enticing a child to go on a date with another person of the opposite sex or enticing other person to go on a date with the child by other means.

Internet isei shoukai jigyou wo riyoushite jidō wo yuin-suru koui no kiseitō nikansuru hōritsu [Act on Regulation of Enticing Children Using an Internet Dating Services], law no. 83 of 2003, art. 6 (Dating Service Regulation Act).

198 Tsubasa Wakabayashi, "Enjokosai in Japan: Rethinking the Dual Image of Prostitutes in Japanese and American Law," 13 UCLA Women's L.J. 143 (2003).

199 Andrew D. Morrison, "Teen Prostitution in Japan: Regulation of Telephone Clubs," 31 Vand. L. Rev. 457 (2021), https://scholarship.law.vanderbilt.edu/vjtl/vol31/iss2/3.

200 Gerald Mclellan, "An Examination of the Causes and Consequences of Compensated Dating (Enjo-Kosai) in Contemporary Japanese Society," 6 J. of Human Environmental Studies 25 (2013), https://www.jstage.jst.go.jp/article/uheoka/6/0/6_KJ00008893939/_pdf/-char/ja.

201 Chizuko Ueno, "Self-Determination on Sexuality? Commercialization of Sex among Teenage Girls in Japan," 4:2 Inter-Asia Cultural Studies 317 (2003); Mutsumi Ogaki, "Theoretical Explanations of Jyoshi Kousei Business ('JK Business') in Japan," 3:1 Dignity 1 (2018), https://digitalcommons.uri.edu/dignity/vol3/iss1/11.

202 Ronald John Weitzer, *Legalizing Prostitution: From Illicit Vice to Lawful Business* (New York/London: New York University Press, 2011); Joyce Outshoorn, ed., *The Politics of Prostitution: Women's Movements, Democratic States and the Globalisation of Sex Commerce* (Cambridge, MA: Cambridge University Press, 2004); Laura Barnett, Lyne Casavant, and Julia Nicol, *Prostitution: A Review of Legislation in*

Selected Countries (Ottawa: Library of Parliament, 2011); Geetanjali Gangoli and Nicole Westmarland, eds., *International Approaches to Prostitution: Law and Policy in Europe and Asia* (Bristol: Policy Press, 2006).

203 *New York Penal Law*, s 230.00 and s 230.02.
204 Ibid., s 230.00 and s 130.00.
205 Tom DeFranco and Rebecca Stellato, "Prostitution and Sex Work," 14 Geo. J. Gender & L. 553, 558–59 (2013). Certain places in Nevada depart entirely from the American pattern, making prostitution legal.
206 Government of the Netherlands, "Prostitution," https://www.government.nl/topics/prostitution; Che Post, Michel Vols, and Jan G. Brouwer, "Regulation of Prostitution in the Netherlands: Liberal Dream or Growing Repression?" 25:2 European J. on Criminal Policy and Research 99 (2019). https://www.researchgate.net/publication/323367667_Regulation_of_Prostitution_in_the_Netherlands_Liberal_Dream_or_Growing_Repression.
207 *German Prostitution Act*, 2001; Federal Ministry for Family Affairs, Senior Citizens, Women and Youth, "Report by the Federal Government on the Impact of the Act Regulating the Legal Situation of Prostitutes (Prostitution Act)," July 2007, https://www.researchgate.net/publication/308914953_Report_by_the_Federal_Government_on_the_Impact_of_the_Act_Regulating_the_Legal_Situation_of_Prostitutes_Prostitution_Act.
208 *Prostitution Reform Act*, 2003; New Zealand Parliament, "Prostitution Law Reform in New Zealand," https://www.parliament.nz/mi/pb/research-papers/document/00PLSocRP12051/prostitution-law-reform-in-new-zealand/.
209 *Swedish Criminal Code*, chapter 6-s 11, https://www.government.se/49ee78/contentassets/7a2dcae0787e465e9a2431554b5eab03/the-swedish-criminal-code.pdf.
210 Ibid., chapter 6-s 12.
211 *Canada (Attorney General) v Bedford*, [2013] 3 SCR 1101.
212 *Criminal Code of Canada*, supra note 110 s 210, made it an offence to keep or be in a bawdy house; s 212(1)(j) prohibited living on the avails of prostitution; and s 213(1)(c) disallowed communicating in public for the purposes of prostitution.
213 *Canadian Charter of Rights and Freedoms*, 1982, s 7.
214 *Bedford*, supra note 211 at [60].
215 Ibid., at [105].
216 Ibid., at [134–36].
217 Ibid., at [140–42]. The SCOC mentioned that the ban would extend to hiring anyone "who could increase the safety and security of prostitutes (for example, legitimate drivers, managers, or bodyguards)" and even to individuals who were "not involved in business with a prostitute, such as accountants or receptionists."
218 Ibid., at [147].
219 Ibid., at [148], [159].
220 Ibid., at [163].

221 *Criminal Code of Canada, supra* note 108 s 286.1.
222 Ibid., s 286.2 and s 286.5(1)(a).
223 Ibid., s 286.3.
224 Ibid., s 286.4 and s 286.5(1)(b).
225 Ibid., s 213.
226 As the Department of Justice explained, the amendment did not legalize prostitution. Department of Justice, "Prostitution Criminal Law Reform: Bill C-36, the *Protection of Communities and Exploited Persons Act*," December 6, 2014, https://www.justice.gc.ca/eng/rp-pr/other-autre/c36faq/.
227 Ibid.,
228 Catherine D. Perry, "Right of Privacy Challenges to Prostitution Statutes," 58 Wash. U. L. Q. 439 (1980).
229 *Erotic Service Provider Legal, Education & Research Project v Gascon*, 881 F.3d 792 (9th Cir. 2018).
230 Ibid.,
231 Ibid.,
232 Arossa H.I. Lunning, "Prostitution: Protected in Paradise?" 30 U. Hawa. L. Rev. 193 (2007) (arguing that the prostitution ban in Hawaii violates the due process clause of the United States Constitution as well as the state Constitution); Dannia Alteminei, "Prostitution and the Right to Privacy: A Comparative Analysis of Current Law in the United States and Canada," 2013 U. Ill. L. Rev. 625 (2013) (privacy should be extended to private acts of prostitution).
233 Julie Bindel, *The Pimping of Prostitution: Abolishing the Sex Work Myth* (London: Palgrave, 2017); Vanessa E. Munro and Marina Dell Guiusta, *Demanding Sex: Critical Reflections on the Regulation of Prostitution* (London/New York: Routledge, 2008); Katie Beran, "Revisiting the Prostitution Debate: Uniting Liberal and Radical Feminism in Pursuit of Policy Reform," 30 L. & Ineq. 19 (2012). See also Emily Bazelon, "Should Prostitution Be a Crime?" *New York Times Magazine* (May 5, 2016), https://www.nytimes.com/2016/05/08/magazine/should-prostitution-be-a-crime.html.
234 U.S. Department of State, "The Link between Prostitution and Sex Trafficking," November 24, 2004, https://2001-2009.state.gov/r/pa/ei/rls/38790.htm.
235 "Legalization" and "decriminalization" might mean the same thing: if prostitution is no longer a crime and no longer entails criminal punishment, it is essentially legal. But since some people support decriminalization but not legalization, decriminalization might mean just removing criminal punishment, while leaving prostitution illegal or even a crime. Then the prostitutes would still be committing a crime by offering an illegal service, but there would be no criminal punishment.
236 Human Rights Watch, "Why Sex Work Should Be Decriminalized," August 7, 2019, https://www.hrw.org/news/2019/08/07/why-sex-work-should-be-decriminalized.
237 See also Sylvia Law, "Commercial Sex: Beyond Decriminalization," 73 S. Cal. L. Rev. 523 (2000).

238 Max Waltman, "Accessing Evidence, Arguments and Inequality in Bedford v Canada," 37 Harv. J. L. & Gender 459 at 474–75 (2014).
239 Ibid., at 466–73.
240 U.S. Department of State, *supra* note 234 ("Where prostitution is legalized or tolerated, there is a greater demand for human trafficking victims and nearly always an increase in the number of women and children trafficked into commercial sex slavery").
241 Jeffrey Gauthier, "Prostitution, Sexual Autonomy, and Sexual Discrimination," 26:1 Hypatia 166 (2011); Shelagh Day, "Prostitution: Violating the Human Rights of Poor Women," Action ontarienne contre la violence faite aux femmes, June 2008, 24, http://www.socialrightscura.ca/documents/publications/shelagh/Prostitution.pdf (the "civil libertarian approach fails to deal with prostitution as a question of women's equality. It ignores the fundamental inequality in the sexual and human transaction between the women and men involved, as well as the very disparate nature of the act for the two parties. This is not a transaction in which a woman and a man together, voluntarily, seek to give and receive sexual pleasure. Prostitution is a transaction in which women provide commodified sexual services to men, in exchange for money. It is a form of social and sexual subordination"). The strongest advocate for this view is Andrea Dworkin, who sees prostitution as "the use of a woman's body for sex by a man, he pays money, he does what he wants." She adds that "prostitution in and of itself is an abuse of a woman's body," which "is the essence and the meaning of male dominance." Andrea Dworkin, "Prostitution and Male Supremacy," 1 Mich. J. Gender & L. 1, 2, 3, 4 (1993). Catharine A. MacKinnon also asserts that, under present conditions, consensual heterosexual relations are inherently oppressive to women: "The wrong of rape has proved so difficult to define because the unquestionable starting point has been that rape is defined as distinct from intercourse, while for women it is difficult to distinguish the two under the conditions of male dominance." Catharine A. MacKinnon, *Toward a Feminist Theory of the State* (Cambridge, MA: Harvard University Press, 1989), 175. Therefore, prostitution is also inherently exploitative and questionable: "prostitution is not something a woman, absent force, would choose to do." Catharine A. MacKinnon, "Prostitution and Civil Rights," 1 Mich. J. Gender & L. 13 at 25 (1993).
242 Norbert Campagna, "Human Dignity and Prostitution," in *Cambridge Handbook of Human Dignity*, ed. by Marcus Düwell, Jens Braarvig, Roger Brownsword, and Dietmar Mieth (Cambridge, MA: Cambridge University Press, 2014), 454. See also Coalition for the Abolition of Prostitution, "Prostitution under International Human Rights Law: An Analysis of States' Obligations and the Best Ways to Implement Them," 2016, http://www.cap-international.org/wp-content/uploads/2016/11/ProstitutionUnderIntlHumanRightsLawEN.pdf; Margaret Jane Radin, "Market-Inalienability," 100 Harv. L. Rev. 1849 (1987); Margaret Jane Radin, "The Pragmatist and the Feminist," 63 S. Cal. L. Rev. 1699 (1990).
243 Lucy Platt, Pippa Grenfell, Rebecca Meiksin, Jocelyn Elmes, Susan G. Sherman, Teela Sanders, Peninah Mwangi, and Anna-Louise Crago, "Associations between

Sex Work Laws and Sex Workers' Health: A Systematic Review and Meta-Analysis of Quantitative and Qualitative Studies," PLoS Med 15(12): e1002680, https://doi.org/10.1371/journal.pmed.1002680.

244 Martha C. Nussbaum, "'Whether from Reason or Prejudice': Taking Money for Bodily Service," 27 J. Legal Studies 693 (1998). See also Lars O. Ericsson, "Charges against Prostitution: An Attempt at a Philosophical Assessment," 90:3 Ethics 335 (1980).

245 Lena Edlund and Evelyn Korn, "A Theory of Prostitution," 110:1 J. of Political Economy 181 (2002). See also Viviana A. Zelizer, *The Purchase of Intimacy* (Princeton/Oxford: Princeton University Press, 2007).

246 On the other hand, if sex should not be commodified, it is strange that most feminists do not support the criminal punishment of prostitutes. Sibyl Schwarzenbach, "Contractarians and Feminists Debate Prostitution," 18 Rev. of L. & Social Change 103 (1990–91).

247 Stewart Cunningham, "Reinforcing or Challenging Stigma? The Risks and Benefits of 'Dignity Talk' in Sex Work Discourse," 29 Int'l J. for Semiotics of L. 45 (2016).

248 Jay Levy, *Criminalising the Purchase of Sex: Lessons from Sweden* (Abingdon/New York: Routledge, 2014).

249 Sex Work and Gender Equality, "Global Network of Sex Work Projects," 2017, https://www.nswp.org/sites/nswp.org/files/policy_brief_sex_work_and_gender_equality_nswp_-_2017.pdf.

250 Bazelon, *supra* note 235. If a prostitute reports the crime to the police, she will face various negative consequences even if prostitution itself is not a crime or unlawful. Amnesty International, "The Human Costs of Crushing the Market: Criminalization of Sex Work in Norway," 2016, https://www.amnestyusa.org/wp-content/uploads/2017/04/norway_report_-_sex_workers_rights_-_embargoed_-_final.pdf.

251 Bazelon, *supra* note 233. See also Canadian Alliance for Sex Work Law Reform, "Safety, Dignity, Equality: Recommendations for Sex Work Law Reform in Canada," March 2017, http://sexworklawreform.com/wp-content/uploads/2017/05/CASWLR-Final-Report-1.6MB.pdf.

252 Amnesty International, "Amnesty International Policy on State Obligations to Respect, Protect and Fulfil the Human Rights of Sex Workers," May 26, 2016, https://www.amnesty.org/en/documents/pol30/4062/2016/en/.

253 "Open Statement of Support for Amnesty International's Draft Policy on Decriminalization of Sex Work," August 5, 2015, https://www.mamacash.org/media/publications/open-statement-of-support-for-amnesty-internationals-draft-policy-on-decriminalization-of-sex-work.pdf. It is sometimes claimed that Amnesty was calling for decriminalization, not legalization. But its position was against criminalization as well as penalization; it defined "criminalization" as "the process of prohibiting consensual adult sex work and attaching punishments in law." As it explained, "Amnesty International considers that to protect the rights of sex workers, it is necessary not only to repeal laws which criminalize the sale of sex, but also to repeal

those which make the buying of sex from consenting adults or the organization of sex work (such as prohibitions on renting premises for sex work) a criminal offence. Such laws force sex workers to operate covertly in ways that compromise their safety, prohibit actions that sex workers take to maximize their safety, and serve to deny sex workers support or protection from government officials. They therefore undermine a range of sex workers' human rights, including their rights to security of person, housing and health." Amnesty International, *supra* note 252 at 2. Clearly, the proposal was not suggesting that the punishment of prostitutes should simply be removed while leaving the ban on prostitution in place.

254 Katherine Shats, "Why I Oppose Amnesty International's Sex Work Policy," August 20, 2015, O'Neill Institute for National and Global Health Law, Georgetown University Law Center, https://oneill.law.georgetown.edu/why-i-oppose-amnesty-internationals-sex-work-policy/.

255 Shinji Miyadai, Naohide Yamamoto, Seiji Fujii, Yukiko Hayami, Toshiko Miya, Hiroo Hirano, Noriko Kanezumi, and Yuuji Hirano, *Sei no jikokkettei genron* [Introduction to Sexual Autonomy] (Tokyo: Kinokuniya shoten, 1998); Chizuko Ueno, Shinji Miyadai, Yukiko Kadota, Seiji Fujii, Tomoko Kawabata, and Mado Chase Onizuka, *Bai baishun kaitai shinsho* [Anatomy of Prostitution and Buying Prostitution] (Tokyo: Tsuge shobou, 2020). See also Usagi Nakamura, ed., *Ecchi na oshigoto naze ikenaino* [Why Is Sex Work Bad?] (Tokyo: Potto shuppan plus, 2017).

256 Yukiko Tsunoda, *Sei to hōritu* [Sex and Law] (Tokyo: Iwanami shoten, 2013), 216–18; Hiroshi Nakasatomi, "Post-gender ki no josei no seibaibai" [Prostitution and Buying Prostitution of Women in the Post-Gender Period], 59:2 Tokyo daigaku shakai kagaku kenkyu 39 (2007), https://jww.iss.u-tokyo.ac.jp/jss/pdf/jss5802_039069.pdf.

257 The exception is Sadami Uemura, "Jinken toshite no seiteki jiyu wo meguru shomondai" [Various Issues on Sexual Freedom as a Human Right] 18:2 Kagawa hougaku 377 (1998), following the discussion in France and attempting to examine the prostitution ban in light of sexual freedom.

258 Nakasatomi, *supra* note 256.

259 Tsunoda, *supra* note 256 at 250.

260 Thus, the U.S. Department of State expressed serious concern regarding the loose enforcement of the human trafficking law in Japan. U.S. Department of State, "2020 Trafficking in Persons Report: Japan," https://www.state.gov/reports/2020-trafficking-in-persons-report/japan/.

261 Seo-Young Cho, Axel Dreher, and Eric Neumayer, "Does Legalized Prostitution Increase Human Trafficking?" 41:1 World Development 67 (2013).

262 Japan accepted the Protocol to Prevent, Suppress and Punish Trafficking in Persons, Especially Women and Children, Supplementing the United Nations Convention against Transnational Organized Crime in 2017 after the Diet approved it in 2005. Under the Prostitution Prevention Act, forcing women and girls to work as prostitutes is already illegal, and a new crime of human trafficking was added to the Criminal Code in 2005. As a result, sex trafficking has been discussed mostly

in connection with gangs, which recruit girls and women from other Asian countries, bring them to Japan to work for a legitimate purpose, and then force them into prostitutions under heavy financial debt, often confiscating their passports to prevent them from running away.
263 Nakasatomi, *supra* note 256.
264 Tsunoda, *supra* note 256 at 252.
265 See *supra* note 94. See also Stuart P. Green, "What Counts as Prostitution?" 4:1 Bergen J. of Criminal L. & Criminal Justice 65 (2016).
266 Tsunoda, *supra* note 256 at 252–53, argues that sexual intercourse and conduct analogous to it come under the heading of human dignity but does not explain why they alone should not be commodified.
267 The ban on customers could be challenged as an infringement of their rights, since both the customer and the sex worker are consenting adults. Moreover, the ban could be challenged as an infringement of the prostitutes' right to engage in prostitution since it would make it more difficult and dangerous for them to offer sex.
268 See supra note 161.
269 Many attribute this absence to the systematic destruction of all documentary evidence immediately after the war.
270 George Hicks, *Comfort Women* (New York/London: W.W. Norton, 1997); Yoshimi Yoshiaki, *Comfort Women: Sexual Slavery in the Japanese Military during World War II* (New York: Columbia University Press, 2002); Toshiyuki Tanaka, *Japan's Comfort Women: Sexual Slavery and Prostitution during World War II and the US Occupation* (Abingdon/New York: Routledge, 2002); C. Sarah Soh, *The Comfort Women: Sexual Violence and Postcolonial Memory in Korea and Japan* (Chicago: University of Chicago Press, 2009); Carmen M. Argibay, "Sexual Slavery and the Comfort Women of World War II," 21:2 Berkeley J. of Int'l L. 37 at 5 (2003); J. Mark Ramseyer, "Comfort Women: The Economics of the Contracts and the Politics of the Dispute," 2020, https://papers.ssrn.com/sol3/papers.cfm?abstract_id=3822439.
271 These stations were established by the Japanese government, and all women were directly recruited. The government called for them to serve the nation and defend the chastity of Japanese women from possible rape or sexual assault by occupying soldiers. Catering to American soldiers, the biggest station was in Tokyo and was called the RAA (Recreation and Amusement Association). There were 55,000 women serving in the RAA, which was abolished in 1946. See Nicholas D. Kristof, "Fearing G.I. Occupiers, Japan Urgesd [sic] Women into Brothels," *New York Times* (October 27, 1995), https://www.nytimes.com/1995/10/27/world/fearing-gi-occupiers-japan-urgesd-women-into-brothels.html?pagewanted=all&src=pm.
272 In 2018, 561 people were sent to the prosecutors for violating the Prostitution Prevention Act (there is no breakdown of which provisions were transgressed), down from 2,164 in 1989. Ministry of Justice (MOJ), Hanzai hakusho reiwa gannendo [Crime Whitepaper, 2019], http://hakusyo1.moj.go.jp/jp/66/nfm/mokuji.html. In 2009, 747 people were arrested for violating the act: among them, 284 were

detained for solicitation, 189 for providing a venue for prostitution, and 224 for mediating the dispatch of prostitutes for rendezvous with customers. National Police Agency (NPA), Keisatsu hakusho heisei22nen [Police Whitepaper, 2010], https://www.data.go.jp/data/dataset/npa_20140905_0005/resource/a933e3a9-7191-4a67-8ef7-542dfdf20f29?inner_span=True.

273 Fujin hodouinhō [Women's Rehabilitation Centre Act], law no. 17 of 1958; "Baishun boushiho ihan no josei wo shobatsu: Fujin hodoin ni haishi motomeru koe" [Punishing Women Convicted of Prostitution Prevention Act Violation: A Growing Call for Abolition], *Tokyo Shimbun* (April 20, 2020), https://www.tokyo-np.co.jp/article/17110 (there is now only one rehabilitation centre in Tokyo; during the present decade, only four women have been sent to a centre).

274 MHLW, "Fujin hogo jigyouno genjou nitsuite" [Current Situation of Women's Protection Service], July 30, 2018, https://www.gender.go.jp/kaigi/kento/shelter/siryo/pdf/1-7.pdf.

275 Gender Equality Bureau (GEB), "Dai4ji danjo kyōdō sankaku kihonkeikaku" [Fourth Basic Gender Equality Plan], December 25, 2015, 78, https://www.gender.go.jp/about_danjo/basic_plans/4th/index.html.

276 Yukiko Kaname, "Seihuzoku de hataraku hitobito to 'josei jiritsu shien'" [The People Working in the Sex Business and Government Support], 19 Rikkyo daigaku gender forum nenpō 117 (2017).

277 In 2022, the Diet passed a statute to reorganize the women's centre and the Women's Rehabilitation Centre. Kon-nan na mondai wo kakaeru josei no shien nikansuru hōritsu [Act concerning Support for Struggling Women], law no. 52 of 2022. The Women's Centre was renamed as "Women's Counselling Support Centre" and the women's rehabilitation centre was renamed as "Facility to Support the Autonomy of Women" and their tasks are not providing helps for prostitutes. However, it did not revise the ban on prostitution.

Chapter 3: Rape

1 Some of these were amply revealed in *Japan's Secret Shame*, a BBC documentary that aired in 2018. British Broadcasting Corporation, "Japan's Secret Shame: Shiori Ito: Japan's Attitudes to Allegations of Sexual Violence Are Locked in the Past," BBC Two, http://www.bbc.co.uk/programmes/articles/3z44Njyr5wzm3wbVMGZ7tFr/shiori-ito-japan-s-attitudes-to-allegations-of-sexual-violence-are-locked-in-the-past.

2 Keihō [Criminal Code], 1907, art. 176.

3 Daishinin [Great Court of Judicature], December 1, 1925, 4:12 Keishu 741 (holding that inserting a finger into a vagina was an assault and a forcible obscene act).

4 Saikō saibansho [SCOJ], 2nd petty bench, March 29, 2005, 59:2 Keishu 54 (chronic headaches caused by extremely loud noises are an injury); Tokyo chihō saibansho [Tokyo DC], August 10, 1979, 947 Hanrei jihō 122 (PTSD caused by repeated harassing calls is an injury).

5 Saikō saibansho [SCOJ], grand bench, November 29, 2017, 71:9 Keishu 467.

6 Criminal Code, *supra* note 2 art. 177. "Definite term" means that the duration of imprisonment is limited. Article 12(1) sets the basic limit at twenty years, but when a rape was committed concurrently with other crimes such as trespass, jail time could be extended to thirty years. Ibid., art. 14(2), 47.
7 Ibid., art. 178(1).
8 Ibid., art. 178(2).
9 Ibid., art. 178-2.
10 Ibid., art. 179.
11 Ibid., art. 180(1) and (2).
12 In order for the public prosecutor to file an official charge, victims need to file criminal complaints within six months, but exceptions were made for complaints involving crimes under article 176 to 178, relieving this deadline. Keiji soshohō [Code of Criminal Procedure], law no. 131 of 1948, art. 235 (revised in 2017).
13 Criminal Code, *supra* note 2 art. 181(1). Imprisonment with labour for an indefinite term is life imprisonment, with the possibility of parole.
14 Ibid., art. 181(2).
15 Ibid., art. 181(3).
16 Ibid., art. 241(1). If death resulted, the punishment was life imprisonment or execution. Ibid., art. 241(3).
17 Ibid., art. 174.
18 Ibid., art. 225.
19 Ibid., art. 226-2(3).
20 Ibid., art. 227(3)
21 In addition, the publication of obscene materials is illegal. Ibid., art. 175.
22 Baishun boushihō [Prostitution Prevention Act], law no. 118 of 1956, art. 3.
23 Ibid.; Mari Kanagawa, "Kon-nichiteki baishun no hōkisei" [Legal Regulation of Modern Prostitution], 11 Ryukoku daigaku daigakuin hougakukenkyu 23 (2009).
24 Jidō kaishun, jidō porn ni kakawaru kouitō no kisei oyobi shobatsu narabini jidō no hogotō nikansuru hōritsu [Act on Regulation and Punishment of Persons Who Had Become Customers of Child Prostitution and Child Porn and the Protection of Children], law no. 52 of 1999 (Child Prostitution Prohibition Act).
25 Ibid., art. 2(1).
26 Ibid., art. 2(2).
27 Ibid., art. 3-2. In October, 2022, the review committee came up with a draft idea of possible further reforms. Shian [Draft], https://www.moj.go.jp/content/001382454.pdf. The draft includes the revision to the requirement for the crime of forcible sexual intercourse, et al. The proposed revised provision would impose criminal punishment when the defendant used one of the listed methods, which would make it difficult for the victim to refuse. The conduct listed includes assaulting or intimidating the victim, forcing them to drink alcohol or take drugs, depriving them of clear consciousness, leaving no time for refusal, terrifying or surprising the victim, causing the victim trauma as a result of the abuse, or taking

advantage of their own position of power. The second clause imposes criminal punishment when the situation was caused by someone else and the defendant simply took advantage of the situation. Both will be subject to definite imprisonment of five years or more. Further tricking the victim into believing obscene conduct is not actually obscene or taking advantage of the victim's resulting confusion is also subject to the same punishment. In addition, the draft would introduce the "Romeo and Juliet" provision, prohibiting all sexual intercourse, et al., with someone under thirteen years of age but allowing someone between thirteen and sixteen years of age to have sexual intercourse, et al., with others less than five years older than them, without their lack of judgment being taken advantage of. The draft would also impose the same punishment for inserting a part of the body (other than the penis) or other objects into a vagina or anus. Lastly, it would further clarify that domestic rape will be subject to criminal charges. If all of these proposals are accepted, they would amount to a significant change to the existing legislation.

28 Ibid., art. 4. The production, provision, possession, and transmission of child pornography are also prohibited. Ibid., art. 2(3) and art. 7.
29 Jidō hukushihō [Child Welfare Act], law no. 164 of 1947, art. 34(1)(vi). Imprisonment with labour for up to ten years or a fine of up to JPY 3 million (roughly US$22,000) will be imposed for a violation. Ibid., art. 60(1).
30 Ibid., art. 3. The act authorizes child services to place the child in protective custody and to issue a restraining order.
31 Tokyoto koushu ni ichijirushiku meiwakuwo kakeru bouryokuteki huryo kouitō no boushi nikansuru jourei [Tokyo Metropolitan Government Ordinance concerning the Prevention of Violent Nuisance Act That Causes Extreme Annoyance to the Public], Tokyo Metropolitan Government ordinance no. 103 of 1962.
32 Ibid., art. 5(1)(i).
33 Ibid., art. 5(1)(ii).
34 Tokyoto seishounen no kenzen na ikusei nikansuru jourei [Tokyo Metropolitan Government Ordinance on Healthy Upbringing of Youth], Tokyo Metropolitan Government ordinance no. 181 of 1964.
35 Ibid., art. 2(i).
36 Ibid., art. 18–6.
37 Punishment consists of imprisonment with labour for up to two years or a fine of up to JPY 1 million (roughly US$7,500). Ibid., art. 24–3. The SCOJ has narrowed down the scope of punishment so as not to penalize individuals who have a genuine romantic relationship with a young person. Saikō saibansho [SCOJ], grand bench, October 23, 1985, 39:6 Keishu 413. Thus, only someone who capitalizes on the immaturity of a young person or who has intercourse with him or her for the purpose of sexual gratification could be punished.
38 Catherine Burns, *Sexual Violence and the Law in Japan* (London/New York: Routledge, 2005), 67–68.

39 *French Penal Code*, art. 222–23, UNODC, https://sherloc.unodc.org/cld/uploads/res/document/french_penal_code_html/french_penal_code.pdf (defining rape as any act of sexual penetration, whatever its nature, committed against another person by violence, constraint, threat, or surprise). Note that an element of surprise could be sufficient in France to find a rape.
40 Mana Shimaoka, "Seihanzai no hogo houeki oyobi Keihō kaisei kosshi no hihanteki kentō" [Interests Protected by Sexual Crime Provisions and Critical Analysis of the Criminal Code Reform], 7 Keio hōgaku 19, 21–22 (2017). It was thus included in a section on crimes against social welfare.
41 Saikō saibansho [SCOJ], 1st petty bench, August 18, 1949, 13 Shukei 307.
42 Shimaoka, *supra* note 40 at 22.
43 Daishinin [Great Court of Judicature], November 19, 1913, 19 Daishinin hanketsuroku 1255.
44 Given that, as legally defined, rape referred only to women, rapists were usually male. But a woman who conspired with a man to rape another woman could also be punishable for rape. In 1953, a male defendant attempted to overturn the conviction of rape as perpetrated solely against women, citing the right to sexual equality under the Constitution, but the SCOJ upheld the limitation. Saikō saibansho [SCOJ], grand bench, June 24, 1953, 7:6 Keishu 1366. See Chapter 2, notes 68–69. When the Criminal Code was radically revised in 2017, the rape provision became a crime of "forcible sexual intercourse et al.," appliable to both men and women.
45 It could, however, be classed as the forcible obscene acts that were prohibited in article 176, but the punishment was much lighter than for rape.
46 Saikō saibansho [SCOJ], 3rd petty bench, May 10, 1949, 3:6 Keishu 711. See Tokyo kōtō saibansho [Tokyo HC], January 24, 2014, unreported; Niigata chihō saibansho [Niigata DC], December 10, 2015, unreported (2015WLJPCA12106006) (threat to life using a knife), upheld Tokyo kōtō saibansho [Tokyo HC], November 11, 2016, unreported (2016WLJPCA11116008), appeal dismissed, Saikō saibansho [SCOJ], 2nd petty bench, April 8, 2018, unreported (2018WLJPCA04086001).
47 Saikō saibansho [SCOJ], 2nd petty bench, June 6, 1958, 126 Shukei 171.
48 Thus, when a girl was surrounded and prevented from escaping by three accomplices in a secluded place late at night, with a hint of threat to her life and safety, and she was incapable of resisting due to fear, this was seen as assault or intimidation. Ibid., In another case, a twenty-year-old virgin was deceived by a defendant who pretended to be a physician working for the police. She had sex with him to allay the suspicion that she had contracted a venereal disease due to engaging in prostitution and in response to his threat to expose these facts to the police and to the public. She felt that she had no options and was therefore unable to resist the sexual intercourse. Tokyo chihō saibansho [Tokyo DC], April 15, 1987, 1304 Hanrei jihō 147. Thus, Burns, *supra* note 38 at 84, is somewhat misleading in suggesting that in Japan "physical resistance to the extent that [the victim] is overcome" is required.

49 Fukuoka kōtō saibansho [Fukuoka HC], August 31, 1966, 19:5 Kokei 575 (sexual intercourse with a fourteen-year-old girl who had a severe mental disability was a quasi-rape).
50 Some cases did hold that the use of force was not sufficient to qualify as assault or intimidation. See, for example, Hiroshima chihō saibansho [Hiroshima DC], March 26, 1969, 235 Hanrei Times 285 (holding the victim down and having sexual intercourse in her unlocked apartment despite her insistence to leave); Osaka chihō saibansho [Osaka DC], March 12, 1971, 267 Hanrei Times 376 (a sixteen-year-old girl did not resist, scream for help, or run away); Osaka chihō saibansho [Osaka DC], March 27, 1972, 283 Hanrei Times 332 (there was no sufficient intimidation to disable resistance, and threatening words were not sufficient); Hiroshima kōtō saibansho [Hiroshima HC], November 20, 1978, 922 Hanrei jihō 111 (although the victim did not consent, pushing her down, ripping off her clothes, and covering her body were not sufficient to constitute assault or intimidation); Urawa chihō saibansho [Urawa DC], October 3, 1989, 1337 Hanrei jihō 150. It may be questioned whether these holdings appropriately applied the "assault or intimidation" standard and whether they should be treated as precedents.
51 Even if a defendant were sentenced to imprisonment with labour for an indefinite term, there was a possibility of parole after ten years (in practice after thirty years). Criminal Code, *supra* note 2 art. 28. There is no life imprisonment without the possibility of parole in Japan. If a perpetrator intended to kill his rape victim, this would be homicide, for which the death penalty is available. Ibid., art. 199.
52 Code of Criminal Procedure, *supra* note 12 art. 250(1) and (2). If an accused were charged with a robbery and rape resulting in death, or with murder, there was no limitation period for filing a charge.
53 Ministry of Justice (MOJ), "Seihanzai nikansuru sougouteki kenkyu" [Comprehensive Research on Sexual Crimes], Kenkyubu houkoku dai55gou, 2016, 3–4, http://www.moj.go.jp/housouken/housouken03_00084.html. There were also 44 cases of concurrent robbery and rape in 2014. Ibid., at 6.
54 MOJ, "Heisei27nendoban hanzai hakusho" [Crime Whitepaper, 2015], http://hakusyo1.moj.go.jp/jp/62/nfm/images/full/h6-2-1-11.jpg.
55 Ibid., at 4. During 2014, there were also 3,439 cases of sexual touching in violation of local anti-nuisance ordinances. Ibid., at 7.
56 It is extremely difficult to determine how many rapes are committed in Japan. In 2013, 0.5 percent of Japanese women reported being a victim of a sex crime. Sixty-five million women live in Japan, meaning that 211,000 were victimized. See MOJ, "Heisei25nendo hanzai hakusho" [Crime Victim Whitepaper, 2013], https://www.npa.go.jp/hanzaihigai/whitepaper/w-2013/html/zenbun/part2/s2_4_2c06.html. This suggests that the number of incidents is far greater than the number of reported cases. On the other hand, if the reporting ratio of sex crimes (18.5 percent) is accurate, as given in the Crime Victim Whitepaper, 2013, that would suggest that the estimated

total number of rape victims in 2013 would be 6,750. One government survey revealed that at least 4.9 percent of female respondents reported that they had been forced to have sex without consent. Gender Equality Bureau (GEB), "Danjokan niokeru bouryoku nikansuru chousa" [Research on Violence between Man and Woman], 2017, 68, https://www.gender.go.jp/policy/no_violence/e-vaw/chousa/h29_boryoku_cyousa.html. These data would suggest that the total number of rape victims could be 3 million.

57 Interestingly, in 2014 however, police identified the suspect in 88.0 percent of rapes and 58.1 percent of forcible obscene acts in Japan. MOJ, *supra* note 54 at 3. This means that they could identify most suspects.

58 In 2014, 1,290 rape suspects were sent to the prosecutors' office. Of these, prosecutors filed charges against 448 (34.7 percent). Of the 3,586 forcible obscene act suspects, prosecutors chose not to file charges against 1,459 (40.7 percent). Ibid., at 20.

59 In 2016, of the 320,488 criminal cases that went to court in Japan, only 104 resulted in an acquittal for the defendant (0.03 percent). MOJ, "Heisei 29nenban hanzai hakusho" [Crime Whitepaper, 2017], http://hakusyo1.moj.go.jp/jp/64/nfm/n64_2_2_3_1_0.html. This high conviction rate has not much changed since then. MOJ, "Reiwa 2nenban hanzai hakusho" [Crime Whitepaper, 2020], https://www.moj.go.jp/content/001363987.pdf (in the 245,537 criminal cases of 2019, only 96 defendants were acquitted).

60 Criminal Code, *supra* note 2 art. 66 and art. 25. The court is likely to suspend a sentence if the defendant is a first-time offender. However, the actual rate of suspended sentences in rape cases was 9.4 percent in 2014, far lower than the average rate for all crimes, which was 59.5 percent. MOJ, *supra* note 54 at 22.

61 Criminal Code, *supra* note 2 art. 236. After a defendant is convicted, the court chooses a particular sentence between the minimum and maximum stipulated in the relevant statute. Even for rape cases, the courts display a clear tendency to opt for the shorter sentences. In 2014, for instance, 11.6 percent of convicted rapists were sentenced to three years in prison, 36.0 percent to three to five years, 33.0 percent to five to ten years, 7.5 percent to ten to fifteen years, and 2.5 percent to longer than fifteen years. MOJ, *supra* note 54 at 22–23.

62 There is no provision in the Criminal Code or other statute that bans publication of the victim's identity or that authorizes or mandates the court to ban it. However, like the police, the media reveal the identity of sex crime victims only if they were killed. Masayo Otsuki, "Hanzai higaisha no joho to hōdō no arikata" [Information of Crime Victims and Freedom of the Press], 2006:8 Reference 53 at 57 (2006).

63 This is well illustrated by Shiori Ito, who recounted her experience with the Japanese police after her alleged rape. Shiori Ito, *Black Box: The Memoir That Sparked Japan's #MeToo Movement,* trans. Allison Markin Powell (New York: Feminist Press, 2021). The original Japanese-language version was published by Bungei shunju in 2017.

64 Nihonkoku kenpō [Constitution of Japan], 1946, art. 82.

65 See *supra* note 48. If a victim's allegation is inconsistent, changes often, or does not accord with the facts, the courts might hold the allegation lacking credibility. Tokyo chihō saibansho [Tokyo DC], December 16, 1994, 1562 Hanrei jihō 141 (the alleged victim's story was not credible, and there was a reasonable doubt on the absence of consent); Osaka kōtō saibansho [Osaka HC], June 19, 2007, unreported.
66 Maebashi chihō saibansho [Maebashi DC], February 7, 2003, courts database, http://www.courts.go.jp/app/hanrei_jp/detail4?id=6320 (the accused drugged a victim, but it was unclear whether the drugs actually had dissolved, how much the victim consumed, and whether it was sufficient to make her lose consciousness).
67 *Criminal Code of Canada*, R.S.C., 1985, c. C-46, s 271 (sexual assault). See also s 272 (sexual assault with a weapon) and s 273 (aggravated sexual assault).
68 Ibid., s 274 ("If an accused is charged with an offence under section ... 271 ..., no corroboration is required for a conviction and the judge shall not instruct the jury that it is unsafe to find the accused guilty in the absence of corroboration"); *R. v Ewanchuk*, [1999] 1 SCR 330; *R. v J.A.*, [2011] 2 SCR 440. See also Lise Gotell, "Canadian Sexual Assault Law: Neoliberalism and the Erosion of Feminist-Inspired Law Reforms," in *Rethinking Rape Law: International and Comparative Perspectives*, ed. Claire McGlynn and Vanessa E. Munro (Abingdon/New York: Routledge, 2010), at 209. The situation in the United States is highly complicated, and certain difficulties in some states resemble those of Japan. Donald Dripps, "Rape, Law and American Society," in McGlynn and Munro, *Rethinking Rape Law*, 224.
69 Maebashi chihō saibansho, *supra* note 66 (the credibility of the victim's testimonies was questionable, and there was no proof that the defendant intended to drug her and rape her).
70 For the meaning of consent, see *Criminal Code of Canada, supra* note 67 s 273.1(1). There is no consent if the complainant is unconscious of incapable of consenting, when the accused induces the complainant to engage in sex by abusing a position of trust, power, or authority, or when the complainant expresses, by words or conduct, a lack of agreement. Ibid., s 273.1(2).
71 In Canada, it is not a defence under s 271 if an accused's belief in consent arose from his or her self-induced intoxication, recklessness, or willful blindness, or any circumstance referred to under section 273.1(2) of the Criminal Code; the accused did not take reasonable steps, in the circumstances known to the accused at the time, to ascertain that the complainant was consenting; or there is no evidence that the complainant's voluntary agreement to the activity was affirmatively expressed by words or actively expressed by conduct. Ibid., s 273.2.
72 Ryan Takeshita and Kaori Sasagawa, "Why a Japanese Journalist Went Public with Her Rape Allegation," *Huffington Post* (November 1, 2017), https://www.huffingtonpost.com/entry/why-a-japanese-journalist-went-public-with-her-rape-allegation_us_59f9f89ae4b0d1cf6e921ec1.

73 In the case of Shiori Ito, the accused, Noriyuki Yamaguchi, did indeed claim that she had consented to having sex with him. Noriyuki Yamaguchi, "Watashi wo uttaeta Ito Shiori san e" [To Ms. Shiori Ito Who Sued Me], *Hanada* (December 2017), 254. The prosecutor eventually decided not to charge Yamaguchi with rape.

74 In the end, Ito filed a civil tort action against Yamaguchi, demanding payment of JPY 11 million (US$82,000) for rape, upon which he launched a countersuit against her, claiming that her false accusation had damaged his reputation. He asked for a staggering JPY 130 million (US$9.7 million) in damages. The Tokyo District Court upheld the damage award for her, dismissed all his counterclaims, and ordered him to pay her JPY 3.3 million (US$24,000). The court was convinced that Ito, who was deeply intoxicated, had not consented to sex. Tokyo chihō saibansho [Tokyo DC], December 18, 2019, unreported (2019WLJPCA12186001); "Shiori Ito: Japanese Journalist Awarded $30,000 in Damages in Rape Case," *BBC News*, December 18, 2019, https://www.bbc.com/news/world-asia-50832524. On appeal, the Tokyo High Court affirmed the basic findings of the District Court and ordered Yamaguchi to pay JPY 3.32 million (US$25,000) for sexual assault, while ordering Ito to pay JPY 550,000 (US$4,100) for accusing that he had used a drug to rape her. Tokyo kōtō saibansho [Tokyo HC], January 25, 2022, unreported; "Itosan seihigai, Tokyo kosai mo nintei, kokuhakuchosho niwa baishoumei meirei" [Tokyo High Court Confirmed the Sexual Damages to Ms. Ito, but Ordered Damage Award for Accusations Made in Her Book], *Sankei Shimbun* (January 25, 2022), https://www.sankei.com/article/20220125-ILQN2DVRRFNLJOXQZJ6MRKOSYU/. The Japanese Supreme Court upheld the decision of the Tokyo High Court. Saikō saibansho [SCOJ], 1st petty bench, judgment of July 7, 2022, unreported; Japan Supreme Court upholds ruling for damages in Ito Shiori rape case, NHK (July 8, 2022), https://www3.nhk.or.jp/nhkworld/en/news/20220708_59/.

75 Criminal Code, *supra* note 2 art. 66 and art. 25.

76 Ibid., art. 236.

77 GEB, "Josei nitaisuru bouryoku nitsuiteno torikumubeki kadai to taisaku" [Agenda and Countermeasures against Sexual Violence toward Women], March 2004, http://www.gender.go.jp/kaigi/senmon/boryoku/houkoku/index_hb004.html.

78 Ibid.

79 Ibid.

80 United Nations Human Rights Committee, "Concluding Observations of the Human Rights Committee, Japan," October 2008, 14, http://www2.ohchr.org/english/bodies/hrc/docs/co/CCPR-C-JPN-CO.5.doc.

81 Ibid.

82 Ibid.

83 Ibid.

84 Ibid., at 27.

85 Ibid.

86 For discussions of the historical development and the current system of victim protection in Japan, see Shigenori Matsui, "Justice for the Accused or Justice for Victims? The Protection of Victims' Rights in Japan," 13:1 Asian-Pacific L. & Pol'y J. 54 (2011); Shigenori Matsui, "Victim Participation in the Criminal Process in Japan," 1 Hastings J. Crime & Punish. 303 (2020).
87 Hanzai higaishatō kyuuhukin no shikyutō niyoru hanzai higaishatō no shien nikansuru hōritsu [Crime Victims Support Benefit Act], law no. 36 of 1980.
88 Hanzai higaishatō no kenri rieki no hogo wo hakarutame no keijitetsuduki nihuzuisuru sochi nikansuru hōritsu [Act concerning Measures with Respect to Criminal Procedure to Protect the Rights and Interests of Crime Victims], law no. 75 of 2000 (Crime Victims Protection Act).
89 Hanzai higaishatō kihonhō [Crime Victims Fundamental Act], law no. 161 of 2004.
90 NPA, "Hanzai higaishatō kihon keikaku" [Crime Victims Protection Fundamental Plan], December 2005, https://www.npa.go.jp/hanzaihigai/kuwashiku/keikaku/basic_plan.html. The NPA subsequently adopted a third fundamental plan. NPA, "Dai3ji hanzai higaishatō kihon keikaku" [Third Crime Victims Protection Fundamental Plan], April 2016, https://www.npa.go.jp/hanzaihigai/kuwashiku/keikaku/pdf/dai3_basic_plan.pdf.
91 NPA, "Keisatsucho hanzai higaisha shien kihon keikaku" [The National Police Agency Crime Victim Support Fundamental Plan], April 1, 2016, https://www.npa.go.jp/higaisya/shiryou/pdf/tsuutatsu/H28kihonkeikaku.pdf.
92 NPA, "Keisatsu niyoru hanzai higaisha shien" [Crime Victim Support by the Police], 2020, https://www.npa.go.jp/higaisya/shien/index.html.
93 Ibid.
94 Ibid.
95 Ibid.
96 Ibid.
97 Ibid.
98 Prosecutors' Office, MOJ, "Hanzai higaisha no katagata e" [For Victims of Crimes], https://www.moj.go.jp/keiji1/keiji_keiji11.html.
99 Ibid.
100 Courts, "Kensatsu shinsakai" [Prosecution Review Board], http://www.courts.go.jp/kensin/seido_gaiyo/index.html.
101 MOJ, "Kouhan dankai deno higaisha shien" [Crime Victim Support during Trials], http://www.moj.go.jp/keiji1/keiji_keiji11-4.html.
102 Prosecutors' Office, *supra* note 98. The court can also allow the prosecutor not to reveal a victim's name in the writ of prosecution if doing so could further endanger his or her safety.
103 Ibid.
104 Ibid.
105 Ibid.
106 Ibid.

107 Ibid.
108 Ibid.
109 Ibid.
110 Ibid.
111 Ibid.
112 Ibid.
113 The definite term for imprisonment was extended from fifteen to twenty years, enabling incarceration to be increased to thirty years if rape had been committed together with other crimes. The minimum imprisonment term for rape was increased from two to three years, and the jail time for other crimes was similarly lengthened.
114 GEB, "Third Gender Equality Fundamental Plan," December 17, 2010, http://www.gender.go.jp/about_danjo/basic_plans/3rd/pdf/3-26.pdf.
115 GEB, "Josei nitaisuru bouryoku wo konzetsu surutame no kadai to taisaku" [Agenda and Countermeasures to Eradicate Violence toward Women], July 2012, http://www.moj.go.jp/content/001162245.pdf.
116 Ibid.
117 "Seihanzai no genbatsuka wo kentō: Matsushima Midori houshō" [Planning a Much Harsher Punishment for Sexual Crimes; Justice Minister Midori Matsushima], *Sankei Biz* (September 27, 2014), https://www.sankeibiz.jp/compliance/news/140927/cpb1409270924001-n1.htm.
118 MOJ, "Seihanzai no bassoku nikansuru kentoukai houkokusho" [Final Report of the Study Committee on the Punishment of Sexual Crimes], August 6, 2015, http://www.moj.go.jp/content/001154850.pdf.
119 The majority supported the removal of the complaint requirement, the expansion of rape to include male victims, the addition of a special provision for rape while taking advantage of power, and the imposition of much heavier punishments. Ibid. On the other hand, the majority did not support the suspension or termination of the statute of limitations for rape, the addition of spousal rape, expanding the definition to include insertion of a finger or object into a vagina, removing the assault or intimidation requirement, raising the age of consent, or transferring sex crime provisions from the "crimes against social welfare" section into the section on "crimes against life and liberty of individuals." Ibid.
120 Housei shingikai [Legislative Council], MOJ, "Yokou (kosshi)" [Draft (Outline)], http://www.moj.go.jp/content/001204028.pdf. See also Kazumichi Toujou, "Seihanzai no bassoku no minaoshi nitsuite" [Reconsideration of Criminal Punishment on Sexual Crimes], 373 Rippou to Chousa 23 (2016).
121 NPA, "Seihanzai higai soudan denwa" [Telephone Centre for Victims of Sexual Crimes], http://www.npa.go.jp/higaisya/seihanzai/seihanzai.html.
122 Ibid.
123 NPA, *supra* note 92.
124 Unless victims die as a result of the assault, the media do not publish their names, though doing so is not illegal.

125 MOJ, *supra* note 53 at 26.
126 Ibid.
127 Ibid.
128 Daniel H. Foote, "Citizen Participation: Appraising the Saiban'in System," 22 Mich. St. Int'l L. Rev. 755 (2013); Kaori Kano and Stacey Leanne Steele, "Japan's Lay Judge System (Saiban-in seido) and Legislative Developments: Annotated Translation of the Act Amending the Act on Criminal Trials with Participation of Saiban-in," 17:2 Asian-Pacific Law & Policy Journal 1 (2016).
129 In contrast to trials by professional judges alone, citizen judge trials tend to impose the longer imprisonment sentences of seven to ten years more often (24.9 percent compared with 15.4 percent) and ten to fifteen years more often (15.1 percent compared with 10.3 percent). They choose incarceration for three to five years less often (15.3 percent compared with 26.5 percent) and five to seven years less often (26.5 percent compared with 29.9 percent). MOJ, *supra* note 53 at 25. See also Yumi E. Suzuki, "Sexual Violence in Japan: Implications of the Lay Judge System on Victims of Sexual Violence," 4:1 J. of L. & Criminal Justice 75 (2016); Mari Hirayama, "Saiban-in seido to seihanzai" [Lay Judge System and Sexual Crimes], 327 Ritsumeikan hogaku 2092 (2009); Mari Hirayama, "Lay Judge Decisions in Sexual Crime Cases: The Most Controversial Area of Saiban-in Trials," 3 Yonsei L.J. 128 (2012).
130 Criminal Code, *supra* note 2 art. 176 ("a person who, through assault or intimidation, commits a forcible obscene act upon another person of not less than thirteen years of age shall be punished by imprisonment with labour for not less than six months but not more than ten years. The same shall apply to a person who commits a forcible obscene act upon another person under thirteen years of age").
131 Ibid., art. 177.
132 Ibid., art. 178(1).
133 Ibid., art. 178(2) ("a person who forcibly commits forcible sexual intercourse et al. by taking advantage of a loss of consciousness or inability to resist, or by causing a loss of consciousness or inability to resist, shall be punished in the same matter as prescribed in [article 177]").
134 Ibid., art. 179(1).
135 Ibid., art. 179(2).
136 Ibid., art. 180.
137 Ibid., art. 181(1).
138 Ibid., art. 181(2). Robbery and forcible sexual intercourse et al. that are committed in tandem can be punished by imprisonment with labour for an indefinite term or a definite term of not less than seven years. Ibid., art. 241(1). If a victim dies as a result of the assault, imprisonment with labour for an indefinite term or the death penalty can be imposed. Ibid., art. 241(3).
139 In 2012, only 6.8 percent of police officers were female. NPA, "Josei kaisatsukan no saiyo/touyo no kakudai nitsuite" [Increase of Appointment of Female Police Officers], https://www.npa.go.jp/hakusyo/h24/honbun/html/ot500000.html. In 2019, the figure

increased to 9.8 percent. NPA, "Reiwa gannen keisatsu hakusho" [Police Whitepaper, 2019], https://www.npa.go.jp/hakusyo/r01/honbun/image/v7z07020.png. In 2020, about 18.5 percent of officers in the Tokyo Metropolitan Police were women. Tokyo Metropolitan Police, "Keishicho niokeru josei katsuyaku suishin no genjō" [Current Status of Female Police Officers in the Tokyo Metropolitan Police], July 2020, https://www.keishicho.metro.tokyo.jp/about_mpd/shokai/women/index.files/17_jyosei.pdf.

140 The police are encouraging medical institutions to cooperate with them in preparing such kits. NPA, "Seihanzai souse niokeru tekiseina shoukohozen nitsuite" [Collection of Evidence for Sex Crimes], notification, July 31, 2019, https://www.npa.go.jp/laws/notification/keiji/souichi/souichi02/010731.pdf.

141 See *supra* note 119.

142 Shimaoka, *supra* note 40 at 22.

143 Unlike in Canada, there was no call to discontinue the legal use of the word "rape" and to integrate it into the category of "sexual assault." Because the word carries such a strong stigma, deleting it from the legal vocabulary was surely beneficial for victims. Even so, rape is seen as the most heinous sex crime, and it receives very strong moral condemnation. If it is subsumed under the heading of sexual assault, no distinction is made between forcible sexual intercourse and sexual touching. This change might trivialize rape, thus reducing the moral condemnation. On the other hand, the phrase "forcible sexual intercourse et al." is somewhat unfamiliar and difficult to comprehend. It is understandable that the legislature wanted to retain the traditional meaning of "sexual intercourse" as penile penetration of a vagina and that adding oral sex and anal sex to the ban thus necessitated the use of "et al." The better approach might be to retain "sexual intercourse" and simply include oral and anal sex in the definition. Also, the call for enhanced protection of crime victims is much stronger in Japan than in Canada. As a result, there was no demand that "victim" be replaced with "complainant."

144 Shimaoka, *supra* note 40 at 29.

145 Ibid.

146 MOJ, *supra* note 118 at 19.

147 Ibid.

148 Ibid.

149 Shimaoka, *supra* note 40 at 31.

150 Ibid. at 34.

151 Hiroshima kōtō saibansho, Matsue Shibu [Hiroshima HC, Matsue branch], June 18, 1987, 1234 Hanrei jihō 154.

152 Shimaoka, *supra* note 40 at 27–28.

153 Ibid., at 35.

154 Ibid., at 35–36.

155 Ibid., at 30. Indeed, the practice of considering a victim's sexual history in determining whether assault or intimidation occurred is utterly inconsistent with a potential shield law that would exclude such evidence during criminal trial.

156 The post-amendment limitation period for prosecution for forcible sexual intercourse et al. is still ten years despite the increased minimum prison term.
157 Ibid., at 25 (at least prosecution should be made possible where a victim was a minor and decided to file a charge after becoming an adult).
158 Gotell, *supra* note 68 at 209.
159 Statistics Canada, "Self-Reported Sexual Assault in Canada, 2014," July 11, 2017, https://www150.statcan.gc.ca/n1/pub/85-002-x/2017001/article/14842-eng.htm. In 2014, there were 636,000 self-reported incidents of sexual assault, which translates to 22 incidents for every 1,000 Canadians. The vast majority of victims were women (87 percent). Ibid.
160 In 2014, one in twenty incidents of sexual assault was reported to the police (5 percent), a proportion that remained unchanged from 2004 (8 percent). Ibid. See also Kirk Makin, "How Canada's Sexual-Assault Laws Violate Rape Victims," *Globe and Mail* (October 5, 2013), https://www.theglobeandmail.com/news/national/how-canadas-sex-assault-laws-violate-rape-victims/article14705289/.
161 In 2014, Statistics Canada recorded 20,735 incidents of sexual assault, but this number was limited to those qualified by police as "founded." Statistics Canada, *supra* note 160. In 2006, the police had stopped collecting data on "unfounded" incidents, because the information was inconsistent and incomplete. In 2017, a *Globe and Mail* article revealed that the chances of being deemed unfounded were significantly higher for sexual assaults than for other offences and that the rates differed among jurisdictions. Robyn Doolittle, "Unfounded: Why Police Dismiss 1 in 5 Sexual Assault Claims as Baseless," *Globe and Mail* (February 3, 2017), https://www.theglobeandmail.com/news/investigations/unfounded-sexual-assault-canada-main/article33891309/. After this revelation, Statistics Canada decided to adopt a more uniform standard and began to collect data again.
162 Statistics Canada, *supra* note 159. Roughly 70 percent of sexual assault incidents involve unwanted sexual touching. Ibid.
163 Ibid. See also Cecilia Benoit, Leah Shumka, Rachel Phillips, Mary Clare Kennedy, and Lynne Belle-Isle, "Issue Brief: Sexual Violence against Women in Canada," December 2015, 5, https://www.swc-cfc.gc.ca/svawc-vcsfc/issue-brief-en.pdf.
164 Between 2009 and 2014, 59 percent of sexual assaults reported by the police led to the identification of suspects, and less than half (43 percent) resulted in a charge being laid. Of those, only half again (49 percent) proceeded to court. Statistics Canada, "From Arrest to Conviction: Court Outcomes of Police-Reported Sexual Assaults in Canada, 2009 to 2014," October 26, 2017, https://www150.statcan.gc.ca/n1/pub/85-002-x/2017001/article/54870-eng.htm.
165 Recently, the Parliament introduced several reforms on the exclusion of evidence regarding a victim's sexual history. *Criminal Code of Canada*, s 276(1), s 276(2), and s 276(3).

166 Of all cases that proceeded to court, just over half (55 percent) resulted in a conviction. Overall, about one in ten sexual assaults reported by the police led to a criminal conviction. Statistics Canada, *supra* note 164.
167 Makin, *supra* note 160.
168 It is reported that 98 percent of all cases ended with prosecution for the least severe category of sexual assault. Ibid.
169 On average, sexual assault offenders are sentenced to two years in jail. Ibid.
170 Ibid.
171 Catharine A. MacKinnon argues that rape needs to be redefined from the perspective of sexual inequality. She rejects the Canadian approach of requiring affirmative consent and proposes that rape should be seen as "a physical invasion of a sexual nature under circumstances of threat or use of force, fraud, coercion, abduction, or of the abuse of power, trust, or a position of dependency or vulnerability." Catharine A. MacKinnon, "Rape Redefined," 10 Harv. L. & Pol'y Rev. 431 at 474 (2016).
172 Benoit et al, *supra* note 163 at 15.
173 Ibid., at 7–9.
174 However, statistics show that the number of reported cases of forcible sexual intercourse, et al. as well as the number of prosecuted persons, trended upward after the 2017 revisions, although the total number of reported cases as well as the number of prosecuted persons dropped. MOJ, "Reiwa 2nen Hanzai hakusho" [Crime Whitepaper, 2020], https://www.moj.go.jp/content/001363987.pdf. In 2019, there were 1,405 reported cases of forcible sexual intercourse et al., and 1,178 persons were prosecuted. In addition, there were 4,900 reported cases of forcible obscene acts, with 2,926 prosecuted persons. Ibid., at 4.
175 Fukuoka chihō saibansho, Kurume Shibu [Fukuoka DC, Kurume Branch], March 12, 2019, unreported, Hanrei Digest, http://www.hanreihisho.com/user-cgi-bin/digest/judgelist.cgi?years=2019.
176 Shizuoka chihō saibansho, Hamamatsu shibu [Shizuoka DC, Hamamatsu Branch], March 19, 2019, unreported (2019WLJPCA03196007).
177 Nagoya chihō saibansho, Okazaki shibu [Nagoya DC, Okazaki Branch], March 26, 2019, unreported (2019WLJPCA03266001).
178 Shizuoka chihō saibansho [Shizuoka DC], March 28, 2019, unreported (2019WLJPCA03286002).
179 Fukuoka chihō saibansho [Fukuoka DC], July 18, 2019, unreported (2019WLJPCA07186003).
180 Fukuoka kōtō saibansho [Fukuoka HC], February 5, 2020, unreported (2020WLJPCA02056008); "Koukyo hunou wo ninshiki to koi nintei" [Defendant Knew That the Victim Was Incapable of Refusing], *Asahi Shimbun* (February 5, 2020), https://www.asahi.com/articles/ASN2566TZN25TIPE01Y.html.
181 Nagoya kōtō saibansho [Nagoya HC], March 12, 2020, unreported (2020WLJPCA03126001); "18sai miman no youjo to seiko, muzai hakishi sashimodoshi, Fukuoka kōsai [Fukuoka High Court Reversed the Acquittal of Case Involving Sexual

Intercourse with Adopted Daughter Less Than Eighteen]," *Asahi Shimbun* (March 11, 2020), https://www.asahi.com/articles/ASN3C6H8HN3CTIPE00G.html.
182 The judgment was confirmed by the SCOJ. Saikō saibansho [SCOJ], 3rd petty bench, November 4, 2020, unreported; "'Teiko hunou' musume ni seiteki boukou: yuzai kakutei e, saikosai" [A Case concerning a Daughter "Unable to Resist" Sexually Assaulted: The SCOJ Affirms Conviction], *Asahi Shimbun* (November 7, 2020), https://www.asahi.com/articles/ASNC700RSNC6UTIL03M.html.
183 Fukuoka kōtō saibansho [Fukuoka HC], March 11, 2020, unreported (2020WLJPCA03118005).
184 Tokyo kōtō saibansho [Tokyo HC], December 21, 2020, unreported; "Chojo eno seiboryoku, jippuni gyakuten yuzai, shougen ni gutaisei aru [Sexual Assault against His Daughter, Father Convicted on Appeal, Testimony Was Found to Be Specific"], *Asahi Shimbun* (Dec. 21, 2020), https://www.asahi.com/articles/ASNDP6JQVNDPUTIL02T.html.
185 Saikō saibansho [SCOJ], 3rd petty bench, November 6, 2020, unreported; "Musume eno seitekiboko, chichioyano yuzai kakuteie, saikosai [Sexual Assault against His Daughter, the Conviction of Father Would Become Final]," NHK Nov. 13, 2020, https://www.nhk.or.jp/gendai/comment/0014/topic028.html.
186 Saikō saibansho [SCOJ], 2nd petty bench, September 15, 2021, unreported; "12sai no choujo eno seiteki boukou, choueki 7nen kakutei e" [Forced Sexual Intercourse against 12-Year-Old Daughter, 7 Year Imprisonment Sentence Is Upheld], *Yomiuri Shimbun* (September 17, 2021), https://www.yomiuri.co.jp/national/20210917-OYT1T50214/.
187 Altamira Pictures, "I Just Didn't Do It," http://web.archive.org/web/20070122114656/http://www.soreboku.jp/eng/; IMDb, "I Just Didn't Do It," https://www.imdb.com/title/tt0794350/.
188 Saikō saibansho [SCOJ], 3rd petty bench, April 14, 2009, 63:4 Keishu 331.
189 Saikō saibansho [SCOJ], 2nd petty bench, July 25, 2011, 304 Shumin 139.
190 Satoshi Sugita, *Nigerarenai seihanzai higaisha* [Victims of Sexual Crime: Simply Cannot Run Away] (Tokyo: Seikyusha, 2013).
191 Osaka chihō saibansho [Osaka DC], October 24, 2008, courts database, http://www.courts.go.jp/app/hanrei_jp/detail4?id=37008.
192 "Goukan jiken de saishin muzai, Osaka chisai, joseirano kyoujutsuwa uso" [Osaka District Court Acquitted the Defendant upon New Trial, Finding the Testimonies Turned out to Be Lies], *Nikkei Shimbun*, October 16, 2015), https://www.nikkei.com/article/DGXLASHC16H3G_W5A011C1000000/. The accused was convicted of raping and assaulting his fourteen-year-old step-granddaughter, largely on the basis of testimony from the girl and her brother. As it turned out, the brother and sister had been very strongly pressured by their mother to lie, and they recanted their testimonies once they became estranged from her. Tsunehiko Maeda, "Seiteki higai wo uketa toiu uso no shougende yaku 6nenmo migarakousoku: Hitoga hitowo sabaku keijisaiban no kowasa" [Detention over Six Years Based on the Lie That She Was the Victim of Sexual Assault: Horror Story of Allowing Persons to Adjudicate

a Person], Yahoo News, January 8, 2019, https://news.yahoo.co.jp/byline/maedatsunehiko/20190108-00110224/. Although the mother told the police that she had taken the girl to see a doctor, they did not attempt to obtain the medical record of the visit and nor did the prosecutor, despite the urging of the defence lawyer. The District Court judge held that such a young girl could not possibly have invented the incident, and the accused was convicted despite his consistent denial. The High Court refused to call the mother to testify or order the production of the medical note. In this rather horrifying situation, everyone involved with the criminal proceedings seems simply to have assumed that the defendant must be guilty. To some extent, this is understandable, as he had admitted to raping the mother of the fourteen-year-old but was never prosecuted due to the statute of limitations. Hiroki Morooka, "Goukan enzai jiken ga okita haikei niwa hukuzatsusugiru kateijijou ga atta" [Complicated Family Background for the Rape Wrongful Conviction Case], Bunshun Online, January 22, 2019, http://bunshun.jp/articles/-/10454.

193 However, the Osaka District Court dismissed the damage claim. Osaka chihō saibansho [Osaka DC], January 8, 2019, unreported; "Goukan enzai, danseino kokka baishou seikyu wo kikyaku: joseino uso de hukueki" [Damage Claim of Wrongfully Convicted Alleged Rapist Dismissed: Imprisoned Because of the Victim Girl's Lie], *Asahi Shimbun* (January 8, 2019), https://www.asahi.com/articles/ASM184FLYM18PTIL018.html?iref=pc_extlink.

194 Richard Klein, "An Analysis of Thirty-Five Years of Rape Reform: A Frustrating Search for Fundamental Fairness," 41 Akron L. Rev. 981 (2008).

195 See also Stephen J. Schulhofer, "Reforming the Law of Rape," 35 Law & Ineq. 335 (2017). Satisfying these requirements places the police, the prosecutors, and judges in a delicate situation. On the one hand, fairness to the accused demands that the investigation be thorough and that sufficient facts are presented in court to secure a conviction. On the other hand, victims must be treated with sensitivity and must not be needlessly traumatized by being asked to relive the experience of sexual assault. Achieving the right balance is no easy feat.

196 *French Penal Code*, *supra* note 39. See also *German Criminal Code*, s 177a.

197 *Code of Virginia*, s 18.2–61. See also *New York Penal Law*, s 130.35, which provides for rape in the first degree when the accused engages in sexual intercourse with another person by forcible compulsion, or who is incapable of consent by reason of being physically helpless, or who is less than eleven years old, or who is less than thirteen years old and the actor is eighteen years old or more. Sexual intercourse without consent can be sexual misconduct (s 130.20), and sexual intercourse with another person who is incapable of consent can be rape in the third degree or rape in the second degree (s 130.25 and s 130.30).

198 Jamie L. Small, "Conceptualizing Consent: How Prosecutors Identify Sexual Victimization in Statutory Rape Cases," 45 L. & Social Inquiry 111 (2020); Eithne Dowds, "Towards a Contextual Definition of Rape: Consent, Coercion and

Constructive Force," 83 Modern L. Rev. 35 (2020). See also New South Wales Law Reform Commission, "Consent in Relation to Sexual Offences," 2020, https://www.lawreform.justice.nsw.gov.au/Documents/Publications/Reports/Report%20148.pdf (attempting to clarify the meaning of consent in sexual offences).
199 Recently, for example, Jian Ghomeshi, a well-known CBC Radio host, was acquitted for sexual assault charges when the judge found that the sworn testimonies of the alleged victims were filled with inconsistencies and were even deceptive and manipulative. Mark Gollom, "Jian Ghomeshi Found Not Guilty on Choking and All Sex Assault Charges," *CBC News*, March 24, 2016, https://www.cbc.ca/news/canada/toronto/jian-ghomeshi-sexual-assault-trial-ruling-1.3505446.
200 Burns, *supra* note 38 at 2.
201 Ibid.
202 Ibid.
203 Ibid.
204 Ibid., at 52.
205 Ibid., at 71.
206 Ibid., at 2–4.
207 The MOJ is now reviewing the reform and discussing whether further amendment is necessary. MOJ, "Seihanzai nikansuru keijihō kentoukai: Torimatome houkokusho" [Review on Criminal Provisions on Sexual Crime: Summary Report], March 2021, https://www.moj.go.jp/content/001348762.pdf. *Supra* note 27.

Chapter 4: Childbirth

1 The Center for Disease Control and Prevention (CDC) in the United States defines infertility as "not being able to get pregnant (conceive) after one year (or longer) of unprotected sex." CDC, "What Is Infertility?," https://www.cdc.gov/reproductivehealth/infertility/index.htm.
2 The CDC definition of "ART," as "all fertility treatments in which both eggs and embryos are handled," excludes artificial insemination. CDC, "What Is Assisted Reproductive Technology?" https://www.cdc.gov/art/whatis.html. But in European countries, as well as in Japan, ART is often seen as including artificial insemination. C. Calhaz-Jorge et al., "European IVF-Monitoring Consortium (EIM) for the European Society of Human Reproduction and Embryology, Assisted Reproductive Technology in Europe, 2012: Results Generated from European Registers by ESHRE," 31 Human Reproduction 1638 (2016), https://academic.oup.com/humrep/article/31/8/1638/2379971. The World Health Organization (WHO) proposes that MAR includes artificial insemination, whereas ART would exclude it. F. Zegers-Hochschild, G.D. Adamson, J. de Mouzon, O. Ishihara, R. Mansour, K. Nygren, E. Sullivan, and S. van der Poel, "The International Committee for Monitoring Assisted Reproductive Technology (ICMART) and the World Health Organization (WHO) Revised Glossary on ART Terminology, 2009," 24:11 Human Reproduction 2683, https://doi.org/10.1093/humrep/dep343. Published: 04

October 2009. See also Patrick Präg and Melinda C. Mills, "Assisted Reproductive Technology in Europe: Usage and Regulation in the Context of Cross-Border Reproductive Care," January 2017, https://link.springer.com/chapter/10.1007/978-3-319-44667-7_14. But MAR is not commonly used in the United States when compared with ART. This chapter follows the Japanese usage and defines ART broadly to include artificial insemination. When ART is used in this way, there is no clear distinction between it and MAR.

3 Gayle Binion, "Reproductive Freedom and the Constitution: The Limits on Choice," 4 Berkeley Women's L.J. 12 (1988); Carter J. Dillard, "Rethinking the Procreative Right," 10:1 Yale Human Rights and Development Law J. 1 (2007), http://digitalcommons.law.yale.edu/yhrdlj/vol10/iss1/1. See *Skinner v Oklahoma*, 316 U.S. 535 (1942).

4 In the United States, it had been well accepted that a woman has the right not to be forced to bear a child, including the right to use contraceptives and to have an abortion (although now the Supreme Court of the United States [SCOTUS] has come to deny the right to have an abortion). It is somewhat controversial whether a man has a constitutional right to be a parent. Joanna Grossman, "'Roe v Wade for Men'? A Men's Rights Group Makes a Farfetched Claim for Avoidance of Child Support," FindLaw, March 22, 2006, https://supreme.findlaw.com/legal-commentary/roe-v-wade-for-men-a-mens-rights-group-makes-a-farfetched-claim-for-avoidance-of-child-support.html. This reluctance is probably triggered by the fear that recognizing his right could deny or restrict women's right not to have children. However, becoming pregnant and giving birth would be strictly consensual and voluntary. Therefore, even if a man has a right to become a father, he does not have a right to force his partner to become a mother. As discussed more fully in the next chapter, a woman has the right not to be forced to give birth.

5 The SCOTUS accepts that parents have a right to make decisions concerning the care, custody, and control of their children as a fundamental right protected as a liberty interest under the Fourteenth Amendment. *Troxel v Granville*, 530 U.S. 57 (2000). This right is meaningless if there is no right to have a child or to become a parent.

6 United Nations, *Universal Declaration of Human Rights*, art. 16 (right to marry and to found a family); United Nations, *International Covenant on Civil and Political Rights*, art. 23 (right of men and women of marriageable age to marry and to found a family); United Nations, *International Covenant on Economic, Social and Cultural Rights*, art. 10 (respect for the establishment of family).

7 *Skinner v Oklahoma*, supra note 3 at 541–42.

8 Charles Scott and Elena del Busto, "Chemical and Surgical Castration," in *Sex Offender Laws*, 2nd ed., ed. Richard Wright (New York: Springer, 2014), at 190; Michael Petrunik, Lisa Murphy, and J. Paul Fedoroff, "American and Canadian Approaches to Sex Offenders: A Study of the Politics of Dangerousness," 21:2 Federal Sentencing Reporter 111 (2008).

9 *California Penal Code*, s 645 (emphasis added). See also Vincent J. Schodolski, "California Passes Chemical Castration Law," *Washington Post* (August 31, 1996), https://www.washingtonpost.com/archive/politics/1996/08/31/california-passes-chemical-castration-law/f87e5174-8cb1-49da-b183-f105d6738432/; Philip J. Henderson, "Section 645 of the California Penal Code: California's Chemical Castration Law – A Panacea or Cruel and Unusual Punishment?," 32 U.S.F. L. Rev. 653 (1997–98).

10 *Florida Statutes on Crimes*, s 794.0235.

11 Elizabeth Thomas, "Alabama Lawmakers Pass Bill Requiring Chemical Castration for Child Sex Offenders," *ABC News*, June 5, 2019, https://abcnews.go.com/US/alabama-lawmakers-pass-bill-requiring-chemical-castration-child/story?id=63503004; Alex Johnson, "Alabama Becomes Seventh State to Approve Castration for Some Sex Offenses," *NBC News*, June 10, 2019, https://www.nbcnews.com/news/crime-courts/alabama-becomes-seventh-state-approve-castration-some-sex-offenses-n1016056.

12 Elena del Busto and Michael C. Harlow, "American Sexual Offender Castration Treatment and Legislation," in *International Perspectives on the Assessment and Treatment of Sexual Offenders: Theory, Practice, and Research*, ed. Douglas P. Boer et al. (Chichester: Wiley-Blackwell, 2011), 543.

13 *Texas Government Code*, s 501.061: Orchiectomy for Certain Sex Offenders.

14 "Poland Okays Forcible Castration for Pedophiles," Reuters, September 25, 2009, https://www.reuters.com/article/us-castration/poland-okays-forcible-castration-for-pedophiles-idUSTRE58O4LE20090925 (pedophiles who are convicted of raping anyone under the age of fifteen or a close relative must undergo chemical therapy on release from prison). Surgical castration is also available upon consent.

15 Leo Cendrowicz, "The Unkindest Cut: A Czech Solution for Sex Offenders," *Time* (February 11, 2009), http://content.time.com/time/world/article/0,8599,1878462,00.html.

16 The Council of Europe urged Germany to stop this practice and repeal the relevant statute. "Germany Urged to End Sex Offender Castration," *BBC News*, February 22, 2012, https://www.bbc.com/news/world-europe-17124604. Although Germany did not repeal the law, the practice appears to have been discontinued. "Germany Praised for Ending Sex-Offender Surgical Castration," *CTV News*, June 1, 2017, https://www.ctvnews.ca/health/germany-praised-for-ending-sex-offender-surgical-castration-1.3438688.

17 "South Korea Introduces 'Chemical Castration' for Paedophiles," *BBC News*, September 28, 2011, https://www.bbc.com/news/av/world-asia-pacific-15100393/south-korea-introduces-chemical-castration-for-paedophiles; Steven Borowiec, "Seoul Puts Castration to the Test," DW, November 1, 2013, https://www.dw.com/en/seoul-puts-castration-to-the-test/a-16513280.

18 Larry H. Spalding, "Florida's 1997 Chemical Castration Law: A Return to the Dark Ages," 25 Fla. St. U. L. Rev. 117 (1998).

19 Zachary E. Oswald, "'Off with His __': Analyzing the Sex Disparity in Chemical Castration Sentences," 19 Mich. J. Gender & L. 471 (2013).

20 C. Rosati, "A Study of Internal Punishment," 123 Wis. L. Rev. 123 (1994); L. Bomann-Larsen, "Voluntary Rehabilitation? On Neurotechnological Behavioural Treatment, Valid Consent and (In)appropriate Offers," 6:1 Neuroethics 665 (2011).
21 W. Green, "Depo-Provera, Castration, and the Probation of Rape Offenders: Statutory and Constitutional Issues," 12:1 U. of Dayton L. Rev. 1 (1986); European Committee for the Prevention of Torture and Inhuman or Degrading Treatment or Punishment, "Report to the Czech Government on the Visit to the Czech Republic Carried Out by the European Committee for the Prevention of Torture and Inhuman or Degrading Treatment or Punishment (CPT)," 2010, Council of Europe, https://rm.coe.int/CoERMPublicCommonSearchServices/DisplayDCTMContent?documentId=090000168069567d. See also Charles L. Scott and Trent Holmberg, "Castration of Sex Offenders: Prisoners' Rights versus Public Safety," 31:4 J. of American Academy of Psychiatry and the L. 502 (2003).
22 Thomas Douglas, Pieter Bonte, Farah Focquaert, Katrien Devolder, and Sigrid Sterckx, "Coercion, Incarceration, and Chemical Castration: An Argument from Autonomy," 10:3 J. Bioeth Inq. 393 (2013), https://www.ncbi.nlm.nih.gov/pmc/articles/PMC3824348/#CR17.
23 C.M. Wong, "Chemical Castration: Oregon's Innovative Approach to Sex Offender Rehabilitation, or Unconstitutional Punishment?" 80 Oregon L. Rev. 267 (2001).
24 Yusei hogohō [Eugenic Protection Act], law no. 156 of 1948, art. 1.
25 Ibid., art. 2(1).
26 Ibid., art. 3. Four family-degree relatives include grand-grand-grand parents, grand-grand parents of one's spouse or cousin.
27 Ibid., art. 4.
28 Ibid., art. 5.
29 Ibid., art. 10.
30 Ibid., art. 11.
31 "16-sai de hunin shujutu wo shiirareta: Kyu-yusei hogohō ga 24911 nin no seishoku kinou wo ubatta rikutsu" [I Was Sterilized at the Age of Sixteen: Why the Old Eugenic Protection Act Deprived 24,911 Persons of Their Reproductive Capacity], *FNN* (April 11, 2020), https://www.fnn.jp/articles/-/29861. For detailed accounts, see *Mainichi Shimbun, Kyosei hinin* [Compulsory Sterilization] (Tokyo: *Mainichi Shimbunsha*, 2019); Yutaka Fujino, *Kyosei hinin to Yusei hogohō* [Compulsory Sterilization and the Eugenic Protection Act] (Tokyo: Iwanami shoten, 2020).
32 Paul Popenoe, "The German Sterilization Law," 25:7 Journal of Heredity 257 (1934); Paul Weindling, "Nazi Sterilization," Eugenicsarchive, April 29, 2014, http://eugenicsarchive.ca/discover/tree/535eed207095aa0000000243.
33 "Remembering the Victims of Nazi Eugenics," DW, July 14, 2003, https://www.dw.com/en/remembering-the-victims-of-nazi-eugenics/a-16945569.
34 Lutz Kaelber, "Eugenics: Compulsory Sterilization in 50 American States," https://www.uvm.edu/~lkaelber/eugenics/ (more than thirty American states had such a law).

35 Sendai chihō saibansho [Sendai DC], May 28, 2019, unreported (2019WLJPCA05286001); "Kyu-yusei hogohō wa iken" [The Court Ruled Compulsory Sterilization under the Former Eugenic Protection Act Unconstitutional], *Asahi Shimbun* (May 28, 2019), https://www.asahi.com/articles/ASM5X4T78M5XUTIL03C.html.

36 Kyu yusei hogohō nimotoduku yusei shujututō wo uketamono nitaisuru ichijikin no shikyu nikansuru hōritsu [Act on Payment of One-Time Benefit for Those Who Received Sterilization under the Former Eugenic Protection Act], law no. 14 of 2019; Motoko Rich and Makiko Inoue, "Japan to Compensate Forcibly Sterilized Patients, Decades after the Fact," *New York Times* (April 25, 2019), https://www.nytimes.com/2019/04/25/world/asia/japan-sterilization-eugenics-compensation.html. However, many victims are suing the government for damages. In one recent landmark judgment, the Osaka High Court acknowledged the manifest unconstitutionality of the mandatory sterilization measure and ordered the government to pay damages, rejecting its argument that the statute of limitations should apply. The accepted damage award was roughly JPY 13.0 million (US$98,000), far larger than the lump sum compensation of JPY 3.2 million (US$24,000) offered by the statute for one patient. Osaka kōtō saibansho [Osaka HC], February 22, 2022, unreported; "Kyu yuseihogohō no hunin shujutu de kunini baishou meirei" [The Court Ordered the Government to Pay Damages to Patients Who Suffered Mandatory Sterilization under the Former Eugenic Protection Act], *NHK* (February 22, 2022), https://www3.nhk.or.jp/news/html/20220222/k10013496251000.html. The Tokyo High Court followed this judgment and also ordered the government to pay damages. Tokyo kōtō saibansho [Tokyo HC], March 11, 2022, unreported; "Kyu yuseihogohō sosho, Tokyo kosai mo genkoku shouso" [Tokyo HC Ordered the Government to Pay Damages: Former Eugenic Protection Act], *Mainichi Shimbun* (March 11, 2022), https://mainichi.jp/articles/20220311/k00/00m/040/112000c.

37 Susan Greenhalgh and Edwin A. Winckler, *Governing China's Population: From Leninist to Neoliberal Biopolitics* (Stanford: Stanford University Press, 2005); Steven W. Mosher, "China's One-Child Policy: Twenty-Five Years Later," 32:1 Human Life Rev. 76 (2006).

38 See, for example, William Yang, "How Has the One-Child Policy Affected China?" DW, July 19, 2018, https://www.dw.com/en/how-has-the-one-child-policy-affected-china/a-44749604.

39 Kristine Sudbeck, "The Effects of China's One-Child Policy: The Significance for Chinese Women," *Nebraska Anthropologist* 179 (2012), http://digitalcommons.unl.edu/nebanthro/179.

40 CBC Radio, "China's One-Child Policy Was Enforced through Abortion and Sterilization, Says Documentary Director," *The Current*, May 2, 2019, https://www.cbc.ca/radio/thecurrent/the-current-for-may-2-2019-1.5118724/china-s-one-child-policy-was-enforced-through-abortion-and-sterilization-says-documentary-director-1.5118738.

41 Nathan Vanderklippe, "The Ghost Children: In the Wake of China's One-Child Policy, a Generation Is Lost," *Globe and Mail* (March 13, 2015), https://www.theglobeandmail.com/news/world/the-ghost-children-in-the-wake-of-chinas-one-child-policy-a-generation-is-lost/article23454402/.

42 Simon Denyer and Annie Gowen, "Too Many Men," *Washington Post* (April 18, 2018), https://www.washingtonpost.com/graphics/2018/world/too-many-men/.

43 United Nations, "Below-Replacement Fertility in China: Policy Response Is Long Overdue," https://www.un.org/development/desa/pd/sites/www.un.org.development.desa.pd/files/undp_egm_201511_policy_brief_no._5.pdf; "Chinese Birth Rate Falls to Lowest in Seven Decades," *BBC News*, January 17, 2020, https://www.bbc.com/news/world-asia-china-51145251.

44 "China's Two-Child Policy," *Bloomberg News* (January 22, 2020), https://www.bloomberg.com/quicktake/china-s-two-child-policy.

45 "China Allows Three Children in Major Policy Shift," *BBC News*, May 31, 2021, https://www.bbc.com/news/world-asia-china-57303592.

46 Steven Lee Myers and Olivia Mitchell Ryan, "Burying 'One Child' Limits, China Pushes Women to Have More Babies," *New York Times* (August 11, 2018), https://www.nytimes.com/2018/08/11/world/asia/china-one-child-policy-birthrate.html; Lily Kuo and Xueying Wang, "Can China Recover from Its Disastrous One-Child Policy?" *Guardian* (March 2, 2019), https://www.theguardian.com/world/2019/mar/02/china-population-control-two-child-polic.

47 Shigenori Matsui, "'Never Had a Choice and Have No Power to Alter': Illegitimate Children and the Supreme Court of Japan," 44 Ga. J. Int'l & Comp. L. 577 (2016).

48 Minpō [Civil Code], 1896, art. 900.

49 Saikō saibansho [SCOJ], grand bench, September 4, 2013, 67:6 Minshu 1320.

50 Japan Association of Obstetricians and Gynecologists, "Huninsho [Infertility]," http://eugenicsarchive.ca/discover/tree/535eed207095aa0000000243.

51 Cabinet Office, "Shoushika shakai taisaku hakusho heisei28nenban [Declining Childbirth Society 2006]" https://www8.cao.go.jp/shoushi/shoushika/whitepaper/measures/w-2006/18webhonpen/html/i1311100.html.

52 Hito nikansuru clone gijutsutō no kisei ni kansuru hōritsu [Act on Regulation of the Use of Cloning Technology in Humans], law no. 146 of 2000.

53 For a discussion of the law and the use of ART or MAR in Japan, see Michiko Ishii, "Medically-Assisted Reproduction and Family Law in Japan," in *Japanese Family Law in Comparative Perspective*, ed. Harry N. Scheiber and Laurent Mayali (Berkeley, CA: Robins Collection, 2009), 175. In Japan, the donation and sale of sperm and eggs are not regulated. With the wide acceptance of artificial insemination, the need for donated sperm has expanded. In the past, it was voluntarily supplied by medical students, and the university that provided ART/MAR collected it. However, with the increase of infertility and the need for sperm, numerous sperm-selling websites have popped up on the internet. Most are dubious. In some instances, women have purchased sperm from these online sources, using it to inseminate themselves.

"Seishi wo morau kau kisei naku susumu genjitsu" [Sperm Donation or Sale: Reality without Legal Regulation], *NHK* (July 13, 2021), https://www3.nhk.or.jp/news/html/20210713/k10013136321000.html. Moreover, in one case, a woman who used provided sperm to give birth has filed a lawsuit against the man who supplied it, claiming that he lied about his academic history and nationality. Although she requested that the sperm be placed in a syringe, he insisted on sex, and she was tricked and forced to have sex to become pregnant. "Seishi torihiki de trouble" [Trouble in Sperm Transaction], *Tokyo Shimbun* (December 27, 2021), https://www.tokyo-np.co.jp/article/151342.

54 Alexander N. Hecht, "The Wild Wild West: Inadequate Regulation of Assisted Reproductive Technology," 1 Hous. J. Health L. & Pol'y 227 (2001); Kirsten Riggan, "Regulation (or Lack Thereof) of Assisted Reproductive Technologies in the U.S. and Abroad," 17:1–2 Dignitas 8 (2010).

55 Francesco Paolo Busardò, Matteo Gulino, Simona Napoletano, Simona Zaami, and Paola Frati, "The Evolution of Legislation in the Field of Medically Assisted Reproduction and Embryo Stem Cell Research in European Union Members," 2014 Biomed Res. Int. 307160 (July 24, 2014), https://www.ncbi.nlm.nih.gov/pmc/articles/PMC4134786/; "Regulation and Legislation in Assisted Reproduction," ESHRE Fact Sheets 2, ESHRE, January 9, 2017, https://www.eshre.eu/-/media/sitecore-files/Pressroom/Resources/2-Regulation.pdf. However, it is important to note that the approach adopted in EU countries is highly fragmented and that some movements toward harmonization are surely underway.

56 Japan Society of Obstetrics and Gynecology, http://www.jsog.or.jp.

57 JSOG, "Teikyo seishi wo mochiita jinkō jusei nikansuru kenkai" [Opinion on Artificial Insemination Using Donor Sperm], June 2015, http://fa.kyorin.co.jp/jsog/readPDF.php?file=74/7/074070749.pdf#page=12.

58 Ibid.

59 JSOG, "Hai teikyo niyoru seishoku hojo iryou nikansuru kenkai" [Opinion on Assisted Reproductive Technology Using Embryo Transfer], April 2, 2004, http://fa.kyorin.co.jp/jsog/readPDF.php?file=74/7/074070749.pdf#page=49. For the Code of Ethics on IVF, see JSOG, "Taigai jusei/hai ishoku nikansuru kenkai" [Opinion on IVF and Embryo Transfer] (1983), https://www.jsog.or.jp/kaiin/html/S58_10.html.

60 JSOG, "Dairi kaitai nikansuru kenkai" [Opinion on Surrogate Motherhood], April 2, 2003, http://fa.kyorin.co.jp/jsog/readPDF.php?file=74/7/074070749.pdf#page=47.

61 MHLW, Kousei kagaku shingikai, Seishoku hojo iryou senmon iinkai [Health Science Council, Expert Subcommittee on Medically Assisted Reproduction Technology], "Seishi, ranshi, hai no teikyotō niyoru seishoku hojo iryou no arikata nitsuiteno houkokusho" [Report on Medically Assisted Reproduction by Using Sperm, Egg, and Embryo Transfer], December 2000, https://www.mhlw.go.jp/www1/shingi/s0012/s1228-1_18.html.

62 MHLW, Kousei kagaku shingikai, Seishoku hojo iryo bukai [Health Science Council, Medically Assisted Reproduction Technology Committee], "Seishi, ranshi, hai no

teikyotō niyoru seishoku hojo iryo seido no seibi nikansuru houkokusho" [Report on the Legalization of Medically Assisted Reproduction Using Semen, Egg, and Embryo Transfer], 2003, http://www.mhlw.go.jp/shingi/2003/04/s0428–5.html.

63 Ministry of Justice (MOJ), "Seishi, ranshi, hai no teikyotō niyoru seishoku hojo iryo niyori shusseishita ko no oyakokankei nikansuru Minpō no tokurei nikansuru youkou chukan shian" [Draft Interim Outline of the Bill Providing for Special Exceptions to the Civil Code on the Parental Relationship for a Child Born by MAR Using Semen, Egg, or Embryo], 11, http://www.moj.go.jp/content/000071864.pdf.

64 MOJ, "Chakushutsu suitei kitei no minaoshi nitomonau seishoku hojo iryou niyori umareta ko no fushi kankeitō no kiritsuno kahi nitsuiteno kento" [Consideration of the Paternal Relationship between Children Born Using Medically Assisted Reproduction in Light of the Reconsideration of the Presumption of Legitimacy], http://www.moj.go.jp/content/001315835.pdf.

65 JSOG, "Taigai jusei/haiishoku/hitohai oyobi ranshi no touketsu hozon to ishoku nikansuru kenkai niokeru kon-in no sakujo nituite" [Deletion of the Marriage Requirement for the Opinion on the IVF and Embryo Transfer/Frozen Storage of Human Embryos and Eggs and Their Transfer] (July 2022) http://fa.kyorin.co.jp/jsog/readPDF.php?file=74/7/074070749.pdf#page=17.

66 Ibid.

67 Japan Society for Reproductive Medicine (JSRM), http://www.jsrm.or.jp/index.html. Although the JSRM was formed in 1956, it was incorporated only in 1970 and admitted into the Japan Medical Association in 1976. JSRM, http://www.jsrm.or.jp/about/aboutus.html.

68 JSRM, "Daisansha haigushi wo mochiiru seishoku iryo nitsuiteno teigen" [Proposal for Assisted Reproduction Using Donor Sperm and Donor Eggs], 2009, http://www.jsrm.or.jp/guideline-statem/guideline_2009_01.html.

69 JSRM, "Dairihaha no mondai nitsuiteno riji kenkai" [Opinion of the Managing Board on Surrogate Motherhood] 1992, http://www.jsrm.or.jp/guideline-statem/guideline_1992_01.html (reporting that there was still no consensus on surrogacy).

70 Science Council of Japan, Expert Committee on Medically Assisted Reproduction, "Dairi kaitai wo chuushin tosuru seishoku hojo iryo no kadai" [Agendas of Medically Assisted Reproduction, Especially Surrogacy], April 8, 2008, https://www.scj.go.jp/ja/info/kohyo/pdf/kohyo-20-t56-1.pdf. This proposed that all surrogacy be banned, except for a few narrowly defined exceptions, and that anyone who engaged in it for profit should be criminally punished. At the time of writing, the Diet had enacted no legislation to this effect.

71 Dr. Nezu of the Suwa Maternity Clinic, a leading ART/MAR expert, was expelled from the JSOG for violating the Code of Ethics prohibition on using donor eggs in 1998. JSOG Special Board Meeting Minutes (Nov. 1998), http://fa.kyorin.co.jp/jsog/readPDF.php?file=to63/50/11/KJ00001745913.pdf. After litigation, both parties settled and Nezu was readmitted to the JSOG.

72 Japanese Institution for Standardizing Assisted Reproductive Technology, "Seishi/ranshi no teikyo niyoru hihaigushakan taigaijusei nikansuru JISART guideline" [Guideline with Respect to IVF Procedure Using Donor Sperm or Donor Eggs] (updated September 4, 2021) https://jisart.jp/about/external/guidline/ (JISART Guideline).

73 JISART, "Seishi/ranshi teikyo jisseki" [Number of Uses of Donor Sperm and Donor Eggs] https://jisart.jp/about/external/proven/. At least, JISART reported ninety-eight cases in which donor sperm and donor eggs were used, as well as the birth of sixty-three babies. Ibid.

74 JISART Guideline, *supra* note 72, limits the use of donor egg IVF to a woman who is medically incapable of conceiving by any other method. It also restricts it to a legally married couple who are healthy and emotionally and economically stable. Surrogacy is neither officially accepted nor flatly banned.

75 The JISART Guideline limits donor egg IVF to a woman under the age of fifty. Ibid. Moreover, the government-provided special grant to cover medical expenses for IVF treatment also has an age limit. MHLW, "Hunin de nayamu huuhu eno shien nitsuite" [Assistance to Couples Who Suffer from Infertility], https://www.mhlw.go.jp/stf/seisakunitsuite/bunya/0000047270.html. For a legally married wife under the age of forty-three, the government provides a special subsidy of JPY 300,000 (roughly US$2,200) for the first IVF or intra-cytoplasmic sperm injection (ICSI) treatment to cover the expensive medical costs. It provides an additional JPY 150,000 (about US$1,100) for subsequent treatment until the age of 43. However, the couple can access this subsidy only a certain number of times: 6 if the woman starts treatment before age forty and three if she starts between the ages of 40 to 43.

76 "Kyuzou ranshi teikyo" [Increasing ART Using Donor Eggs], *NHK* (January 10, 2013), https://www.nhk.or.jp/gendai/articles/3292/index.html; "Kyuzou dairishussan: Kisei to genjitsu no hazamade" [Increasing Surrogacy: Caught between the Regulation and Reality], *NHK* (September 30, 2014), https://www.nhk.or.jp/gendai/articles/3558/index.html. Moreover, although selling and buying sperm or eggs are not officially permitted in Japan, an increasing number of Japanese couples are now purchasing sperm from the world's largest sperm bank, in Denmark. "Sekai saidai no seishi bank kara kounyu, kokunai ni 150nin-cho [Over 150 Persons Bought Sperm from the Biggest Sperm Bank in the World]," *Yomiuri Shimbun*, November 24, 2020, https://www.yomiuri.co.jp/medical/20201124-OYT1T50110/.

77 "Taigai juseiji, 16nin ni hitori," [One in 16 Children Were Born by IVF] *Asahi Shimbun* (October 1, 2020), https://www.asahi.com/articles/ASNB15J73NB1ULBJ008.html.

78 The number is not, however, especially discouraging. In the United States, whose population is 2.5 times larger than that of Japan, 330,773 ART cycles performed at 448 reporting clinics in the United States during 2019, resulting in 77,998 live births and 83,946 live born infants. Approximately 2.0% of all infants born in the United States every year are conceived using ART. Centers for Disease Control (CDC), "Assisted Reproductive Technology (ART)," https://www.cdc.gov/art/artdata/index.html.

79 Juntendo University, "Chiryorei goto no hiyou" [Costs of Treatment], https://www.juntendo.ac.jp/hospital/clinic/reproduction/about/treatment/cost.html.

80 JSOG, "Seishoku hojo iryo (assisted reproductive technology) no jissai" [Practice of Assisted Reproductive Technology] http://www.jsog.or.jp/to_medics/miryoku/miryoku04.html; Cabinet Office, "Sanko shiryo" [Relevant Data], 2020, https://www5.cao.go.jp/keizai2/keizai-syakai/future2/20200327/shiryou1.pdf (the success rate for a single IVF cycle is about 7 percent, and the accumulative success rate is 25 percent).

81 See *supra* note 75.

82 Cabinet Office, "Dai203kai kokkai niokeru Suga naikaku souridaijin shoshin hyoumei enzetsu" [Opening Statement of Prime Minister Suga in the 203th Diet], October 26, 2020, https://www.kantei.go.jp/jp/99_suga/statement/2020/1026shoshinhyomei.html.

83 Seishoku hojo iryo no teikyotō oyobi koreniyori shusseishita kono oyako kankei nikansuru Minpō no tokurei nikansuru hōritsu [Act on the Provision of Medically Assisted Reproduction and on the Special Rule for the Parental Relationship between Parents and Children Born Using Such Procedures], law no. 76 of 2020.

84 "Medically assisted reproduction" as used in this act means "artificial insemination, in vitro fertilization, and in vitro fertilized embryo transfer." Ibid., art. 2(1).

85 Ibid., art. 3.

86 Ibid., art. 4(1).

87 Ibid., art. 4(2).

88 Ibid., art. 5.

89 Ibid., art. 6.

90 Ibid., art. 7.

91 Ibid., art. 8.

92 Ibid., addendum art. 3. There is an increasing call for protection of the right to know the identity of the sperm donor. However, opinions remain divided. Many fear that the mandatory disclosure of a donor's identity will drastically diminish the rate of donation. The government decision to reserve this matter for further discussion was a disappointment for those who favour mandatory disclosure. "Houan ni shitsubo: Shutsuji wo shiru kenri wa hairazu" [Huge Disappointment Caused by the Bill: No Protection of the Right to Know the Identity of the Sperm Donor Was Included], *Tokyo Shimbun* (December 2, 2020), https://www.tokyo-np.co.jp/article/71706.

93 *Supra* note 82.

94 The MHLW decided to apply national health insurance coverage to ART/MAR from April 1, 2022. MHLW, "Hunin tiryou ni kansuru shien nitsuite" [Support for Infertility Treatment], https://www.mhlw.go.jp/content/000901931.pdf. It will cover artificial insemination (excluding AID) and IVF (including ICSI and TESE) if pregnancy cannot be achieved by any other means and if the woman is under forty-three. There is a limit on how many times a patient can use public health insurance

coverage for ART/MAR. If the treatment is covered, a patient will pay only 30 percent of the costs. Nevertheless, some procedures have been omitted: AID, IVF using donor gametes, and surrogacy. To use some of the more advanced technology would require individual application for support. Moreover, public health insurance coverage will pay only the standard fee to doctors.

95 This is only one of the legal issues presented by ART/MAR. Jenna Casolo, Campbell Curry-Ledbetter, Megan Edmonds, Gabrielle Field, Kathleen O'Neill, and Marisa Poncia, eds., "Assisted Reproductive Technologies," 20 Ger. J. of Gender and L. 313 (2019).

96 Kosekihō [Family Registration Act], law no. 224 of 1947.

97 Ibid., art. 6. In addition to the family registry address, information to be recorded includes the name and birthdate of an individual, the date that person was added to the register and the reason why, the names of his or her legal father and mother and their relationship with the person, the names of any adoptive parents and their relationship with the person, distinct men of a husband and a wife in the case of a married couple, any previous register in which the person may have been listed, and other information stipulated in the MOJ regulation. Ibid., art. 13.

98 Ibid., art. 9, 14.

99 Minpō [Civil Code], 1896, art. 750. The SCOJ recently upheld this requirement for a married couple. Saikō saibansho [SCOJ], grand bench, December 16, 2015, 69:8 Minshu 2586.

100 A birth registration application (or notification of birth) must give the name of the child, its sex (male or female), whether it is legitimate or illegitimate, the date and place of birth, the names of the legal father and legal mother, their place of family registry, and other information stipulated by the MOJ regulation. Family Registration Act, *supra* note 96 at art. 49(2). Basically, the birth certificate issued by the physician or midwife must be added to the application. Ibid., art. 49(3).

101 Ibid., art. 49(1) and 52(1).

102 Ibid., art. 18(1).

103 Ibid., art. 52(2). If the mother is incapable of filing the application, a person with whom she lives can deliver it. Ibid., art. 52(3).

104 Ibid., art. 18(2).

105 Ibid., art. 17.

106 Civil Code, *supra* note 99 at art. 779. Filiation can be accomplished by filing an application or in a will. Ibid., art. 781; Family Registration Act, *supra* note 96 at art. 60 and art. 64. The child or his or her descendants can file a suit for filiation in court, but this must occur within three years after the death of the father. Ibid., art. 787.

107 For a brief overview of the rule on parentage in Japan, *see* Ishii, *supra* note 53 at 186–92.

108 Actually, the Civil Code presupposes that the mother can filiate her own illegitimate child. Civil Code, *supra* note 99 at art. 779. This suggests that when the Civil Code was written in 1896, the legislature assumed that establishing parentage for an

illegitimate child would start with filiation by the mother. Yet, this provision became meaningless because the very fact that she must file the birth registration application confirmed that she was the legal mother.
109 Saikō saibansho [SCOJ], 2nd petty bench, April 27, 1962, 16:7 Minshu 1247.
110 In situations where a baby is born at home and there are no medical professionals to provide confirmation, the mother must persuade the municipal government that it is hers.
111 If a baby is abandoned and the identity of the mother is not known, a police officer must notify the head of the municipal government, who will create a family register for a baby. Family Registration Act, *supra* note 96 at art. 22, 57. If the mother comes forward later, she must file a birth registration application and supply proof of childbirth to have the family register changed. Ibid., art. 59.
112 Civil Code, *supra* note 99 at art. 772(1). The bill to amend the Civil Code was introduced into the Diet in October, 2022, and would drastically change many provisions on parental relationship. Revised article 772 stipulates that "a child conceived by a wife during marriage, is presumed to be the child of her husband in that marriage. A child conceived by a wife before marriage and born after the formation of marriage is similarly treated." Article 772(1) (if amended).
113 Ibid., art. 772(2). For a legislative history of this provision, see Atsushi Hirata, "Minpō 772jou (chakushutsu no suitei) no keihu to kaishaku" [Pedigree and Interpretation of Civil Code Article 772], 18 Meiji daigaku houka daigakuin ronshu 1 (2016). If the new amendment were to be passed, the revised article 772(2) will stipulate that "for the purpose of the previous section, a child born within 200 days after the formation of marriage is presumed to be conceived before the marriage. A child born after 200 days from the formation of a marriage ... is presumed to be conceived during that marriage." Article 772(2) (if amended).
114 Civil Code, *supra* note 99 at art. 772(2). The new amendment would stipulate that "A child born ... within 300 days of the divorce or dissolution of a marriage is presumed to be conceived during the former marriage." Article 772(2) (if amended). Since the amendment will remove the waiting period for a woman who wishes to remarry after divorcing, a new section will be created to stipulate that "if a woman is in more than two marriage relationships between the conception of a child and the birth of the child, that child is presumed to be a child of the husband of her most recent marriage, at the time of the childbirth." Article 772(3) (if passed).
115 Ibid., art. 774. The newly amended article 774 will allow both the father and the child to challenge the legitimacy of the father. In addition, the mother is allowed to challenge it as well, except when the child does not stand to benefit from her doing so. Article 774 (if amended).
116 Ibid., art. 775. The newly amended article 775 will mandate that the denial of legitimacy needs to be filed as lawsuits in the courts against specified defendants. Article 775 (if amended).

117 Ibid., art. 777. The newly amended article 777 will stipulate that suits in which the father seeks to deny legitimacy need to be filed within three years of him becoming aware of the birth of the child. Similarly, the child and mother wishing to file a suit for the same purpose must do so within three years of the child's date of birth itself. Article 777 (if amended).
118 Ibid., art. 776. New amended article 776 will stipulate that the father or mother will lose the right to deny legitimacy when he or she has once acknowledged the legitimacy of the child.
119 It must be noted, however, that the SCOJ has developed the suit for confirmation of the absence of a parental relationship by case law. Saikō saibansho [SCOJ], 1st petty bench, May 29, 1969, 23:6 Minshu 1064.
120 Daishinin [Great Court of Judicature], January 23, 1940, 19:5 Minshu 54. Since the legal presumption is not applicable, the interested parties could easily deny paternity. Daishinin [Great Court of Judicature], September 20, 1940, 19:18 Minshu 1596. For a development of the doctrine of "children not covered by the presumption," see Hirata, *supra* note 113 at 17–19.
121 Civil Code, *supra* note 99 at art. 773. The newly amended article 773 will allow the court to decide who the father is when the woman has violated article 732 and married more than two husbands at the same time and when the father of the child cannot be decided in accordance with article 772. Ibid. (if amended).
122 Ibid., art. 733 (prior to the 2016 amendment).
123 Saikō saibansho [SCOJ], grand bench, December 16, 2015, 69:8 Minshu 2427.
124 Civil Code, *supra* note 99 at art. 733 (after the 2016 amendment). The new amendment to the Civil Code would remove article 733 altogether, allowing a woman to get remarried any time after divorcing. Doing so, however, presents a conflict for the presumption of paternity. When a child is born over 200 days after the date of marriage, then conception will be presumed to have occurred during the marriage (article 772(2)), and the woman's current husband will be presumed to be the father of the child (article 772(1), if amended). If this marriage is a woman's first, and a baby is conceived before she entered into it, her husband at the time of childbirth will be presumed to be the father of the child. If she remarries between the time of conception and childbirth, it would be her second husband, the husband at the time of childbirth, who is presumed to be the father (article 772(3), if amended). In all cases, the presumed father can deny the legitimacy of the child (article 774(1), if amended). The first husband, as such, can challenge the second husband's legitimacy as father (so long as it would not harm the best interests of the child) (article 774(3), if amended). In that case, the woman's first husband would be presumed to be the father (article 774(4)), and he could not deny his legitimacy as father any further (article 774(5), if amended).
125 Ibid., art. 792.
126 Ibid., art. 793.
127 Ibid., art. 796.

128 Ibid., art. 797.
129 Ibid., art. 798.
130 Ibid., art. 800; Family Registration Act, *supra* note 96 at art. 66.
131 Family Registration Act, *supra* note 96 at art. 13, item 5.
132 Ibid., art. 13, item 3 and item 7.
133 Civil Code, *supra* note 99 at art. 809.
134 Ibid., art. 810.
135 As a result, when the natural parents pass away, the child can inherit a portion of their estate.
136 In 2020, 101,311 adoptions were reported. E-Stat, https://www.e-stat.go.jp/dbview?sid=0003322640.
137 Taimie L. Bryant, "Sons and Lovers: Adoption in Japan," 38:2 Am. J. Comp. L. 299 (1990); Lianna Brinded, "98% of All Japanese Adoptions Are Employers Adopting the Adult Men on Their Staff, Not Children," *Independent* (January 12, 2017), https://www.independent.co.uk/life-style/japanese-adoption-rates-majority-adult-men-a7524301.html.
138 MOJ, "Kon-in no kaisho matawa torikeshigo 300nichi inaini umareta ko no shussei no todoke no toriatsukai nitsuite" [Treatment of the Birth Registration Application for a Child Born within 300 Days after a Divorce or Cancellation of Marriage], http://www.moj.go.jp/MINJI/minji137.html.
139 See *supra* note 120. For a development of this doctrine of "children excluded from presumption," see Hirata, *supra* note 113 at 22–26.
140 Saikō saibansho [SCOJ], 1st petty bench, May 29, 1969, *supra* note 120. See also Saikō saibansho [SCOJ], 2nd petty bench, August 31, 1998, 189 Shumin 497.
141 Saikō saibansho [SCOJ], 2nd petty bench, August 31, 1998, 189 Shumin 437 (no clear objective evidence indicating the total absence of marital relationship); Saikō saibansho [SCOJ], 1st petty bench, July 17, 2014, 247 Shumin 79 (the same).
142 Civil Code, *supra* note 96 at art. 1(3) ("no abuse of rights is permitted").
143 Saikō saibansho [SCOJ], 2nd petty bench, October 3, 1952, 6:9 Minshu 753.
144 Saikō saibansho [SCOJ], 2nd petty bench, July 7, 2006, 220 Shumin 673.
145 Saikō saibansho [SCOJ], 2nd petty bench, July 7, 2006, 60:6 Minshu 2307. *See also* Ishii, *supra* note 53 at 190–91.
146 Toshikazu Inaguma, "Seishoku hojo iryo eno houteki kisei wo meguru shomondai" [Issues on the Legal Regulation on Medically Assisted Reproduction], 263 Rippou to Chousa 128 (2007). But recently, the Diet has at least clarified some issues. See *infra* notes 201 and 202.
147 "Mago dairi shussan mata jisshi, Nezu ishi, kokunai 4reime"[The Granddaughter Was a Child Born through Surrogate: Dr. Nezu Performed Fourth Surrogacy in Japan], Shikoku News (Feb. 29, 2008), http://www.shikoku-np.co.jp/national/medical_health/20080229000408. According to the Suwa Maternity Clinic where Dr. Nezu works, before 2014 the clinic attempted 21 surrogacies that resulted in 14 childbirths and 16 children, but since then it has stopped offering surrogacy services. Suwa Maternity Clinic, http://temporary.e-smc.jp/info/.

148 Saikō saibansho [SCOJ], 2nd petty bench, March 23, 2007, 61:2 Minshu 619. *See* Ishii, *supra* note 53 at 196.
149 See *supra* notes 126–36.
150 See *supra* note 131.
151 Civil Code, *supra* note 99 at art. 817–2. This procedure could be allowed under certain circumstances, such as when the biological parents would have extreme difficulty in raising the child. In all instances, it must be authorized by a family court. Ibid., art. 817–7 and art. 817–2.
152 Family Registration Act, *supra* note 96 at art. 20–3. Although the municipal office is aware of the special adoption, it is not recorded in the register, where the baby is simply listed in the normal way.
153 Civil Code, *supra* note 99 at art. 817–9.
154 Therefore, Mukai and her husband were forced to adopt their twins as special adopted children. This is a unique precedent, however, because Mukai was a celebrity who made it public that she had retained a surrogate. As a result, it was common knowledge that she had not given birth to the twins. However, if a woman is not a famous celebrity and does not reveal the facts, the municipal government will have no way of knowing that she asked for a surrogate while she was overseas. The birth certificate issued by the foreign country is usually sufficient to register the child. Given this, women who use surrogacy abroad could easily register their children without disclosing the truth of the matter.
155 See *supra* note 110.
156 As mentioned, the JSOG initially limited ART/MAR to legally married couples, who were also required to supply an official copy of their family registry. Although the JSOG has abandoned this requirement, it still limits ART/MAR to married couples, who must at least be in a common law marriage. See JSOG, *supra* note 65.
157 Tokyo kōtō saibansho [Tokyo HC], September 16, 1998, 51:3 Kateisaibansho geppo [Kagetsu] 165.
158 Ibid.
159 Chapter 2, note 69.
160 Saikō saibansho [SCOJ], 3rd petty bench, December 10, 2013, 67:9 Minshu 1847.
161 Saikō saibansho [SCOJ], 2nd petty bench, September 4, 2006, 60:7 Minshu 2563. See Ishii, *supra* note 53 at 194.
162 Saiko saibansho [SCOJ], 2nd petty bench, June 5, 2019, unreported: "Juseiran no mudan shiyou: Saikosai mo husikankei wo nintei [Using the Frozen Embryo without Consent: SCOJ Sustained the Paternal Relationship]," *Sankei Shimbun*, June 7, 2019, https://www.sankei.com/article/20190607-Q7MLNFVKDBIV7J3TQ5LYBSYPRM/.
163 But the SCOJ have not clarified its position on this issue. See also Osaka katei saibansho [Osaka FC], November 28, 2019, unreported (2019WLJPCA11286021).
164 "Seibetsu henko, oyakokankei mitomezu, touketsuseishi de shussan – tokyo kasai" [Tokyo Family Court Denied Parental Relationship between the Child Using Frozen Sperm of Transgender Woman], *Jiji tsushin* (February 28, 2022), https://www.jiji.com/jc/article?k=2022022801066&g=soc.

165 See also Ishii, *supra* note 53 at 175.
166 *Michael H. v Gerald D.*, 491 U.S. 110 (1989).
167 Jana Singer, "Marriage, Biology, and Paternity: The Case for Revitalizing the Marital Presumption," 65 Md. L. Rev. 246 at 246–47 (2006).
168 Ibid., at 248.
169 Ibid.
170 Ibid., at 247.
171 *California Family Code (CFC)*, s 7610(a). See also s 7650 (action for declaration of the existence or non-existence of the parental relationship between the child and the mother).
172 *Johnson v Calvert*, 851 P. 2d 776 (Cal. 1993). See also *CFC*, s 7962; "The Aftermath of *Johnson v Calvert*: Surrogacy Law Reflects a More Liberal View of Reproductive Technology," 6 St. Thomas L. Rev. 191 (1993–94).
173 *CFC, supra* note 171 at s 7611(a) (a "person is presumed to be the natural parent of a child if the presumed parent and the child's natural mother are or have been married to each other and the child is born during the marriage, or within 300 days after the marriage is terminated by death, annulment, declaration of invalidity, or divorce, or after a judgment of separation is entered by a court").
174 Ibid., s 7611(d).
175 Ibid., s 7540 ("except as provided in Section 7541, the child of a wife cohabiting with her husband, who is not impotent or sterile, is conclusively presumed to be a child of the marriage").
176 Ibid., s 7630(a)(2).
177 Ibid. See also s 7541.
178 Ibid., s 7571.
179 Ibid., s 7573; California Courts, "Establishing Parentage (Paternity)," http://www.courts.ca.gov/1201.htm.
180 *CFC, supra* note 171 at s 7630(a)(1) (mother's action for declaration of the parental relationship between the child and the father), s 7634 (the child support agency's action); *Uniform Parentage Act*; California Courts, "Disputing Parentage," http://www.courts.ca.gov/1202.htm.
181 *CFC, supra* note 171 at s 7541.
182 Ibid., s 7575.
183 Ibid., s 7576 and s 7578(d).
184 Ibid., s 7636.
185 Ibid., s 7613(a) and (b).
186 Ibid., s 7601(c).
187 Ibid., s 7612(c).
188 For example, the California Family Code speaks generally of mother and "parent" (s 7611) and "parentage" (s 7550 and s 7570), although it still refers to "father" (s 7500) or to "husband" (s 7540 and s 7541).
189 United Nations, *Convention on the Rights of the Child*, http://www.ohchr.org/EN/ProfessionalInterest/Pages/CRC.aspx.

190 Ibid., art. 3(1) ("in all actions concerning children, whether undertaken by public or private social welfare institutions, courts of law, administrative authorities or legislative bodies, the best interests of the child shall be a primary consideration").
191 Saikō saibansho [SCOJ], grand bench, December 16, 2015, *supra* note 124.
192 See *supra* notes 110 and 156.
193 Teiko Kiyosue, "Dairi shussan niokeru boshi kankei" [Legal Mother of a Child Born through Surrogacy], 18 Hokudai housei journal 1 at 8 (2012).
194 In Japan, women have sometimes asked their mothers to be surrogates for them. In such cases, the surrogate will be the legal mother (and grandmother) of the baby, and its biological mother will also be its sibling. If she wishes to become its legal parent, she must adopt it. This is a bit strange.
195 Kiyosue, *supra* note 194 at 20 (proposing to allow the intended mother to filiate the baby and become its natural mother). On the other hand, once the baby is born, the surrogate might decide to keep it, especially if her own egg was used in its conception. Then, some kind of system needs to be introduced to grant an intended mother the legal status of birth mother in addition to that of legal mother, if doing so serves the best interests of the child.
196 The current rule sometimes precludes judicial challenges as an abuse of rights while leaving the underlying legal status of father and child uncorrected. Such a situation puts the child in an unstable position. It is doubtful that this would respect the wishes of parents or conform to the best interests of the child.
197 If a man who has no intention of becoming a father has a sexual relationship with a woman who becomes pregnant as a result, he is the legal father. This would hold true even if he erroneously believed or was tricked into believing that she could not conceive, because conception was not absolutely impossible. If she decides not to have an abortion, he should not be allowed to object (because the choice is up to her). Nor, as the legal father, should he be permitted to refuse her the abortion if she decides to have one (because it would not be in the best interests of the child to deny her this natural right).
198 In one Japanese case, the court upheld the paternity relationship between the husband and the child, who was born using his frozen embryo without his explicit consent during the couple's somewhat incomplete separation. Nonetheless, the court granted a damage award order against his wife, who had failed to ask for his consent. Osaka chihō saibansho [Osaka DC], March 12, 2020, unreported; "Juseiran de mudanshussan wa jikoketteiken shingai: Moto tsuma ni baisho meirei" [Giving Birth to a Child Using an Embryo without Consent Was an Infringement of the Right of Autonomy: Ordering the Ex-Wife to Pay Damages], *Asahi Shimbun* (March 13, 2020), https://www.asahi.com/articles/ASN3D6TKWN3DPTIL027.html.
199 In 2005, the SCOJ dealt with a case involving the denial of the franchise to Japanese citizens who lived abroad, finding that the failure of the legislature to grant the voting rights was unconstitutional and ordering the government to pay damages for deprivation of their rights. Saikō saibansho [SCOJ], grand bench, September 14, 2005, 59:7 Minshu 2087. In light of this decision, the courts could confirm the

failure of the legislature to update its law of parentage to respond to the development of ART/MAR and even order it to pay damages because it had failed to adopt necessary measures despite the unconstitutionality.
200 Medically Assisted Reproduction Act, *supra* note 83 at art. 9.
201 Ibid., art. 10.
202 As in the case of the child born to the lesbian couple, one of whom was transgender, the legislature needs to allow same-sex marriage (discussed further in Chapter 6). If this were to occur, the transgender partner could receive the presumption of fatherhood despite being legally female.

Chapter 5: Abortion
1 Keihō [Criminal Code], 1907 at art. 212.
2 Botai hogohō [Mother's Body Protection Act], law no. 156 of 1948.
3 Masato Taniwaki, "Dataizai nitsuiteno jakkan no kousatsu" [Several Comments on the Crime of Abortion], 20:2 Toin hougaku 1 (2014).
4 Tiana Norgren, *Abortion before Birth Control: The Politics of Reproduction in Postwar Japan* (Princeton, NJ/Oxford: Princeton University Press, 2001); Lynn D. Wardle, "Crying Stones: A Comparison of Abortion in Japan and the United States," 14 N.Y.L. Sch. J. Int'l & Comp. L. 183 at 187–89 (1993); Hiromi Maruyama, "Abortion in Japan: A Feminist Critique," 10 Wis. Women's L.J. 131 at 132–34 (1995); Kenzo Matsuzaki, "Datai (chuzetsu)/mabiki nimiru seimeikan to rinrikan" [View of Life and Ethics in Abortion (Termination of Pregnancy) and Infanticide], 21 Nihon jomon bunka kiyo 119 (2000), http://id.nii.ac.jp/1109/00000457/; Marco Gottardo, "Pregnancy and Infanticide in Early-Modern Japan: The Role of the Midwife as a Medium," 54 Tamagawa daigaku bungakubu kiyo 213 (2013); Yoshie Toyoshima, "The Lives of Children and the Conditions of Abortion and Infanticide in the Late Edo Period," 10 Bulletin of Ryotokuji University 77 at 78–81 (2016). During the early Edo Period, female abortion doctors performed abortions, but the method was not sophisticated and used mostly natural herbal medicines. Many poor women took a natural poison, applied pressure to the abdomen, or soaked in cold water in hopes of provoking a miscarriage. Many families killed babies immediately after birth by suffocating them. Norgren and Christiana, *supra* note 4 at 78–80.
5 During the Edo Period, farmers paid their taxes in the form of rice. Therefore, maintaining their numbers was integral to supporting all government spending.
6 Norgren, *supra* note 4 at 81; Wardle, *supra* note 4 at 189–92.
7 Wardle, *supra* note 4 at 192.
8 Keihō [Old Criminal Code], dajokan hukoku no. 36 of 1880, art. 330–335, https://ja.wikisource.org/wiki/刑法_(明治13年太政官布告第36号).
9 Keihō [Criminal Code], 1907, *supra* note 1.
10 Wardle, *supra* note 4 at 193. There was heated debate among women as to the abortion ban, even during the Meiji era. Yumiko Ehara, "Josei mondai to jinkō mondai" [Women's Issue and Population Issue], 28:3 Shakaihosho kenkyu 261 at 262 (1992).

11 Kokumin yuseihō [National Eugenics Act], law no. 107 of 1940, National Archives of Japan Digital Archive, https://www.digital.archives.go.jp/DAS/meta/MetSearch. cgi?DEF_XSL=default&IS_KIND=summary_normal&IS_SCH=META&IS_ STYLE=default&IS_TYPE=meta&DB_ID=G9100001EXTERNAL&GRP_ ID=G9100001&IS_SORT_FLD=&IS_SORT_KND=&IS_START=1&IS_TAG_ S1=fpid&IS_CND_S1=ALL&IS_KEY_S1=F00000000000000037670&IS_ NUMBER=100&ON_LYD=on&IS_EXTSCH=F9999999999999900000%2BF2009 121017005000405%2BF200502182055460067 0%2BF20050218205549 00671%2BF 2005021905352400960%2BF2005021909315601055%2BF2005021909323501057% 2BF00000000000000037670&IS_DATA_TYPE=&IS_LYD_DIV=&LIST_ TYPE=default&IS_ORG_ID=F00000000000000037670&CAT_XML_FLG=on.
12 Ibid., art. 1.
13 Ibid., art. 2 art. 13.
14 Ibid., art. 16.
15 "Sengo, Hakatakou hikiageshara no taiken" [After the War: Experiences of Withdrawers], *Yomiuri Shimbun* (January 21, 2007), https://hogetest.exblog.jp/4979697/.
16 Kiyoko Yamamoto, "Sengo nihon niokeru jinkoseisaku to kazokuhendou nikansuru rekishi shakaigakuteki kousatsu" [Historical and Sociological Comments on Population Policy and Family Changes in Post-War Japan], 39 Sonoda gakuen joshi daigaku ronbunshu 85 at 88 (2005), https://id.ndl.go.jp/bib/7239337.
17 Eugenic Protection Act.
18 Maruyama, *supra* note 4 at 135; Wardle, *supra* note 4 at 194.
19 Eugenic Protection Act, *supra* note 2 at art. 1.
20 Ibid., art. 2(2).
21 Ibid., art. 14(1). When the act was passed in 1948, it authorized designated doctors to apply for review by the local genetic protection commission when they believed that ATP was necessary. Women who qualified fell into four categories:

1 the patient is suffering from a disease listed in appendix 1 or appendix 2,
2 the patient became pregnant within one year of giving birth and there is a risk that her health will be seriously endangered,
3 the patient already has several children and there is a risk that her health will be seriously endangered,
4 the patient became pregnant because she was raped with assault or intimidation, or when she could not resist or refuse.

Ibid., art. 13, para 1 (revised), http://www.shugiin.go.jp/internet/itdb_housei.nsf/ html/houritsu/00219480713156.htm. The second medical opinion was necessary for the first three grounds, and the opinion of the local human rights commissioner was necessary for the fourth. Ibid., art. 13, para 2 (revised). Once these were in place, the local genetic protection commission decided whether ATP were appropriate, art. 14, and the doctor was allowed to perform it based on this decision. Ibid., art. 15.

Therefore, designated doctors were not at liberty to perform ATP without consultation. The review system was abolished in 1952. Yusei hogohō no ichibuwo kaiseisuru hōritsu [Act to Amend Parts of the Eugenic Protection Act], law no. 141 of 1952. Thereafter, the decision as to whether ATP criteria were satisfied was made solely by the designated doctor.

22 The leprosy patient was placed in mandatory isolation under another statute. Rai yobohō [Leprosy Prevention Act], law no. 214 of 1953 (repealed in 1996).
23 Yusei hogohō no ichibu wo kaiseisuru hōritsu [Act to Amend Parts of the Eugenic Protection Act], law no. 216 of 1949.
24 Forcible sexual intercourse with assault or intimidation constituted a criminal rape, and sexual intercourse with a victim who was unconscious or unable to resist was a quasi-rape. See Criminal Code, *supra* note 9 at art. 177 (before the 2017 amendment). Victims of these crimes could ask for ATP if they had conceived as a result. Now, forcible sexual intercourse et al. and quasi-forcible sexual intercourse et al. are prohibited. See texts accompanying Chapter 3, notes 131 and 133.
25 Masahiro Morioka, "Yusei hogohō kaisei wo meguru seimei rinri" [Ethic of Life in the Discussion of the Amendment to the Eugenic Protection Act], 16 Nihon kenkyu 221 (1997). The dominant political party in Japan, the LDP has been in office almost constantly since it was founded in 1955. Its basic political stance is liberalism and anti-socialism, but some of its members are extremely conservative.
26 For information about Seicho-no-ie, see its homepage at http://www.seicho-no-ie.org/eng/.
27 Morioka, *supra* note 25.
28 Ibid.; Ehara, *supra* note 10 at 265; Maruyama, *supra* note 4 at 140.
29 Ehara, *supra* note 10 at 265; Maruyama, *supra* note 4 at 141–42.
30 Morioka, *supra* note 25.
31 Mother's Body Protection Act. The title is sometimes translated as Maternal Protection Act, Maternal Health Protection Act, or Motherhood Protection Act.
32 Morioka, *supra* note 25 at 215. The Leprosy Prevention Act was abolished by the enactment of the Hansen byō mondai no kaiketsu no sokushin nikansuru hōritsu [Act on Facilitation of the Solution to Leprosy Problems], law no. 28 of 1996, addendum art. 2.
33 Criminal Code, *supra* note 1 at art. 212.
34 Daishinin [Great Court of Judicature], October 19, 1909 (Meiji 42), 15 Keiroku 1420; Daishinin [Great Court of Judicature], December 8, 1911 (Meiji 44), 17 Keiroku 2183.
35 Criminal Code, *supra* note 1 at art. 213.
36 Ibid., art. 214.
37 Ibid., art. 215(1).
38 Ibid., art. 215(2).

39 Ibid., art. 216. The crime of injury carries imprisonment with labour for no more than fifteen years. Ibid., art. 204.
40 Taniwaki, *supra* note 33 at 1–2.
41 Ibid., at 3–4. Since the fetus does not have the sufficient capacity to give consent, it could never give consent anyway.
42 Ibid., at 6.
43 Ibid., at 7.
44 Ibid., at 8. It is assumed that anyone should be held liable only for abortion and not for causing the death of the fetus as a result of the abortion.
45 Mother's Body Protection Act, *supra* note 2 at art. 2(2).
46 Ibid., art. 14(1).
47 Ibid., art. 14(2).
48 Ibid., art. 25.
49 Criminal Code, *supra* note 1 at art. 35.
50 Therefore, they are also excused from liability for the death of the fetus. Taniwaki, *supra* note 3 at 12. But if ATP delivers a live baby, it is then seen as a person, and the doctor has a legal responsibility to save its life unless it is incapable of surviving. Ibid., at 11–12.
51 Ibid., at 10–11.
52 Criminal Code, *supra* note 9 at art. 37. Moreover, when a fetus dies during pregnancy, any doctor can extract it at any time.
53 Ministry of Health, Labour and Welfare (MHLW), "Yusei hogohō niyori jinkō ninshin chuuzetsu wo jisshi suru jiki no kijun nitsuite" [On the Period for Performing ATP under the Eugenic Protection Act], March 2, 1990, MHLW notification no. 55 on health and medical affairs, notification of vice health secretary general, https://www.mhlw.go.jp/web/t_doc?dataId=00ta9691&dataType=1&pageNo=1.
54 MHLW, "Yusei hogohō niyori jinkō ninshin chuuzetsu wo jisshi suru jiki no kijun no henkō nitsuite" [On the Change of the Period for Performing ATP under the Eugenic Protection Act], March 20, 1990, Health, Medical Affairs Bureau, Psychological Health Division Head notification no. 12, https://www.mhlw.go.jp/web/t_doc?dataId=00ta9692&dataType=1&pageNo=1.
55 Maruyama, *supra* note 4 at 139. But since the calculation depends on the woman's recollection of when she last menstruated, the cut-off line is not rigid. Ibid., at 140.
56 Japan Association of Obstetricians and Gynecologists (JAOG), jinko ninshin chuzetsu nituite osietekudasai [Could you Tell me about the ATP?], http://www.jaog.or.jp/qa/confinement/ninsinshusanqa6/.
57 "All About, Jinkō ninshin chuzetsu shujutsu no hiyō kingaku no meyasu/hoken wa tsukaeru?" [Estimated Cost of Artificial Termination of Pregnancy/Could It Be Covered by Health Insurance?], https://allabout.co.jp/gm/gc/465142/.
58 Early ATP will cost about JPY 100,000 to 250,000 (roughly US$750 to $1,800). Ibid.
59 Ibid.

60 It can cost roughly JPY 300,000 to 600,000 (about US$2,300 to $4,700). Ibid. See Kumi Tsukahara, "Ninshin chuzetsu gijutsu no doukou to nihon no genjō" [Development of Abortion Technology and the Current Situation in Japan], 70 Monthly Journal of Sex Education 1 (2017), https://www.jase.faje.or.jp/jigyo/journal/seikyoiku_journal_201701.pdf. The dead fetus must be reported to the local municipality via a death notification and must be buried or cremated as a dead person as required.

61 National Police Agency (NPA), "Heisei27nen no hanzai" [Crime Report, 2015], https://www.npa.go.jp/toukei/soubunkan/h27/pdf/H27_02.pdf.

62 Saikō saibansho [SCOJ], 3rd petty bench, January 19, 1988, 42:1 Keishu 1. In this case, the court upheld the conviction of a doctor for professional abortion. At the urging of the mother, he had performed the procedure when she was in her twenty-sixth week. Recently, a physician was arrested for aborting a fetus without the consent of the mother, causing injury. "Hudouidatai utagaide ishi taiho" [A Doctor was Arrested for Performing Abortion without Getting Consent], Reuters (August 9, 2020), https://www.reuters.com/article/idJP2020080901002709. Evidently, the baby was his, even though he was engaged to another woman. He was afraid that its birth would ruin his future, so he decided to do the abortion without getting the mother's consent. A similar case occurred in 2010 at the Jikei University School of Medicine's Hospital. A physician who worked there injected an abortifacient into a woman who was carrying his baby because he feared that its birth could ruin his marriage. Tokyo chihō saibansho [Tokyo DC], August 9, 2010, unreported; "Hudoui dataide ishi ni yuzaihanketsu" [Physician Was Convicted for Performing an Abortion without Getting Consent], *Nihonkeizai Shimbun* (August 9, 2010), https://www.nikkei.com/article/DGXNASDG0901I_Z00C10A8000000 (sentencing him to imprisonment for three years following the outcome of an initial five-year suspension period in which, if the defendant manages to maintain good behaviour for the duration of this time, the three-year prison sentence will cancelled altogether).

63 GEB, "Danjo byoudou sankaku hakusho Heisei28nen ban" [Gender Equality Whitepaper, 2016], http://www.gender.go.jp/about_danjo/whitepaper/h28/zentai/html/zuhyo/zuhyo01-04-03.html.

64 Ibid.

65 MHLW, "Heisei 28nendo eisei gyousei houkokusho no gaiyou" [Summary of the Report on Health Administration, 2016], https://www.mhlw.go.jp/toukei/saikin/hw/eisei_houkoku/16/dl/gaikyo.pdf; GEB, "Danjo byoudou sankaku hakusho reiwa 2nen ban" [Gender Equality Whitepaper, 2020], https://www.gender.go.jp/about_danjo/whitepaper/r02/zentai/html/zuhyo/zuhyo01-05-05.html (Gender Equality Whitepaper, 2020).

66 Gender Equality Whitepaper, 2020, *supra* note 65.

67 E-Stat, "Botaihogo toukei" [Mother's Body Protection Act Statistics], age group statistics, 2001, https://www.e-stat.go.jp/stat-search/files?page=1&layout=datalist&toukei=00450029&tstat=000001024040&cycle=7&year=20010&month=0&tclass1=000001030988.

68 Ibid.
69 Maruyama, *supra* note 4 at 144. It is often claimed that the actual number of abortions is two or three times larger than the reported number. Wardle, *supra* note 4 at 220–21, points out, however, that the rate of underreporting might not be this low.
70 E-Stat, "Botaihogo toukei houkoku" [Mother's Body Protection Act Statistics], ATP procedure period statistics, 1991, https://www.e-stat.go.jp/stat-search/files?page=1&layout=datalist&toukei=00450029&tstat=000001024040&cycle=7&year=20010&month=0&tclass1=000001030988.
71 Ibid.
72 The suspicion has been raised that some clinics offer ATP for much more advanced pregnancies. In such cases, the doctor may claim that the fetus had already died and that because the extraction was not ATP, the Mother's Body Protection Act had not been violated. According to MHLW statistics for 2019, there were 8,997 natural in utero deaths. MHLW, "Reiwa 2nen (2020) Jinkō doutai toukei" [2020 Population Shift], 6, https://www.mhlw.go.jp/toukei/saikin/hw/jinkou/kakutei19/dl/04_h2-1.pdf.
73 E-Stat, "Eiseigyousei houkokurei" [Health Administration Report], 2018, https://www.e-stat.go.jp/stat-search/files?page=1&layout=datalist&toukei=00450027&tstat=000001031469&cycle=8&tclass1=000001132823&tclass2=000001132824&tclass3=000001134083&stat_infid=000031873760&tclass4val=0 (among 161,741 ATP in 2018, only 224 involved pregnancy as the result of sexual assault).
74 National Institute of Population and Social Security Research, "Dai15kai shussei doukō kihon chousa" [Fifteenth Survey on the Basic Tendency of Childbirth], 2016, 37, 40.
75 JAOG, "10dai no jinkō ninshin chuuzetsu nitsuite no enquête kekka kara" [Results of the Questionnaire on ATP by Teenagers], February 17, 2003. http://www.jaog.or.jp/sep2012/JAPANESE/MEMBERS/TANPA/H15/030217.htm.
76 Mitsuo Sakaihara, "Nihon niokeru wrongful birth sosho to shougaitaiji no ninshin chuzetsu" [Wrongful Birth Action in Japan and the Abortion of a Disabled Fetus], 12:1 Seimei rinri 183, 186 (2002).
77 Taniwaki, *supra* note 33 at 9.
78 Falsifying consent or forging the consent form could constitute the forgery of a private document. Criminal Code, *supra* note 9 at art. 159. But it is highly unlikely that anyone would be arrested or prosecuted for falsifying the ATP consent form. Theoretically, a doctor who performed ATP without the consent of the husband could be charged for violating the Mother's Body Protection Act. But this too is highly unlikely. Doctors who insist on acquiring consent from the husband are more concerned about the litigation risk from a husband who did not consent. "Chuzetsu haigusha no doui youken, sanhujinkai 7 wari teppaisugeki" [Requirement for Husband's Consent for ATP: 70 Percent of Gynecologists Argue for a Repeal], *Yomiuri Shimbun* (February 20, 2022), https://www.yomiuri.co.jp/medical/20220219-OYT1T50381/.

79 Kyouko Tanebe, "Botai hogohō ni okeru haiguusha no doui to reproductive health/right" [Requirement for Consent of the Husband under the Maternal Health Protection Act and Reproductive Health/Right], 2013 http://www.toyama.med.or.jp/wp/wp-content/uploads/2013/03/26.2.15_ishindenshin.pdf. Some hospitals and clinics apparently required consent from the biological father even when the pregnancy was the result of rape. The MHLW clarified that the intent of the Mother's Body Protection Act was not to require consent from the assailant and revised its instructions. MHLW, "Botai hogohō no sekou nitsuite no ichibu kaisei nituite (tsuchi)" [Revision to the Instruction on the Enforcement of the Mother's Body Protection Act], October 2020, https://www.mhlw.go.jp/hourei/doc/tsuchi/T201022N0010.pdf.
80 United Nations Committee on the Elimination of Discrimination against Women, "Concluding Observations on the Combined Seventh and Eighth Periodic Reports of Japan," March 7, 2016, https://tbinternet.ohchr.org/Treaties/CEDAW/Shared%20Documents/JPN/CEDAW_C_JPN_CO_7-8_21666_E.pdf.
81 See *supra* note 65.
82 GEB, "Danjo Byoudo Sankaku Hakusho Heisei 30nendo ban" [Gender Equality Whitepaper, 2018], http://www.gender.go.jp/about_danjo/whitepaper/h30/zentai/html/zuhyo/zuhyo01-00-37.html.
83 N. Hashimoto et al., "Sexuality Education in Junior High Schools in Japan," 12:1 Sex Education 1 (2011), https://www.researchgate.net/publication/254339294_Sexuality_education_in_junior_high_schools_in_Japan.
84 Rika Nakagoshi et al., "A Report on Sexual Knowledge and Learning among Senior High School Students," 7:1 Ehime kenritsu iryou gijutu daigaku kiyo37 (2010), http://www.epu.ac.jp/library/kiyou/file/1021.pdf. At the third grade level, 83.3 percent knew this fact.
85 Ministry of Education, Culture, Sports, Science and Technology (MEXT), "Ninshin shita seitoeno taioutō nitsuite" [Treatment of Students Who Become Pregnant], http://www.gender.go.jp/kaigi/senmon/jyuuten_houshin/sidai/pdf/jyu13-04-1.pdf. Forty percent of these students left the school voluntarily or withdrew due to its advice. The MEXT instructed all schools not to force such students to withdraw and instead to provide reasonable care for them. Ibid.
86 Yuko Konno and Miharu Mishiwaki, "Relationship of Knowledge about Sex and Sexual Morality to Sexual Activity in University Students," 9 Yamagata Journal of Health Science 33 at 38 (2006), http://www.yachts.ac.jp/off/library/kiyou/ronbun/0904.pdf.
87 Japanese Organization for International Cooperation in Family Planning (JOICFP), "Nihon no hinin houhou kara kangaeru" [Reconsidering the Contraception Method in Japan], June 5, 2017. https://www.joicfp.or.jp/jpn/2017/06/05/37254/. The third most popular was the calendar method. Ibid.
88 CDC, "Contraception," https://www.cdc.gov/reproductivehealth/contraception/index.htm.
89 Evy F. McElmeel, "Legalization of the Birth Control Pill in Japan Will Reduce Reliance on Abortion as the Primary Method of Birth Control," 8 Pac. Rim. L. & Pol'y 681 (1999).

90 Ibid., at 688.
91 Ibid., at 689–90.
92 Ibid., at 688, 691. McElmeel also speculates that the declining birthrate, the possible environmental impact of estrogen, and the loss of income for doctors who performed ATP might be counted as additional reasons for the reluctance but questions their persuasiveness. Ibid., at 693–97.
93 JAOG, "Keikō hininyaku (OC) no shohō no tejun" [Procedure for Prescribing Contraception Pills], http://www.jaog.or.jp/sep2012/JAPANESE/jigyo/JYOSEI/PILL/doctor/section_2.htm.
94 Prescription medication is covered by national health insurance, which could cover the pill if prescribed for treatment of menstrual pain or endometriosis but does not extend to prescription for contraception. The pill costs roughly JPY 2,000 to 4,000 (about US$23 to $35) a month. Medley, "Contraception," May 11, 2020. https://medley.life/diseases/topics/57b6586f3ee3ba32008b4569/details/pill/cost/.
95 JOICFP, *supra* note 87.
96 Nihon kazoku keikaku kyoukai [Japan Family Planning Association], "Kinkyu hinin Q&A" [Emergency Contraception Q&A], November 2020. http://www.jfpa.or.jp/women/emergency.html. Any doctor can prescribe the morning-after pill, but not all do, so patients are advised to check in advance. Moreover, since most hospitals and clinics are closed on weekends, a woman who needs a morning-after pill on Saturday or Sunday could have difficulty in acquiring it. In the United States, some types of morning-after pill, such as levonorgestrel, which must be taken within seventy-two hours after sex, are available over the counter. Others, such as ulipristal acetate (brand name Ella), require a prescription from a doctor or nurse. Planned Parenthood, "Which Kind of Emergency Contraception Should I Use?" 2022, https://www.plannedparenthood.org/learn/morning-after-pill-emergency-contraception/which-kind-emergency-contraception-should-i-use.
97 Mamari, "After pill no nedan wa" [How Much Will It Cost to Get After Pills?], October 18, 2017. https://mamari.jp/13046. The average price is JPY 100,000 to 200,000 (roughly US$75 to $150). Ibid.
98 Although ulipristal acetate, or Ella, was approved by the Federal Food and Drug Administration in the United States, Japan has not yet followed suit, https://www.usa.gov/federal-agencies/food-and-drug-administration. MHLW, "Beikokude shouninzumide, Nihonde mishounin no iyakuhin nitsuite" [Drugs Approved in the US but Not in Japan], https://www.mhlw.go.jp/topics/2013/07/tp0730-3.html.
99 The MHLW had accepted the practice of issuing online prescriptions and produced a guideline. One doctor launched an online prescription service for the morning-after pill, including ulipristal acetate, sending the products by courier since they must be delivered in time. The MHLW warned him that providing online prescriptions was inappropriate because such practice was not accepted by the guidelines on online prescriptions at that time. Yuriko Izumiya, "After pill (kinkyu hininyaku) no online shohō wo ishi ga kaishi: Kouroushō wa hutekisetsu to keikoku suruga" [One Doctor Started Online Prescription of After Pill (Emergency

Contraception) Despite a Warning from the MHLW as Inappropriate], *HuffPost* (September 14, 2018), https://www.huffingtonpost.jp/2018/09/13/after_a_23516027/. With the COVID-19 pandemic, the MHLW eventually decided to liberalize the practice, including the online dispensation of morning-after pills. MHLW, "Kinkyu hinin nikakawaru online shinryo nitsuite" [Online Prescription of the Emergency Pill], https://www.mhlw.go.jp/stf/seisakunitsuite/bunya/0000186912_00002.html.
100 Some individuals imported it from overseas, but the MHLW clamped down on this practice. MHLW, "Kojin yunyuu sareru keikō ninshin chuuzetsuyaku (iwayuru keikō chuuzetsuyaku) nitsuite" [Personal Import of Abortion Pills], press release, October 25, 2004, https://www.mhlw.go.jp/houdou/2004/10/h1025-5.html.
101 Maruyama, *supra* note 4 at 155.
102 McElmeel, *supra* note 89 at 681; Maruyama, *supra* note 4 at 131.
103 Kyokai kenpo, "Shussan nikansuru kyuuhu" [Childbirth Benefit], https://www.kyoukaikenpo.or.jp/g3/cat320/sb3170/sbb31712/1948-273.
104 WHO, "Global Abortion Policies Database," https://abortion-policies.srhr.org/?mapq=q1i; Center for Reproductive Rights, "The World's Abortion Laws," https://reproductiverights.org/worldabortionlaws?category[294]=294&category[325]=325&category[297]=297.
105 Katie O'Malley, "Abortion Law: Which Countries Have the Strictest Laws and What Are the Punishments?" *Independent* (May 30, 2019), https://www.independent.co.uk/life-style/women/abortion-ban-alabama-bill-countries-strictest-laws-punishments-prison-a8916496.html. It must be noted, however, that the difficulty of accessing abortion cannot be determined merely by taking a look at the relevant statutes. Indeed, the danger to the health of the mother as one reason for seeking a lawful abortion can be both broadly and narrowly construed, thus making the distinction a bit ambiguous.
106 *The Family Planning, Human Embryo Protection and Conditions of Permissibility of Abortion Act of 7 January 1993*, https://www.reproductiverights.org/sites/crr.civicactions.net/files/documents/Polish%20abortion%20act–English%20translation.pdf.
107 Ibid., art. 1.
108 Ibid., art. 4a.
109 "Poland Rules Abortion Due to Foetal Defects Unconstitutional," *Guardian*, October 22, 2020, https://www.theguardian.com/world/2020/oct/22/poland-rules-abortion-due-to-foetal-defects-unconstitutional.
110 Monika Pronczuk, "Poland Delays a Near-Total Ban on Abortion," *New York Times*, November 4, 2020, https://www.nytimes.com/2020/11/04/world/europe/poland-abortion-law-delay.html. Since many Polish women go elsewhere in Europe to have an abortion or are forced to obtain it illegally at home, the fetal defect had become the most popular grounds for requesting a lawful abortion. Many claim that the elimination of this clause would make abortion practically impossible in Poland.
111 *New York Penal Law*, s 125.05. New York also criminalized abortion unless it was justifiable in accordance with section 125.05(3) (abortion in the second degree, s

125.40), abortion in the first degree (s 125.45), self-abortion in the second degree (s 125.50), and self-abortion in the first degree (s 125.55).
112 *Roe v Wade*, 410 U.S. 113 (1973).
113 *New York Consolidated Laws*, Public Health Code, s 2599-AA and s 2599-BB.
114 Ibid., s 2599-AA.
115 Ibid., s 2599-BB.
116 Since this development, questions have arisen about whether abortion without consent or that does not satisfy the Reproductive Health Act would in fact be a crime. Moreover, since homicide is now applicable only to a person after birth, no separate prosecution may be filed for the charge of killing an unborn baby. This decision thus might backfire against women for removing legal protection for their pregnancies and their bodies.
117 *German Criminal Code*, s 218, http://www.gesetze-im-internet.de/englisch_stgb/englisch_stgb.html#p1957.
118 Ibid., s 218a.
119 BVerfGE 39, 1.
120 *Criminal Code of Canada*, s 287 (repealed in 2019).
121 *R. v Morgentaler*, [1988] 1 SCR 30.
122 Nihonkoku kenpō [Constitution of Japan], 1946, art. 31.
123 Wardle, *supra* note 4 at 214.
124 Ibid., at 215.
125 Ibid., at 215–17.
126 JAOG, "Jinkō ninshin chuzetu no teigi" [Definition of ATP], https://www.jaog.or.jp/sep2012/JAPANESE/teigen/teigi.htm.
127 McElmeel, *supra* note 89 at 683; Kumiko Ishimura, "Chuzetsu kiseito yusei shiso" [Abortion Regulation and the Perspective of Eugenics], 11 Nigen kagaku kenkyu shuroku 25 at 31 (2002).
128 Maruyama, *supra* note 4 at 147–50.
129 Japan Medical Association, "Botai hogohō shitei ishi no shitei kijun model no kaitei nitsuite" [Revised Model Guideline for Designation of Designated Doctors under the Mother's Body Protection Act], April 2013, http://dl.med.or.jp/dl-med/teireikaiken/20130424_2.pdf. According to this guideline, a doctor who provides ATP must have five years of experience after obtaining a medical licence, training as a gynecologist for more than three years or certification as a gynecology expert, and a history of participating in more than twenty ATP and miscarriage operations, over ten of which must be ATP. He or she must also receive instruction from the local medical association.
130 "Ishira 3nin shorui souken e: Mushikaku chuszetsude ninpu shibou [Three Doctors Are Sent to Prosetutor for Prosecution: A Pregnant Woman Died as a Result of ATP without Qualification]," *Sankei Shimbun*, March 30, 2017. https://www.sankei.com/article/20170330-QFKGJXBEDNMCPDAB7F7IXVJUWM/. Evidently, the doctors erroneously believed that because the head doctor at their hospital was designated

to perform ATP, they could as well. The Tokyo Prosecution Office, Tachikawa Branch, however, decided not to file charges. "Datai, shorui souken ishi wo hukiso: Tokyo chiken tatikawa Shibu" [Prosecutor Decided Not to File Charges against Doctor for Performing Unqualified ATP], *Asahi Shimbun*, June 15, 2018. https://www.asahi.com/articles/DA3S13540739.html. The reason for this decision is not known.
131 Japan Medical Association, *supra* note 129.
132 According to one private website, designated doctors work at 4,874 hospitals. Caloo, "Zenkoku no Botai hogohō shitei ishi no haichi sareteiru iryo kikan" [Hospitals with Designated Doctors under the Mother's Body Protection Act], https://caloo.jp/hospitals/search/all/e22. The number of facilities that can handle ATP after twelve weeks is far smaller.
133 JAOG, "Nihon sanfujinka ikai no korekara" [Future of the Japan Association of Obstetricians and Gynecologists], January 9, 2013. http://www.jaog.or.jp/wp/wp-content/uploads/2017/01/61_130109.pdf (pointing out the concentration of gynecologists in Tokyo, Osaka, and Kyoto).
134 See *supra* note 57.
135 Emiko Kinefuchi and Mari Takahashi, "Jinkō ninshin chuzetsu wo keikenshita josei no shinri katei" [Psychological Process of Women Who Have Undergone Induced Abortion], 1 Ishikawa Journal of Nursing 39 at 44–45 (2004).
136 Anne Page Brooks, "*Mizuko Kuyō* and Japanese Buddhism," http://nirc.nanzan-u.ac.jp/nfile/2226/; Elizabeth G. Harrison and Igeta Midori, "Women's Responses to Child Loss in Japan: The Case of 'Mizuko Kuyō,'" 11:2 Journal of Feminist Studies in Religion 67 (1995); Sheryl Wudunn, "In Japan, a Ritual of Mourning for Abortions," *New York Times* (January 25, 1996), https://www.nytimes.com/1996/01/25/world/in-japan-a-ritual-of-mourning-for-abortions.html. On the other hand, Buddhism views abortion as temporarily sending the life of the fetus to another world, where it waits until it is born again. In other words, abortion is a suspension of life, not a termination, thus making it easier for women to accept. Maruyama, *supra* note 4 at 147. Therefore, Buddhist tradition apparently does not encompass commemorating or praying for an aborted fetus. Yet Japan gradually accepted a tradition of establishing the baby Buddha (*jizō*) as a guardian of small children who predeceased their parents and praying for their safety and happiness. Kazuo Takemura, "Toshi niokeru jizō shinkō to community keisei" [Belief in Jizō in Urban Areas and the Creation of Community], 35:3 Soshioroji 87 (1991). This tradition was converted into the practice of memorializing and praying for an aborted fetus at temple, which became very popular during the 1970s. William R. LaFleur, *Liquid Life: Abortion and Buddhism in Japan* (Princeton, NJ: Princeton University Press, 1992); Shigeichi Morikuri, "Mizuko kuyōbirth no hassei to genjō" [Origin and Current Status of Mizuko Memorialization], 57 Kokuritsu rekishi minzoku hakubutsukan kenkyu houkoku 95 (1994). It must be noted that temples and business operators encouraged the practice for their own benefit, prompting many to condemn their exploitation of women who had lost a baby or been forced to abort a fetus. Ibid.

137 Yuko Yasuda, Ayumu Arakawa, Saori Takada, Ayae Kido, and Tatuya Sao, "Mikon no jakunen josei no chuzetsu keiken" [ATP Experience for Unmarried Young Women], 7 Shituteki shinrigaku kenkyu 181 (2003).
138 Sachie Mizohata, "Nippon Kaigi: Empire, Contradiction, and Japan's Future," 14:21:4 Asia-Pacific Journal 1 (2016).
139 Max Fisher, "Japanese Politician Wants to Boost the National Birthrate by Banning Abortion," *Washington Post* (February 26, 2013), https://www.washingtonpost.com/news/worldviews/wp/2013/02/26/japanese-politician-wants-to-boost-the-national-birthrate-by-banning-abortion/?noredirect=on&utm_term=.f9015a28bc3f.
140 "Noda Seiko giin, shoushika taisaku toshite chuzetsu kinshi tonaeru?" [Is MP Seiko Noda Arguing for the Ban on ATP in Order to Cope with the Declining Child Population?], J-cast News, February 25, 2013, https://www.j-cast.com/2013/02/25166877.html?p=all.
141 Fisher, *supra* note 139.
142 Minpō [Civil Code], 1896, art. 792.
143 Ibid., art. 817–2, authorizing the family court to allow the special adoption procedure, terminating the family relationship between the adopted child and its natural parents, and treating the child as a natural child of the adoptive parents.
144 In 2015, 710 children were adopted, and 512 were approved for special adoption. MHLW, "Satooya oyobi tokubetsu youshi engumi no genjō nitsuite" [Current Situation of Foster Families and Special Adoption], 2016, https://www.mhlw.go.jp/file/05-Shingikai-11901000-Koyoukintoujidoukateikyoku-Soumuka/0000147429.pdf. The ratio of adopted children is far lower than in the United States and Europe. Ibid.
145 The courts assume that this occurs once a part of its body is exposed outside the mother's body. Daishinin [Great Court of Judicature], December 13, 1919, 25 Keiroku 1367.
146 Taniwaki, *supra* note 3 at 3; Tamotsu Saegusa, "Jinkō ninshin chuzetsu to taiji no seimei" [ATP and the Life of the Fetus], 29 Shinshudaigaku hougakuronshu 1 at 7–9 (2012). Therefore, a fetus is not simply a part of the mother's body.
147 Civil Code, *supra* note 142 at art. 3, para 1.
148 Ibid., art. 886, para 1. When the fetus is stillborn, the presumption is not applicable. Ibid. at para 2.
149 Ibid., art. 721.
150 Criminal Code, *supra* note 9 at art. 199.
151 Saikō saibansho [SCOJ], 3rd petty bench, February 29, 1988, 42:2 Keishu 314.
152 Kinko Nakatani, "Taiji nitaisuru kagai to kashitsu chishishouzai no seihi" [Could an Assault toward a Fetus Lead to a Negligent Injury Leading to Death?], 53:12 Keio J. of L., Politics and Sociology 1737 (1980).
153 *Roe v Wade*, *supra* note 112.
154 597 U.S. – (2022.)
155 BVerfGE, *supra* note 119.

156 Ibid. In a highly controversial German case of 1992, a brain-dead pregnant woman was kept alive until the fetus was capable of surviving birth. Christoph Anstötz, "Should a Brain-Dead Pregnant Woman Carry Her Child to Full Term? The Case of the 'Erlanger Baby,'" 7:4 Bioethics 340 (1993), DOI: 10.1111/j.1467-8519.1993.tb00224.x.
157 Saegusa, *supra* note 146 at 12.
158 Ibid., at 11.
159 Ibid., at 12–13.
160 Ibid., at 13–15.
161 It might also preclude the legalization of ATP, while it could justify non-punishment of abortion due to legitimate reasons. In Germany, the legislature was mandated to impose criminal punishment but allowed to refrain from enforcement when there was a compassionate grounds.
162 Nobuo Kurata, "Sentakuteki jinkō ninshin chuzetsu no rinriteki kyoyou jouken" [Ethical Conditions for Selective Abortion], 8:1 Seimei rinri 35 (1998); Eisuke Yamamoto, "Sentakuteki jinkō ninshin chuzetsu wo meguru rinriteki mondai" [Ethical Issues concerning Selective Abortion], 36:1 Ryutsu Keizai daigaku ronshu 29 (2001).
163 Yoshimi Kakimoto, "Chuzetsu no jiyu wa sentakuteki chuzetsu wo hukumunoka" [Does Freedom of Abortion Include Selective Abortion?], 9 Kyoto joshi daigaku gendaishakai kenkyu 79 (2006). So far, doctors do not offer genetic testing unless there is a significant risk that the baby could have a serious hereditary disease or that a miscarriage could occur. However, if a mother catches measles during pregnancy, the baby could potentially become disabled. If amniocentesis reveals that the fetus has an extra chromosome, the baby could have Down syndrome. In such situations, the mother must make the difficult choice of whether to give birth or seek an abortion. Moreover, several wrongful birth suits have been filed, seeking damages from doctors who failed to inform parents of the possible disability of the fetus. On this subject, courts are divided between two positions: The first holds that economic difficulty is a permissible ground for ATP of a disabled fetus, thus finding that the mother's right to autonomy was infringed. The second denies the permissibility and grants damages only for the negligent failure of doctors to allow mothers to prepare for a disabled baby. Sakaihara, *supra* note 76 at 186; Masahiro Hayashi, "Shougai wo riyu tosuru jinkō ninshin chuzetsu nitsuiteno keijihouteki ichikousatu" [Legality of Induced Abortion from the Reason of Fetal Impairment under Japanese Criminal Law], 12 Musashino daigaku seijikeizai kenkyusho nenpo 1 (2016).
164 NIPT involves taking a blood sample from a pregnant woman and trying to detect the very small amounts of fetal DNA that naturally circulate in her bloodstream, mostly to identify an abnormal number of chromosomes, such as a trisomy (Down syndrome is a trisomy of chromosome 21). However, NIPT can also be used to uncover other abnormalities, as well as the sex of the fetus. National Human Genome Research Institute, "Noninvasive Prenatal Genetic Testing," 2018, https://www.genome.gov/dna-day/15-ways/noninvasive-prenatal-genetic-testing.

165 MHLW, "Botaiketsu wo mochiita atarashii shusseizen idengakuteki kensa no shishintō ni tsuite (shuchi irai)" [Guidelines for NIPT], March 13, 2013, Kojibo hatsu 0303 dai1gou, https://www.mhlw.go.jp/web/t_doc?dataId=00tb9274&dataTy pe=1&pageNo=1. Under the guidelines, NIPT is reserved only for cases in which ultrasound has revealed an abnormality, for patients who have already carried a fetus with a genetic abnormality, and for those who are at high risk.
166 NIPT Consortium, https://niptconsortium.nl.
167 "NIPT: Inochi no senbetsu teichaku kenen" [NIPT: Concern with the Increase in Choosing What Life to Keep], *Mainichi Shimbun* (January 28, 2018), https://mainichi.jp/articles/20180128/ddm/002/040/069000c?inb=ys; "NIPT: Gakkai ga kakudai shishin ni doui" [NIPT: Association Agreed on the Guideline's Expansion], *Mainichi Shimbun* (June 20, 2020), https://mainichi.jp/articles/20200620/k00/00m/040/184000c; "NIPT, taisho kakudai e: Seijingo ni hasshousuru byoukimo [NIPT: Applicable Cases Expanded to Include Diseases Which Could Manifest After Grownup] *Asahi Shimbun*, June 26, 2021, https://www.asahi.com/articles/ASP6V5D8DP6TULBJ014.htm.
168 "NIPT: Ijo hanmei no 96% chuzetsu" [NIPT: 96 Percent of Pregnant Women Chose Abortion after Finding an Abnormality], *Mainichi Shimbun* (April 25, 2016), https://mainichi.jp/articles/20160425/k00/00m/040/119000c?inb=ys.
169 JSOG, "Jutokuna identesei shikkan wo taishotoshita chakushoumae idenshi kensa nikansuru kenkai" [Position on Pre-implantation Testing for Patient who Has Serious Hereditary Diseases], revised January 9, 2022, http://fa.kyorin.co.jp/jsog/readPDF.php?file=74/7/074070749.pdf#page=22 (limiting pre-implantation testing for medical reasons only to patients who have a serious genetic abnormality that could be passed on to the baby or who have a history of miscarriages due to a genetic abnormality). For the turbulent history of pre-implantation testing and screening in Japan, see Keiko Toshimitsu, "1990nendai iko no nihon niokeru chakushomae shindan wo meguru ronsō no suii" [History of the Controversy over Pre-implantation Testing since the 1990s in Japan], 25 Ritsumeikan daigaku seizongaku kenkyu center houkokusho (2016), https://www.ritsumei-arsvi.org/publication/center_report/publication-center25/publication-363/.
170 One individual was stripped of his expert reproductive doctor status for violating the self-regulatory code that bans the use of preimplantation testing for non-medical reasons. Japan Society for Reproductive Medicine, "Chakushomae screening kensa wo jisshishita seishokuisenmon-i no shogu nitsuite" [Disciplinary Action against a Reproductive Expert Doctor Who Implemented Preimplantation Screening], November 4, 2016, http://www.jsrm.or.jp/announce/113.pdf.
171 Tomohide Ibuki, "Should PGD for Sex-Selection Be Allowed in the Japanese Context? A Literature Review and Critical Analysis of the Biotechnical Arguments," 24:1 Bioethics 244 (2014). Interestingly, one recent study found that, although the preference for boys has traditionally been the norm, many pregnant women now prefer girls. Shingo Kodani, "Nihon niokeru seisenko no keiko sono youin" [Tendency and Factors of Sex Preference in Japan], 5:2 Chiiki seisaku kenkyu 31 (2002).

172 Or the government could introduce legal regulations on genetic testing before birth. Kazunori Yasui, "Shogaikokuniokeru shusseizen-shindan/chakushouzen-shindan nitaisuru houtekikisei nitsuite" [Legal Regulations on Genetic Testing before Birth], 779 Chousa to joho 1 (2013).
173 Marvin Olasky, *Abortion Rites: A Social History of Abortion in America* (Wheaton: Crossway, 1992); Z. Acevedo, "Abortion in Early America," 4:2 *Women Health* 159 (1979).
174 James C. Mohr, Abortion in America: The Origins and Evolution of National Policy, 1800–1900 2nd Edition (Oxford: Oxford University Press, 1978); Leslie J. Reagan, *When Abortion Was a Crime: Women, Medicine, and Law in the United States, 1867–1973* (Berkeley, CA: University of California Press, 1998).
175 For instance, the Model Penal Code, which was proposed by the American Law Institute in 1962. As an influential model for state law, it introduced the following limitations:

230.3 Abortion

(1) Unjustified Abortion. A person who purposely and unjustifiably terminates the pregnancy of another otherwise than by a live birth commits a felony of the third degree or, where the pregnancy has continued beyond the twenty-sixth week, a felony in the second degree.
(2) Justifiable Abortion. A licensed physician is justified in terminating a pregnancy if he believes there is substantial risk that continuance of the pregnancy would gravely impair the physical or mental health of the mother or that the child would be born with grave physical or mental defect, or that the pregnancy resulted from rape, incest, or other felonious intercourse. All illicit intercourse with a girl below the age of 16 shall be deemed felonious for purposes of this subsection. Justifiable abortions shall be performed only in a licensed hospital except in case of emergency when hospital facilities are unavailable ...
(4) Self-Abortion. A woman whose pregnancy has continued beyond the twenty-sixth week commits a felony of the third degree if she purposely terminates her own pregnancy otherwise than by a live birth, or if she uses instruments, drugs or violence upon herself for that purpose. Except as justified under Subsection (2), a person who induces or knowingly aids a woman to use instruments, drugs or violence upon herself for the purpose of terminating her pregnancy otherwise than by a live birth commits a felony of the third degree whether or not the pregnancy has continued beyond the twenty-sixth week.

American Law Institute, Model Penal Code, 1962, 230.3, https://archive.org/details/ModelPenalCode_ALI/page/n266/mode/1up.

176 *Roe v Wade, supra* note 112.

177 Article 1191 of the Texas Penal Code stated, "If any person shall designedly administer to a pregnant woman or knowingly procure to be administered with her consent any drug or medicine, or shall use toward her any violence or means whatever externally or internally applied, and thereby procure an abortion, he shall be confined in the penitentiary not less than two nor more than five years; if it be done without her consent, the punishment shall be doubled. By 'abortion' is meant that the life of the fetus or embryo shall be destroyed in the woman's womb or that a premature birth thereof be caused." Article 1196 specified that "nothing in this chapter applies to an abortion procured or attempted by medical advice for the purpose of saving the life of the mother."
178 *Roe v Wade, supra* note 112 at 152–53.
179 Ibid., at 153–54.
180 Ibid., at 155.
181 Ibid., at 162.
182 Ibid., at 156–58.
183 Ibid., at 162.
184 Ibid., at 162–63.
185 Ibid., at 163.
186 Ibid.
187 Ibid.
188 Ibid.
189 Ibid., at 160.
190 Ibid., at 164.
191 *Griswold v Connecticut*, 381 U.S. 479 (1965).
192 *Doe v Bolton*, 410 U.S. 179 (1973); *Planned Parenthood v Danforth*, 428 U.S. 52 (1976); *Colautti v Franklin*, 439 U.S. 379 (1979); *City of Akron v Akron Center for Reproductive Health*, 462 U.S. 416 (1983); *Thornburgh v American College of Obstetricians and Gynecologists*, 476 U.S. 747 (1986). On the other hand, the SCOTUS held that the state can refuse to offer abortion at public hospitals as well *Maher v Roe*, 432 U.S. 464 (1977); https://supreme.justia.com/cases/federal/us/432/464/. *Harris v McRae*, 448 U.S. 297 (1980); *Webster v Reproductive Health Services*, 492 U.S. 490 (1989).
193 Lawrence Tribe, *Abortion: The Clash of Absolutes* (New York/London: W.W. Norton, 1992); Jack Balkin, *What Roe v Wade Should Have Said: The Nation's Top Legal Experts Rewrite America's Most Controversial Decision* (New York/London: NYU Press, 2005); Mary Ziegler, *Beyond Abortion: Roe v Wade and the Battle for Privacy* (Cambridge, MA: Harvard University Press, 2018); Mary Ziegler, *Abortion and the Law in America: Roe v Wade to the Present* (Cambridge, UK: Cambridge University Press, 2020).
194 *Planned Parenthood of Southeastern Pa. v Casey*, 505 U.S. 833 (1992).
195 Ibid., at 844–65.
196 Ibid., at 870–76.

197 Compare *Stenberg v Carhart*, 530 U.S. 914 (2000); *Whole Woman's Health v Hellerstedt*, 579 U.S. _ (2016); and *June Medical Services v Russo*, 591 U.S. _ (2020) with *Gonzales v Carhart*, 550 U.S. 124 (2007).
198 Caroline Kelly, "States Passed a Flurry of New Abortion Restrictions This Year. Here's Where They Stand," CNN, October 29, 2019, https://www.cnn.com/2019/10/27/politics/abortion-laws-states-roundup/index.html.
199 "What's Going On with the Abortion Laws? A State-by-State Look," *NBC News*, June 1, 2019, https://www.nbcnews.com/news/us-news/guide-anti-abortion-laws-state-n1012566.
200 595 U.S. – (2021).
201 597 U.S. – (2022), *supra* note 154.
202 Ibid., at –.
203 "Tracking the States Where Abortion Is Now Banned," *New York Times* (updated July 27, 2022), https://www.nytimes.com/interactive/2022/us/abortion-laws-roe-v-wade.html.
204 *Criminal Code of Canada*, s 287 (repealed in 2019).
205 *R. v Morgentaler*, [1988] 1 SCR 30.
206 Ibid., at 51.
207 Ibid., at 53–61. The SCOC found that an average of eight weeks could elapse between the woman's initial contact with a physician and the abortion itself. Ibid., at 57. According to the Criminal Code, a woman who desired an abortion had to apply to a "therapeutic abortion committee" in either an accredited or an approved hospital. The former, which must be capable of offering "diagnostic services and medical, surgical and obstetrical treatment," was accredited by the Canadian Council on Hospital Accreditation. The latter was approved by the provincial minister of health. The abortion committee must consist of "not less than three members each of whom is a qualified medical practitioner" and all of whom were appointed by the hospital's administrative board. As a result of these requirements, the number of eligible hospitals was greatly reduced, and it became pretty hard for a pregnant woman to obtain approval. Ibid., at 65–71.
208 Ibid., at 73, 76, 79–80.
209 Shelley A.M. Gavigan, "Beyond Morgentaler: The Legal Regulation of Reproduction," 1992, http://digitalcommons.osgoode.yorku.ca/scholarly_works/98. Nevertheless, various obstacles remain. For details, see Mark Gollom, "Abortion Barriers in Canada Are Back in Spotlight Following Passage of Abortion Bans in U.S.," *CBC News*, May 18, 2019, https://www.cbc.ca/news/health/abortion-access-canada-us-bans-1.5140345; Chris Cummins, "Decades Later, Abortions in Canada Are Still Hard to Get," Policy Options, August 13, 2019, https://policyoptions.irpp.org/magazines/august-2019/decades-later-abortions-in-canada-are-still-hard-to-get/.
210 *German Basic Law*, art. 1 and art. 2(1).
211 BVerfGE 39, 1, *supra* note 119; Robert E. Jonas and John D. Gorby, trans., "German Constitutional Court Abortion Decision, BVerfGE 39, 1," 9 John Marshall J. of Practice and Procedure 605.

212 Ibid.
213 Ibid.
214 Ibid.
215 Ibid.
216 Ibid.
217 "BVerfGE 88, 203 – Abortion (Schwangerschaftsabbruch II)," https://germanlawarchive.iuscomp.org/?p=1190.
218 Donald P. Kommers, "The Constitutional Law of Abortion in Germany: Should Americans Pay Attention?" 10 J. Contemp. Health L. & Pol'y 1 (1994); Vanessa MacDonnell and Jula Hughes, "The German Abortion Decisions and the Protective Function in German and Canadian Constitutional Law," 50:4 Osgoode Hall L.J. 999 (2013).
219 Krishna K. Upadhya, John S. Santelli, Tina R. Raine-Bennett, Melissa J. Kottke, and Daniel Grossman, "Over-the-Counter Access to Oral Contraceptives for Adolescents," 60:6 J. Adolesc. Health 634 (2017).
220 Setsuko Sugano, "Sentakuteki Chuzetsu to Feminism no Iso" [The Phases of Selective Abortion and Feminism], 64:1 Shakaigaku hyoron 91 (2013).
221 Ibid., at 93.
222 Ibid.
223 See Kinefuchi and Takahashi, *supra* note 135.
224 Sugano, *supra* note 216 at 93.
225 Ibid., at 94.
226 Ehara, *supra* note 10 at 265; Maruyama, *supra* note 4 at 140.
227 Nobuyoshi Ashibe, with Kazuyuki Takahashi, *Kenpō* [Constitution], 7th ed. (Tokyo: Iwanami shoten, 2019), 128 (accepting the right to abortion as a privacy right); Koji Satoh, *Nihonkoku kenpōron* [Japanese Constitution], 2nd ed. (Tokyo: Seibundo, 2020), 212, 216 (accepting the right to abortion as a right to autonomy).
228 Nihonkoku kenpō [Constitution of Japan], 1946, art. 13.
229 Ibid., art. 24.
230 Hideki Shibutani, *Kenpō* [Japanese Constitutional Law], 3rd ed. (Tokyo: Yuhikaku, 2017), 467.
231 Shuichi Kato, "Josei no jikoketteiken no yougo" [In Defence of the Right to Autonomy of a Woman], 15 Sociologos 14 (1991), http://www.l.u-tokyo.ac.jp/~slogos/archive/15/kato1991.pdf.
232 Maruyama, *supra* note 4 at 156. The author argues for the abolition of the abortion ban in the Criminal Code and for making contraceptives broadly available, while keeping for-cause requirements for abortion so long as it is permitted for general reasons, such as "distress" or "physical, emotional or economic reasons" to be determined solely by the women independent of her physicians. Ibid., at 156–57. Ikuko Nie, Jinkō ninshin chuzetsu no hōkisei [Legal Regulation of Elective Abortions: Legal Issues on Elective Abortions Due to Fetal Abnormalities], 7 Rikkyo daigaku hukushi gakubu kiyo 137 (2005), https://www.jstage.jst.go.jp/article/jalps/52/2/52_95/_pdf/-char/ja (arguing for the right to abortion to include aborting a disabled fetus).

233 Dobbs, 597 U.S. –, (2022).
234 Ibid., at –.
235 Ibid., at –.
236 Wardle argues that the Japanese approach allows women to mourn for the aborted fetus, which could be beneficial for them. Wardle, *supra* note 4 at 239. The American approach, which invokes the constitutional right to abortion and thus insists that there is nothing wrong with it, may be uncomfortable for many American women. Ibid., at 239–40. But we can leave the moral questions to the women themselves. We need to allow them to assert their constitutional right, even if many might feel guilt for doing so.
237 The Japanese government is now considering the approval of the abortion pill, which would be used by designated doctors for the first time. "Keiko chuzetsuyaku no yakuji shounin ryoushou, kokunaihatsu, ninshin 9shu made taisho [The Government is Going to Approve the Abortion Pill for the First Time, to Be Available for Pregnancy during First 9 Weeks], Jiji (Jan 27, 2023), https://www.jiji.com/jc/article?k=2023012700843&g=soc.

Chapter 6: Sex, Childbirth, and the Government

1 The current situation is well summarized in Cabinet Office, "Shoushikashakai taisaku hakusho, 2020" [Declining Childbirth Whitepaper, 2020], https://www8.cao.go.jp/shoushi/shoushika/whitepaper/measures/w-2020/r02pdfhonpen/r02honpen.html (Declining Childbirth Whitepaper).
2 Ministry of Health, Labour and Welfare (MHLW), "Jinko doutai souran no nenji suii" [Annual Trends in Population Change], https://www.mhlw.go.jp/toukei/saikin/hw/jinkou/suii09/soran2-1.html.
3 Ibid.
4 Ibid.
5 MHLW, "Jinko doutai souran (ritsu) no nenji suii" [Annual Trends in Population Change Rate], https://www.mhlw.go.jp/toukei/saikin/hw/jinkou/suii09/soran2-2.html.
6 OECD (2016), "Fertility," in OECD Factbook 2015-2016: Economic, Environmental and Social Statistics, https://www.oecd-ilibrary.org/docserver/factbook-2015-2-en.pdf?expires=1659290597&id=id&accname=guest&checksum=B87D5139988182F11DA05BC8BDC253C7.
7 Ministry of Internal Affairs and Communications, Tokeikyoku [Statistics Bureau], "Heisei27nen kokuseichousa (kekka no gaiyo)" [2015 National Census (Summary)], http://www.stat.go.jp/data/kokusei/2015/kekka/kihon1/pdf/gaiyou1.pdf.
8 Ibid.
9 Cabinet Office, "Reiwa 2nen ban kourei shakai hakusho" [Aging Society Whitepaper, 2020], https://www8.cao.go.jp/kourei/whitepaper/w-2020/zenbun/pdf/1s1s_01.pdf (Aging Society Whitepaper).
10 Ibid.

11 Ibid.
12 Ibid.
13 Ibid.
14 Statista, "The Countries with the Largest Percentage of Total Population over 65 Years in 2021," https://www.statista.com/statistics/264729/countries-with-the-largest-percentage-of-total-population-over-65-years/.
15 According to Statista, "The 20 Countries with the Lowest Fertility Rates in 2021," https://www.statista.com/statistics/268083/countries-with-the-lowest-fertility-rates/, Japan ranked eleventh, with a TFR of 1.38. Four other Asian countries scored lower: Taiwan (1.07), South Korea (1.09), Singapore (1.15), and Macao (1.21). Other developed countries also scored extremely low, such as Greece (1.39), Portugal (1.42), and Italy (1.47). According to a CIA database, Japan ranked fifth-lowest among 228 countries, with only 6.95 births per 1,000 population. Central Intelligence Agency, "A World Factbook, Country Comparison: Birth Rate," https://www.cia.gov/the-world-factbook/field/birth-rate/country-comparison. The lowest was Saint Pierre and Miquelon (6.47).
16 Ministry of Economy, Trade and Industry, "2050 nen made no keizaishakai no kouzo henka to seisaku kadai nitsuite" [Possible Structural Change and Accompanying Policy Agenda for Social Economy until 2050], 2018, https://www.meti.go.jp/shingikai/sankoshin/2050_keizai/pdf/001_04_00.pdf.
17 National Institute of Population and Social Security Research, "Nihon no shourai jinkou suikei" [Future Estimate of the Population of Japan], 2017, http://www.ipss.go.jp/pp-zenkoku/j/zenkoku2017/pp29_ReportALL.pdf.
18 In 2022, tax revenue totalled JPY 65.3 trillion (about US$400 billion), a significant improvement from JPY 38.7 trillion (roughly US$280 billion) in 2009, yet it covered only 60 percent of all government expenditures of JPY 107.5 trillion (roughly US$760 billion). Ministry of Finance (MOF), "Zaisei nikansuru shiryō" [Data on the Government Budget], 2022 https://www.mof.go.jp/tax_policy/summary/condition/a02.htm; MOF, "Zeishu nikansuru shiryō" [Tax Revenue Data], 2022 https://www.mof.go.jp/tax_policy/summary/condition/a03.htm. The government relies heavily on income tax revenue, which was JPY 20.3 trillion (approximately US$16 billion) in 2018, also a significant improvement from JPY 12.9 trillion (roughly US$76 billion) in 2009. Sales tax revenue in 2022 was JPY 21.5 trillion (about US$160 billion). The sales tax was raised in 2019, partially to cover the ever-increasing social security expenses.
19 The health insurance system in Japan is highly fragmented. Health care contributions from public employees are managed by a mutual help co-op, a health care association handles small-business employees, a national health care company does the same for employees of large corporations, and everyone else contributes directly to the national health insurance. All residents must somehow be insured, however, and the national health insurance premium is collected either by local tax or a local mandatory premium.

20 MHLW, "Wagakuni no iryo seido no gaiyō" [Summary of the Health Care System of Japan], https://www.mhlw.go.jp/bunya/iryouhoken/iryouhoken01/dl/01a.pdf?_fsi=nHURi7Pw. To reduce the burden on patients, there is a cap on very expensive costs. On the other hand, seniors whose income is higher than a certain maximum now pay 30 percent of their medical bills.
21 Ibid.
22 MHLW, "Nihon no iryo no gaiyō" [Summary of the Medical Care System of Japan], 2017, https://www.mhlw.go.jp/toukei/saikin/hw/k-iryohi/17/dl/kekka.pdf.
23 As a result, though they did not need medical treatment, a huge number of seniors ended up living in hospitals for indefinite periods, raising medical costs and occupying beds that should have been allocated to sick patients. The government is now encouraging hospitals to discharge these seniors to group homes or elder care facilities.
24 Minpō [Civil Code], 1896, art. 877.
25 Kaigo hokenhō [Elderly Care Insurance Act], law no. 123 of 2007; MHLW, "Kouteki kaigo hoken seido no genjō to kongo no yakuwari" [Current Situation and Future Role of the Public Elderly Care System], 2015, https://www.mhlw.go.jp/file/06-Seisakujouhou-12300000-Roukenkyoku/201602kaigohokenntoha_2.pdf.
26 The central and local governments supply half of the fund, and the remaining half is furnished by contributions from residents. Ibid. Residents between age forty and sixty-four pay 28 percent of the fund, and those sixty-five years and older, pay 22 percent.
27 The fund covers 80 to 90 percent of all necessary spending, while users pay the remaining 10 to 20 percent (with a cap on the their own expenses). The care provided includes home visits, in-patient care, and short and extended stays in senior homes and senior health facilities. Ibid. Residents who qualify for care can use the available services, depending on the degree of disability.
28 Aging Society Whitepaper, *supra* note 9.
29 Ibid.
30 At the time of writing, the pension system in Japan remained highly fragmented. Public employees pay into a mutual help co-op pension, and many other employees pay into company pensions. In both instances, the employers contribute as well. Half of the contribution goes to the company pension and half to the national pension system. Everyone else pays into the national pension system. MHLW, "Kouteki nenkin no gaiyō" [Summary of the Pension System in Japan], https://www.mhlw.go.jp/file/05-Shingikai-12601000-Seisakutoukatsukan-Sanjikanshitsu_Shakaihoshoutantou/0000086292.pdf. Dependent spouses will be covered by the company pension of the employed spouse and are exempt from contribution. Upon reaching age sixty-five, everyone receives old-age pension payments from the national pension system, and retired company or government employees can receive further stipends from their own pension system. But now the various pension systems are integrated into the national pension system and company pension system, and the recipient can decide when to start receiving the pension (from ages 60 to 75). Japan Pension Service, Rourei nenkin no seido [Old-Age Pension System]. https://www.nenkin.go.jp/service/jukyu/roureinenkin/index.html;

Nenkin seido no kinou kyouka notameno kokumin nenkinhōtō no ichibu wo kaiseisuru hōritsu [Act to Amend Parts of the National Pension Act et al. to Intensify the Pension System], law no. 40 of 2020.
31 Aging Society Whitepaper, *supra* note 9.
32 Ibid.
33 Ibid.
34 According to a 2019 Financial Agency report, a retired couple that received the old-age pension would require an additional JPY 50,000 (roughly US$375) per month simply to survive. If both lived for thirty years after retirement, they would need at least JPY 20 million (about US$150,000) in savings or assets to sustain a reasonable standard of living. Financial Agency, Kin-yu shingikai [Finance Council], "Kourei shakai niokeru shisan keisai/kanri" [The Creation and Management of Assets for an Aging Society], 2019, 16, https://www.fsa.go.jp/singi/singi_kinyu/tosin/20190603/01.pdf.
35 Seikatsu hogohō [Welfare Assistance Act], law no. 144 of 1950.
36 In 2020, some 1.6 million families (about 2 million people) were receiving welfare. Of these, 0.9 million were senior families, or some 55.5 percent of all recipients. It is reported that their numbers are on the rise, indicating that the old-age pension payment is not enough. MHLW, "Seikatsuhogo no hihogosha chousa no kekka" [Result of Recipients of the Welfare Payment], July 2020, https://www.mhlw.go.jp/toukei/saikin/hw/hihogosya/m2020/dl/07-01.pdf.
37 MHLW, "Shakai hoshō no kyuhu to hutan no genjō" [The Current Situation and the Burden of Social Security Spending], 2020. https://www.mhlw.go.jp/stf/newpage_21509.html.
38 MOF, "Shourai no shakai hoshō kyuhu no mitooshi" [Prospect of Future Social Security Spending], 2019, https://www.mof.go.jp/about_mof/councils/fiscal_system_council/sub-of_fiscal_system/proceedings/material/zaiseia310423/01.pdf.
39 In 2019, the government raised the sales tax from 8 to 10 percent, in order to partially cover the increase in social security spending. MOF, "Shouhizei no shito nikansuru shiryō" [Data on How Revenue Obtained by Sales Tax Raise Will Be Used], https://www.mof.go.jp/tax_policy/summary/consumption/d05.htm. But apparently, it was not enough.
40 MOF, "Nihon no zaisei wo kangaeru" [Japanese Government Finance], https://www.mof.go.jp/zaisei/current-situation/situation-debt.html.
41 MOF, "Futsu kokusai zandaka no ruiseki" [Accumulated National Bond Debt], https://www.mof.go.jp/tax_policy/summary/condition/004.pdf.
42 MOF, *supra* note 41, https://www.mof.go.jp/zaisei/current-situation/situation-comparison.html.
43 Shoushika shakai taisaku kihonhō [Fundamental Act on Declining Childbirth Countermeasures], law no. 133 of 2003.
44 Cabinet Office, "Kodomo/kosodate honbu" [Child and Child Raising Headquarters], https://www8.cao.go.jp/shoushi/index.html. The government even decided to create the Children and Family Agency on April 1, 2023, as a leading agency on children

and family policies. Cabinet Secretariat, Kodomo kateicho nitsuite [Children and Family Agency], https://www.cas.go.jp/jp/seisaku/kodomo_seisaku_suishin/pdf/betu2_kodomo_siryou.pdf.
45 Declining Childbirth Whitepaper, *supra* note 1.
46 Cabinet Office, "Shin shoushika taisaku taikō" [New Outline of Declining Childbirth Countermeasures], Cabinet decision, May 29, 2020, https://www8.cao.go.jp/shoushi/shoushika/law/pdf/r020529/shoushika_taikou.pdf.
47 Ibid., at 63.
48 Declining Childbirth Whitepaper, *supra* note 1 at 17 (85.7 percent of single men and 89.3 percent of single women between the ages of eighteen and thirty-four plan to marry someday).
49 In Japan, 22.4 percent of all male employees work informally, as do 57.1 percent of all female employees. Ibid., at 20. However, for males between the ages of fifteen and twenty-four, the percentage is particularly high, at 47.6. Ibid. Many young workers earn less than JPY 1.5 million (roughly US$11,000). Indeed, among those between the ages of twenty and twenty-four, 8.3 percent of those who have permanent jobs are married, whereas 2.8 of those who work informally are married. Among workers between twenty-five and twenty-nine, 30.5 percent of those with permanent jobs are married, whereas 12.5 percent of informal workers are. Ibid., at 22. It is generally true that the higher the income, the higher the marriage rate. Ibid.
50 Roudou keiyakuhō [Labour Contract Act], law no. 128 of 2007, art. 18.
51 Tanjikan roudousha oyobi yuukikoyō roudousha no koyoukanri no kaizentō nikansuru hōritsu [Act concerning the Improvement of Employment Management of Part-Time and Fixed-Term Workers], law no. 76 of 2003.
52 Hatarakikata kaikaku wo suishin surutame no kanren hōritsu no seibi nikansuru hōritsu [Act concerning the Adjustment of Relevant Acts to Promote the Way of Work Reform], law no. 71 of 2018 (Way of Work Reform Act).
53 Roudousha haken jigyō no tekisei na un-ei no kakuho oyobi haken roudousha no hogotō nikansuru hōritsu [Act on the Establishment of Adequate Management of Worker Dispatch Business and the Protection of Dispatch Workers], law no. 88 of 1985 (Dispatch Workers Act). The government published the "Guideline for Prohibition of Unfair Treatment toward Part-Time Workers, Fixed-Term Workers, and Dispatch Workers." "Tanjikan, yukikoyo roudousha oyobi haken roudousha nitaisuru hugouri na taigu no kinshitō nikansuru shishin" [Guidelines for Prohibition of Unfair Treatment of Part-Time or Fixed-Term Workers and Dispatch Workers], MHLW public notice no. 430 of 2018.
54 Couples who are eligible must be under the age of thirty-four and have a combined income of less than JPY 3.4 million (roughly US$25,000). The central and local governments split the subsidy, which can be as much as JPY 300,000 (about US$2,200).
55 In Japan, anyone who inherits assets must pay a hefty progressive inheritance tax, and a substantial donation tax also applies when one receives a monetary gift from a living parent or grandparent. These taxes are designed to prevent the accumulation of profits or assets, to ensure that people cannot give away their fortune to their children or grandchildren, and to achieve an egalitarian society. Exemptions to the

donation tax are allowed only up to some predetermined amount, and the recipient needs to satisfy certain income requirements.
56 "Nippon ichioku soukatsuyaku plan" [Japan All the People Revitalization Plan], Cabinet decision, June 2, 2016, https://www.kantei.go.jp/jp/headline/ichiokusoukatsuyaku/index.html#plan.
57 "Jinko mondai kihon chousa: Gendai nihon no kekkon to shussan" [Marriage and Childbirth in Japan Today], 2015, 69, http://www.ipss.go.jp/ps-doukou/j/doukou15/NFS15_reportALL.pdf (Marriage and Childbirth).
58 Declining Childbirth Whitepaper, *supra* note 1 at 23.
59 Marriage and Childbirth, *supra* note 58 at 75 (56.3 percent).
60 Ibid. (23.5 percent). Other reasons for limiting the number of children included being too old (39.8 percent), the burdensomeness of the responsibility (17.6 percent), and added pressure on work (15.2 percent).
61 Boshi hokenhō [Mother and Child Health Protection Act], law no. 141 of 1965; Jidō hukushihōtō no ichibuwo kaiseisuru hōritsu [Act to Amend Parts of the Child Welfare Act], law no. 63 of 2016.
62 Seiiku katei niarumono oyobi sono hogosha narabini ninsanpu ni taisi hitsuyouna seiiku iryou wo kiremenaku teikyō surutame no sesaku no sougoutekina suishin nikansuru hōritsu [Act on Comprehensive Promotion of Various Measures to Provide Necessary Support without Disruption to Children, Families, and Pregnant Mothers], law no. 104 of 2018.
63 This measure was necessitated by the sudden decrease of gynecologists who specialized in caring for pregnant women and handling childbirth, due to the risk of litigation. Giving birth can be dangerous, with possible complications and even death, so gynecologists can find themselves being sued after something goes badly wrong. Since many hospitals lost gynecologists and became unable to take on pregnant women as patients, numerous women feared that no gynecologist would be available to them. To deal with the situation, the government introduced a no-fault insurance system for childbirth, provided some assurance for patients and gynecologists, and actively facilitated the increase of the latter.
64 Jido teatehō [Child Benefit Act], law no. 73 of 1971.
65 Infants and children who are abandoned or in need of care due to neglect or abuse live in a public care facility until the age of eighteen, after which they are supposed to move out. The fact that most have nowhere to go is a serious issue.
66 Many Japanese employers request a personal guarantee from new recruits simply to ensure that they can be trusted and that they have someone to vouch for them.
67 Shougaisha kihonhō [Fundamental Act for Persons with a Disability], law no. 84 of 1970.
68 Shougaisha kihon keikaku (dai4ji) [Fourth Fundamental Plan for Persons with a Disability], Cabinet decision, March 30, 2018, https://www8.cao.go.jp/shougai/suishin/pdf/kihonkeikaku30.pdf.
69 Shougai wo riyu tosuru sabetsu no kaishouno suishin nikansuru hōritsu [Act on the Elimination of Discrimination Based on Disability], law no. 65 of 2013.
70 The government reported that though 2,890,000 spots were available, 16,772 infants were still waiting for admission. MHLW, "Hoikushotō kanren joukyō torimatome"

[Current Childcare Situation], September 6, 2019, https://www.mhlw.go.jp/stf/houdou/0000176137_00009.html.
71 Declining Childbirth Whitepaper, *supra* note 1, https://www8.cao.go.jp/shoushi/shoushika/whitepaper/measures/w-2020/r02pdfhonpen/pdf/s1-3.pdf.
72 Ibid., https://www8.cao.go.jp/shoushi/shoushika/whitepaper/measures/w-2020/r02pdfhonpen/pdf/s1-2.pdf.
73 In 2018, the TFR for Canadian women was 1.499, better than 1.488 in 2000, but still a steep drop from 3.811 in 1960. World Bank, "Fertility Rate, Total (Births per Woman) – Canada," https://data.worldbank.org/indicator/SP.DYN.TFRT.IN?locations=CA. Canada admitted 284,390 immigrants in 2020. Statista, "Number of Immigrants in Canada from 2000 to 2020," https://www.statista.com/statistics/443063/number-of-immigrants-in-canada/. It accepts more or less 250,000 immigrants every year.
74 Shutsu nyukoku kanri oyobi nanmin ninteihō [Immigration Control and Refugee Approval Act], law no. 319 of 1951, art. 7 (Immigration Control Act).
75 Ibid., appendix 1. The government adopted the policy of accepting skilled professional foreign workers, while rejecting the idea of accepting unskilled foreign workers in 1999 and has continued this policy ever since. "Dai9ji koyotaisaku kihon keikaku" [Ninth Fundamental Plan for Employment Measures], Cabinet decision, August 13, 1999, https://www.mlit.go.jp/singikai/kokudosin/keikaku/lifestyle/3/shiryou3-4.pdf; MHLW, "Gaikokujin koyo mondai kenkyukai houkokusho" [Foreign Workers Employment Problems Study Report], July 2002, https://www.mhlw.go.jp/topics/2002/07/tp0711-1.html (Foreign Workers Report).
76 In 2018, Canada accepted the most refugees (some twenty-eight thousand), followed by the United States (some twenty-three thousand), Australia (some thirteen thousand), and the United Kingdom (some six thousand). World Economic Forum, "These Are the Countries That Accept the Most Refugees in the World," June 27, 2019, https://www.weforum.org/agenda/2019/06/canada-now-leads-the-world-in-refugee-resettlement-surpassing-the-u-s/.
77 MOJ, "Reiwa gan-nen niokeru nanmin ninteishasutō nitsuite" [Number of Refugees Accepted in 2019], http://www.moj.go.jp/nyuukokukanri/kouhou/nyuukokukanri03_00004.html. Generally speaking, the number of applicants is on the rise, but the acceptance rate remains very low. In 2017, only 94 of the 19,629 applicants were admitted (22 came under protected refugee status). MOJ, "Wagakuni niokeru nanmin higo no joukyōtō" [Acceptance of Refugees in Japan], https://www.moj.go.jp/isa/content/930004128.pdf.
78 Immigration Control Act, *supra* note 75, appendix 2.
79 Toshio Kondo, "Nikkei Brazil-jin no shurō to seikatsu" [Work and Life of Japanese Brazilians], 40 Bukkyo daigaku shakaigakubu ronshu 1 at 2 (2005).
80 Their numbers increased to some 300,000, dropped due to the economic slowdown, and subsequently rose again, with the result that about 200,000 Japanese Brazilians currently live in Japan. In 2018, the government announced that it would accept

fourth-generation Japanese descendants, under strict conditions. Immigration Services Agency of Japan, "Nikkei 4sei no saranaru ukeire seido [Program for Further Acceptance of Fourth-Generation Japanese Descendants]," https://www.moj.go.jp/isa/publications/materials/nyuukokukanri07_00166.html. The primary goal of the settled foreigners program was to allow Japanese children who were marooned in China at the end of the Second World War and who became Chinese to return to Japan as Japanese descendants.

81 Ministry of Education, Culture, Sports, Science and Technology (MEXT), "Gaikokujin ryugakusei zaiseki jokyō chosa" [Enrolment Survey on Foreign Students], April 22, 2020, https://www.mext.go.jp/a_menu/koutou/ryugaku/1412692.htm.

82 Immigration Services Agency of Japan, "Shikakugai katsudō kyoka nitsuite" [Permit for Work Outside of the Official Status], https://www.moj.go.jp/isa/applications/guide/nyuukokukanri07_00045.html.

83 Gaikokujin no ginō jisshuu no tekiseina jisshi oyobi ginō jisshusei no hogo nikansuru hōritsu [Act on Proper Implementation of the Foreign Trainee System and on the Protection of Trainees], law no. 89 of 2016.

84 Immigration Control Agency, "Aratana gaikokujin ginō jisshu seido nitsuite" [New Foreign Trainee System], https://www.mhlw.go.jp/file/06-Seisakujouhou-11800000-Shokugyounouryokukaihatsukyoku/0000204970_1.pdf.

85 MHLW, "Indonesia, Philippines oyobi Vietnam karano gaikokujin kangoshi/kaigohukushi kouhosha no ukeire nitsuite" [Acceptance of Candidates for Nurses and Care Workers from Indonesia, the Philippines, and Vietnam], https://www.mhlw.go.jp/stf/seisakunitsuite/bunya/koyou_roudou/koyou/gaikokujin/other22/index.html.

86 However, the government exam was so challenging that very few people passed it. The government subsequently revised it, making it somewhat less onerous, but it remains the greatest barrier for candidates to stay in Japan.

87 In 2019, it was revealed that some seven hundred foreign students were missing from the Tokyo Welfare University. Like various other private universities, it accepts huge numbers of foreign students. Apparently, once they are admitted, many leave to find work. Yasuhiro Ide, "Nihonjin ga mewo mukenai kieta ryugakusei no shinso" [Truth about the Missing Foreign Students That Have Been Unnoticed], Wedge, November 1, 2019, https://wedge.ismedia.jp/articles/-/17753.

88 MHLW, "Gaikokujin koyo joukyou" [Employment of Foreigners], January 31, 2020, https://www.mhlw.go.jp/stf/newpage_09109.html.

89 MOJ, "Reiwa gan-nen matsu genzai niokeru zairyu gaikokujinsu nitsuite" [Number of Foreigners Staying in Japan by the End of 2019], March 27, 2020, http://www.moj.go.jp/nyuukokukanri/kouhou/nyuukokukanri04_00003.html.

90 Shutsu nyukoku kanri oyobi nanmin ninteihō oyobi houmushō secchihō no ichibu wo kaiseisuru hōritsu [Act to Amend Parts of the Immigration Control and Refugee Recognition Act and Ministry of Justice Establishment Act], law no. 102 of 2018, amending the Immigration Control Act, *supra* note 75, appendix 1.

91 MHLW, "Aratana zairyu shikaku 'Tokutei ginō' nitsuite" [New Status to Stay in Japan: Specified Skill], March 6, 2019 https://www.mhlw.go.jp/content/12601000/000485526.pdf.
92 Foreign Workers Report, *supra* note 76 at 10.
93 Ibid., at 17 (necessity of achieving consensus on the kind of society or country to which Japan should aspire).
94 Ibid., at 10.
95 MHLW, *supra* note 89.
96 In 2015, the United States had the highest number of immigrants, with 48.0 million, followed by Russia (11.6 million), Saudi Arabia (10.8 million), Germany (10.2 million), and the United Kingdom (8.4 million). But when the number of immigrants is compared with the total population, the picture changes. For example, 87.3 percent of residents in the United Arab Emirates are immigrants. Australia followed with 21.0 percent, Canada 17.2, the United States 12.9, and the United Kingdom 12.7. At 1.7 percent, Japan ranked much lower. World Economic Forum, "Which Countries Have the Most Immigrants?" March 13, 2019, https://www.weforum.org/agenda/2019/03/which-countries-have-the-most-immigrants-51048ff1f9/.
97 Ibid., at 9. Moreover, the acceptance of foreign workers might delay the innovation and upgrading of work environments in Japan. Ibid.
98 Ibid.
99 See Masahiro Morioka, "Yusei hogohō kaisei wo meguru seimei rinri" [Ethic of Life in the Discussion of the Amendment to the Eugenic Protection Act], 16 Nihon kenkyu 221 (1997); Max Fisher, "Japanese Politician Wants to Boost the National Birthrate by Banning Abortion," *Washington Post* (February 26, 2013), https://www.washingtonpost.com/news/worldviews/wp/2013/02/26/japanese-politician-wants-to-boost-the-national-birthrate-by-banning-abortion/?noredirect=on&utm_term=.f9015a28bc3f.
100 "Dokushinzei, zaimushou ga kentouchu?" [Tax for Being Single: Is the Ministry of Finance Really Considering It?], J-cast, September 8, 2017, https://www.j-cast.com/tv/2017/09/08307948.html.
101 When you are married with a full-time salaried worker, the spouse is entitled to receive the benefit as a dependent, is exempt from paying social security contributions, and is entitled to receive the spousal tax break unless the income of the spouse reaches the maximum limit.
102 Nihonkoku kenpō [Constitution of Japan], 1946, art. 24.
103 Motoko Rich, "Craving Freedom, Japan's Women Opt Out of Marriage," *New York Times* (August 3, 2019), https://www.nytimes.com/2019/08/03/world/asia/japan-single-women-marriage.html.
104 There has been heated debate on whether we as a species need to limit our growth. Many people do believe that the human population has grown too much to for the earth to sustain and that there is a much more urgent need to limit the human

population. For obvious reasons, attention has then tended to focus on birth control. Diana Coole, *Should We Control World Population?* (Cambridge, UK: Polity Press, 2018); Jade S. Sasser, *On Infertile Ground: Population Control and Women's Rights in the Era of Climate Change* (New York: NYU Press, 2018); Paige Whaley Eager, *Global Population Policy: From Population Control to Reproductive Rights* (London/New York: Routledge, 2017). However, while birth control may be necessary in countries where population has grown out of control, in countries, such as Japan, which are facing a rapid population decline, there is an urgent need to increase the population. In any case, it is apparent that the population policy is important, to varying degrees, in all countries.

105 Moreover, instead of restricting abortion, the government could more actively promote adoption. Sometimes, mothers simply abandon a newborn baby that they are incapable of raising. In response, one hospital hit on the idea of setting up a cradle in which a mother could anonymously leave her newborn without running the risk of prosecution. Because abandoning a child is a crime, the government was not willing to accept this scheme. Nevertheless, it could save lives and could increase the possibility that the babies could be raised by someone else. This is surely a possible way of increasing childbirth. Kumamoto City, Kounotori no yurikago senmon bukai [Special Committee on Stork's Cradle], "Kounotori no yurikago kenshou houkokusho" [Review of Stork's Cradle Operation], September 2014, https://www.city.kumamoto.jp/common/UploadFileDsp.aspx?c_id=5&id=6463&sub_id=1&flid=43570 (during the two and a half years before the review, twenty babies were placed in the cradle).

106 MHLW, "Hunin chiryō to shigoto no ryōritsu nikakawaru shomondai nitsuite no sougouteki chousa kenkyu jigyō" [Comprehensive Research on the Proper Balance between Infertility Treatment and Work], 7, https://www.mhlw.go.jp/file/04-Houdou happyou-11910000-Koyoukankyoukintoukyoku-Koyoukikaikintouka/0000197931.pdf (only 9 percent of the companies surveyed stated that they had a special system for workers who were undergoing infertility treatment, whereas 21 percent reported that they responded on an individual basis).

107 Ibid., at 39. In addition, 11 percent had discontinued the treatment. Ibid.

108 Ibid., at 53–54.

109 Rodou kijunhō [Labour Standards Act], law no. 49 of 1947, art. 65.

110 Ikuji kyugyou, kaigo kyugyotō ikuji matawa kazokukaigo wo okonau roudousha no hukushi ni kansuru hōritsu [Infant and Elder Care Leave Act], law no. 76 of 1991, art. 5.

111 Koyou no bunya niokeru danjo no kintō na kikai oyobi taigu no kakuhotō nikansuru hōritsu [Act to Secure the Equal Employment Opportunity and Equal Treatment in the Employment Fields], law no. 113 of 1972, art. 11–3 (Equal Employment Opportunity Act, EEOA).

112 Ibid., art. 9.

113 Josei no shokugyou seikatsu niokeru katsuyaku no suishin nikansuru hōritsutō no ichibu wo kaiseisuru hōritsu [Act to Amend Parts of the Act on Promotion of

Women's Professional Life], law no. 24 of 2019, art. 4, adding new art. 11–4 to the EEOA (effective in June 2020).
114 MHLW, Koyo kankyo kinto kyokuchō [Employment Environment Equality Division Chief], "Kaisei koyo no bunya niokeru danjo no kintō na kikai oyobi taigu no kakuhotō nikansuru hōritsu? no sekou nitsuite" [Enforcement of the Revised Equal Employment Opportunity Act], February 10, 2020, 39–40, https://www.mhlw.go.jp/hourei/doc/tsuchi/T200213M0040.pdf.
115 Infant and Elder Care Leave Act, *supra* note 111 at art. 5. Although 82 percent of employed women asked for maternity leave, only 6 percent of male partners requested paternity leave. MHLW, "Dansei no ikuji kyugyo no shutoku joukyo to shutoku sokushin notameno torikumi nitsuite" [Ratio of Male Partners Who Applied for Infant Care Leave and Measures to Improve the Low Ratio], July 3, 2019, https://www8.cao.go.jp/shoushi/shoushika/meeting/consortium/04/pdf/houkoku-2.pdf.
116 Hoping to cut down on the waiting list, the government enabled approved facilities to admit more children, but many infants are still waiting for admission. *Supra* note 71.
117 Way of Work Reform Act, *supra* note 53.
118 Ibid., art. 1, amending Labour Standards Act, *supra* note 110 at art. 36.
119 Ibid., art. 3, amending Koyō taisakuhō [Employment Stabilization Act], law no. 132 of 1966, to carry a new title, Roudou seisaku no sogoutekina suishin narabini roudousha no koyōno antei oyobi shokugyou seikatsu no juujitu ni kansuru hōritsu [Act concerning Comprehensive Promotion of Labour Policies and Implementation of Stable Employment of Employee and Fulfillment of Work Life], law no. 132 of 1966, and amending its art. 4.
120 Ibid., art. 5, amending the Dispatch Workers Act, *supra* note 54 at art. 30–3, and art. 7, amending Tanjikan roudousha no koyōkanri no kaizento nikansuru hōritsu [Part-Time Workers Act] to a new title of Tanjikan roudousha oyobi yuki-koyou roudousha no koyoukanri no kaizentō nikansuru hōritsu [Act concerning the Improvement of Labour Management of Part-Time Workers and Fixed-Term Workers], law no. 76 of 1993, and amending its art. 8.
121 Gender Equality Bureau, Danjo kyodo sankaku hakusho [Gender Equality Whitepaper], 2021, https://www.gender.go.jp/about_danjo/whitepaper/r03/zentai/html/honpen/b1_s02_01.html. Only 53.1 percent of married working women remained at work after the birth of their first child. Of those who held a permanent job, 69.1 percent continued to work, whereas only 25.2 percent of informal workers did. Declining Childbirth Whitepaper, *supra* note 1 at 25. These figures clearly show the difficulties for working women to keep working while raising children.
122 More than 25 percent of male employees in their thirties and forties work more than sixty hours a week. Ibid., at 27.
123 Gender Equality Bureau, "Kaji, ikuji, kaigo to shigoto no balance" [Balancing Household, Childcare, and Elder Care Duty and Work], 2020:9 Kyodou sankaku 2, https://www.gender.go.jp/public/kyodosankaku/2020/202009/202009_02.html.

124 See *supra* note 123.
125 A 2019 report estimated that raising just one child to university age will cost JPY 31,500,000 (roughly US$236,000). If the child attends private school from kindergarten to university, the cost will be JPY 35,000,000 (about US$260,000). In Japan, parents are responsible for funding their children during their time at university or college, including paying tuition, rent, and living expenses. This is an estimate just for one child. Shogakkan, "Hagukumu," May 27, 2019, https://hugkum.sho.jp/56608.
126 Kaku Sechiyama, "Japan, the Sexless Nation," *Oriental Economist*, December 19, 2014, https://toyokeizai.net/articles/-/56360. Citing survey data from Durex, a leading British condom manufacturer, this article concludes that "Japan has the lowest sexual frequency in the world, and it is the only country where the percentage of people who are not happy with their sex life is higher than that of those who are."
127 Japan Family Planning Association, "Sex Survey Japan 2020," https://www.jfpa.or.jp/pdf/sexservey2020/JexSexSurvey_p3-4.pdf.
128 National Institute of Population and Social Security Research, "Dai15kai shusseidoukou kihonchousa" [Fifteenth Research on the Birth Trend], 2015, 21, http://www.ipss.go.jp/ps-doukou/j/doukou15/NFS15_reportALL.pdf. A closer look at the statistics in this document shows that 64.0 percent of men in their early twenties and 49.7 percent of those in their late twenties had no regular partner of the opposite sex. For women in the same age ranges, the figures were 50.5 percent and 34.4 percent. Ibid., at 23.
129 Kevan Wylie, "A Global Survey of Sexual Behaviours," 3:2 J. of Family and Reproductive Health 39, July. 2009. https://www.researchgate.net/publication/228641949_A_Global_Survey_of_Sexual_Behaviours.
130 Japan Family Planning Association, *supra* note 129.
131 Additionally, increasing numbers of women feel unsatisfied by sex. Overall, 42.2 percent of them were not satisfied; 30.7 percent in their twenties and 34.1 percent in their thirties felt unsatisfied. Interestingly, 77.9 percent of men wanted to have sex, whereas 22.1 percent did not (69.9 percent in their twenties and 77.6 percent in their thirties did). For their part, 41.4 percent of women wanted to have sex and 58.6 percent did not (60.2 percent in their twenties and 57.3 percent in their thirties did). Ibid.
132 For example, because a married couple must share the same family name, some women are forced to avoid legal marriage and choose de facto marriage. Moreover, divorced women were required to wait for six months, now 100 days, before getting remarried. Furthermore, due to a judicial doctrine that precluded cheating spouses from filing for divorce, some people are prevented from getting married with new partners. Without the blessing of marriage, the couples are naturally discouraged from having sex and children. The government should abandon all of these practices in order to facilitate marriage.
133 In the past, the laws discriminated against illegitimate children. Although these statutory discriminations were struck down by the SCOJ and removed, nevertheless,

legitimate and illegitimate children are still treated differently, and there still remains a strongly persistent prejudice against them. Both of which serve to surely deter single women from having children.

134 Although the Sapporo District Court recently held that the exclusion of same-sex marriage was unconstitutional, Sapporo chihō saibansho [Sapporo DC], March 17, 2021, https://www.courts.go.jp/app/hanrei_jp/detail4?id=90200; "Douseikon no hujuri, hatsu no iken handan: Sapporo chisai sabetsuteki atsukai" [First Unconstitutional Holding against Exclusion of Same-Sex Marriage: Sapporo DC Viewed It Discriminatory], *Asahi Shimbun*, March 17, 2021, https://www.asahi.com/articles/ASP3K3F63P3JIIPE02H.html, the Osaka District Court sustained its constitutionalitu, Osaka chihō saibansho [Osaka DC], June 20, 2022, unreported: "Douseikon mitomenai no wa goouken" [It is Constitutional to Exclude Same-Sex Marriage], *Asahi Shimbun*, June 20, 2022, https://www.asahi.com/articles/ASQ6N41M4Q68PTIL00V.html?iref=pc_rellink_01. We must wait for the decision of the SCOJ to settle this issue.

135 In 2018, a transgender woman who worked for the government sued it for not permitting her to use a nearby women's washroom. She had not yet received sex reassignment surgery and was thus legally defined as male. On appeal, the Tokyo High Court noted that her employer had considered both her plight and the possible uneasiness of other women who used the restroom, and had instructed her to use a women's washroom two floors above her workspace. It ruled that this was not unreasonable. Tokyo kōtō saibansho [Tokyo HC], May 27, 2021, unreported; "Sei douitsusei shougai no toilet shiyo seigen, kousai ihou dewanai" [Limitation on the Use of a Restroom for a Transgender Woman: The Tokyo HC Held It Not Unreasonable], *Asahi Shimbun* (May 27, 2021), https://www.asahi.com/articles/ASP5W5228P5TUTIL04B.html.

136 Moreover, treating transgender people as if they have a disorder (sexual identity disorder), is no longer acceptable. In the past, they were offered various treatments to "straighten" them up or were forced to undergo them. Individuals should be free to live as their own sexual or gender identity, and any attempt to impose cisgenderism on transgender people, as in conversion therapy, needs to be banned. *Criminal Code of Canada*, s 320.101 to s 320.104. Christine Hauser, "Canada Bans 'Conversion Therapy,'" *New York Times* (January 6, 2022), https://www.nytimes.com/2022/01/06/world/canada/canada-conversion-therapy-law.html.

Index

abortion, 6, 17, 18, 22, 28, 154, 158, 212; its actual practice, in 160; ban Canada, 170; ban in Germany, 169, 184; comparative analysis of the constitutionality of its ban, 180; comparative perspective on its ban, 166; constitutional right, 185, 187, 188; discriminatory, 178; and government aids, 165; history of its ban in Japan, 155; permissible as an artificial termination of pregnancy (ATP), 152, 159; practical difficulty, 174; pill, 165. *See also* pill (morning after pill)
adoption, 138, 176
adultery, 32, 52, 56
aging, 12, 192
artificial insemination, 127
artificial termination of pregnancy (ATP), 14, 154–63, 165, 172, 174–80, 187, 190–91, 210, 219, 293n21, 294n24, 295n50, 295nn53–54, 295n58, 297n72, 297n78, 299n92, 301nn129–30, 302n132, 304n161, 304n163
assisted reproductive technology (ART), 6, 17, 117, 127, 201, 213, 218

Beate Sirota Gordon, 40
Bedford, 68
best interest of the child, 150
bigamy, 56
birth control policy, 163
birthrate, 13, 176, 192; attempt to increase, 197

castration, 118
Child Abuse Prevention Act, 41, 42, 86
Child Prostitution Prohibition Act (Japan), 41, 42, 86
Child Welfare Act (Japan), 41, 42, 86
childbirth, 8; promotion 197
citizen judge, 99
Civil Code (Japan), 11, 36, 37, 40, 136, 153, 177
comfort women, 81
consent, 49, 92, 103, 115; and use of ART/MAR 145, 153

Constitution of Japan (Japan), 11, 16, 39, 91, 139
contraception, 6, 17, 28, 164, 186
Crime Victim Protection Act (Japan), 95
Crime Victims Fundamental Act (Japan), 95
Criminal Code (Japan), 11, 36, 37, 41, 52, 53, 84, 99, 154, 155, 158, 172, 189, 212
criminal complaint, 86, 100

DNA testing, 148, 152
Dobbs v Jackson Women's Health Organization, 22, 29, 183, 189

enjokōsai (compensated dating), 65
Entertainment Business Regulation Act (Japan), 64, 65
Equal Employment Opportunity Act (EEOA) (Japan), 214
equality, 11, 26
escort service, 65
Eugenic Protection Act (Japan), 124, 156, 172, 174; renamed as the Mother's Body Protection Act, 158

family, 10, 17, 27, 37, 148, 218
family law, 10, 37, 40
family registration (family registry), 36, 40, 43, 135
Federal Constitution Court of Germany (FCCG), 30, 178, 188
fetus, 125, 127, 133, 154, 158, 159, 166, 167, 175, 178, 179, 180, 181, 182, 185, 187, 188, 190; its dignity, 155, 177
forcible obscene act (sexual assault), 84, 99, 100
forcible sexual intercourse, et al., 58, 99, 100, 102; criticism of, 102; and evidence of sexual history, 104
foreign immigrants, 8, 203; government's reluctance to accept, 204; increased acceptance, 206

foreign trainees, 205
foreign workers, 204; government's limited acceptance, 204
freedom of choice on childbirth, 5
Fundamental Act on Declining Birthrate Countermeasures (Japan), 197
fundamental human rights, 11

gay: couples, 21, 45, 54, 218
Gender Equality Bureau of the Cabinet Office (GEB), 82, 93, 97
gender identity. *See* sexual or gender identity

homosexual, 21, 39, 45, 54, 218
housemaster, 36, 40
human dignity, 76, 79

immigrants, 8, 14, 15; immigration policy, 203–4, 206–9, 316n73, 318n96
in vitro fertilization (IVF), 127, 129, 130, 132, 135, 143, 146, 180, 213, 218
incest, 53
indecent sexual conduct, 42

Japan Society of Obstetrics and Gynecology (JSOG), 128, 139, 179
Japan Society for Reproductive Medicine (JSRM), 130
JK business, 66

law of parentage, 6, 118, 135, 136, 213
Lawrence v Texas, 19, 24, 49, 52, 56, 71, 72–73, 228, 237n8, 238n12, 238n14, 243n43, 246n86, 246n89, 248n119; the SCOTUS in, 19, 21–22, 33, 39, 45–46, 54, 72, 240n52
lesbian, 146

marriage, 16, 27, 38, 57; promoting, 197
medically assisted reproduction (MAR), 6, 17, 117, 127, 201, 212, 218

Medically Assisted Reproduction Act (Japan), 135, 153
Meiji Constitution (Japan), 10
Meiji Restoration, 9, 36, 155
morality, 33
R. v Morgentaler, 184
morning-after pill, 165. *See also* abortion; pill (contraception pill)
Mother's Body Protection Act (Japan), 154, 159, 172, 174, 190, 212

pill (contraception pill), 154, 165, 186, 212. *See also* abortion; morning-after pill
population, 12; policy 4, 8, 209
privacy, 21, 26, 29
proportionality, 30
prostitution, 22, 42; Amnesty International's position 77; constitutionality 68; constitutionality challenged (Canada) 68; constitutionality challenged (United States) 71; constitutionality reconsidered 77; history 61; divided opinions, 73; international comparison, 67; meaning of, 63; Nordic model, 68, 69, 71, 76, 77
Prostitution Prevention Act (Japan), 41, 42, 63, 65, 86

"quasi-forcible obscene act," 85, 100
quasi-forcible sexual intercourse et al., 100
"quasi-rape," 85; renamed as quasi forcible sexual intercourse et al., 100

rape, 31, 41, 42, 46, 84; renamed as forcible sexual intercourse et al., 99; renamed as sexual assault in Canada, 92, 105
requirements for punishment, 88

revenge porn, 46
right: to be treated as a parent, 147; to become a parent, 118, 132; to decide one's own sexual or gender identity, 3, 28, 35, 44; to have a child, 17, 117; to have sex, 3, 17, 35, 39, 40; not to be forced to have a child, 3, 28, 118, 154, 180; not to be forced to have sex, 3, 28, 84, 101; not to have a child, 28
Roe v. Wade, 18, 168, 178, 181
Romeo and Juliet Law, 61

same-sex marriage, 44, 57, 218
settled foreigners, 204
sex: with animals (bestiality), 55; in the broader sense, 47; in the broadest sense, 47; with children, 58; with the dead (necrophilia), 55; deviant or atypical, 33, 54; as distinguished from activities that might stimulate sexual desire, 48; exploitation, 73; group, 51; meaning, 42, 44; in the narrow sense, 47; practical difficulties caused by the family system, 56; in public, 49; with unmarried persons (fornication), 51; violent and dehumanizing, 49; workers, 68, 69
sexual autonomy, 3, 7, 16, 18, 25; freedom, 3, 4, 16, 17, 35, 39, 41; intercourse, 42, 47, 63, 88, 218; minorities, 31; new perspective for declining birthrate, 211; service special business, 64; touching, 109
sexual or gender identity, 3, 4, 14, 28, 35, 43–44, 57, 126, 220, 221, 222, 237n1, 322n136
soapland, 65
sodomy, 21, 33, 39, 54
spousal rape, 103

Supreme Court of Canada (SCOC), 30, 33, 49, 51, 68, 171, 184
Supreme Court of Japan (SCOJ), 25, 39, 42, 57, 59, 86, 110, 126, 150, 177
Supreme Court of the United States (SCOTUS), 18, 26, 27, 29, 39, 45, 54, 178, 181, 188, 189
standard of review, 28
sterilization, 122
strict scrutiny, 29
surrogacy, 131, 133, 142

total fertility rate (TFR), 193
transgender, 41, 43, 56, 57, 218
2SLGBTQ+, 54, 218

UN Committee on the Elimination of Discrimination against Women (DEDAW), 163